The Privatization
of Public Utilities

Leonard S. Hyman

Public Utilities Reports, Inc.
Vienna, Virginia

1995

First printing, May 1995

ISBN 0-910325-59-6
Library of Congress Catalog Card No. 95-67746
Printed in the United States of America

DEDICATION

To the senior branch of the family,
my father, Dr. Milton Hyman,
my mother, Elsie Hyman, and
my uncle, Victor Hyman.

Table of Contents

The Privatization of Public Utilities

Preface

Leonard S. Hyman

I first experienced the ins and outs of privatization when Merrill Lynch's London bankers told me that I was going to help them make a pitch (indelicately phrased, perhaps, but that's what we were doing) to secure a management position for Merrill in the first British Telecom sale. I went over, dutifully rehearsed, learned about "beauty contests" first hand, tried to fathom what people in the not-yet-privatized British Telecom dining room were putting on my plate, and, even worse, what the proper eating utensil might be for food that I could not identify (a difficult decision for a graduate of Stuyvesant High School rather than Eton or St. Somebody). I also learned that watching *Masterpiece Theatre* and *Monty Python's Flying Circus* was not sufficient training to deal with British civil servants and junior ministers. Subsequently, I worked on privatization projects on several continents, but none sported as colorful a cast of characters as that found in Thatcherite Britain.

The word "privatization," incidentally, so often associated with the Thatcher years, originated earlier. According to that fount of truth, the *Oxford English Dictionary*, the word first appeared in English print in 1959, in a story in the *News Chronicle* about the West German government's plan to sell a state-owned mining concern to private owners. The word found some use in the 1960s and 1970s, in the United States and Canada, again in the sense of selling state-owned assets to the private sector, or of allowing private enterprise to perform functions that were previously handled by the state. "Privatization" seemed a more popular word, though, among philosophers and theologians who spoke of the privatization of death, the privatization of God, and even privatization as an activity of the nuclear family. However, the ascendancy of Prime Minister Thatcher brought the word back into the economic arena. Since the early 1980s, governments all over the world (with the outstanding exception of those in the United States) have been selling off state-owned businesses or entrusting to the private sector the expansion of activities formerly monopolized by the government.

Why Is this Book Different?

Academic economists, philosophers, political scientists, and international bankers have produced scores of excellent books on the phenomenon of privatization. What makes this book different?

- **The book focuses entirely on public utilities** — In developing countries, the lack of telecommunications, energy and water infrastructure holds back the modernization process. Governments in those nations turned to privatization of those sectors because: they lacked the resources to expand the sectors, they believed that private owners would run the utilities more efficiently, and utility properties are not only saleable but bring in large sums needed for other purposes. In the industrialized world, hard pressed governments are turning to privatization for the same reasons, although the desire to raise money may be the controlling factor. We all can learn from the experiences of others, and this book tells about those experiences.

- **The authors have hands-on experience** — The contributors are business executives, financiers, and consultants who have worked in the utility industries, advised government, managed successful privatizations, taken part in the financial deal-making, marketed the securities, and worked with the privatized companies and their shareholders after the privatization. They are insiders willing to discuss their experiences, procedures and strategies. To the extent that the devil is in the details, those insights may help planners and investors do better privatizations in the future.

- **The book discusses the basics of the process** — Getting it right (whether that means planning the privatization, or deciding to make the investment, or running the company in a new environment) requires an understanding of the basics, meaning: how and why the industry is organized as it is, whether there are alternatives, what the regulator should do, how the banker fits into the process, what private sector finance and accounting are like, and especially, how the capital markets work. Most people are embarrassed to ask about the basics. Most writers assume that the reader knows. Well, here is everything that you need to know but were afraid to ask.

- **This is not an ideological tract** — It may take decades to establish that privatizations actually produce the hoped-for results. Some analyses of the virtues or evils of privatization, therefore, tend toward ideological or self-serving discussions, because of the lack of long term data. The purpose of this book is not to prove that privatization is a winner or a loser, but rather to discuss the reasons for privatization, the hazards and rewards of the process, what one should know when privatizing, and what one should do afterwards, using actual privatizations as examples, whenever possible.

Organization of the Book

The organization of the book follows a simple format. The first section, *Setting the Stage*, examines why governments privatize, and then looks into the huge capital needs that are pushing the process. The section also considers that the utility industries can be reorganized to produce desired results, and that the regulatory process plays a key role in successful privatization. Readers who already possess sophisticated knowledge of these topics should move onward.

The second section, *Views from the Field*, examines industry frameworks for privatization, and specific instances of privatization, where it worked, why it should work, and how the process is playing out.

The third section, *Doing the Private Deal*, focuses on the project, mainly within the context of Latin America. The developers need to structure the deal, which is a different story from simply selling shares of an existing entity to the public.

The fourth section, *The Public Offering and Beyond*, looks at the process of selling shares in the stock markets, and then dealing with shareowners afterwards.

The fifth section, *Management and Finance*, discusses the new industry factors that require different approaches to operations and finance, as well as a look at how the newly private corporations can raise capital in the bond markets.

The sixth section, *The United Kingdom Experience*, is a thorough look at the restructuring and sale of Britain's industry, with emphasis on the electricity supply sector, and then examines the changes required in a newly privatized firm, and whether the government really succeeded in its efforts.

The seventh section, *The Telefonica Experience*, looks at two case studies of privatizations accomplished by Telefónica de España, and then considers how and why that company makes such extensive use of strategic alliances to accomplish its goals.

The *Appendices* provide analyses of utility usage throughout the world, a chronology of major privatizations, and examination of the market performance of privatized firms, and a brief bibliography. Finally, the Appendices include a detailed review of financial and accounting basics, and a discussion of how the capital markets value securities.

Acknowledgments

The writers of the chapters, of course, made the book possible. Many other people were also instrumental in the creation of this book. John Hunter of Management Exchange helped me snare several authors. John Arcate of Complan Associates not only recommended several authors but also contributed invaluable insights that improved their articles. Angel García Cordero of Anta Internacional also recommended several authors and helped with translation. Eileen Toole did much of the word processing, with an astounding eye for accuracy and meaning. Linda Fukuchi helped when the Spanish seemed to go in circles. Katie Jay and Susan Johnson of Public Utilities Reports, in the capacity of editor and publisher respectively, made the process of putting together the book as easy as possible. On the information gathering front, Mary Galvin Casale of Merrill Lynch found a number of sources. On the home front, younger son Robert compiled and organized much of the statistical material, elder son Andrew put together the bibliography, and wife Judith again demonstrated that what she teaches second and third graders about computers has commercial applications.

A Final Word

Privatization, nowadays, is trumpeted as the cure for all ills, denounced as a give-away of the public wealth, seen as a means of filling the state's coffers, a sure-fire way to get rich quickly, a means to bring efficiency to the public sector, the road to environmental ruin, and a way of either incenting or firing employees. In the past decade, most privatizations shared several of those characteristics. Privatization, itself, should neither be demonized nor beatified. Privatization is, simply, a powerful tool to use in trying to reach specific goals. I hope that this book makes a modest contribution to helping the reader use that tool better.

Leonard S. Hyman
North Tarrytown, N.Y.
January 22, 1995

PART I
Setting the Stage

➤

Chapter 1

The Privatization and Restructuring of Utilities: Why and How

Leonard S. Hyman

Once upon a time, long ago, private entrepreneurs established the public utilities. Then, later on, misguided socialists and nationalists took over those enterprises, turning them into unproductive state agencies. Finally, in the 1980s, people saw the light. Governments sold those utilities back to private investors. Everyone lived happily ever after.

That, truly, was a fairy tale. Many utilities started as government-owned agencies that showed as much energy and acumen as their privately-owned counterparts. Some governments, in fact, socialized the utilities because of the inadequacies of their private owners. Consider two examples:

- In the United Kingdom, both Conservative and Labor governments advocated government participation in, or ownership of, the electric industry to increase its efficiency. A Conservative government set up the state-owned National Grid in the 1920s in order to create a transmission and least cost generation system that the industry seemed incapable of creating on its own. The Churchill wartime government discussed nationalization of the electricity industry, but the postwar Labor government did the deed, principally, to bring about economies of scale lacking in the industry and to prevent an increasing fragmentation of the industry.

- The Mexican government took control of Teléfonos de México as late as 1972 only when it became apparent that the private investors that ran the company could not finance the expansion of the system. Although Telmex remained a quoted company with outside shareholders, after taking control the government furnished approximately half of the share capital with money raised through a telephone tax. As in the British case, nationalization was not a reaction to foreign control because the major shareholders were Mexican, but rather a reaction to the inadequacy of the private company.

During the era of the advance of socialism, too, economists argued that society as a whole would benefit if the state owned or subsidized the utilities that would then price their output in a certain manner:

- In a famous article published in 1938, "The General Welfare in Relation to Problems of Taxation and of Railway and Utility Rates" (6 *Economica* 242-269), Harold Hotelling argued that society is better off when a regulated monopoly, whose costs decrease with output, prices its output at marginal cost. Of course, if the monopoly did that, it would lose money. The solution, it follows, would be to provide a subsidy to the monopolist to cover its losses. Furthermore, asked some socialists, if the government has to subsidize the private monopolist, why not make the monopolist a government agency? It amounts to almost the same thing. If the government must support the utility, why not own it outright and have better control over costs? From the time when Hotelling wrote the article to well into the 1960s, the declining cost curve prevailed in the utility industries. This, too, was a period of increasing government ownership of utilities. While the economists gave the socialists a ready theoretical reason to take over utilities, the socialists did not necessarily follow the economic advice on how to price the utility's output in order to maximize the general welfare.

So much for theory. In the period after World War II, when socialism was in its glory, everyone—except in the United States—took it for granted that the government should own or control public utilities. The state-controlled utilities demonstrated the same range of accomplishment as the private-sector companies, running the gamut from innovative excellence to incompetence. Somehow, history is not as simple as it is supposed to be.

Margaret Thatcher's government, in the 1980s, started the privatization movement in earnest, selling Great Britain's state-owned utilities to private investors. As a matter of dogma, the Thatcher government assumed that private companies would run more efficiently than state-owned firms, that the price of service would decline as a result of privatization, and that it was important to encourage ordinary citizens to own stock. Other countries followed the British lead, although without the same thoroughness or conviction. Japan sold some of its shares in Nippon Telephone and Telegraph. The Spanish government decreased its holdings in the nation's largest electric company, although it also encouraged that still state-controlled system to take over a greater share of the national market. At the end of 1990, Mexico made a spectacular disposal of shares of Teléfonos de México. An avalanche of sales and industry reorganizations followed.

It is easy—but misleading—to lump together all this activity under the heading of "privatization." To most people, "privatization" means the sale of a government-owned asset or company to private investors. What actually ensues may encompass reorganization of the industry, breaking up existing entities, rewriting the rules of regulation, bringing in new owners, selling assets, and encouraging private firms to supply services to government-owned utilities. Perhaps "restructuring" is a more descriptive term for the process than "privatization." The former term encompasses alteration of industry structure while the latter focuses on ownership. There is more to this business than just changing owners.

Reasons to Privatize

The government that plans to restructure or privatize its utility sector may have one or many motives for the move:

- **The government needs money**—This is the simplest motive. Utilities may be the largest, most profitable assets owned by the government, assets that can be easily sold, assets that will produce more cash upon sale than anything else the government has to sell.

- **The utility system must expand, but the government lacks the funds to finance the expansion**—Once the government sells the system, the new owners have to find the capital for the expansion. Why doesn't the government-owned utility raise prices enough to allow it to finance its expansion? Sometimes the government does not have the political will to raise the price. Other times the budget rules include utility capital expenditures in the total government budget, and overall budget constraints limit those expenditures. In either case, selling the utility may be easier than raising prices or changing budget rules.

- **The government believes that private management is inherently more efficient than a government bureaucracy**—Certainly in many cases, state companies over staff in order to placate strong unions and place political appointees in top managerial positions without regard for their lack of business acumen. Again, the government could make the utility more efficient without selling it, but someone else might do the job more easily.

- **The government desires to build capitalism by encouraging widespread share ownership**—To do so, the government needs to sell the type of large, well-known, stable, dividend-paying company (such as a utility) that would appeal to new investors. The government might even sell the stock at a price low enough to guarantee a profit to this group of investing novices, in order to entice them to buy.

- **The government wants to restructure the industry in order to eliminate monopolies, and encourage competition between suppliers**—Through those measures, the government hopes to force the utilities to run more efficiently and to lower prices. The government decides that introducing competition is a better way to control the utilities than by means of heavy-handed regulation. As part of the process, the government has to break up the existing state-owned monopoly or to introduce new firms into the business. Firms all owned by the government might not compete vigorously. Thus, the government must sell some or all of the industry's assets to private investors in order to introduce competition.

Different Goals Yield Different Policies

A government needs to determine first why it wants to privatize a company, and then plan the privatization around that goal. Too often, the government has contradictory goals, and as a result, it muddles through the process without extracting the optimal results. Consider these goals and their consequences:

- **Obtain the highest price from the sale**—To accomplish this, the most straightforward goal, the government may have to avoid restructuring, probably should not introduce competition to the industry, and should set up a tariff and regulatory system favorable to the utility. Reform plays second fiddle to the pocketbook. Yet a highly profitable utility has the cash flow required to expand and improve service. Giving the utility what is required in order to get a high price when selling the utility may also accomplish another goal—building infrastructure.

- **Restructure the industry in order to improve its performance**—Restructuring, though, might break up comfortable monopolies, or introduce competition, or create an effective regulatory system. Those steps could reduce the profits of the existing utility. Investors may pay less when they buy firms that face keen competition or effective regulation. Society might be better off with a restructured utility industry but not the government treasury which will receive less from selling the utility to investors.

- **Create widespread share ownership**—To enlarge the participation of small investors in the capital markets, the government might offer shares to individual investors and to employees at low prices with favorable payment terms, possibly at a price below the market value in order to assure investors that the stock's price will rise after it is purchased. That would please the purchasers, encouraging them to buy subsequent share offerings. The government, however, sells an asset presumably owned by all citizens (represented by the government) at a price below its value only to those citizens who can afford to buy the new shares. The process transfers wealth, in a sense, from those who do not have it to those who do. The government does not maximize the proceeds of the sale, but hopes, as an offset, that the country's economy will gain from having more shareholders. As an alternative, the government might give vouchers that convey a right to purchase shares in privatized companies to all citizens. Those vouchers would have value whether the citizen decided to buy the shares or to sell the voucher to someone who did want to make the purchase. An even simpler plan is to give away shares in the new companies to all citizens.

- **Maintain government control of the industry**—As long as the government keeps control, it has not really privatized, but it can still accomplish some of the goals of privatization. The state, for instance, could raise funds by disposing of some of its shares in the utility. Yet the price of the shares sold might be lower than if the sale were part of a full privatization. Investors would wonder if the utility were a real commercial entity or still just an arm of the government. The government could retain control in another way: the state retains the utility, but the utility begins to buy services and output from private vendors such as independent power generators. The vendors raise the capital, build the new facilities, and sell their output to the government utility. This is *de facto* privatization. The government maintains the appearance of ownership and control, but private firms really account for much of the output, and possibly for all incremental output and services.

Ownership and Control

It is bad enough when opponents accuse the government of selling the family jewels at cut-rate prices to a privileged few or to politically influential cronies of the ruling party's leaders. It is worse when the government sells highly visible public service entities to foreigners. Ownership matters. Consider these variations on ownership and control:

- **The government maintains a majority or controlling shareholder position**— Thus the state (which regulates the company) also shares in the utility's profits. That arrangement, one could argue, protects the other shareholders, because the government has a proprietary interest in the well-being of the utility. Many investors would counter that governments do not always act in a rational, economic manner, that they place the wrong people in charge of the utility, and that the company is not a private enterprise if the government remains in control. If enough investors take a negative view, the price of the utility's stock reflects that lack of confidence.

- **The offering spreads share ownership, leaving no group with a large enough position to control the company**—This diffused ownership is typical of large corporations in the United States, Canada and the United Kingdom. In effect, professional management holds control, at the sufferance of a board of directors that supposedly represents (and is elected by) shareholders, but sometimes acts as if it is beholden to the management. Divorcing ownership from control may separate the interests of the professional managers from those of the shareowners.

- **A strategic investor or group of investors controls the business**—In Latin America and Continental Europe, a family or investment group typically owns enough stock (or enough voting stock) to control the corporation. In theory, management should take greater care when making decisions because its own money is at stake. The arrangement, though, has disadvantages. Outside shareholders have no way of dislodging poor management because management controls the vote. The government, though, may feel that the new corporation must have an experienced business group in control in order to turn a bureaucratic monopoly into an efficient business. The government may require, as one of the major shareholders, a corporation with operating experience in the utility sector. This strategic investor would help upgrade the newly privatized utility's service levels.

- **Foreign vs. domestic control**—Many governments insist upon a domestic group as the controlling shareholder. Where there is no control group, the government may limit the percentage of the voting shares owned by foreigners.

- **The government keeps ownership of a golden share after privatization**—In order to prevent the newly privatized utility from taking actions antithetic to government policy, or to prevent undesirable investors from taking control of the company, the government retains ownership of a "golden share," i.e., a share with special voting rights that allow the government to veto activities that it does not approve of. The government, thus, manages to maintain the rights of a controlling shareholder without any of the financial risks of ownership.

Getting the right shareholder group in place does make a difference, especially when the utility needs new management, direction and technological expertise. If the control group does not have enough capital to buy an absolute majority of the stock, the government might divide up the capital into voting and non-voting shares, selling the voting shares to the control group and non-voting shares to others. The government, in addition, must make sure that the employees are significant shareholders so that they have enough of a financial stake in the business to want it to succeed. If the employees do not have the money to buy the stock, the government might have to lend it to them, or even give them the stock. The Mexican government, in its sale of Teléfonos de México, provided a model:

- The government first created voting and nonvoting shares. Then it sold control of the voting shares to a group whose majority partner was an entrepreneurial Mexican company, Grupo Carso. The minority partners in the group, Southwestern Bell and France Telecom brought technical and marketing experience. The government also lent to employees enough money to buy a large bloc of shares at the same price as the control group. Then the government sold the balance of its shares to Mexican and international investors over a period of several years.

At the same time, some schemes to keep the government in control of decisions show misunderstanding of regulation. The government sets the rules through the regulatory process, and therefore does not need to own shares or control votes in order to achieve certain ends. The government does need to specify those ends in the regulatory rules, and then enforce them. In the United States and in Canada, the governments rarely own any shares in investor-owned utilities. They control policy through the regulatory process. Regulators in the USA and Canada are limited by the rules, so the shareholders have the protection of an established regulatory process followed by right of appeal to the courts. Governments that maintain control of utilities through ownership can change policies for any reason, at the expense of non-government shareholders.

Regulatory System

Formal regulatory systems often are absent where the state owns the utility industry. In those places, the government writes the rules, changes them whenever it wishes, picks the utility's managers, guarantees the utility's debts, and sets the price of service. The government chooses whether to make a profit in the utility business, or to use the utility to serve social or political purposes instead.

Private investors, however, will not buy a utility company whose existence is subject to the changing whims of the government. Investors need to know the rules so that they can estimate the cash flows and profits, decide the price that they wish to pay for the utility, and make a bid.

The government that plans to privatize its utility sector must set the rules to allow them to achieve and prioritize the goals of regulation:

- **Protect consumers**—The utility may have monopoly power as the only provider of a particular service. If so, the regulators must protect the consumer from too high or discriminatory pricing, or from inadequate service.

- **Attract capital**—Many utilities face enormous demand for their services. The utility is a vital part of the nation's infrastructure. If it cannot raise enough capital to expand its operations in order to meet rising demand for its services, that shortfall may stifle the economy's growth. The utility must earn a high enough profit to attract the new capital that it requires to finance its expansion. Thus, regulators may have to set tariffs that permit high profits if they want to encourage expansion of the utility system.

- **Encourage competition**—In some instances, the utility sector no longer exhibits the characteristics of a natural monopoly. If that is so, then consumers might benefit from the introduction of competition. Making room for competitors where none existed before may require rules that specifically encourage competition.

- **Advance the goals of public policy**—The government, for instance, might want to channel service to certain customer groups, avoid environmental degradation, or choose fuels in a way to assure national security. As long as the investors know the rules, they can determine how the public policy goals affect profitability and, therefore, determine the worth of the utility in the marketplace. Over time, public policy goals shift. Utility investors expect that. All they want is to maintain a reasonable level of profitability however the rules may change.

Before privatization, the government officials who write the rules must understand the conflicts between the goals. If the primary goal is to attract enough capital to build infrastructure, then the regulations have to emphasize profitability over competition or the protection of consumers or the achievement of public policy aims. If the goal is to make the utility more efficient, then the regulator might want to introduce competition or set the pricing rules so that the utility earns more money if it cuts costs while still maintaining set standards of service.

Governments with little experience of utility regulation need to be sensitive about what can go wrong with the process. They can lose sight of the difference between form and substance. As an example, the British government created a regulatory framework in which the regulators set the price of the product, not the rate of return. Yet the price formulas were devised with an acceptable rate of return on investment in mind, and the regulators adjusted the formulas to correct the problem of potentially too high profits, although they never formally addressed the question of what constituted an unacceptably high return. Some investors may have been surprised, which brings up another issue: investors want consistency. If the host country develops a reputation for inconstancy, investors will hesitate to put more money into the country, and may withdraw the funds that they have there. Admittedly, sometimes the host country strikes a poor deal for itself when it sets the rules, but the host government may want to consider that if it reneges on the deal after luring in investors with the attractive arrangement, future investors may stay away out of fear that they too could lose out under similar circumstances. To reiterate, countries unused to regulation or long-term planning have to understand one simple fact: they cannot privatize the utility sector until rules are in place.

Selling the Utility

First, the government enacts the regulatory rules. Then the government either reorganizes the utility in order to get it into shape for the sale, or sells the utility as is. There are many types of sale:

- **Private (or trade) sale**—The government chooses to sell the utility or the utility plant to a large investor, possibly to a corporation or partnership that has the experience to run the utility well and the money to improve and expand the property. The government sells through an auction process in which qualified firms submit their bids, one of which the government chooses as the best bid. The government may also sell the property through a process of negotiation between it and potential buyers. The private sale can be made more quickly than a full-blown public stock offering, which requires months of preparations.

- **Public stock offering**—Selling shares to the public is a long and elaborate procedure. In order to get the best price, the government might have to take a year to fix up the utility in order to make it presentable for the offering, in the same way that the owner of a house fixes it up in order to attract buyers. Then, with the aid of highly-paid bankers and lawyers, the government prepares the documents necessary for the sale. Finally, the sale of stock to thousands of investors takes place, with an outcome that is by no means assured. Some public offerings fail even after all the expensive preparations, to the great embarrassment of all those involved.

- **Combination sale**—Recently, a number of countries have tried to achieve the benefits of private and public sales by combining the processes. First, the government sells part of the utility's shares in a private sale, often to a group that includes a strategic investor with the technological expertise needed to run the business. Later, after the investor group has overhauled the utility, the government sells its remaining shares in a public offering, often at a higher price than at which the control group bought its shares.

- **Local or international sale**—If the local capital market is large enough, the government might prefer to sell the utility to local investors. Where the local investors do not have the resources to buy the utility, the government has to seek foreign buyers. If the government sells shares in a public offerings, it has to comply with the securities laws of numerous countries. Despite that disadvantage, offering some stock in the international markets may help the government get a better price for the shares, because the international market opens the way for more buyers to compete for the shares.

- **All or partial sale**—If the nation needs cash fast, or wants to place the utility unequivocally in the private sector, it sells the entire utility at once. If the government wants to realize the maximum proceeds over time, it may sell part of its holdings to start the privatization process, and then sell the rest of the shares later, after the utility has become a successful enterprise, and its shares reflect that success through higher prices. Conceivably, the government might want to sell only part of the utility's shares, and remain in control. But that is not true privatization. What might be worse, though, would be for the government to sell some of its shares to the public with the understanding that it would sell the rest later, and then decide to keep the remaining shares rather than sell them. Buyers who purchased the stock expecting a full privatization, might feel betrayed. So far, this reversal of intention has not taken place.

The government must understand that its conduct at the initial privatization sale, and the operating performance of the utility, and the market performance of the shares afterwards, all will influence the attitude of investors toward any subsequent privatizations in that country.

After the Sale

The sale of the utility is the beginning—not the end—of the process. The utility and the regulators now have to deal with new audiences: the investors who bought the shares of the privatized utility and the consumers of the utility's output who now have to makes their wishes known through the regulatory process.

Investors want a flow of information that helps them value their investment on a daily basis. They want clear and timely financial statements, translated into accounting procedures that are acceptable in the leading industrialized countries. They want access to management and to government officials, many of whom grew up in a tradition of secrecy, never before having had to deal with persistent outside investors. Most of all, investors want a steadily rising flow of income and dividends.

While they realize that the utility has to earn enough of a profit to maintain and expand its plant and equipment, the utility's customers desire good service at the lowest possible price. Each customer group, too, attempts to gain advantages over other customer groups. Formerly, the customers made their requests through the political process. After privatization, they may have to take their complaints to the regulatory agency.

The regulator has an odd position. Investors want an independent regulator, one who will make decisions based on the merits of the issues, rather than one who is swayed by political pressures. Investors also want a regulator who follows the direction implied by the government or the bankers during the privatization process. A regulator who does not follow such direction is a risk that investors must consider. Customers want an independent regulator, as long as the system favors them, but they will apply political pressure to get what they want when the regulator does not comply with their wishes. Countries without a long tradition of independent judiciary, regulatory bodies, or legal continuity may find it hard to resist changing or bending the rules when expedient to do so.

Making the first sale, privatizing the utility, is the easiest part of the process. Governments must make sure that they follow up the sale in such a way that the first privatization is not the last.

Conclusion

For ideologues, privatization is an end in itself. For most people, it is a procedure designed to help a country achieve a set of goals, which include more participation on the part of small investors in the economy, greater efficiency, encouragement of entrepreneurial activities, attraction of needed capital, and the introduction of technological expertise to the sector.

Perhaps public utilities seem unlikely candidates for privatization. Public utilities do not require as much entrepreneurial management as do firms in other sectors, and are not technological pioneers, but provide a public service. Yet utilities do require huge sums of capital. Governments rarely have the money at hand to expand the utilities. Private owners with more business experience than civil servants can make even public utility firms more efficient. On those grounds alone, privatization of utilities could provide benefits to the host country. Any other benefits are icing on the cake.

Chapter 2

Financing the Expansion of Utilities

Leonard S. Hyman

The expansion of utility infrastructure will demand huge but uncertain amounts of capital. Those regions with the least ability to pay for that capital will need the most capital, because they have the greatest requirements to expand and upgrade their utility systems. Bankers will say that they can raise the money in international markets: no problem. The fact remains, though, that the customers for the service eventually pay for it, and the price includes not only operating costs but also cost of capital. In other words, the bankers may raise the needed money up front from outside investors, but the locals eventually pick up the tab.

Investors expect a return on and of capital. The utilities have only one way to achieve that return: by charging the customers a price high enough to cover all operating costs plus that return. If the customers do not have the income to pay that price, smart investors do not build the utility facilities. Then the customers do without the service, or some governmental body subsidizes the service, paying to investors what the customers cannot afford to pay. In poor countries, expansion of the utility infrastructure must provide enough value to society and enough impetus to the country's development to produce the income needed to pay for the expansion.

Development and Utility Infrastructure

Is the expansion of utility services a prerequisite for economic development or does economic development create the demand for utility services and the funds necessary to finance that expansion? (One could show how the lack of those services has created bottlenecks that thwarted economic development, but one could just as easily demonstrate that countries grew despite the appalling nature of some of their utility services.) The fact is, though, that the expansion of utility services is associated with economic development. (See Tables 2-1 and 2-2, and Figures 2-1 and 2-2. Water and sanitation data, unfortunately, is not available on the same basis as that for other services. Natural gas usage, which is not shown in the tables, may be associated more with availability of supply than with income levels.) Developing countries must prepare for the huge financial burden that accompanies the expansion of utility systems.

Table 2-1. Utility Services and Economic Development

	Low Income Economies	Middle Income Economies	High Income Economies
Economy and Population (a)			
Gross domestic product ($ billion)	1147	3549	18312
Population (millions)	3191	1419	828
GDP/capita ($)	359	2501	22116
Energy (a)			
Commercial energy use per capita			
(kg oil equivalent)	338	1812	5101
GDP per kg oil equivalent ($)	1.1	1.4	4.4
Electricity (b)			
Generating capacity per capita			
(MW per million inhabitants)	53	373	2100
Power percentage of infrastructure			
investment (%)	22	39	51
Telecommunications (b)			
Main lines per 1000 inhabitants	6	81	442
Telecommunications percentage			
of infrastructure investment (%)	2	6	9
Water and Sanitation (b)			
Percentage of population with access to:			
Water (%)	62	75	94
Sanitation (%)	42	68	95
Water and sanitation percentage			
of infrastructure investment (%)	18	16	6

Notes: (a) 1992
*   (b) 1990*

Source:
World Bank, World Development Report 1994 *(New York: Oxford University Press, 1994).*

Table 2-2. Electricity and Telecommunications by Region and Income Level (1990)

Region	GDP per Capita (1990 $)	Electricity Consumption per Capita (MWH)	Telephone Access Lines per 100 Inhabitants
North America	$22270	12.60	54.9
Latin America	4880	1.34	5.8
Western Europe	12325	5.44	37.6
Central and Eastern Europe	5165	3.61	11.4
Commonwealth of Independent States	6970	5.95	12.0
Middle East and North Africa	3690	1.15	4.9
Sub-Saharan Africa	1250	0.45	1.0
Centrally Planned Asia	1695	0.56	0.8
Other Pacific	6770	2.52	16.2
South Asia	1090	0.30	0.6
World	4765	2.19	9.8

Sources:
World Energy Council, Energy for Tomorrow's World *(New York: St. Martin's Press, 1993).*
Siemens AG, 1993 International Telecom Statistics *(Munich:Siemens AG, 1993).*

Historically, though, the returns on utility investment (other than for telecommunications) have been low. (See Table 2-3.) Investors will avoid such long-term commitments in the future unless they can earn better returns than they have in the past, which may indicate higher prices for utility customers in the future.

Table 2-3. Economic Rates of Return for World Bank Projects 1983–1992

Type of Project	Average Return (5)
Urban development	23
Transport	21
Telecommunications	19
Power	11
Water and sanitation	9

Source
World Development Report 1994.

Figure 2-1. Utility Services and Income Levels

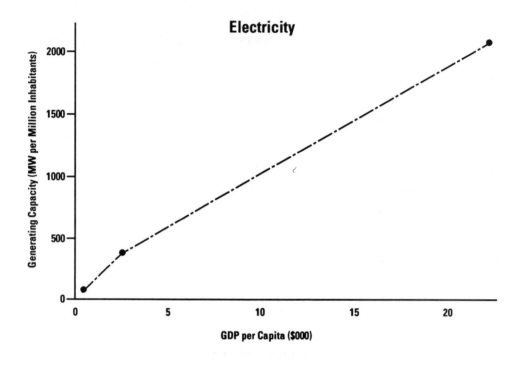

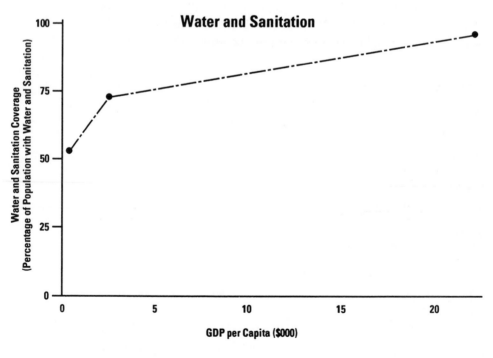

Figure 2-1. Utility Services and Income Levels

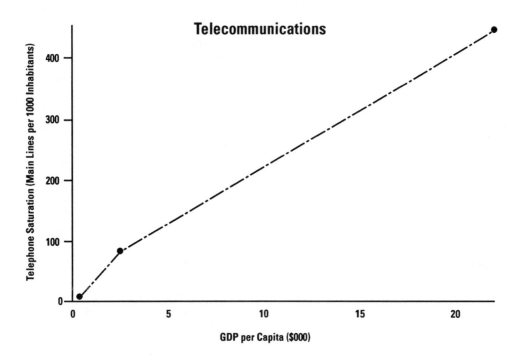

How Much Will It Cost?

Utilities are capital intensive entities. The builders of the infrastructure may have to spend money on projects that take years to complete yet bring in no profits during the construction process. They have to put into place backbone infrastructure that will not be fully utilized for years. Plant put into the wrong place cannot be moved, so the utility may have underutilized plant in one place while it has to build new facilities elsewhere where the demand has grown. That lack of mobility of assets affects investors, too. Once they have sunk their money into the assets, they have no way to escape political or economic instability. Thus, they insist on higher returns than one would normally expect in a stable business.

Based on the projections of income levels and electricity usage made by the World Energy Council in *Energy for Tomorrow's World,* and on the current cost of electric utility facilities, it appears as if the electric utilities and other power producers could spend $4281 billion (in real terms) over a 30-year period, excluding funds to rehabilitate or replace existing facilities. Based on the same income projections per region, using a declining cost model for installation of plant that attempts to take into account the gradual commercialization of technology now being introduced for the installation of plant, and assuming that telephone saturation moves up with income levels as shown in Figure 2-2, the expansion of the telecommunications system might require $1840 billion in the same period. (See Table 2-4 for projections.) If water and sanitation coverage increases with income level, as shown in Figure 2-1, then the expenditures for that industry could reach $427 billion in the three decades. Based upon projections of usage by the World Energy Council, capital expenditures for the natural gas industry could exceed $315 billion in the same period. Admittedly, these estimates require heroic assumptions about technology and costs, and should be viewed in terms of order of magnitude, but whatever their faults, they indicate the vast size of infrastructure investment needs. The total of utility capital expenditures, based on the estimates, could exceed $6863 billion, or $229 billion per year on average. Of the total, the five poorest regions (as measured by GDP per capita in Table 2-2), which account for only 28 percent of the world's GDP, may make 53 percent of the expenditures. That percentage works out to $122 billion per year for poorest regions. (See Table 2-5.)

Table 2-4. Expected Electricity and Telecommunications Investment by Region 1990–2020 (1990 $ Billions and %)

| Region | 1990 GDP % | 30 Year Capital Spending | | | |
| | | $ Spending Program | | % of 1990 GDP | |
		Elec	Telecom	Elec	Telecom
North America	6145	441	380	7	6
Latin America	2185	657	195	30	9
Western Europe	5595	537	280	1 o	5
Central and Eastern Europe	515	93	20	18	4
Commonwealth of Independent States	2010	257	114	13	6
Middle East and North Africa	1000	390	120	39	12
Sub-Saharan Africa	625	179	71	29	11
Centrally Planned Asia	2115	732	300	35	14
Other Pacific	3780	617	300	16	8
South Asia	1250	378	60	30	5
World	25220	4281	1840	29	7

Source:
Author's estimates. GDP data from Energy for Tomorrow's World, *adjusted by the author to 1990 price levels.*

Figure 2-2. Electricity and Telecommunications Usage by Region (1990)

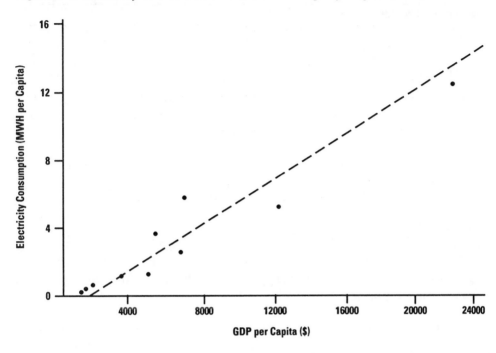

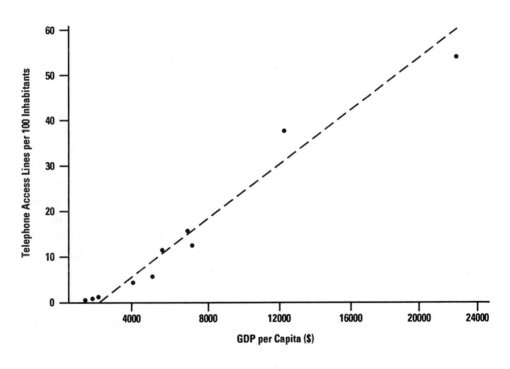

Table 2-5. Projected Utility Capital Spending for Five Poorest Regions (1990–2020)

Percentage of World:	
Population (1990)	68%
Gross domestic product (1990)	28
Capital expenditures (1990–2020)	
Electricity	55
Telephone	41
Water and sanitation	90
Natural gas	57

Source:
Author's estimates.

Who Has the Money?

The richer regions will find ways to finance their expansion programs, as they always have. The poorer regions may have to scramble, tapping every likely source of funds. At least six types of sources come to mind, although they are not equally plausible or rich:

- **Local governments** — These institutions want to foster development. They may already control the utility. The capital needs of the utilities, though, often weigh heavily on overburdened government budgets. The governments want to redeploy cash out of the utilities into other infrastructure and social investments that cannot run as businesses, or that may produce greater returns on the investment made. While some local governments may want to put more money into utilities, the trend seems to be in the opposite direction.

- **Local private investors** — Local ownership seems an ideal solution. Local investors know local business practices. They are not interlopers. But local investment has its own drawbacks. The capital market of the country may be too small to handle the huge needs of the utility. Local managements may not have the expertise to run the utilities well; And, investment in utilities may not provide the returns that local investors desire. Nevertheless, the utility should tap local markets for as much capital as possible. They can do so by selling control shares to wealthy local investors, by offering stocks and bonds in the local market, and by requiring that new subscribers buy a combination of stock and bonds that provides at least some to the funds required to add that subscriber to the system.

- **International development agencies** — The World Bank, its affiliates, and regional development banks have poured large sums into utility projects. Those agencies, however, have limited resources and almost unlimited demands on those resources. The agencies prefer, when possible, to push for private enterprise solutions, when possible. They may act as a catalyst for investment, and put some funds into the projects in order to give comfort to private investors, though.

- **Vendors** — In order to secure orders, manufacturers and the countries in which they are located often extend loans to purchasers of equipment. They may even invest in the common stock of the purchasing utility, if doing so makes the deal work.

- **International private investors and lenders** — Lending institutions and equity investors control enormous pools of capital. They have a long history of financing the acquisition of existing assets and of the construction of plant for expansion, in developed countries, whether by state-owned or investor-owned utilities. Lending money to or investing in newly-privatized utilities, though, is a recent phenomenon, without a long track record in the developing countries. Investors who get in on the ground floor, at the time of privatization, usually underpay and then make speculative profits. How they will do over several decades is an open question. Those investors may view a greater range of opportunities than local investors, so the utility has to offer a competitive potential profit. Those investors, too move in and out of holdings with speed, for short-term reasons, and doing so may disrupt the market. Those traits are not ideal for investment in long-lived projects whose payoff may occur years in the future.

- **Utilities in developed nations** — Those organizations face slowly growing and increasingly competitive markets at home. They have operating and financial (but not international) expertise. They want to branch out, to seek better opportunities for growth and profit. They do have choices, though. They may prefer the safer markets of the middle and high income countries. They may wish to invest only in existing facilities, in order to avoid construction risks and to earn immediate profits from a going operation.

Clearly, none of the potential investor groups is ideal, on its own, but, in combination, they may provide the necessary combination of operational, financial, and political skills.

Are There Alternatives to Big Spending Programs?

In the past, utility planners, operating under rigid regulation or under political control, assumed that price was given, they had to meet their customers inflexible demands by adding to supply, and also that however the utility normally did it was the only way. The utilities had little incentive to think otherwise. This supply-side mentality caused enormous problems in developed countries, and could do the same in developing countries. Radical alternatives exist:

- **Raise the price high enough to cover costs** — World Bank studies indicate enormous underpricing of utility services. One could calculate that some utilities need to raise prices 50 percent. A price increase of that size would: alleviate pressure on government budgets, create resources for utility expansion, and reduce the demand for the utility service (due to price elasticity of demand) perhaps enough to diminish or eliminate the need for outside financing.

- **Operate facilities more efficiently** — If the utilities made better use of existing assets, they could cut back on orders for new equipment, diminishing need for new capital.

- **Make use of pricing to control demand** — There are two pricing strategies: keep price stable and demand will fluctuate, or allow price to fluctuate in order to keep demand stable. In most of the world, utility regulators have, historically, fixed the price. When demand rises, rather than raise prices, as would normal businesses, utilities maintain the price and meet rising demand by building more facilities. When demand falls (possibly because the utility finally raises prices in order to pay for the new facilities), the utility rarely lowers price to encourage demand, as would a normal business. Use of market clearing price ahead of building programs could induce customer activities that would, to some degree, obviate the need for the new plant. Lowering the price when demand is down, would encourage greater economic activity in the country. A better pricing policy would reduce the risk of the utility building surplus facilities. A real time market clearing pricing policy, by controlling demand, could also diminish the need for expensive reserve plant.

- **Look for unconventional solutions** — Perhaps the introduction of Western-style utility supply systems in every underdeveloped region is a hopelessly uneconomic endeavor. Poor rural areas may require simple solutions that emphasize distributed systems, possibly isolated from the main network, with low levels of reliability, run by local entrepreneurs and agents, rather than by distant bureaucrats, and, perhaps service to the community rather than to private individuals. Where resources are scarce, perhaps the emphasis should be on renewable resources and greater efficiency of use rather than in attempting to expand supplies. Privatization and expansion programs seem to be designed to ignore those opportunities in favor of standard supply side options.

Capital Markets Needed

Due to fast depreciation, quick deployment, high returns, and improving technology, the telecommunications firms could come close to financing all needs from internal sources, within a reasonable period of years after the rampup of the expansion program. The other utility operators, however, suffer from longer lead times during construction, often inadequate depreciation allowances, and lower returns. The external financing needs of those utilities could exceed $40 billion per year in the five poor regions. That sum equals two-thirds of the annual official development assistance received by those countries. It constitutes over five times the average amount received in privatizations over the past few years, most of which money has gone to buy existing assets rather than to expand facilities.

Adjusting for commonly accepted capitalizations, the utilities in the poor regions would need to raise about $20 billion per year in the form of new common equity, if they were private enterprises. Ironically, the governments, as sellers of existing utility assets, will compete against the utilities as sellers of equity for purposes of expansion. Both will attract the same buyers. The market value of the equity of the government-owned utilities in the poorer regions, if capitalized in the normal fashion and brought up to accepted levels of profitability, could approach $400 billion. Obviously, selling off a substantial portion of those assets could siphon off funds from the expansion financing, creating a competition for investors and lowering the market valuations of the assets. Worldwide capital markets may be large, but are not limitless. The market for the securities of utilities in poor countries is only one part of the market, and it has to compete with others, including the market for utility privatizations in wealthier and more stable nations. (The sale of the German telecommunications system alone could drain $40–$60 billion from the markets in the next few years.) So far, so good, but it would take only a few disasters to sour investor sentiment, and with so many firms out there seeking money, a few disasters are inevitable.

Conclusion

Raising the money needed to expand and improve utility facilities will strain the resources of less developed countries. They will have to attract the huge sums from abroad or raise prices sufficiently to allow self financing of the projects, or most likely, raise the initial sums abroad and gradually raise prices to levels that allow self financing once the systems are larger and more modern. They could also consider the unthinkable: develop imaginative ways to control demand through pricing and deal with supply in a manner appropriate to the needs of the local population, rather than replicating what was done in richer countries. The richer countries have demonstrated how to build and run utilities without regard to economic rationality. Perhaps where money is scarce, necessity will be the mother of invention, and the customer will be better off and so will investors.

Chapter 3

Structuring the Utility

Leonard S. Hyman

Not so long ago, almost every utility was fully integrated vertically. That is, the utility owned and ran all aspects of the process of producing and selling its product. Sometimes the government controlled the manufacturer of the utility's equipment, the utility's fuel supplier (if an energy utility), and the utility itself. That was another sort of vertical integration. Nowadays, students of business as well as policy makers question the need for vertical integration. Reengineering consultants commonly promote the notion that corporations need to outsource, specifically to buy inputs from others who can produce it more economically than the corporation itself. Policy makers now believe that competition more effectively protects the public against exploitation than does regulation. Therefore, policy makers advocate breaking up the utility into components, keeping the parts that are natural monopolies under regulation and turning loose the others in a competitive market.

Governments considering privatization may have other reasons to contemplate breaking up the utility. Selling one huge entity may attract fewer qualified buyers than selling off many parts. In the former case, not many firms have enough money to buy a large corporation, and many potential bidders may not have the interest in or expertise to run the entire business. Buyers may prefer to purchase those parts that they can run the best, in size that is prudent for the purchaser. Furthermore, the government may wish to retain control of the utility but not of all the utility's functions, so it splits off the nonstrategic functions and sells them.

The various utility industries differ in possible structure, although some of the similarities are startling.

Electric Utilities
The fully integrated utility owns its source of fuel, the generating station that produces the electricity, the transmission line that carries the electricity to the centers of population, the distribution lines that carry it through the city to the customers, and the meter that measures the electricity that the customer buys. Generally the customers own the lines and electrical appliances on their side of the meter.

In the past decade, many electric utilities have sold or deemphasized their fuel businesses, having concluded that private operators provide ample, reliable, and economical fuel supplies.

The generating plant, exhibiting economies of scale, used to be a key part of the utility monopoly. Now, economies of scale seem to have expired for many types of power stations, independent power producers have entered the generation business, and many believe that power generation should be a competitive business, separate from the rest of the utility. Generators can and should compete against each other to sell their output to the utility or directly to the utility's customers. That model, though, may not work well if the generating stock consists of huge nuclear and hydroelectric stations or if small, new generating stations cannot acquire fuels at economical prices.

The transmission lines act as common carriers, as highways that bring the output of all producers to the market. Most policy makers think that transmission needs to remain a regulated monopoly, and should not be owned by a generator that could run it in a manner that would disadvantage competitors. Transmission could remain as a government entity, in the same way as highways, or be an independent corporation, or be owned by local electric distribution companies.

The local distribution part of the business retains all the characteristics of a regulated, local, natural monopoly. Nobody would want to build another set of wires when one already exists. The new question is whether the local distribution utility can function differently than before. For instance, rather than sell electricity to consumers, the utility could rent its lines to suppliers who would compete against each other to sell their electricity to consumers.

In France, Japan, Canada, Mexico and the United States, integrated utilities dominate the marketplace. In the United Kingdom, Chile, Argentina and New Zealand, the industry has been split into functional components.

Natural Gas

Natural gas is produced at wells. Gas gathering systems, which are small pipelines, take the gas from the wells to the big pipeline that will carry it to the centers of population. There, at the city gate, the local distribution utility moves the gas through a web of smaller pipes under the streets to the customer. The local distribution company owns the meter that measures the flow of gas to each customer, but rarely anything on the customer's side of the meter.

Originally, many of the gas systems were fully integrated. (In fact, at one time the local utility manufactured gas from coal, in the same way that the electric utility manufactures electricity from fuel.) Utilities owned the gas wells, the pipeline and

Figure 3-1. Electricity

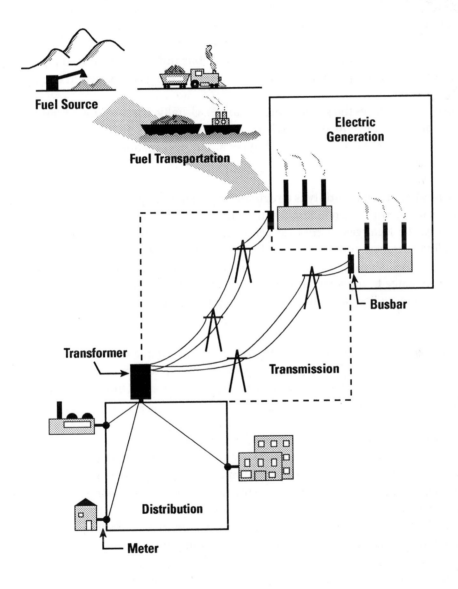

the local distribution company. The regulators set prices for every aspect of the business, including that of the gas at the wellhead.

The production of natural gas in many parts of the world is a competitive business, in which case there is no need for the government to set prices. Gas utilities need not own their own well in order to procure reliable supplies in a really competitive market.

The gas gathering systems may operate as public utilities, as part of the pipeline, on its own as a competitive business, or as part of the gas production facility.

The pipeline carries the gas for long distances. Usually, it is a regulated public utility, supposedly open to all who wish to use its system. The utility may buy the gas from producers, carry it, sell it to buyers along the pipeline, or simply transport the gas for others for a fee.

The local distribution utility is a regulated natural monopoly. As in the case of the electricity distributor, nobody wants to duplicate the existing delivery network. Usually, the local gas distributor arranges to buy gas from producers, pays the pipeline to transport it, and then sells that gas to its own customers. Increasingly, though, large consumers of gas have decided to buy the gas directly from the producer, arrange to transport it by pipeline, and then pay the local gas distribution utility no more than a fee to transport the gas from the pipeline to the consumer who owns the gas.

Integration from the wellhead to the consumer may have been the model in the past, but is becoming less and less prevalent. An industry of brokers can find the gas, arrange transportation, and assure the right price for those consumers that cannot do it themselves.

Telecommunications

In the old days, the telephone company owned the manufacturer of telephone equipment (or the manufacturer of equipment owned the telephone company), all the switching equipment, all the terrestrial and radio transmission plant, and even the wires and telephones in the customers' homes and offices. Rapid changes in technology as well as customer dissatisfaction with the existing system have forced major changes in the structure of telecommunications.

Basically, the telecommunications system is now divided into local exchange and long distance (interchange) services. The local exchange connects all the customers (usually by means of wires) to the switch, which directs the call within the local exchange. If the destination for the call is outside the local exchange, the switch directs the call to the switch of a long distance (interexchange) carrier. The

Figure 3-2. Natural Gas

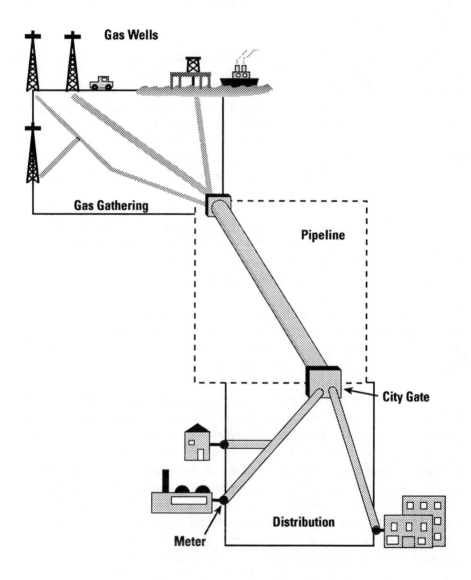

interexchange carrier then carries the call over its transmission system to the local exchange carrier at the destination of the call. That carrier then connects the call to the designated number. The customer who makes the call might only pay the local telephone company for the call, but the local telephone company will share the revenue with the long distance carrier and the local exchange at the destination of the call. That process, of course, was simple when one firm owned all the companies in the business.

Until recently, most people viewed the local exchange as a monopolist that had to be regulated. After all, nobody could or would duplicate all those lines and switches. The local exchange carrier was viewed as the only conduit to the customer, like a highway. Now, however, other carriers are finding ways to link up with the customer. Cable television systems, competitive fiber optic systems, and cellular telephony provide the means to do so. Eventually, the cable and cellular and local exchange telephone networks will be interconnected, so that the customer of one service can talk to a customer of one of the other services. (Cellular customers, of course, do this already.)

Some telephone users bypass the local exchange carrier when they make long distance calls. Rather than send the call to the long distance carrier through the local exchange system (and pay the local carrier for the service), the customers connect their calls directly to the long distance carrier.

In a number of countries, the long distance market is competitive, with numerous carriers offering their services. Customers choose their long distance carrier, although they may still pay the bill through the local exchange carrier, which acts as the collecting agent for the long distance companies.

Many countries have set low prices for local exchange service and high prices for long distance service, on the theory that large businesses and wealthy individuals make most of the long distance calls, and they can afford to pay the overcharges. The extra money earned on the long distance business is used to subsidize the local service, keeping its price down so that as many people as possible can afford to have a telephone, even if they cannot afford to make expensive long distance calls. Where such cross subsidy arrangements exist, the government may be reluctant to let competitors into the long distance market, because they might skim off some of the revenue that is providing the subsidy. Equally, the government may not wish to break up the telephone system into local and long distance firms because doing so might make it harder to transfer the profits from long distance to local. Modern technology, though, makes it easier for customers to evade subsidy arrangements. Governments might have to ban new technologies in order to retain old arrangements.

Figure 3-3. Telecommunications

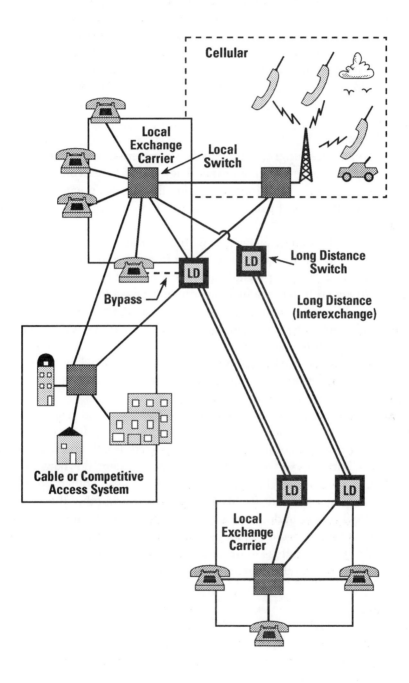

The telecommunications industry is moving in the direction of a market in which several competitive, interconnected providers furnish local service, some providing services over the lines of the existing local exchange carrier. Under those circumstances, only part of the local exchange service will require regulation. The long distance market, which already has the characteristics of a competitive should require little regulation once the competitors have established themselves. As long as a multiplicity of service providers can interconnect with each other, there seems little reason to keep all telecommunications services under one corporate roof.

Water and Sewage

These two services, seemingly, will retain the characteristics of public utilities and natural monopolies long after the others. They might benefit from outsourcing and from less integration, and from regulation that creates greater incentives for efficiencies, but little of the business could be put into the competitive sector.

The function of collection of water and its transportation often requires government control of land use, of extraction of water from the aquifer, and of riverways. The huge capital needs may preclude any benefits from competitive duplication of facilities. Enough different water sources may not exist in an area to allow competition, either. The water distribution system has all the characteristics of a classic public utility, too. Providing several sets of water pipes would represent a colossal waste of resources and cause disruption in the streets. In many places, the collection and long distance transport of water is accomplished by a different entity than its local distribution, so vertical integration is not a necessity.

Many of the same comments apply to sewage collection and disposal. The city does not need competing underground lines carrying sewage from the same localities. Due to the difficulty of finding sites for the facilities, the need to safely dispose of wastes, and the fixed nature of the transport system, it is hard to envisage numerous sewage treatment facilities competing with each other. Envisioning a system in which the treatment facility is owned by a firm other than the sewage collection entity is easier to do. In fact, when the need for a treatment facility arises, the sewage company could call for bids for a contract to serve it, and award the contract to the firm that agrees to provide the treatment for the lowest price. The sewage firm gets some of the benefits from competition through outsourcing.

Figure 3-4. Water and Sewage

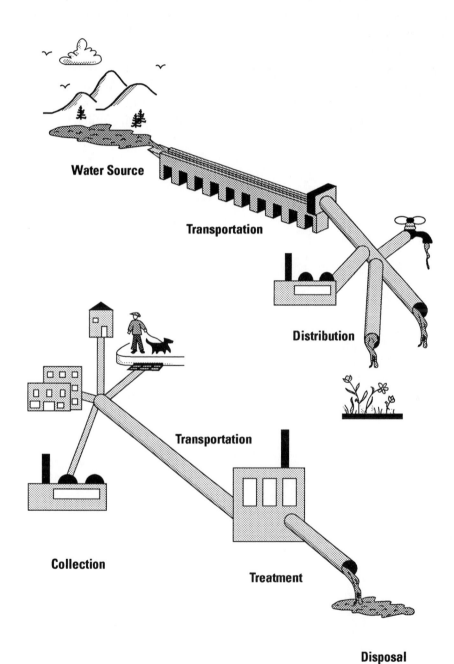

Conclusion

The era of the monolithic, regulated, vertically integrated utility has ended. Policy makers can structure privatizations in a way to take advantage of competitive forces in two ways. First, competition should do a better job than regulation of forcing the utility to operate efficiently. Second, the government may find only a limited number of potential buyers for a huge utility, but many buyers could emerge for smaller portions of the utility business, thereby giving the government more flexibility in selling off all or part of the business at the best prices. Getting the structure right might not only benefit the customers of the utility, but also the buyers and sellers.

Chapter 4

The Role of the Regulator

Leonard S. Hyman

The world turns away from government control over the economy. Central planning has failed. Capitalism has triumphed. Yet the regulator of public utilities remains on the scene, although in a diminished role. Successful privatization, in fact, requires a well-balanced regulatory structure. That is one in which the regulators take into account the needs of utilities to earn sufficient income to attract investors, as well as the requirement that the utilities provide reliable services in adequate quantities at the lowest possible price. Inordinate attention to assuring high levels of profit may attract investors initially, but could lead to a backlash against those investors afterwards. Too much emphasis on low price could frighten away potential investors, thereby hindering a successful privatization.

Regulation vs. Competition

Traditionally, governments either owned or minutely regulated the utility. Those ownership or regulatory arrangements often inhibited investment. Often, the government did not have the money needed to invest in the utility's expansion. Its regulatory policies, too, may have set prices for service that were too low to produce sufficient profits to attract capital and that discouraged efficiency and innovation (because the regulators provided little or no reward for either). As a result of those experiences, governments have chosen to remove the utilities from the state budget through privatization, and to set up industry and regulatory structures that depend as much as possible on competitive market forces to discipline and control the privatized utilities. Most commonly, the governments free from regulation sectors of the market that can operate competitively. Those include the generation of electric power, long distance and cellular telephony, acquisition of natural gas supply on a large scale, or dealings with large customers who have the ability to produce or obtain their own utility services. By and large, governments have retained regulatory power over all aspects of water supply, transmission and distribution of natural gas and electricity, and the local telephone network.

Regulatory Mechanics

Regulators operate under laws that may spell out in detail how they should regulate, or under laws that leave the regulators with great discretion. Some regulators work within a government department. The minister of the department appoints, instructs, and dismisses the regulators. Clearly, those regulators cannot act independently of political control. In the United States, Canada and the United Kingdom, the government appoints (or the people elect) independent regulators or panels of regulators who hold office for fixed terms, and can act on their own, without fear of dismissal.

The rules of operation and regulation may be set by law, a contract negotiated between the utility and the government (called the franchise or license agreement), or through rules issued by the regulators. Those rules may have set terms or continue until changed. In the United States, utility regulation must operate within a framework of constitutional law. The courts will overturn regulatory decisions they deem unconstitutional. That layer of legal protection may not exist in other countries. In fact, one of the dangers that investors face is the possibility that the government decides to change the rules once it discovers that the old rules, for instance, allow the privatized utility to earn a larger profit than anticipated. Make no mistake about it. In some countries, when the government wants to change the rules, it changes the rules, and the unhappy investor can do little but protest.

Separating Competitive from Regulated

Public utilities exhibit the characteristics of natural monopolies. They have economies of scale in operation. As public utilities expand and serve more customers, costs per unit of output decline. One large utility, serving the area, operates at a lower cost level than would many smaller firms competing for customers. Furthermore, utilities put in extensive networks or distribution systems to carry the service offered. Duplication of those networks would be extraordinarily expensive, and few cities or regions have the space for multiple distribution systems. In order to secure the lowest cost service for consumers, the government selects one firm to provide service in the region (usually called a "franchise area"), and that firm moves down the cost curve by reaching economies of scale. That utility is now a monopolist.

In competitive markets, the price of the product acts as the rationing device. If the price is high enough, and a high price is accompanied by high profits, new capital enters the market, to supply more product. The new supply eventually lowers the price of the product. If price is too low, and the profit on the sales is too low as a result, then producers leave the market, and as supply falls, price rises to a level that might attract competitors back into the market.

In competitive markets, firms cannot overcharge or provide poor service for long, because customers will take their business to other firms that offer better prices and service. Competition gives the customer choice. The customer of a monopolist has no choice. In order to prevent the utility monopolist from taking advantage of its customers, the government sets up a regulatory entity to act as a substitute for the competitive forces of the marketplace. The forces of competition would prevent the firm from overcharging, from making exorbitant profits, or from providing shoddy service. Market forces would induce the firm to operate as efficiently as possible, to innovate, to offer new and better products and services. The actions of the market would attract new capital needed to expand output, or cause capital to leave the industry. The regulators try to do for the consumers what the competitive market would do. Unfortunately, regulators seem to have concentrated the most on keeping down profits and assuring minimum standards of service, and they have done a poor job of attracting capital, or encouraging efficiency and innovation. Many people believe that the marketplace produces better results for consumers than do regulators. Therefore, when reorganizing the public utility for privatization, they try to regulate as little as possible and depend on market forces wherever possible.

As a start, the government may want to break up the utility, so that the natural monopoly elements of the business remain under regulation, and other segments operate in a competitive marketplace. Those segments that retain economies of scale, or which could be duplicated only at great expense, or act as common carriers that provide the competitive service with access to the customers, are the services that normally remain under regulation. The other services furnished by the utility may or may not remain regulated, depending on particular circumstances, including whether competitors are likely to enter the market. There is no point in deregulating a business that remains in the hands of monopolists or oligopolists, because under those circumstances, the customer will gain few benefits from the deregulation.

The government may, also, continue to regulate the utility, but authorize the utility to contract for output and services from unregulated entities. Free market force would determine what price the utility has to pay to elicit the services or product from the unregulated supplier. The government would continue to control the price that the utility charges to its customers. That arrangement may be detrimental to the regulated utility whose cost of inputs is determined by market forces but whose price of output is set by the government.

How are regulators dividing up assets and functions? The answer differs from place to place, so the chart that follows shows trends rather than statistical analysis.

Deregulation, though, need not mean a complete absence of governmental supervision. For the government will want to assure that the companies in the business compete fairly, follow operating rules, and meet minimum service standards. If the deregulated market does not produce the expected results, the government might have to reintroduce regulation.

Table 4-1. Where Do Utility Sectors Fall in the Competition Spectrum?

	Regulated	Moving toward Competitive	Competitive
Electricity	Distribution Transmission	Generation	
Natural Gas	Distribution	Transmission	Production
Telecommunications		Local exchange	Cellular Cable TV Long Distance
Water	All sectors		

Formulas for Regulation

Regulation falls, roughly, into five categories. All have their virtues and drawbacks:

- **Rate of Return** — This procedure has dominated regulation for almost a century. The regulator determines how much money has been invested to serve the public (the "rate base"). Then the regulator sets an appropriate return on that investment after considering what capital costs in the marketplace. Rate base multiplied by rate of return equals the income the utility should earn from which it can pay those who provided the money to build the rate base. The utility is entitled to collect enough money from customers to pay all costs of doing business, including that return on investment. The system focuses attention on the profit that the utility needs to attract capital, so an expanding utility that needs new capital can invest money knowing that the new investment will earn a profit. However, rate of return regulation has serious drawbacks. The first is that utilities might be tempted to make unnecessary investments because regulators let them earn a return (profit) on those investments. The second—and more serious—objection is that rate of return regulation does not provide the utility with incentives to run more efficiently. The utility collects all costs plus a profit. If the costs decline, then the utility has to lower prices, and therefore does not collect a bigger profit.

- **Standard Costs** — Regulators may like rate of return regulation, but they also want to reward utilities that operate more efficiently. To do so, regulators analyze the cost structure of the industry, and then set up a cost and investment model for a hypothetical utility. A price is set for electricity that provides an adequate rate of return for the utility. The price derived from that model is then applied to all the utilities. Utilities whose costs are lower than the standard used in the model earn a higher return than those whose costs are higher than the standard. Utilities that manage to serve customers with less capital than the standard utility earn a higher return than those who require larger amounts of capital than the standard. In effect, the utility that is more efficient in its operations or in its use of capital earns a higher return than that set by the standard model. This method of regulation encourages efficiency, but it may not provide the means for regulators to deal with specific problems at a utility. It may not produce lower prices for customers for long periods of time, either, until the period of the formula runs out and a new one is set that brings down prices to reflect efficiencies.

- **Incentive** — Many plans fall under this rubric. The simplest is to set a range of returns around a designated number. If the utility earns less than the designated return, but within the range, it cannot request a price increase. If the utility earns more than the designated return, but within the range, it can keep the extra profit over the designated return. This procedure induces the utility to run efficiently and to spend less time seeking price changes from regulators, because the utility loses profits if it cannot earn the designated return and because it collects extra profits if it can exceed that return. The second type of incentive regulation involves profit sharing. The regulator, again, sets a range of returns. If the utility earns above that range, it can keep some of the excess profit, and it turns the rest of the excess back to customers through a refund. In this way, customers immediately gain some of the benefits of the increase in efficiency. The third type of incentive plan requires the regulators to set up an elaborate array of performance indices. The utility's level of profit depends on how well it performs against the indices. While the idea seems sensible, in principle, devising the right indices is not a simple task, and the utility might find a way to game the indices without necessarily producing lower costs overall that benefit customers.

- **Price Cap** — This method has become fashionable, due in part to its seeming simplicity. Regulators tie the annual price increase to the cost of living index for a given period of years. Then, in order to encourage more efficient operations, they normally subtract a productivity index from the cost of living index to arrive at the price increase for the year. (For instance, cost of living rises 4 percent and the productivity index is 3 percent, so prices rise 1 percent). If the utility can increase its real productivity by more than the productivity index, it makes an extra profit that it can keep. The procedure has faults, too. The prices and costs at the utility may be poorly connected to the moves in the cost of living index. The rigid productivity index takes no account of sudden and dramatic change in costs. The formula provides no incentive to add to investment in a major way (because revenues are tied to sales volume which may grow slowly). Finally, although the price cap formula was designed to avoid the problems caused by rate of return regulation, the results of price cap are often judged on a rate of return basis. In other words, if the price cap formula produces too high a return on investment, it may be changed to produce a lower return.

- **Ad hoc** — Often, the regulator has to deal with a specific problem. Rather than attempt to bend one of the standard regulatory methods in order to produce satisfactory results, the regulator formulates a solution to the problem. The utility, for instance, may have to borrow large sums of money in order to meet demand for service. The regulator would then set prices in such a way to produce enough profit to cover borrowing costs by a given margin. Or, the regulator might want to encourage a merger that would help reduce costs, so the regulator gives the utility special profit incentives to make the merger. A few regulatory agencies have resisted regulatory formulas altogether, and set prices by bargaining with the utility every year. To the extent that ad hoc procedures solve problems, they are good. To the extent that they create uncertainty because of their impermanent nature, they may discourage investment.

Service Standards

Most investors concentrate their attention on the regulatory rules that affect profitability. Consumers, on the other hand, pay attention to the rules that affect service standards. Regulators must assure that utilities do not increase profits at the expense of reliable service to customers. At the same time, excessively high service standards might raise costs and prices to levels that customers cannot afford to pay. In developed countries, the regulators often set uniform standards for all customers in a particular category, and charge all customers the same price for that service. That practice does not let the customers choose the level of service that they desire. Some may be paying for service levels that they do not want, and others might be willing to pay more for a higher level of service. In less developed countries, some consumers might want a basic level of service that they can afford to pay for, rather than a high level of service that is too expensive for their limited budgets. Thus, regulators and utilities need to tailor standards and prices to the social and economic needs of the population.

Regulators may do more than set minimum standards for operations. They may set goals for improvement of service, and most commonly, goals for the expansion of service to a greater part of the population. In fact, the franchise contract or the regulatory rules may require the utility to add a certain number of customers every year, or to expand service to rural areas. Without those rules, the utility might limit its services to the most affluent or the most populated parts of the country, which would produce the greatest profit per dollar of investment.

Poor utility service is endemic to less developed economies, and without adequate utility service, the economy cannot develop. Naturally, planners and investors want to put in the best of everything, to make the system look like that of a developed country. At times, though, flexible, imaginative and economic solutions to underdevelopment might require less high technology.

Conclusion

Investors want certainty and high profits. They do not want to invest funds unless the regulatory scheme is clearly set forth in advance of investment. They want regulators who are independent of political pressure. Utility managements want profits sufficient to allow the utility to expand, and to meet the demands of customers. Governments want the local utility to aid the expansion of the economy, not to retard growth, but they also want the utility to charge the lowest price possible. In addition, governments want the utility to help solve environmental, social and developmental issues; and want regulators who do not embarrass them politically, yet who are not independent of the will of the politicians. Customers want the best possible service for the lowest possible price. The regulator has to balance all those pressures.

PART II
Views from the Field

➤

Chapter 5

Telecommunications Privatization and Beyond: A Global Perspective

Leo A. Sozzi

The ability to send, receive, and manage information is critical to the economic, political, and social well-being of all nations. United States (US) vice president Al Gore highlighted this fact to representatives from 132 countries during his presentation at the March 1994 United Nations Telecommunications Conference. Gore stated, "A planetary information network should be created to promote economic growth, foster democracy, and link people around the world." Nations must establish priorities, set goals, allocate resources, and plan the development of their telecommunications infrastructure accordingly.

With the possible exception of oil-rich Arab Emirates, all nations lack the resources to provide for at least some of their important needs, e.g., education, health care. In all probability, most nations also lack the resources to build the infrastructure required to satisfy all of their critical information movement and management (IM&M) needs.

The question faced by nations that have a lack of resources for IM&M and other needs is whether they can and should try to get the resources they require from sources outside of their own government. This chapter considers the privatization of a nation's IM&M infrastructure as a means of satisfying its IM&M needs, and as a means of providing a source of capital to meet other, critical needs. Nations considering privatization can use this discussion, its insights and frameworks, to make effective decisions in the pursuit of more resources.

However, for privatization to work as a solution to the problem of scarce resources, the seller, i.e., the nation, and the prospective buyers, i.e., financial and strategic investors, must negotiate a "deal"—price and conditions that are satisfactory to both parties. Success in such negotiations is a function of the value and risk each party ascribes to the deal. This chapter presents a framework that can be used by sellers and buyers to define a range of acceptable prices and risks.

In addition, this chapter explores the fact that some nations may have to go beyond privatization to maximize the performance of their IM&M industries. For instance, analysis may show that an existing industry structure will be more effective when converted from a regulated monopoly to open competition.

Finally, this chapter explains that nations have a variety of resources and varying resource needs. Therefore, each nation must assess its own privatization opportunities and determine an effective structure for its IM&M industry.

Furthermore, this chapter puts the IM&M industry in a global perspective. A nation, independent of its size, cannot effectively plan the development of its IM&M infrastructure without a complete understanding of how that infrastructure will integrate with the world's networks and the IM&M industry's economic structure.

Keep in mind that this chapter addresses only the ability to send, receive, and manage information. The development and ownership of content, e.g., data, entertainment, will also play a major role in shaping the industry...but is beyond the scope of this discussion.

A Global Information Movement and Management Industry

All the current evidence; e.g., the General Agreement on Tariffs and Trade (GATT), multi-national alliances; indicates that a global economy is developing. The need to move and manage information among the world's economic centers is growing at a rapid rate.

An evolving oligopoly of service providers will serve as the primary force shaping a global IM&M industry. Competing forces will focus on satisfying the needs of government, business, and individual consumers in and among the top 50–100 economic centers of the world, i.e., "city-states" like New York, London, and Hong Kong. These "city-states" are the markets and geographic areas that hold the promise for the most attractive economic returns.

The competitors in this global industry will be alliances of many of today's largest, leading-edge telecommunications and cable companies, equipment manufacturers, and software developers. They will include Post, Telephone, and Telegraph companies (PT&Ts) and US Local and Interexchange Carriers (LECs and IECs).

The oligopoly will create a global infrastructure that will consist of competing, yet inter-operable, wireline, and wireless networks and provide the capability to have one competitor's customer seamlessly and transparently communicate with a rival's customer. In essence, competitors will be "networks of networks" similar to those that currently serve the United States long distance market. In fact, the US long distance oligopolists, e.g., AT&T, MCI, Sprint, are among the leading-edge firms shaping this global oligopoly. Each is allying with foreign carriers while simultaneously expanding into the provision of local service in locations where they envision attractive economic returns.

Current international activities support the vision of a global oligopoly. Such activities include AT&T's creation of World Partners and its entry into England's marketplace, the MCI and British Telcom (BT) alliance; and Sprint's partnering with the German and French PT&Ts. Within the US, examples of consolidation and industry merging include the US West and Time Warner alliance and the NYNEX, Air Touch, Bell Atlantic, and US West wireless joint venture.

As currently envisaged, when fully developed, these global competitors will be vertically-integrated, full-service providers, with the ability to offer consumers "one-stop shopping" in the markets they choose to serve. In targeted areas/markets, these global oligopolists will provide consumers with a wide array of wireline and wireless services from which to choose. These services will enable consumers to implement many new applications, and increase the capabilities and user-friendliness of existing ones. Examples of the types of wireline and wireless services available include:

- one-way narrowband services that will enhance paging

- two-way wideband services enhancing existing and introducing new store and forward data applications

- asymmetrical broadband services that enable shop-at-home and video-on-demand

- symmetrical broadband enabling interactive video-telephone and games.

In other targeted areas/markets, these competitors will provide a more limited set of services. In all cases, the decisions of where, when and how much to provide will be driven by economic motives and the regulations in the geographic areas/markets the oligopolists may have an interest in serving.

In all probability, the services provided by these oligopolists will be commodities, i.e., consumers will not be able to discern any significant differences among competing services. The primary reasons for this conclusion are the assumptions that technology will be available to all, and that several different types of technology will allow all service providers to offer services with virtually the same capacity, capabilities, and quality of service characteristics. Therefore, technology will not provide a competitive advantage for any particular player, ceteris paribus.

This idea that technology will not provide competitive advantages is important, because, based on accepted economic theory, the nature of competition is focused on the ability to price competitively and to provide a full array of services. Yet, meeting these two criteria will not guarantee success. In this type of competitive environment, marketing and sales skills will also be critical success factors. However, in the final tabulation, an oligopolist cannot hope to be a leading player without a cost structure that allows competitive pricing.

The oligopolists will have to reach people and machines, e.g., computers, faxes, beyond their targeted areas in order to provide global connectivity. These are the areas where other, more locally focused, providers of services will operate. These local providers will offer consumers connectivity to the global oligopolists, in addition to providing intra-area services.

Within these local areas, it is envisioned that the industry structure can take several forms, including oligopolies; regulated monopolies of privately-owned, for-profit companies; and government-controlled, operated, and possibly subsidized, providers of service. Existing examples of these forms are:

- Local Oligopolies: provision of long distance access services in the US, provision of local service in England

- Privately-owned, Regulated Monopolies: provision of local services in many parts of the US, provision of service in Argentina and Chile

- Government Controlled: most PT&Ts around the globe.

Some governments will have to create monopolies and provide subsidies if services are to be made available in parts of, or even in an entire nation. The reason for this is the existence of markets and geographic areas around the globe, including in the US, which will not provide sufficient economic incentive for incumbent providers to upgrade facilities, to attract new entrants, or in the extreme case, for anyone to provide service of any kind.

Potential hope exists in these extreme cases from the promise offered by the worldwide, wireless, satellite networks that are currently on drawing broads. However, unless there are significant technological breakthroughs, the wireless technology will not provide the same service capabilities as the wireline alternative. Specifically, limitations will exist in the higher bandwidth services. In any event, even if the wireless networks become a reality, government subsidies will be required in certain corners of the globe.

A second conclusion can be drawn from this brief discussion of wireless capabilities. In areas where the demand for broadband services is high enough to provide attractive economic returns, wireline access means, e.g., fiber, coaxial cable, will be available.

The net result of all this activity will be a world market that is much more competitive than it is today. The world market will consist of:

- a global oligopoly in which competitors directly serve government, business, and individual consumers in the most economically attractive areas and along the most attractive routes

- secondary oligopolies serving the areas beyond, and sometimes overlapping, those of the global oligopolists

- regulated, privately-owned, and possibly subsidized, monopolies, in areas where demand and/or government mandates will not support more than one network

- government controlled, operated, and possibly subsidized, monopolies in areas that cannot provide an attractive return on the investment required to provide services

- areas without any services at all.

In some countries, all of the above conditions may exist. Whirling around in this global market will be many niche players, primarily resellers and wireless access providers, and new entrants trying to profitably make their way into the market.

The rate of speed and extent of this global evolution are a function of many variables and therefore are extremely difficult to predict. These variables include:

- status of the existing infrastructures and networks

- prices and the demand they generate

- speed, nature, and sequencing of deregulation

- technological advancements and their price/performance characteristics

- amount of capital, technical, and managerial resources available to the industry.

Planning for a National IM&M Industry

The value ascribed to the IM&M industry by a nation is extremely important in establishing effective overall national policies and priorities. Calculating the value of the IM&M industry requires a comprehensive understanding of a nation's current and potential future positioning in the global web of networks and regulation. With this information, a nation can define how it can participate in the global industry and, in turn, generate plans that will maximize value within the country.

When calculating value, it must be recognized that the movement and management of information, i.e., communications, is an enabling capability whose value extends well beyond the national industry itself. The benefits to be derived will be seen in many areas, such as in the economic growth of other industries as well as in education, health, and national security. This value-creating capability must not be overlooked when establishing national priorities and investing in the nation's IM&M infrastructure.

Assuming that the development of an IM&M infrastructure has now been assigned a high priority, the task becomes one of establishing specific objectives for the infrastructure and defining the plans that will have the highest probability of achieving them.

Outlined below is a systematic, four-step process which, if properly applied, will provide some of the critical information required to establish objectives and plans. The process focuses on the existing and anticipated demand emanating from the national markets and the nation's ability to satisfy the demand using only its own, internally-available resources and capabilities. If unmet demand exists, it is defined. Also identified are the additional resources and capabilities, i.e., beyond those internally available, required to meet the unmet demand.

Much of the data and information required in this process should be in the nation's IM&M business plan, should one exist. If a business plan does not exist, one should be created. A process to develop a business plan is described in the following four steps:

Step 1. Develop a thorough understanding of the demand side of the marketplace.
Those who are developing the business plan need to identify and quantify market segments so that existing and future consumer needs can be identified and quantified. All of the needs should be clearly identified as either existing or anticipated. The planners must also define the services required to satisfy consumer needs, including quality of service expectations. For instance, planners must find out whether narrowband services are required to enable ordinary audio communications (telephony) and/or symmetrical broadband services to enable interactive, multi-media communications.

Planners must understand each market segment's ability to pay, in addition to determining the government's plans and ability to subsidize services. Planners must also identify existing prices and estimate price- and cross-elasticities of demand. This information provides the basis for calculating the units of service that will be in demand at different price levels, as well as the revenue that may be generated.

The geographic distribution of the demand and potential revenue, e.g., areas of dense and sparse concentrations, must be identified. This is required for the efficient design of the network and operations support systems. In all cases, planners need to quantify the variables and forecast a range of potential values. In addition, estimates must be made of the points in time at which the values are expected to be achieved.

All of this information is required to determine whether the network investment will create economic value, i.e., be "profitable" and the degree of risk associated with the investment.

Step 2. Develop a thorough understanding of the supply side of the marketplace.
Planners also need to take a comprehensive inventory of the nation's existing service provisioning capabilities. In addition, a detailed definition of the capabilities that are planned to be put in service, with their expected timing, should be prepared. This information must be aggregated in a manner that will allow a comparison of these capabilities with the demand for services derived in Step 1.

The costs associated with providing service must also be thoroughly understood. This requires a knowledge of the investment in inservice facilities with their on-going cost for maintenance and repair and the investment in new facilities with their on-going costs.

Planners need to aggregate costs into arrays that allow correlations to be drawn to revenues and any non-financial benefits, e.g., increased national security, which are being or are projected to be derived. This means aggregation by service type, by market, by geographic area, and by combinations of these factors.

The availability of this information will allow planners to determine important factors such as:

- the price that must be charged to cover the cost of providing specific services

- the amount of subsidy required at different price levels

- the economic value created or lost as a result of providing a specific array of services to a market or geographic area

- the economic value of the entire, national IM&M industry.

The quality of service and price levels are two additional dimensions that planners must consider from the supply side. The nation's planners must ask, "Are existing quality of service levels meeting consumers' needs and expectations?" and "Are prices reasonable in light of consumers' ability to pay?" The answers to these questions must also be aggregated in a way that will allow conclusions to be drawn when used in conjunction with the demand information developed in Step 1.

The information derived in Steps 1 and 2 will provide all the data required for planners to establish priorities of needs and to generate the plans for satisfying them.

Step 3. Define unmet needs.
A nation must understand the needs it cannot satisfy and the possible benefits it may be foregoing. This information is required in deciding whether to seek assistance from sources outside of the national government.

In Step 1, the national market was segmented into customer groups that possessed common needs. Step 2 provided the ability to define the needs that would be met with the resources available to the government. A comparison of the two will identify unmet needs.

Planners must analyze the benefits to be derived from satisfying each of the unmet needs that are identified. The benefits must be fully described. Wherever possible, the benefits should be quantified and estimates made of their timing.

With this information, the nation's planners must decide whether or not they want to investigate the attractiveness of obtaining outside assistance to satisfy the unmet IM&M needs. However, the information required to make this decision has not been completely developed. Planners must identify the additional resources required to satisfy the needs beyond those currently allocated to the IM&M industry.

A nation could decide not to pursue additional needs satisfaction and stop at this point in the analysis, but this is not recommended. The analysis outlined in the final step will provide valuable information. However, if planners stop the planning process after Step 3, a decision must be made on the advisability of "selling" equity shares in the IM&M assets as a means of raising the capital required for achieving other national goals.

Step 4. Determine the additional resources required to satisfy unmet needs.
Two broad classes of resources are critical in the early stages of satisfying needs:

- knowledgeable people who can define the optimal plan for meeting needs with an explicit definition of the costs of implementation and the plan's economic consequences

- the cash to cover the capital investments and on-going expense required to implement the plan.

The optimal plan may require the introduction of an entirely new network architecture and the wholesale replacement of existing technology with the latest, state-of-the-art equipment. In fact, it may be determined that the plan may offer the best method for serving all needs not just the ones that are currently unmet. The nation will need to have access to individuals with knowledge of the latest technology and the expertise to use it in designing new and enhancing existing networks.

After the plan is developed and funds secured, people with other skills are required. These people include technicians to install, maintain, and repair the network and supporting operating systems; marketers to establish price and sell; and managers to coordinate overall operations. In this new, global industry, they must possess up-to-date skills.

Clearly, a nation should conduct a thorough assessment and inventory of its people skills. The skills of the workers should be benchmarked against the skills that industry experts deem necessary for a nation to successfully operate in the global IM&M industry.

With regard to the additional investments and on-going costs, each must be identified and associated with the needs they satisfy and the benefits they will produce. Again, the market segmentation developed in Step 1 should be used. In this way judgements can be made as to the economic attractiveness of the various investment alternatives available to the country. Going through this process will also be of value in establishing national IM&M priorities and goals and making resource allocation decisions. Most nations probably require human and cash resources beyond those available if they are to effectively plan, build, and manage a modern IM&M network.

Define Alternatives for Obtaining the Additional Resources
A nation may secure the resources required to satisfy unmet IM&M needs in numerous ways. They include:

- divert funds from other areas of the national budget

- seek loans, e.g., from the World Bank

- Build, Transfer, Operate options (BTO)

- alliances with other countries or companies

- various forms of privatization (normally a requirement for World Bank loans)

- combinations of the above.

In the ensuing discussion, it is assumed that privatization, specifically the sale of equity in the national IM&M infrastructure, has been selected as the most attractive alternative for the nation. Further, it is assumed that the nation is willing to accept cash and/or the use of the experienced people required to create the IM&M infrastructure in exchange for the equity.

Telecommunications Privatization

Privatization can be an effective tool to achieve many national objectives. Key among the objectives are:

- infusion of capital that can be used for a wide range of purposes, e.g., communications, security, education, health

- infusion of the technical and managerial skills required for the planning, development, and operation of the IM&M infrastructure

- separation from government control the management and operation of the infrastructure under the belief that private management and control is superior to that of the government.

To start, a nation must establish a privatization strategy. For instance, should the nation privatize its entire infrastructure or only a portion? Should wireline and wireless be sold separately or as a package? The alternative combinations and permutations will be virtually unlimited for some nations, while for others privatization opportunities will be limited or nonexistent.

The value and risk ascribed to the privatization by the seller (the nation) and the potential buyers (strategic and/or financial investors) should be the primary drivers of a strategy. The estimation of these variables can be systematically approached and requires a thorough understanding of the global industry and the conditions that exist within the country. The approach must be applied to each of the privatization strategies under consideration and the information gathered must be used to select the optimal strategy.

Value and Risk to "The Seller"

At this stage, the nation has decided to "sell" all or a portion of its IM&M assets if the price is acceptable and the risks are manageable. The bounds for an acceptable price can be established by valuing the assets to be sold from two perspectives:

- the economic value that will be derived strictly within the IM&M industry

- the economic, non-economic, and/or unquantifiable value to be accrued to the entire country.

Due to the enabling nature of IM&M services, the second value will probably be higher than the first. If this is the case, the first value represents the highest price a nation can expect to receive, ceteris paribus. The second value provides the basis for determining the lowest price they should accept.

For some countries, the economic value generated within the industry will be negative. A country may be subsidizing the industry in order to realize other benefits. As a result, the rates charged for services are probably below the level required to produce a positive economic return. If this condition exists, it could preclude privatization unless special concessions are granted by the government. If privatization is not a viable alternative and other means of obtaining resources prove fruitless, the nation will be forced to maintain the status quo.

In defining value, the nation must include the anticipated explosive growth in the global demand for IM&M services. The nation must assess how it will fit into the world economy and the global IM&M industry. For instance, the "valuators" must understand whether the nation contains any of the city-states and/or routes that may be targeted by the global oligopolists, i.e., potential strategic investors.

Understanding risk is critical to the decision making process, and a major consideration in establishing price. A thorough risk assessment provides the basis for determining the need for contingency planning.

An effective method to assess risk requires the identification of all of the significant assumptions, e.g., the magnitude and timing of revenues. A review of these assumptions and an assessment of their possible consequences provides the required risk information. A nation should use this information to develop contingency plans.

An example of the risk to the seller is the potential of the nation losing control, i.e., the ability to manage and operate the infrastructure, of a critical industry. This loss of control could occur if the country uses foreigners or has strategic investors assume the responsibility to plan, manage, and operate the infrastructure. Should these individuals leave, the nation could have a problem unless it had developed plans to address this risk. To understand the potential consequences of losing control, all one must do is study the events that occurred in Iran after the 1979 revolution.

Value and Risk to "Buyers"

Buyers come in two forms: financial and strategic investors. They all have a common objective. They want to create "shareowner value," i.e., the appreciation of their investment and the dividends it pays must produce an economic return that is equal to or exceeds a level commensurate with the risk they will incur. The value and risk calculated by the two types of investors can be significantly different.

Financial Investors

Financial investors buy ownership positions in the IM&M infrastructure. Their return is based solely on the performance of that "business." In estimating potential return and risk, they must take the same "strictly within the IM&M industry" perspective that the seller's evaluation took. The results produced by these two evaluations can vary significantly if different assumptions are made.

In any event, the financial investor should ask for, and the seller should be prepared to provide, a detailed plan for the "business." The plan should clearly identify and support assumptions, costs, and benefits. In addition, an on-site inspection and a due diligence should be conducted by IM&M experts on behalf of the investors.

The financial investors will also identify and assess the potential consequences of the risks involved. Some of the potential risks may include: the nation does not have, nor can it obtain, the required technical and managerial skills; revenue projections are too high; and cost estimates are too low.

Strategic Investors

In estimating value and risk the strategic investor must perform exactly the same tasks as the financial investor. However, a major difference could exist since the strategic investor will probably be one of the global oligopolists. As a result, the strategic investor may have a source of value that neither the seller nor the financial investor possesses. Value could be derived from synergies that may be realized with other assets. The net result is that the strategic investor may be willing to pay a higher price than the financial investor, ceteris paribus.

A second significant difference could exist between the two types of investors. The strategic investor will probably be in a position to provide planning, technical, managerial, and operational skills. In this case, a fair market price must be established for these skills.

Finally, the strategic investor will incur all of the risks incurred by the financial investors with the possible exception of the concern over the availability of people skills. Yet, if the strategic investor pays a premium in anticipation of realizing synergies, there may be an additional risk associated with achieving the synergies.

Sources of Information Required to Calculate Value

Two types of information are required to quantitatively calculate value: analytical methods and input data. The analytical methods can be found in any good economics, finance, or mergers and acquisitions textbook. Furthermore, most of the input data required to perform the valuation can be derived from the four-step planning process described earlier in this chapter and the financial and operational reports of the nation's telecommunications company.

Beyond Privatization

Privatization by itself may not engender the marketplace behavior required to achieve national IM&M goals. The industry structure, e.g., regulated monopoly, open competition, will have a significant impact on marketplace behavior and the relationships that can be established with potential financial and/or strategic investors.

Up to this point, this chapter's discussion has been based on the assumption that there has been no change in the industry structure within the nation. For most of the world, this means a regulated monopoly controlled by the government. This structure may not produce the desired results. US vice president Al Gore made this clear at the United Nations Telecommunications Conference when he stated, "Privatization is not enough, competition is needed as well." He added, "Today, there are many more technology options, and it is not only possible but desirable to have different companies provide competing but interconnected networks."

The need for competition is clearly highlighted when the experiences of countries like Argentina, Chile, and England are considered. In these cases, huge amounts of capital have been raised and the required management and technical expertise have been obtained through privatization. Yet, in Argentina and Chile an effective monopoly was granted to the buyer. The result has been increasing prices and a slower-than-desired introduction of advanced technologies and capabilities.

In England, the market has been opened and competition encouraged through the enactment of government policy and regulation. The result has been that advanced technology is being rapidly introduced, new services are being offered, consumer choices are increasing, prices are falling, and demand is up. The desired results are being achieved.

Therefore, a nation should include industry structure as part of its privatization planning. Various alternatives must be defined and analyzed for their impact on the benefits to be derived by the nation, and the price potential strategic and financial investors would be willing to pay under the different structures. In some cases, this analysis may result in the conclusion that the only way a nation can privatize is by awarding an effective monopoly to the investors. Decisions must then be made as to what is best for the country.

Recommendation and Summary

Any nation contemplating the privatization of its IM&M assets should follow a disciplined, systematic process in its decision making. The process outlined in this chapter and summarized below, if properly implemented, will provide all the information required for effective decision making.

- establish overall national priorities to include a thorough assessment of the value of the IM&M industry

- develop a comprehensive picture of the global IM&M industry and a vision of it in the future

- conduct a thorough evaluation of the national IM&M industry by looking at its existing and projected demand and supply components, unmet needs, and the additional resources required to satisfy those needs

- calculate the value of the industry to the country and to potential financial and strategic investors

- investigate the different national industry structures that are possible and select the one that will be most beneficial to the country.

Chapter 6

Chile and Beyond: Privatization in Latin America

M. Mario Zenteno

(Translated by Emily Aitken)

In the underdeveloped world, the reduction of entrepreneurial activities on the part of the state is part of a process of modernization or rather adaptation of the country's economy to the globalization phenomenon now shaping the world economy. Because of the extraordinary upswing in international investment, finance and trade, countries who do not want to be left out of this process must change their economic structures, and seek a sustained increase in productivity that enables them to compete successfully in international markets. This is the great challenge faced by developing countries and met successfully by some countries of the Far East and to a less extent by Chile in Latin America.

A major objective of privatization is, therefore, to increase productivity through an optimum allocation of resources based on market forces. In the economic arena, the state is limited to a subsidiary and normative role and its activities should focus on social aspects such as health, education and housing.

A market economy operates effectively when proper conditions exist. Ultimately, it will be necessary to make radical changes in the country's economic structure. In Chile, the chief measures taken were as follows:

- deregulation of prices, abolishing all types of control, except for monopolies;

- elimination of indirect subsidies;

- opening up to external trade; low and uniform custom duties;

- equal treatment for foreign and domestic investment;

- realistic exchange rates;

- rationalization of state investments consistent with the state's economic system;

- commercial administration of public enterprises;

- fiscal policies that stimulate investment;

- appropriate labor legislation;

- privatization of pension funds;

- an end to earmarking of taxes; and

- autonomy of the country's Central Bank.

The political importance of such changes depends on the extent to which the economy is state-controlled. In Latin American countries with a long tradition of state interference with the economy, those changes constitute a formidable challenge, requiring a high degree of consensus and political will if they are to be successful. At the beginning, these changes might have a severe impact, however transitory, on politically sensitive issues such as unemployment, higher prices, and the rate of inflation. This combination of negative factors gives rise to social unrest, which in turn brings strikes, riots, and political instability, as we have seen in many countries in the region. In Chile, in the late seventies and early eighties unemployment rose to 30 percent, the highest since the thirties, due to massive personnel reductions in state-owned companies being privatized and the bankruptcy of many industrial concerns that were previously protected from foreign competition by high custom duties.

Electricity prices in most underdeveloped countries are usually heavily subsidized. Privatization, then, can cause price increases that provoke strong complaints from every category of consumer, such as large industrial consumers who may bring strong political pressures to bear against privatization to avoid such price increases, because it is far easier to obtain subsidies from public than from private enterprises.

In addition, some countries have legal and even constitutional restrictions that prohibit the sale of companies at prices below their actual value or the purchase of public enterprises by foreign investors.

The above reasons could explain the slowing down of economic reforms observed in some Latin American countries. In particular, governments' attitudes towards privatization today are more cautious, and it seems that although the advantages of privatization are widely recognized, governments have decided not to implement the process too quickly or extensively.

If privatization is to be successful, two basic requirements must be met: ownership of enterprises must be primarily private and the preconditions for competition must exist. If a company is not controlled by the private sector, it can't really be termed privatized. Moreover, if privatization is to result in more efficient companies, they must operate in a competitive market. Competition is the best stimulus for effective private action. In the case of natural monopolies, such as electricity distribution, competition can be stimulated by setting price levels that ensure a reasonable rate of return if the company operates in accordance with levels of efficiency corresponding to standard costs. Greater efficiency is rewarded, consequently, with higher rates of return. On the other hand, the punishment for lower efficiency is a lower rate of return. In other words, the rate of return is not guaranteed, but neither is it limited. This system, which stimulates efficiency, has been successfully applied in Chile.

The state-owned electric companies in most Latin American countries are in a very precarious situation, financially, technically and administratively. Rates are below costs and costs are beyond reasonable limits due to political interference in investment decisions, over staffing, poor management, and exorbitant demands from politically-motivated unions. Lack of adequate maintenance and financial restrictions have originated acute power shortages in countries like Argentina, Bolivia, Colombia, the Dominican Republic, Jamaica, and Mexico.

Governments agree that an effective way to remedy this situation is privatization. Therefore, many Latin American countries, with the help of international loan organizations are currently revising rates criteria and the institutionality of the sector as preliminary steps towards an eventual privatization or, at least, as a means to improve power utilities performance.

When the privatization process began in Chile, the electric power sector was concentrated in two state-owned companies that could be considered reasonably efficient. Their rate of return averaged 5 percent and never, with the exception of one year under the Marxist regime, registered operating losses. Therefore, the decision to privatize these companies was based on economic principles supported by the military government of the time.

Some characteristics of the electricity industry, like capital intensity, long construction periods, price regulation and long periods of capital recovery have often been used to justify public ownership and may now create obstacles to its privatization. Some believe that the private sector is not interested in acquiring electric companies for reasons that might be beyond its control, as are financial matters. They also estimate that already privatized companies will not sustain the investments needed to expand the sector. From a market-economy perspective, if the private sector refuses to participate in developing the electric power sector, one can surmise that the economy offers other more interesting investment alternatives. It will thus be necessary to revise tariff levels. In developing countries, privatization of the electricity industry may be the greatest challenge faced by the private sector, which will have to demonstrate its ability to assume responsibility for a service that is vital to its economic and social development.

In Chile, after eight years of private involvement in the electric power sector, this challenge has been met quite successfully. The quality of service has improved, rates have decreased in real terms, and electric companies' shares are the blue chips of the capital market. Two of these companies have crossed the Andes to Argentina and are now controlling and operating distribution and generation companies in the Buenos Aires area.

The Institutional and Regulatory Framework
Private sector participation in the Latin American electric power industry can take place in two forms: acquisition of companies already in operation or the building and operation of new facilities. The former is valid for any type of company: generation, transmission or distribution. In practice, the latter is restricted to generation through the formation of new companies or through special deals like Build-Operate-Transfer (BOT) or Build-Lease-Transfer (BLT).

As is usual elsewhere, the electric industry in Latin America is controlled by specific laws. In most countries, however, current legislation is outdated and not suitable for privatizing the electric sector. Fundamental issues like tariffs, return on investment, and operational costs are vaguely treated and can be interpreted to suit the prevailing political interests of the government. In this way, rates are easily manipulated in order to grant subsidies.

With the exception of BOT or BLT schemes, which operate under specific contracts with other electric companies or large industrial consumers, in a similar way as qualifying facilities (QFs) operate in the United States, it is advisable for private investors to choose their investments after the rules of the game are clearly stated and endorsed by law.

Most Latin American countries have now decided to make the necessary reforms to ensure that electricity producers and consumers rights and obligations are duly protected. To this end, the two key issues are the institutional and the regulatory frameworks. Since the 1980s, Chile has pioneered in this field and the knowledge of what this country has achieved is being used by other countries as a basis for their own reforms.

In most third world countries, state-owned electric power utilities are the sole suppliers, or are substantially larger than other suppliers if they exist. In addition, the functions of distribution, transmission and generation are most often integrated vertically. Both characteristics are hindrances to privatization. Large size gives rise to two problems. First, the capital market may not have sufficient capacity to undertake to purchase the company. Second, excessive concentration of capacity in a single company thwarts competition. Vertical integration mingles different activities. Electricity supply comprises three functions whose marketing needs to be regulated in different ways.

Distribution is a natural monopoly because economies of scale increase rapidly in relation to customer density. Consequently, distribution should be subject to price regulation for small consumers and should be based on concessions.

Transmission also has the characteristic of a natural monopoly. The capacity of a transmission line varies with the square of the voltage, whereas the cost is proportional to voltage. Wheeling arrangements should then be price regulated.

Generation, however, offers no significant economies or scale. Usually, the magnitude of demand far exceeds the maximum power that can be concentrated in one power station owing to reasons of reliability and economics of supply. In a given interconnected electrical system it is therefore possible for several generating companies to operate competitively. Because distribution companies sell energy at regulated prices to small consumers, the energy bought from generation companies for this purpose is paid at regulated prices.

Large consumers do not have to contend with a monopoly situation because they have enough power to negotiate the prices of electricity furnished with various producers. Consequently, the buying prices for large consumers need not be regulated. In Chile, consumers whose demand is over 2,000kW negotiate their rates directly with the producers.

In most Latin American countries, legislation does not differentiate between the three functions discussed above. Fixed prices integrate the three functions. The importance of this situation to prospective investors will be better understood after the rate problem is analyzed—in line with this philosophy, the first step to privatization is to separate distribution, transmission, and generation as separate businesses, followed by the horizontal decentralization of these three activities into separate companies. In Chile all these changes were carried out between 1982 and 1985.

The most radical change needed by the Latin American electric power sector involves rates. Apart from not reflecting costs, rates are so structured that heavy cross subsidies exist among different kinds of customers. For the last 15 years the World Bank and the Inter American Bank have been promoting more efficient, economic rate schemes. Marginal cost-based rates were recommended. Almost all Latin American countries intended to follow this advice and made the necessary studies; consulting firms were hired and a great number of papers and even books were published. At the time, the idea was to improve state-owned electric companies' performances. Unfortunately, from a practical perspective, the results have been mediocre, largely because of political considerations. The same studies are being made today. Now the idea is to privatize the state-owned companies, in as much as privatization is not possible without a rational and efficient rate system with clear formulas of calculation, explicit variables, and automatic indexation. Hopefully, governments' openly-declared intentions to make the necessary reforms of the institutional and regulatory framework of electric power utilities will now produce positive results. Besides, big industrial consumers have realized that this inefficiency is menacing them with power shortages due to the growing difficulty in obtaining financing for new projects; they seem willing to pay more reasonable prices.

In general, regulated prices criteria can be classified in two categories: those setting the rate of return, like the cost-plus system, and those setting the price, like standard or marginal cost-based rates. The former do not stimulate operating-cost efficiency and the latter could lead to more than reasonable reductions in operating costs, thus negatively affecting quality of service. In both cases, the Government must exert some degree of control over the companies. In Chile the price-setting criterion was selected because it was considered more appropriate for creating better competitive conditions.

Nevertheless, whatever criterion is selected, what is really important is that the rate system should be based on technical concepts in order to make it impervious to political manipulation. It is extremely important that the Government pledge to maintain the tariff system's stability by passing a law rejecting any pressure to distort it no matter where the pressure comes from. Prices can be based on marginal costs or standard costs. In Chile, the choice was marginal costs for generation, standard costs for distribution, and a mix of marginal and standard costs for transmission wheeling charges.

Since marginal costs look to the future, their values depend on expansion plans conceived by the agency that sets the regulated prices. Expansion plans arise from a series of disputable factors, such as demand growth rate, investment costs, future fuel costs, technological advances, management improvement, dates of commissioning new installations, and many other minor factors. These factors will involve regulatory bodies and companies in much analysis and discussion before they reach agreement. Eventually, political considerations may creep into these discussions in the absence of a law that clearly defines the standards and procedures.

Nevertheless, marginal pricing is economically efficient in the sense that it reflects future costs that do not depend on present or past management of companies and thus enables consumers to evaluate their future energy needs. In addition, since marginal costs are equivalent to market prices in a competitive economy, the optimum operation of a power system is automatically achieved when there are several generation companies operating on the same system, even when operating decisions are decentralized. Each power plant increases its output until its marginal cost equals that of the system. Financial equilibrium is attained when the electric system is optimally adapted to the demand, that is, when demand is met at minimum cost and capacity matches demand. In this way, marginal pricing induces efficiency on the part of producers and consumers and thus constitutes the most logical choice from an economic point of view.

There are different ways of using marginal costs to establish prices. In Chile, short term marginal costs, averaged over the next three years, are used to set regulated prices at which generation companies sell energy. Short-term marginal costs were selected because they are more closely linked to the operation of the system. Instantaneous system marginal costs are used for generation dispatch. For the purpose of setting rates, electric power system expansion plans are prepared by a government authority based on information provided by the electric companies themselves. Load dispatching is carried out by the companies themselves without any interference by the government.

In Chile, regulated distribution prices for sales to small consumers are based on the standard costs of an idealized company deemed adequate to serve the region where the real distribution company operates. In this way an "added value of distribution" can be defined that can be calculated through mathematical formulas that are revised every four years by the regulatory agencies and the companies' representatives, together with local and foreign consulting firms. In case of discrepancy, a weighed value is adopted; Government's values are worth two and company's values are worth one. Inflation is considered through indexation formulas that are applied automatically by the companies themselves, without any further consultation with the authorities. The final price to consumers equals the high-voltage price at which the energy is acquired from generating companies plus the distribution added value. The standard values so calculated can be shown to coincide with the long-term marginal costs of distribution. This system allows relatively rapid privatization of distribution companies because their regulated rates are independent of the rates in the generation sector. Marginal cost analysis for the transmission network is a long and complex process, whereas distribution added values can be determined relatively quickly—no more than six months for most Latin American cities. In Chile, the differentiation of rates according to consumer category—residential, industrial, commercial, rural—has been replaced by a group of rate options. Each consumer freely chooses the option that minimizes his bill.

Transmission rates pose a very complicated problem when established as a function of short-term marginal costs based on losses. Since the base capacity of transmission lines rarely lends itself to their loads, prices based upon transmission losses do not cover capital and operating costs. Therefore in Chile transmission rates are calculated as a mixture of marginal and average costs. Shared use of transmission lines involves payment of tolls calculated through formulas fixed by the electricity law.

The institutional reforms and rates described above are contained in an electricity law passed in 1982. Until now, the law has worked reasonably well. Besides improving the efficiency of the sector, the most important consequence has been the active participation of private investors. In 1985, when Chile's privatization process began, about 90 percent of the electricity industry was state owned; today, about 90 percent is in private hands, and the Government has announced additional sale of property to the private sector.

Distribution has proved to be the least risky business in the electric industry; investments are made gradually and the planning horizon does not exceed two years. Consequently its privatization was fast and expeditious. Generation, on the other hand, requires large investments over a relatively short time period and power plants take much longer periods of construction; investment decisions are therefore made with a higher degree of uncertainty. However, the Government's attitude towards maintaining the rules of the game, regardless of political contingencies, has encouraged the private sector to take control of the ownership of generation and transmission companies. Such encouragement illustrates the importance of the longstanding rules of the game for gaining the confidence of private investors.

Forms of Sale
The types of sales currently being used in Latin America for the privatization of existing public businesses are:

- public auction of majority share packages,

- sale on the domestic and foreign stock exchanges, and

- popular capitalism.

In practice, most sales have used a mixture of these three types.

From the outset of the privatization process, the most controversial aspect in public opinion was the economic evaluation of the companies. Since the commercial value of a business must be measured by its ability to generate profits, it is equal to the present value of the future flow of projected net earnings. It is thus necessary to formulate a business plan for the company and establish a viable financial structure. With this information it is possible to prepare financial projections and to calculate the flow of expected future earnings.

The next controversial aspect is the adoption of the discount rate, which naturally had to be consistent with other investment options offered by the economy. The discount rate must reflect the different perception of the risk associated with private and public investments. Sectors that traditionally have been in state hands, with regulated prices and a long history of political interference, are considered by the private sector to carry a much greater risk than other investment alternatives. Thus, at least at the outset of the privatization process, private investors must be attracted by prospects of rates of return higher than the market average. Anyhow, it is advisable to hire the assistance of well known financial consulting firms in order to avoid future criticism about the prices at which the public companies were sold.

In many cases, expected business plans show that the company is not financially viable either in the present or in the near future; the risk perception of private investors is then greater. The best decision for the Government is to absorb the necessary amount of the company's liabilities to make it viable. Experience shows that the cost of these liabilities is significantly less than the price increase that can be obtained. However, the political implications of this situation are clear. The state appears to be absorbing a loss to the benefit of private investors. Protests frequently flow from the most varied quarters.

However, in Latin America many still argue that the selling price should be equal to the book value, including high government officials and even Supreme Court judges. Such ideas obviously make privatization much more difficult. The argument has no economic justification because book value is merely an accounting figure that reflects past events. Thus, old hydro plants, almost fully depreciated, can be sold at prices far above their book values, whereas relatively new installations might not be worth more than half their book values. This shows the inconsistency of evaluation criteria based on book value.

In Chile, the implicit discount rate of the first power plants sold to private investors was as high as 24 percent. Later on, the discount rate gradually decreased to less than 10 percent. At the beginning of the process, electrical companies' shares were sold in the stock market at 40 percent of their book value. Given the difference between the book value and the market value of shares, it was not desirable to capitalize the companies through the issuance of new shares. A good solution was to establish subsidiaries for the building of new facilities and invite other private investors to participate in their financing. Today power utilities' share prices are above book value and securing financing for new projects is no problem.

Auctions of majority or of all share packages are conducted in accordance with the usual rules for such transactions. Since the electric sector has great economic and social importance, interested private investors must prequalify by demonstrating their financial solvency and technical ability to manage the business properly. In Argentina and Chile, no limitations whatsoever are placed on foreign investors, who apply on exactly the same conditions as nationals. In other countries, however, foreign investors are subject to numerous restrictions and prohibitions. Given the limited capacity of capital markets in Latin America, such restrictions make privatization of the sector difficult.

The documentation for the bid calls must be complete and cover technical and financial information, as well as issues related to rate bases and future development plans for the electricity sector. This information is expected to give the process the greatest possible transparency and so avoid a situation in which influential economic groups can get additional information not available to other interested parties.

Popular capitalism, the sale of public enterprises shares to government employees, has two basic objectives: to spread ownership of companies among all segments of the population and to expand the capital market. When a broad spectrum of society becomes co-owners of the major state-owned enterprises, these enterprises gain great political stability, especially in the case of monopolies with regulated prices. Any attempt to manipulate these prices would cause grave economic damage to thousands of small investors. Financing the stock purchases of government employees is achieved by pre-payment and using some of the reserves that all companies maintain in their balances sheets for retirement benefits. This measure frees up a significant amount of capital and enables the workers to acquire ownership of state-owned enterprises.

Given the socio-economic objectives of popular capitalism, the shares to be sold to workers are usually subsidized in relation to their commercial value, as has been done even in some developed countries. In Chile, shares sold to small investors (popular capitalists) were offered at about a 10 percent discount in relation to their stock market values. Popular capitalism has been very successful in Chile, where around 30 percent of the electrical companies shares belongs to small investors and workers. In Argentina the same percentage has been reserved by the Government for popular capitalism. These percentages constitute a comfortable guarantee for the majority stockholders in the sense that they ward off political interference. A sole owner, especially a foreigner, can be a useful target for the objectives of certain politicians.

Labor Situation

Most state-owned electric power utilities in Latin America are over staffed. New owners, in Argentina and Chile, have reduced personnel, in some cases up to 40 percent. In addition, the employees have acquired various benefits that depend on the size of the enterprise and the degree of political influence wielded by their respective labor unions. When companies are privatized, some of these benefits have to be reduced or eliminated due to financial constraints. Labor's resistance to privatization is therefore not surprising. They see the process as synonymous with unemployment and the loss of union victories.

Benefits and layoff issues require long and complex negotiations with union leaders. Loss of employment is usually compensated through the payment of special allowances and early retirement programs. Complementary efforts include the privatization of certain company activities (cleaning, transportation, security, cafeterias, etc.) and helping workers start their own small businesses. Benefits obtained by collective bargaining is trickier. Negotiating the agreement requires arduous negotiations with labor unions and may even lead to strikes. Nevertheless it is essential to gain the support of employees. They have a natural distrust of a system that is unfamiliar to them and prefer the comfortable security that, in their opinion, is offered by the state as an employer. Public sector workers feel secure in their jobs, either because of the clout of their labor unions or because of the labor policies followed by the government. Besides, in many third world countries, there are private companies that are not a good examples to imitate. A frequent error that many governments make, including Chile and Argentina, is to proclaim the advantages of privatization only in terms of macroeconomic gains, forgetting the personal concerns of most workers. To them, an increase in the gross national product or exports is less important than job security and raises.

An intense information campaign has to be carried out by the top management who must, in direct and frank conversations with the employees, clearly and informally explain the advantages of the new system, particularly with regard to opportunities for promotion for unskilled workers and more equitable compensation levels. Private enterprise values effort over diplomas, and salaries are set by the market. State-owned companies promote employees based on seniority, academic credentials, or political influence; salaries are determined by purely administrative decisions. Besides, government authorities usually adopt across-the-board salary policies that apply to all employees, including under a single umbrella the most diverse enterprises with totally different activities, structure, and objectives. Regarding compensation, most state-owned enterprises have a very typical structural deformity, the average wage for unskilled personnel is higher than the market value, and at the high levels and especially for executives the reverse is true.

For their part, labor unions must realize the necessity for a radical change in their attitude toward the enterprise's management. The demands of the labor unions in public enterprises do not consider their possible impact on the financial situation and, in addition, union leaders are well aware of the significant role political influences play in the results of such negotiations. In private companies, labor unions must know and understand the financial position of the company and accept the natural limitations that this imposes on their demands—a difficult situation to explain to union members. The management/union relationship is another privatization problem that must be resolved. The traditional antagonistic attitude of labor unions toward management must give way to forthright cooperation and their activities must aim to improve productivity as the only means of raising salaries.

If the intention to privatize the economy is truly serious, such labor problems should, ideally, be resolved before the privatization process begins. Private prospective investors should urge the government to do so. Otherwise, the new owners will have to confront the situation, and the private sector will suffer a negative image. After all, government is responsible for labor problems due to past wrong decisions. Transferring these problems to the new owners is unfair, to say the least. These measures clearly represent a great political risk for the government but, these are the major challenges of privatization that must be confronted from the start.

At Endesa, in Chile, the most effective measure in gaining the understanding and cooperation of the employees was to sell them a distribution company through direct negotiations. Financing came in part from employee benefits funds and in part from loans. An agreement was reached after rapid negotiations. Later on the employees acquired another distribution company sold through public bidding. Financing was provided by private banks. By securing a majority holding of two distribution companies, Endesa workers became participants in the privatization process. They later formed investment groups and acquired other distribution companies. For the record, the management of the companies, up to now, has been very efficient and has made investments in Argentina. Lastly, an interesting change occurred in the attitude of the electricity sector workers regarding the new economic system that now prevails in the country. Groups of workers had set investment companies and obtained commercial loans to acquire additional shares of electricity companies and purchase small distribution companies.

Managing the Privatization Process
Once the institutional reforms and regulatory frameworks are established, state-owned companies must submit themselves to the new rules of the game and operate as if they were private, thus proving that the new system works. Any mistrust that the private sector might have will be assuaged and, additionally, the government will obtain a better price.

The process of adapting state-owned companies to a free-market economy is painful and politically complicated, and requires a complete reorganization of the company's different functions. Some functions, like engineering and construction, must be drastically scaled back or transferred to other private companies. The necessity to take harsh measures in relation to layoffs and wages has already been explained. Management must make financial adjustments in light of new realities, both within the company and without. Financial analysis of new projects takes on new importance: Financing has to be secured for the new projects without the backing of the state and solely on the basis of the project's economic efficiency and the financial solvency of the company. Preparing the company for the shift to a market economy and subsequently selling it, must be overseen by top executives who clearly understand the objectives of privatization and are committed to its success.

Owing to the highly complex technical, financial, and administrative aspects of the electric industry, company management must be entrusted to people with relevant expertise and experience. Countries with a long tradition of state ownership of the electricity sector have difficulty in finding chief executive officers who, in addition to knowing the industry, can successfully steer the privatization process and make the necessary changes that will ultimately cost them their jobs. Nonetheless, the success of privatization hinges to a large extent on finding such executives. Privatization failures in Chile of certain state-owned enterprises can be attributed to a lack of adherence to government economic principles from their executives. This meshing of objectives between the government and senior officials of public enterprises is key to the success of the process.

Perhaps the most important change that needs to be made in privatizing a state-owned enterprise is the change of attitude among senior managers and, in particular, the general manager, who oversees the process. The most marked difference between state-owned and private enterprises lies in the origin of initiatives that define their future course. In the former, the most significant decisions regarding investments, budgets, and personnel benefits generally originate with government authorities (who base their decisions on criteria that may conflict with the company's best interest) or, at least, are reviewed, modified and approved by the authorities using criteria that may conflict with the interests of the enterprise itself.

In private companies, on the other hand, a key task of the management is to prepare business plans, formulate strategies, suggest policies, and promote the future development of the company. Management at a private company is also accountable for the results.

The senior officials of state-owned enterprises are not usually prepared for this radical change in managerial style, much less to act in a competitive environment. Experience with a market-based economic system is lacking in most developing countries, where the state traditionally managed the economy. This situation presents a major obstacle in countries that now opt for a market economy, and may explain the rabid opposition of public business groups to privatization.

A Sample Case: Privatization of Endesa, Chile

Still the largest electric power utility in Chile, Endesa was created by the government in 1943 to develop the country's abundant hydro resources. Although a public company, Endesa was organized in the legal form of a private company, all the shares were owned by the government and were not sold in the stock market. The intention was to endow the company with enough autonomy to liberate it from government bureaucracy and give it a much greater flexibility in decisions involving investments and salaries.

At the time it was privatized, the company was reasonably efficient and enjoyed an excellent reputation at home and abroad. As a consultant firm, its services were hired by many developing countries in matters such as power system planning and operation, power plant and transmission lines design and construction and maintenance of electrical equipment. Endesa's rate of return oscillated between five and seven percent, in spite of performing many tasks that should have been undertaken by the government, like national hydrological programs, irrigation works, and free electrification of the country's underprivileged areas.

Therefore, many people, within and without the government, did not see the need to privatize Endesa because as it happens today in most countries of Latin America, privatization was only considered useful as a cure for bad management or administrative and financial problems. However, for Chile's government at the time, privatization was the means to a much broader objective: To liberalize the economy so that market forces could assign the resources. The government would only be an arbiter in this process, not a participant. Privatization would therefore extend to all sectors of the economy.

Endesa followed the steps explained in the preceding points. First, distribution and generation-transmission were separated as different companies. Then each area was deconcentrated. Distribution was divided into seven companies and generation into four companies. Six distribution companies and two small generation companies were sold at public auctions, one of the latter to American private investors. At the end of this stage, Endesa was reduced to a generation-transmission company with only 60 percent of its original installed generating capacity. What remained of the company was to be sold on the stock exchange.

Before Endesa's privatization, certain financial arrangements had been extended to the company. Just before deciding to privatize Endesa, the government made unexpected changes in its foreign exchange policy and the financial position of the company deteriorated. Financial projections showed that it was not financially viable. The ratio of long-term liabilities to equity rose beyond the limit stipulated by Endesa's agreements with credit institutions.

Instead of selling the company in such a condition, the government decided to capitalize the company through the acquisition of a new issue of shares for a total of $500 million. This substitution of a large share of Endesa's debt by the government was bitterly criticized. Even today, government officials and members of parliament consider it an unjustified subsidy of the new owners. The truth is that a large percentage of that debt represents Endesa losses caused by the changes in exchange policy. Furthermore, without improvement in its financial position, Endesa's sale price would have dropped by more than $500 million due to private investors' perception of major risk. In any event, economic authorities had the courage to take the measure which from a political standpoint, was unpopular. The selling of Endesa's shares in the stock market began in early 1989 at a price of 40 percent their book value. In 1994, the price is more than five times that original price, in real terms, due to the rapid expansion of the capital market and the excellent performance of the now private Endesa. Stock market price exceeds book value.

Conclusion

Many people argue that the Chilean privatization process was possible thanks to the dictatorial nature of the military government ruling the country at that time. In a democracy, they say, such a fast and drastic privatization process would have been impossible. There is some merit in this argument, but considering what is happening in the world economy today, one might infer that Chile's particular situation merely permitted the anticipation of the process. In any case, the task was not as easy as some imagine. Many highly placed government officials put up a strong fight against privatization. Furthermore, most military officers favored public ownership of large companies, probably because of the nationalist bias inherent in their organization.

There was also a widespread belief that the electric power sector was "strategic" and therefore must belong to the state. The "strategic" label applied to certain businesses has often served to justify their public nature. Also, Latin American countries prohibited the privatization of certain public enterprises considered "strategic." However, it was not possible to arrive at a precise definition of what is meant by "strategic enterprise." After analyzing and comparing different definitions that had been put forward, *The Economist* magazine concluded that the term could apply to activities involving national security or functions necessary to the development of normal productive activities. According to *The Economist*, none of these cases justifies nationalizing these industries. As regards the first case, it is enough to remember that in time of war or catastrophe, the contribution of private business has been decisive. And in the second case, private ownership of essential economic sectors, such as energy, transportation, and communications, has proved that it can serve the interests of the country more effectively than the public.

Privatization produces profound changes in the economic structures of countries. When we speak of changes, we must also accept the need to overcome many difficulties that will be more or less important depending on their extent and nature. Otherwise, the changes will arrive spontaneously. In confronting these difficulties, the involved parties act in different manners. Some oppose the changes and offer a million "good reasons" why they aren't viable. These generally end up as the residue of the process. The vast majority remain expectant and passive; they neither add nor restrict. Finally, some leaders appear who are capable of providing solutions to the problems posed by the changes. During the process of privatization, one must find these leaders and hand them the reins. The modernization of Chile's economy was possible because the country was lucky enough to find a group of young economists who, with creativity and tenacity, were able to achieve what had previously appeared impossible; between them, they privatized the electric power system.

Chapter 7

The Privatization Payoff

Don D. Jordan

Countries worldwide are embracing privatization, driving growth, and creating opportunities for Western firms. Houston Industries tapped Argentina's electric power sector while adapting to economic, cultural, and political challenges.

A phenomenon is sweeping across the world stage that is unique in the annals of business. Its financial and geopolitical impact will be worldwide. Through it, technology will improve the economies of nations and the lives of ordinary citizens. And participating investors and politicians might alter the course of history. This process is the large-scale privatization of government-owned industries. Virtually overnight, countries and their governments in every region of the world have repudiated socialistic, "managed" economies and have embraced private investment and free enterprise. As a result, the business and investment communities now are confronted with an unprecedented opportunity and challenge.

Among major industries being privatized are electric services, telecommunications, petroleum exploration and development, railways, steel production, and mining—each a critical part of the infrastructure needed to build or sustain economic success. I will focus on electric power production and distribution, one of Houston Industries' key businesses. But my comments, particularly those on risk analysis, are pertinent to any industrial privatization.

Why Privatize?
Through privatization, poor countries are finding it possible to leapfrog decades ahead in building infrastructure required for development. Newly industrializing nations are using privatization as a means to speed the spread of prosperity among their citizens, bolstering lagging economies or adding momentum to those that are taking off. Even highly industrialized countries are getting into the act to enhance their positions in an increasingly competitive and ever-more-open world marketplace.

In many countries, state-owned enterprises such as electric utilities have been big money losers, requiring massive subsidies. Being extremely capital-intensive, they often have burdened governments with crushing debt. And, in many cases, the inability of governments to finance needed expansion has hampered industrial- ization. In India, for example, an official with the United States (US) Agency for International Development (AID) estimates that inadequate and unreliable elec- tric supply costs industry 1.5 percent of Gross National Product; in Pakistan the figure could be 1.8 percent. In other cases, frequent blackouts or brownouts have undermined political support and the credibility of the government.

For some nations, the sale of utility and other assets also offers a way out of an international debt problem. By privatizing, the government not only attracts investment and operating expertise, it raises hard currency that is used to reduce international debt. In turn, this may reduce pressures from the International Monetary Fund, the World Bank, and private lenders, and facilitate loans needed for other purposes.

Finally, in an increasing number of nations, the decision is being made to let business handle what it does best, while the government focuses on areas such as defense, public health, and education, where it is the logical large-scale provider.

Wanted: Capital Transfusions
The scope of the investment needed is staggering. There are at least 50 major nations in the process of privatizing, ranging from Argentina to Australia, Bangladesh to Brazil, Italy to India, Peru to Pakistan, Turkey to Thailand, Mexico to Malaysia, and China to Colombia).

In the electric supply sector, the US Agency for International Development estimates that developing nations' demand for electric power is increasing at an annual rate of 6.5 percent. In the US, the Edison Electric Institute forecasts a more modest annual rise of only 1.9 percent over the next decade.

According to AID, the electricity requirements of developing and industrializing nations over the decade will amount to a whopping $100 billion a year, "...sums which are not now and are unlikely to be available in the future from developing nations' treasuries."

These figures only address known, new additions to the existing power supply. Add to this the expected value of government-owned generating, transmission, and dis- tribution system assets where these are being sold. This process has just begun, but to date these asset sales have raised about $140 billion of private investment. CS First Boston estimates that additional sales of existing government-owned electric facilities in the next decade could exceed $500 billion.

Figure 7-1. The Need for Electric Power In Latin America

**Power consumption per capita in many Latin American countries has doubled in the past 20 years.
Rapid industrialization may result in doubling again in the next seven to eight years.**

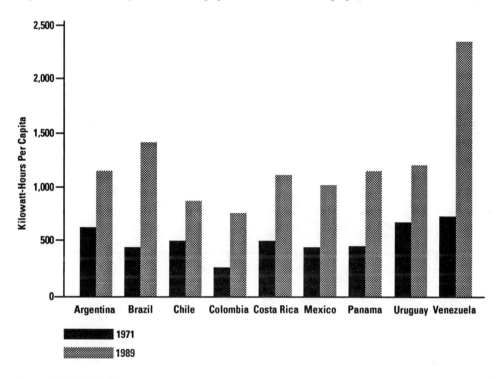

Source: The World Bank.

In Latin America, according to the Latin American Energy Organization, "...there is a $13 billion a year investment deficit in the electricity sector which has forced some countries to ration power and threaten(s) economic growth." As shown in Figure 7-1, in some South American countries, the consumption of electricity per capita has more than doubled in the past 20 years. In some, it is forecast to more than double again in the next seven to eight years. This is fairly typical: Electric consumption usually matches or exceeds growth in Gross Domestic Product until a country reaches a level of development typical in the US or Western Europe. (See Figure 7-2 for projected growth of US and developing nations.)

Latin American countries have undertaken a major effort to attract private investment. Several already are successfully privatizing, and Argentina, Bolivia, Brazil, Chile, Colombia, Ecuador, Mexico, Peru, and Venezuela all have adopted legislation geared to attract foreign investment.

Figure 7-2. Projected GDP Growth

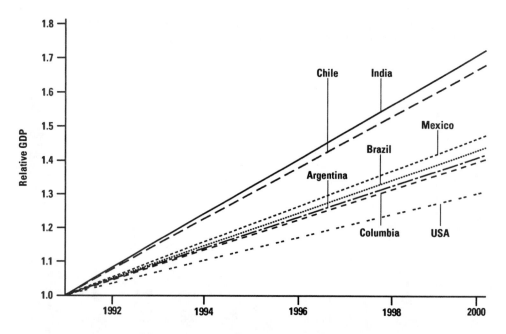

Forecasts depend on projected levels of infrastructure investment.
Source:
The Economist.

Asia faces similar problems with electricity supply. According to the World Bank, if Asia is to sustain the average 8.4 percent growth rate it realized in the 1980s, generating capacity will need to double by 1999. This alone would require the equivalent of $450 billion. China, India, the Philippines, Indonesia, Thailand, Malaysia, and others are struggling with economies that are being restrained by electric supply shortages.

Add these ingredients to the recipe, and the full scope of private investment needed just for electric system privatization over the next decade approaches $1.5 trillion. Such an outlay is analogous to a modern-day, private-sector Marshall Plan.

Where's the Push?
These opportunities represent the "pull" luring investors. But why would chief executives consider leaving the safety of the US or Western European business environment for less familiar territories abroad—the "push" factor in the economic equation?

Many companies like my own face a maturing market in existing operations. Our forecast for our subsidiary, Houston Lighting & Power, for example, parallels the national electric demand forecast—approximately 2 percent growth compounded over the next decade. That contrasts with as much as 13.8 percent in some years, during decades when sales at our utility could more than triple.

If we're to achieve the earnings growth needed to sustain attractive dividends and total return for our investors, we have little choice but to explore new markets with our other subsidiaries.

Other companies in the electric sector are coming to the same conclusion. At least 12 other US electric utility affiliates currently are bidding on privatization projects. Utilities in Spain, France, Chile, and Belgium also have entered the market. And independent power producers in the US, which have built about half the new generation here for the past several years, are starting to move into the privatization arena, as lower domestic growth and competition have consistently whittled away their returns.

Entering the Market

For many companies, mature markets and the size of new privatization opportunities abroad will provide ample initial attraction. However, a more detailed analysis will be required to identify particularly appealing market niches and to see if a firm has strengths that can provide a competitive advantage. Methods of privatization can affect this analysis.

- Share distribution. Some governments have chosen to distribute shares on the stock exchange. This model has been used extensively in Europe and is being adopted in some Asian markets. It is probably appropriate if a business—or the broader industry of which it is a part—is reasonably well-run and efficient, and if there is a viable stock exchange to serve as a vehicle for trading.

- Asset sales. This method involves either the outright sale of assets, or the sale of a controlling interest in them, to an investor, along with a concession or franchise. This is probably most appropriate where improvements to the operation are needed. This approach is the one most typical in Latin American markets.

- Market liberalization. In some countries, the government is partially privatizing by retaining existing assets but opening the market to new private suppliers to meet expanding needs.

Analysis of our strengths convinced us that our 110-year experience in designing, building, and operating large utility facilities would allow us to enhance existing utility operations where they are being privatized. We could add value and realize efficiencies through a hands-on approach. Ownership of a controlling interest ourselves, or as part of a consortium in which we would be involved in operations, became one targeted approach.

Our second thrust is in the area of new power additions. And we're taking a different approach than most competitors.

Governments that are privatizing often call for and receive bids from scores of potential generating firms when new plants are needed. There's often little to differentiate these bidders.

Rather than respond to every request for proposals for a power station, our focus is to build on existing expertise with familiar industries. Our utility subsidiary has long served some of the largest facilities in the petrochemical, refining, oil services, transportation, and biomedical industries. We not only understand their power requirements, but their internal plant processes. Just as important, they know us and our capabilities; we're a proven quantity. We tell these firms we'll build and operate dedicated power facilities, on their plant sites if appropriate, anywhere in the world they wish to locate or expand their facilities. This offers advantages in cost, reliability, and scheduling, even in areas where power supply is inadequate or unreliable.

By selecting these two approaches, we've both differentiated ourselves by focusing on our strengths and expertise, and effectively narrowed the market niches in which we wish to compete.

Risk Analysis

Having completed a competitive analysis, we proceeded to a series of risk analyses.

Any investment involves risks, but offshore investments—particularly those in countries in the early stages of privatization—involve additional concerns (see Figure 7-3).

Obviously, country risk is a prime consideration. By this I mean the overall stability of a given nation. Established governments that enjoy popular support and facilitate free enterprise are likely to attract capital. On the flip side, investors probably won't beat down the doors of nations where terrorism, armed opposition factions, and coups are the norm. Unfortunately, some nations continue to face these difficulties, and the returns for investors in these situations will have to be very high for them to tolerate the risk.

Figure 7-3. Privatization Risk Analysis Factors

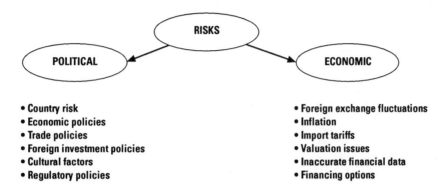

- Country risk
- Economic policies
- Trade policies
- Foreign investment policies
- Cultural factors
- Regulatory policies

- Foreign exchange fluctuations
- Inflation
- Import tariffs
- Valuation issues
- Inaccurate financial data
- Financing options

For us, highly volatile political situations are unappealing. Others may have more tolerance for such risks.

Other considerations include national trade and foreign investment policies. Is there a provision for repatriating profits from an investment? And if you buy a company that needs upgrading, will you be able to import equipment without encountering monstrous tariffs? Will the government permit the renegotiation of union or supply contracts? Is inflation in the country under control? If free enterprise policies are relatively new in that locale, does the government (and the population) have a long-term commitment to them?

Culture and economic history also may affect a company's decision. In some former socialist states, for example, companies aren't familiar with the basic principles of Western accounting and finance. In some instances, AID has enlisted American firms to show countries interested in privatizing how to install generally accepted accounting, budgeting, and audit systems, so that an acceptable book value can be established for assets to be privatized. This was the case when Houston Industries worked with AID to assist a utility in the Czech Republic. (The utility has since been privatized through share distributions.)

Taking the Plunge
Houston Industries' initial privatization investment was in the electric distribution system in La Plata, Argentina, a city of 700,000 that is the capital of the Buenos Aires province. We're part of a consortium of two US and two Argentine firms that bought majority ownership of this system. A review of why this investment was attractive to us may be a useful example of risk analysis for privatization.

We were attracted to an investment in Argentina, because, among other reasons, the government is stable, and legislation provides protection for private property and enterprise.

Initially, we completed a technical analysis on several properties the government offered for bids. Some of these we rejected out of hand because we didn't feel the risk-adjusted returns would he adequate, or because they would have required the infusion of too much additional capital.

However, we were attracted to three distribution systems. Besides the La Plata system—also known as Edelap—there were two distribution systems in Buenos Aires called Edenor and Edesur. In addition to clearing our hurdle rates, the bid packages for these properties offered investor safeguards, including a management contract that effectively provided a revenue floor; an allowance for renegotiating union and other existing contracts; and provisions for protection against currency fluctuations and for the repatriation of profits.

Also important: We were able to link up with large, well-respected Argentine firms— Techint Compania Tecnica Internacional and Los W S.A.—as well as with Citicorp S.A. We knew these companies could provide legal expertise and intelligence on the Argentine culture and politics. Their contribution to analyzing service area economies and local demand forecasting was invaluable.

Although unsuccessful on bids for Edenor and Edesur, our consortium was the winning bidder for La Plata's Edelap. The bid price was $138 million for a 51 percent ownership (39 percent of the system was retained by the government, and 10 percent was given to employees). The range of bids on all these properties was surprisingly broad, perhaps because they reflected widely different bidding strategies and return requirements. There was a spread of about $250 million between the winning and low bids on both Edenor and Edesur; the spread on the smaller Edelap system was about $90 million.

In any acquisition, you receive some surprises. And ours was no exception. We expected "non-technical" losses—including power diversion or theft—in the neighborhood of 16 percent of generation. The actual figure was somewhat closer to 21 percent.

We also have been subject to greater natural gas fuel curtailment in the winter than we anticipated because of inadequate pipeline capacity. That means slightly lower revenue from the power station that was part of our purchase.

In addition, damage from severe storms in a system with predominantly overhead power lines is worse than we expected. In some cases, to make post-storm repairs, we've tied two trucks together to create four-wheel drives. In Argentina, four-wheel drive trucks are scarce.

Nonetheless, the La Plata investment is performing. The equipment is proving to be sound, employees are technically competent, we substantially reduced non-technical losses, an early retirement program has helped alleviate overstaffing, and the reliability of service to customers in La Plata is improving steadily. At the bottom line, the system is reporting profits.

Window of Opportunity

The scale of privatization represents an unprecedented investment opportunity. Yet the window of opportunity is relatively small. In what will probably be only a decade, governments worldwide will attempt to privatize and modernize a staggering array of industrial enterprises.

The US government, under the auspices of AID and other agencies, is doing what it can to expedite and encourage the process, because it embraces privatization as a means to stabilize the global economy and to demonstrate the viability of free enterprise.

Done successfully, privatization will play a key role not only in improving the quality of life of millions, but also in ushering in an era of international cooperation and coexistence as we move into the 21st century.

Chapter 8

Privatization of Water Supply and Sewage

Jose Kochen

(Translated by Leonard S. Hyman)

What will happen when oil becomes scarce? We are already developing alternative sources of energy, so we will surely have substitutes when they are needed. One cannot say the same about another scarce resource, water. Not only is water in short supply but there are no substitutes for it. With this in mind, international environmental organizations have been advocating programs to rationalize administration of water supply, discourage wasteful use, and diminish losses in the supply process. Perhaps privatization may be one of the methods of reaching those objectives.

Water Supply: What is it and Why is it Important?

Remember the oft-repeated phrase that sums up water's essentiality: water is life. Potable water is not only indispensable for our physical necessities but also essential to improve public health. Providing drinkable water reduces illnesses, infant mortality, and the propagation of waterborne diseases. Industry requires sufficient water for its processes, and, clean bodies of water are important recreational assets. Thus, water supply service is important not only to the maintenance and improvement of public health but also to the community's industrial and commercial development.

A good water supply service provides its product continually, in accord with sanitary standards, without interruptions or shortages, at an adequate pressure, and at a price that is affordable to the community served.

No regional plan or development program is credible or stands any chance of success if it does not include the mechanism to provide water supply and the resources needed to finance that supply.

Organization of Water Supply

Water suppliers come in many forms. Most suppliers have been operated by government entities, such as directly by departments of the government, government authorities, corporations in which the government is the majority shareholder, and what are referred to as mixed economy corporations in Brazil (the government joins with private capital but is not necessarily the majority shareholder).

These entities may serve the entire country, a state or region, and most frequently, a municipality.

The predominance of government ownership may be due to water not only being a scarce resource, but also one not always located nearby. In the past, building the necessary facilities may have been beyond the capabilities of local private investors but the community needed the facilities nonetheless. Local interests petitioned the government to make the investment in water supply, which was recovered from subscribers in the form of a tariff for services rendered. This model for development was common, and it led many to the comfortable but false belief that water, as an essential for life, was the exclusive obligation of the government to furnish, which induced many people to not bother to pay for the service when the water entities were poorly organized or administered.

This misunderstanding about the obligations of government has led to the deterioration of many governmentally owned water suppliers. In a vicious cycle, a tariff set for political reasons at an unrealistically low level plus inability to collect the bills creates an operating deficit for the water supplier. That, in turn, leads to a scarcity of funds for investment and a deterioration of maintenance, which produces, as a consequence, a drop in the quality and continuity of service, and finally, a water shortage, which, in turn, makes it impossible to charge a realistic tariff because the service is so bad. At this point, the cycle repeats, each time producing worse results.

The government is not the best organizer, operator or administrator, and the burden of these bureaucratic deficiencies and overheads ends up on the customers, in the form of higher taxes required to cover the operating deficit, or in the form of an unnecessarily high tariff for water services.

In developed nations and in those in which free markets thrive, privatization of public services is seen, increasingly, as a means of eliminating deficiencies in operations and improving the quality of service. This trend has been most evident in Europe, especially in the United Kingdom. As the experiences of privatization become better understood, more governments may adopt it as a solution.

The Structure of Government Water Suppliers

Normally, the governmental utility has four distinct divisions of management:

1) **The presidency or chief executive**—representing the top management by means of the president or general manager, and the executive directors.

2) **Operations**—responsible for the end product of the entity, which is to produce and distribute water.

3) **Finance**—charged with financial and economic matters and with the collection of revenues.

4) **Administrative**—in charge of support and personnel. Yet, thanks to the almost constant necessity of modernization and expansion, principally in developing countries, two additional divisions almost always are present, one for planning and design, the other for construction. These two activities, as a result of the resources applied to them, end up assuming an importance even greater than the activity that produces the end product of the business, operations. The bulk of the resources of the corporation, including the best personnel, end up directed to these two areas, to the extent that they almost deform the service provider into a construction firm. The political dividends derived from public works projects end up making construction more important than providing an essential public service.

The planning and design, and construction activities, which are outside the main purpose of the water entities, can be contracted out and executed by private firms that specialize in those fields, probably at lower costs, especially when one considers the factors that influence costs, including the likelihood that these divisions end up as permanent parts of the government entity, even after the construction becomes less important or ends.

For this reason, private water companies do not ordinarily have planning and design, and construction divisions, other than to supervise those activities, and therefore, they are proportionally smaller and less costly. When those activities are required, they are contracted out to private firms. This difference is one of the factors that weighs in favor of the privatization of water supply.

Providing the End Product

Furnishing potable water involves a series of activities in a process that can be visualized as follows:

1) **Collection**—The water is collected from sources, which may be surface runoffs, rivers, lakes, reservoirs created by dams, or subterranean natural deposits.

2) **Treatment**—The water receives chemical and mechanical treatment that brings it to the standards of drinkability.

3) **Storage**—The treated water is conducted and accumulated in tanks to constitute a reserve for use during peak hours of consumption, and also to guarantee supply during emergencies.

4) **Distribution**—This system carries the water to the various supply zones of the city.

5) **Supply**—Pipes transport the water from the distribution network, passing in front of houses, buildings and industrial firms, and connecting to the water installations on private property.

Each of the stages of the process are connected together by pipe systems that range from the large diameter water mains between the collection, treatment, and storage stages, and from there through successively smaller diameters down to the pipe under the streets serving the supply function. In each of the stages, there may or may not be a mechanical elevation of water by means of pumping stations, depending on topography.

All the activities which make the entire system function properly and provide the end product to the customer constitute the operational activity.

A good water supply service is one that guarantees the continuity of supply and the quality of the product that is supplied. Continuity of service is guaranteed by effective, corrective and protective maintenance of all the equipment that constitutes the supply system. The physical, chemical and bacteriological quality of the product is guaranteed by adequate control through sampling from collection—and even before—through to final delivery.

The supply of water is, then, basically an industrial activity, and private enterprise has the means to run it. The stages of activity discussed involve equipment commonly used in industrial activities, and the labor needed is available in the marketplace. Private initiative has demonstrated better managerial performance than the government (in many forms), which leads one to conclude that those activities in which the government plays a role as business manager should be privatized, and water supply is one such industry. The benefits of privatization—derived from greater productivity—should accrue to the community in the form of better service and lower prices.

Difficulties that Public Water Suppliers Face

Lack of resources for investment is one of the difficulties commonly faced by governmental water agencies. There are four principal causes:

1) Competition from other government sectors for the limited budget resources of the government.

2) Inability to convince society of the importance of investment in the sector in order to improve public health or develop the community as a whole.

3) The water sector's lobby in the political arena is unconvincing and unable to raise the sector's visibility or get it the needed recognition.

4) Government interest in putting money into more obvious projects—such as roads, port facilities and subway systems—that produce more electoral dividends, to the detriment of the water sector.

The shortage of investments, over time, reduces levels of service, leaving part of the population without water and at the mercy of the consequent public health problems. Lack of resources, too, leads to deterioration of equipment, of work habits, of controls, with repercussions on cost and quality of service.

The extended organization structure—with an excessive number of managers and advisors who work largely to accommodate each other and who resist change—is another issue that needs to be addressed. These structural deformations often originate with an inadequate salary policy, and the need to get around it. The majority of employees, who are not favored by the policy, have no incentive to work productively, show a general lack of interest in the employer, resulting in a bad reflection on the water agency's image. What makes matters worse is the susceptibility of government agencies to external factors that encourage nepotism, which results in crews of personnel far greater in size than needed, and often without the necessary qualifications.

These disequilibrating factors are difficult to correct in a government agency. Not only do private firms have fewer of these problems to deal with, but when they do occur, they can be corrected more promptly. The private firms can line up resources more quickly, are less sensitive to political pressures, are free to determine the size of crews and salary policy, and to guide themselves by the real needs of the enterprise and by the situation of the labor market.

Principal Failings of Government Water Agencies

Certain deficiencies are common among government water suppliers. They are most easily corrected through privatization. These are the most common failings among the government water suppliers:

1) **Loss of water in the system**—It is common to come across water supply systems that lose over 25 percent of the water produced. This loss is the difference between the volume impounded at the source and that billed. The losses take place at all stages of production through to billing, and are of a size that is unacceptable in any industrial process, especially in an era in which industrialists seek total quality control and reduction of waste to as close to zero as possible. Those high losses require the utility to spend more money for electricity, chemicals, personnel, and capital. The reduction of losses, though, is important not only to eliminate

those excess costs, but also to free up productive capacity that can be placed at the disposal of unserved areas and new customers, which also implies the postponement of new (and unneeded) investment.

2) **Automation and remote control**—Entirely automatic equipment for such purposes as pumping, measurement, pressure control and treatment is available on the market. When installed, it provides the system with greater security, allows a reduction of personnel, and lowers costs. Equipment may be operated by remote control, using radio or telephone links, with the same assurances of security and efficiencies. Yet many systems still lack these improvements.

3) **Operational control**—Whoever controls the operations of the supply system—increasing or decreasing volume, directing the water to where it is required, handling emergencies—needs an information system that provides real time data on rate of flow, volume, elevation, pressure, state of repair, and standards of quality. Such a system permits the operator to rapidly identify alternative actions, make improvements, produce greater efficiency, and more rapid and surer decision making in the operation of the water supply system. The use of such information systems is not that common.

4) **Elimination of areas and points of critical problems within the system**—At times, intermittent service or water shortages become chronic problems in certain areas. The solutions for these deficiencies are often postponed either for lack of resources needed to invest in the solution, or because even worse problems take precedence. Chronically poor operations in a particular area is one of the failings that most often depresses the quality of service. Many times, the utility will adopt palliatives such as shifting the supply from one area to another, with the intention of minimizing rather than resolving the problem.

5) **Constant modernization of work procedures and materials**—What ought to be routine may not be done at all by government water suppliers. The application of new work procedures, and the utilization of modern machinery and equipment and materials is often slowed down almost always because of shortages of money or unwillingness of the staff to make changes.

6) **Billing and collection**—No economic activity can survive if it cannot identify and know in detail its clientele and costs, and cannot collect enough to cover the costs of the service that it sells. Unfortunately, these pitfalls of the billing and collection process are common. As an example, non-payment for service is a serious problem, unless the water company systematically applies coercive collection techniques such as shutting off service. Activities so basic to survival, billing and collection, can be greatly improved by setting standards for them similar to those of private enterprises.

7) **Work rules**—The enterprise must control the productivity of the service crews, by setting the number of members of the crew, time standards for each type of service, and by rationalization of these activities. Doing so not only reduces costs but also improves the public image of the firm.

8) **Information management**—The company should pursue the extensive application of information management to all areas, with the objective of simplifying and speeding procedures, furnishing necessary information rapidly and correctly, and accelerating the decision-making process.

9) **Training**—Constant training and updating of skills should be a part of personnel policy. Workers need to be stimulated by their jobs, have pride in the services they provide, and be certain that their careers will advance based on their own merits.

The deficiencies discussed may seem surprising in that they should not exist in a well organized firm, but they are commonplace in government water service entities.

Privatization of Water Supply and Reflections on Service

We have described the deficiencies of and the difficulties confronting government water suppliers, many of which could be reduced or eliminated through privatization. The natural struggle to produce a return on investment stimulates the search for efficiencies, and the reduction of losses and wastes. These two objectives, return on investment and reduction of costs, ought to stimulate the utilization of modern work procedures, rationalization of activities, and reduction of crew sizes, but not at the expense of security and quality of service. Reaching these objectives rapidly will not be possible, but long term actions should be successful.

Private enterprise may be able to move resources into capital investments more rapidly, raising the percentage of the population that is served, modernizing plant and equipment and control systems, all of which should improve quality and security of service. As a private enterprise, the water service company should be less vulnerable to the influence of politicians, who at times could be seen interfering with the organization and its decision-making, interference not always coincident with the interests of the community. The personnel situation should improve too from diminished political influence, because, with privatization, the internal groups that represent one or another politician should disappear.

Overall, management of the private enterprise will be more transparent to the community, as a result of the audits and controls that will be legally required, and the rules of conduct established by the concession.

Guarantees to the Community

The decision to privatize a government-owned water service agency should be taken only after the new concessionary organization agrees to adhere to conditions involving:

1) **Water quality**—The company must agree to standards set by the law.

2) **Continuity of service**—Service must be furnished in a manner that assures uninterrupted service and adequate pressure.

3) **Prices**—The tariff structure ought to be set up in advance, be appropriate to the needs of the community, with specific rules for residential, industrial, commercial and other groups. Furthermore, the tariff may have to take into account the social needs of the community, including access to service for those with low incomes.

4) **Investment capacity**—Finances are needed that allow the firm to invest quickly when required to expand service within the community.

5) **Quality of materials and services**—The company must utilize materials and follow work procedures in a manner that adheres to manufacturers' technical recommendations.

6) **Emergencies**—To guarantee the continuity of service, the company needs an organization that deals with emergencies, something indispensable for all good service.

7) **Customer relations**—The water company must respect time limitations for the provision of services, and provide quality services to the consumer.

If the water supplier is unwilling or unable to comply with the regulations, the community should have the power to seek immediate correction, to levy penalties and, if necessary, to cancel the concession.

Deciding to Privatize

The decision to privatize a governmental water service agency, in order to reap the benefits of market mechanisms acting on an activity directly linked to collective well-being and public health, should have been vigorously discussed by representatives of the community, so that the decision reflects the views of the majority.

The debate over the advantages and disadvantages of privatization ought to include alternative methods of making the change. The topics discussed in the four preceding sections of this chapter provide the bases for the debate. A resolution must also be reached before the final decision, as to whether the government should privatize the entire activity or part of it, and whether the government should continue to participate in the ownership of the corporation.

The privatization model should be tailored to the peculiar circumstances of each service and to the concerns of the respective communities. The entire process of privatization, from the decision to make a change, to the rules on how to set up the new system, to the choice of the enterprise to do the job, must result from a transparent and open process.

The rules of choice must clearly define the goals to be reached, the parameters of performance, the responsibilities, the penalties, the channels of communication with the community, the previous experience of the competitor for the concession, and in fact, almost every aspect that will regulate the relationship between the enterprise and the community. Privatization will succeed only if the parties develop a climate of familiarity and mutual respect.

Benefits of Privatization to the Community

We can enumerate the results that we would expect from privatization of water supply specifically, although they should be expected in any type of privatization. First, though, note that water supply is a permanent need for society, and it cannot be interrupted or stopped if the private enterprise fails, as would be the case with an industrial activity. The privatization must be accomplished in a way that gives the government sufficient powers and flexibility to act in case the public interest is endangered.

These are the benefits that we expect:

1) Privatization should stem the hemorrhaging of public funds that result from the need to cover the operating losses of water suppliers. That should free up funds for social purposes and other community needs.

2) Privatization will also liberate government funds for capital investment in other sectors.

3) Privatization will reduce the role of the government in the economy, on the road to eliminating the state corporation. The state, in turn, could dedicate itself to what are truly governmental functions.

4) Privatization should stimulate the growth of new enterprises that will provide services to the concessionaire.

5) Finally, privatization should provide the motive to produce lower costs.

Sewage: The Difficulties

The first request of the inhabitants of a newly incorporated area is for water service. However, as the population becomes denser, sanitary problems grow, and the residents start to demand installations for the collection and removal of sewage. The existence or lack of this service directly affects public health and the environment. Lack of sewage services usually causes pollution of waterways and of the water table, as well as of the local environment as a whole, and a deterioration of the quality of life in the area. As a consequence of the priority given to investment in water supply for reasons of public health, the level of sewage service may be much lower than that of water. Usually the same governmental entity that operates water supply to also run the sewage service. While there are a variety of types of agencies that furnish sewage, most are municipally owned, although some are on the regional or state level.

The sewage service function may be divided into five stages:

1) **Connections**—Pipes that connect the sanitary installations in the house, building or factory, to the collecting network of the sewer system.

2) **Sewer collecting network**—The network of pipes to which are attached the connections that carry the sewage (normally by gravity flow) to the trunk collectors which take all the flows from the drainage basin.

3) **Removal**—The assemblage of large trunk pipelines and mains that receives the flow from the trunk collectors and brings the sewage to the treatment station.

4) **Treatment station**—Facilities that treat the sewage, remove the solid waste in suspension, and bring the liquid up to standards that permit its reintroduction into the environment, so that it may be reused.

5) **Final disposition**—Discharge of the liquid effluent from the treatment station, in accord with regulations that take into account the levels of treatment, at carefully determined points, so that the final elimination of impurities and inorganic materials takes place helped by natural processes, without environmental damage. Solid wastes are normally transformed into fertilizer with restricted use.

A well run sewage service is one that maintains its network for collection and discharge permanently free of obstructions and leakages, that treats the entire volume collected, and does so in a manner adequate to preserve the waterways, water sources, and the environment as a whole.

If the need to invest in water facilities is great, the needs are even greater for sewage. The necessary investments are large, involve expensive construction and equipment, and the industry is far behind the demand for its service.

The difficulties facing government sewage industries are, basically, the same as those facing the water industry (See section titled Difficulties that Public Water Suppliers Face). Reasons to privatize sewage services are the same as those for water supply, but the most important reason to do so is to raise the capital for new treatment stations and the network.

Conclusion

Economic policy in the majority of countries encourages the formation of a market economy, in order to stimulate entrepreneurial creativity, and by doing so, raises the standard of living.

One of the ways to attain this goal is to reduce the role of the state as an owner of businesses, diminishing its interference in private business, and reserving for the state its proper role in education, welfare, preservation of the environment and social services.

The water and sewage industries are, without doubt, enterprises that are privatizable. The benefits of privatization are derived from the rationalization of services, improved water quality, greater efficiency, and reduction of costs. As long as the privatization respects the needs of the community, privatization will be a good solution for the users of the service as well as for the water companies themselves.

Chapter 9

Why Restructure INTEL?

The Proposal of the Government of Dr. Ernesto Pérez Balladares
Presented by Dr. Juan R. Porras, General Manager of INTEL

(Translated by Leonard S. Hyman and Angel García-Cordero)

Note: This proposal was originally presented in newspaper supplement format. We have made minor changes in formatting and have transformed some of the graphics into tables and text.

Why Restructure INTEL?
Because we all win!
- The People: Economical communications and public works

- The State: Funds for social investments

- The Private Enterprise: Profits on investment

- The Workers: Guarantees for what the worker has already achieved and stability

INTEL: Autonomous State Enterprise?
INTEL is autonomous in name only. It functions as one more ministry, and it has to submit its decisions to the bureaucracy of the Ministry of Planning and Political Economy, to the Ministry of Finance and Treasury, and to the Controller General of the Republic. Although providing a service that today functions at the speed of light, INTEL functions at the speed of a state bureaucracy...

BASIC DATA (rounded):

- Number of telephone lines   300,000*

- Unsatisfied demand   60,000

*Capacity of switches.

Between the people who have asked for service and the numbers already granted in excess of the operating capacity of the central offices (80 percent) we are behind demand by 60,000 telephone lines. Studies, moreover, indicate that if we double the number of lines in service, the community would absorb them.

- Telephone density: 11 telephones per 100 inhabitants

That is not bad in comparison with Latin American neighbors, but if we want to be an advanced country, we should aspire to a density of at least 25.

- Number of workers   3,800

Each worker takes care of an average of 70 lines, half the worldwide average. In a few words, we have a ratio of workers-to-lines twice the worldwide average. We ought to at least double the number of telephone lines to put ourselves on a par with international competition.

B/. millions*

- Revenues (1994 budget)   280

  From basic service   60

  From national long distance   40

  From international long distance   130

  From previous fiscal year   50

* *One balboa (B/.) equals one US dollar*

International service, as a result of its high and uncompetitive rates, provides the bulk of INTEL's earnings. High rates not only inhibit economic development but also encourage the piracy of so-called "Call-Back."

- Operating expenses   B/.80 million

- Investments   B/.80 million

Those investments are far below what is needed for expansion and improvement of service. INTEL should invest at least B/.120 million per year to bring its service up to date technologically and to expand service.

- Contribution to the state   B/. 115 million

Present Situation of INTEL

We have neither cellular mobile nor fixed (public rural) cellular.

According to Law 17 of 1991, the "A" band should be put up for public auction and INTEL should develop service on the "B" band. So far, neither of the two bands has been put into service. Nowadays, one can use the cellular system to provide public and private telephone service in remote and inaccessible regions faster and more economically.

We do not have telephone lines.

We have a serious deficit of 60,000 lines, taking into account the real demand of the people who have requested a telephone, and telephone numbers handed out in excess of the 80 percent standard of saturation of switch capacity. As a result, at peak hours (9:00 AM to 4:00 PM) subscribers have to wait to obtain a dial tone, the call fails to go through, or they encounter a busy signal. The desired level of unsatisfied demand ought to be less than 1 percent (in the case of INTEL, that represents 3,000 lines at present.)

If INTEL, like any other business, is paying a salary to its workers, and paying for energy and rents, etc., it should have at its disposal the means to provide the service that it sells: telephone lines. Not having enough lines to meet demand inhibits economic growth and is bad business for both INTEL and for the community.

We do not have a totally digitalized network:

Forty-five percent (136 thousand lines) are analog (dinosaurs) and cause problems not only for the subscriber but also for INTEL:

1) They cannot offer value added services such as call waiting, conference calls, call identification, transfers, etc., all of which prevents the customer from fully utilizing modern systems in the most economical manner. For example, call waiting is as if the customer had two lines instead of one for only B/. 1.00 more, and INTEL would be collecting that additional money without adding another line.

2) Quality of transmission is poorer, causing line noise, etc.

3) Repairs are costlier and slower.

We do not have a modern, centralized trunk dispatch communication system:

Half of INTEL's employees work outside the company offices, but they do so without a central system of radio communication that permits them to maintain contact with their offices. Such a system would save INTEL many man-hours by dispatching staff efficiently for installation and repair orders.

We do not have tools for work:

Sixty percent of the vehicular fleet is more than five years old and virtually destroyed. It is inconceivable that with half of the workers on the road, they cannot count on vehicles in good condition. INTEL also lacks other tools of the trade as basic as boots, helmets, etc., all of which contributes to the inefficiency of the enterprise.

We do not have a competitive international service:

The bulk of INTEL's profits are derived from international service, owing to tariffs that are not only excessively high but also inhibit economic development. It is well known that the most developed countries are those that offer the lowest telephone rates. The high rates also encourage the piratical business known as "Call-Back," which is robbing INTEL of business and defrauding the Treasury of taxes on long distance calls.

In the last three years, INTEL has lost B/.30 million to those criminal activities. They use INTEL's network, but with advanced technology they reverse the call and the client receives a dial tone in Miami and pays a much lower rate. If we do not take urgent measures, this system could force INTEL into the position of having to raise its basic rates in order to offset the losses, to the detriment of most subscribers. INTEL must rebalance tariffs in order to become competitive, but doing so requires huge investment in technology, sums which are presently not at our disposal.

We do not have a modern billing system:

1) This is another one of the dinosaurs that INTEL has to deal with, and it causes difficulties to customers as well as losses to INTEL because it produces a delayed and out-of-date billing. On occasion, bills arrive at the subscriber for long distance calls made three or four months before the close of the billing period.

2) Customers who want to lodge complaints or request information must do so personally at one of INTEL's offices. With a modern system, they would be able to do so by telephone, without having to show up personally and to waste valuable time.

3) This anachronism prevents the managers and executives of INTEL from having an efficient, instantaneous, paperless electronic mail communication system.

We cannot opportunely and economically make investments:

1) At INTEL, it takes an average of three years to implement a bid, and many times the process results in all sorts of suspicion of corruption, and lack of ethics among suppliers who employ dishonest means to oppose their competitors. This delay implies higher costs and out-of-date technology for the subscribers. For example, an installed telephone line cost B/.1600 four years ago. In the last bidding that INTEL conducted, each line cost B/.450 installed and the technology was more advanced.

2) The most palpable example is the international central office that was opened to bids four years ago, recently inaugurated, and is already saturated. With a business-like system of purchasing, INTEL would be able to acquire modern technology at a lower cost.

We do not have motivated executives or workers:

The comparatively low salaries on an international basis, the lack of tools and of investment, all keep our workers unmotivated. The evaluations to which workers are entitled, are often delayed in the bureaucracy for a year before they are implemented. The partisan political situation negatively affects the moral of INTEL's highly professional workers.

Alternatives

1) **Status quo:** To leave things the way they are or only to try to achieve more autonomy, would be irresponsible— in light of the accelerated deterioration of INTEL—to its workers and to the to the community which has expectations of better service.

2) **Restructure INTEL:** The proposal of the government of Dr. Ernesto Pérez Balladares, which takes into account the public interest, that of the workers, and the drive inherent in private capital.

3) **Total sale:** This represents the other extreme, in which the state would have no participation nor would it represent the balance between the public interest, and that of private profit.

Restructure INTEL (Our Proposal)
Law that authorizes the formation of INTEL, S.A.:

First Stage: As a result of this law, one can make the following advances, while still maintaining in the first stage 100 percent state ownership of shares:

1) Eliminate the purchasing red tape.

2) The Controller would audit in place of direct intervention.

3) Substitute enterprise planning for government central planning.

4) Substitute dividends for contributions dictated by the central government.

Second stage: While beginning the preparation of INTEL, S.A. for the auction of 49 percent of its shares, a special procedure should begin that would involve:

1) Prequalification of the proposed bidders: taking into account three basic requirements:

   a) Capability and operating experience in the field of telecommunications;

   b) Financial capacity not only to buy the 49 percent of INTEL, S.A., but also to invest in activity to improve the corporation;

   c) Technical capability.

2) Agreement on and signing of the bidding document: The prequalified bidders will receive portfolios of the bidding documents shown below, with the end that they will negotiate among themselves a uniform version and then sign an unconditional acceptance of the same:

   a) The telecommunications concession;

   b) The operating contract;

   c) The conditions of the bidding document;

   d) A draft of the telecommunications law;

   e) Proposals for the modification of the articles of incorporation of INTEL, S.A.

3) "Due Diligence": That is the name of the procedure in which INTEL, S.A. allows all the prequalified bidders to examine, without restrictions of any kind, all of its books, assets and properties, in order to allow them to evaluate the enterprise.

4) Public bidding: Once the special preliminary procedures—which eliminate the subjective evaluations or provisional judgments that invite corruption and unethical competition by the bidders—are completed, the act of open and public bidding takes place. All who desire may be present at the bidding, including the news media. In the decision, the only consideration for choice of winner will be the highest price, payable in cash, guaranteed by a bank, upon delivery of 49 percent of the shares of INTEL, S.A. This proportion of the shares gives the buyer the right to name two directors to the board and to operate the enterprise.

5) The State retains 49 percent of the shares: With the right to appoint two members on the board of directors of INTEL, S.A., to receive dividends on its shares, and to collect a tax on the income from operations of the company.

6) The workers receive 2 percent of the shares deposited in an irrevocable trust: They may not sell the shares and they remain beneficiaries as long as they are employees or retirees of INTEL, S.A. Those shares will have a right to appoint one member to the board.

Highlights of the Concession

1) Twenty years: Renewable by means of a new negotiation that should begin five years before the expiration of the concession.

2) Commitment to invest B/.581 million in telecommunications.

3) Orderly and gradual opening up of exclusive services: In the negotiation for the concession, the period of exclusivity for basic and long distance services (between 5 and 8 years) will be determined.

4) Operation of the cellular mobile "B" band: Law 17 of 1991 gives this right to INTEL. No operator of one band may operate the other band, in order to maintain competition and reasonable prices to the public.

Table 9-1. National Telecommunications Institute Program of Investments

		Five Year Total in B/. Thousands
Replacement of vehicles		7,000
Computer and automation equipment		5,000
Financial terminals		1,700
Switching		173,150
Replacement of electromechanical central offices	39,150	
Unsatisfied demand	44,000	
Future demand	90,000	
Energy		5,982
External plant		104,393
Project Darien		1,823
Project San Blas		800
Land and buildings		11,560
Transmission		76,929
Radio networks	44,429	
Fiber optics	30,300	
Multiplexers	2,200	
Trunk system		2,375
Terminal equipment		14.098
Special equipment and PABX	1,625	
Telephone booths	1,258	
Telephone instruments	9,545	
Testing and measuring equipment	1,670	
International system		10,000
Public telephones		5,800
National cellular telephony band B		14,000
Subtotal		434,610
ITBM/ Customs and sales tax		63,884
Labor loans made		7,900
Improvement in salary system		75,000
Total of investments		581,394

New Labor Relations

1) Negotiation and signing of a collective bargaining agreement in place of Law 8 of 1975 that, as a minimum, provides the same benefits as that law;

2) At the option of the employee:

   a) Liquidation the existing labor contract and institution of a new contract,

   b) INTEL, S.A. assumes responsibility for the pension fund and other obligations to labor,

3) Labor stability.

Effects of the Plan

1) Investments of 581 million balboas for the development of telecommunications;

2) One thousand million balboas for investments by the State in highways, schools, housing, health centers, crime control, and infrastructure for ports and airports.

Present and Future

The restructuring project, as it is conceived, guarantees the community access to all telecommunications services, even in remote and unprofitable areas, at reasonable prices.

- Cellular mobile telephony

- Cellular fixed telephony

- Satellite cellular telephony

- Value added services

- Video communication

- Interactive TV

- Communications superhighway

Finally, the restructuring will have a multiplier effect on the national economy in industry, electricity, private construction, employment and competitive efficiency, food production, tax collections, and commerce.

Chapter 10

Telecommunications in Europe

Sylviane Farnoux-Toporkoff

New technology, competition, deregulation and customer demand have been the driving forces behind change in telecommunications since 1987. These drivers have led the European Commission to adopt January 1, 1998 as the date for full liberalization of Europe's telecommunications markets, including voice telephony services. The Commission will liberalize through two types of directives:

- Those based on Article 90-3 of the Treaty, which gives the Commission the power to open markets to competition. Following up on its earlier directive on liberalization of terminal equipment (May 16, 1988), the Commission adopted a new directive in 1990 concerning the liberalization of almost all services other than voice telephony.

- Those of harmonization based on Article 100-A of the Treaty, relating to the implementation of an Open Telecommunications Network (Open Network Provision or ONP). The Commission always considered that steps toward liberalization of telecommunications services went hand in hand with those aimed at the harmonization of those services in the context of the single European market.

Finally, on July 22, 1993, the Commission decided to establish January 1, 1998, as the date for the full liberalization of the European Telecommunications Market, including voice telephony services and infrastructure. To encourage this liberalization, a group of leading European representatives of the industry, including both operators and users, under the chairmanship of Mr. Martin Bangemann, recommended in a July 1994 report, that member states accelerate their ongoing processes of liberalization of the telecommunications sector by:

- opening infrastructures and services still in the monopoly realm to competition.

- removing non-commercial political burdens and budgetary constraints imposed on telecommunications operators.

- establishing timetables and deadlines for the implementation of practical measures to achieve these goals.

As a consequence of the liberalization, new and existing operators will want to interconnect with one another, in order to provide telecommunications services throughout the Community. Such interconnection implies the need to establish ongoing principles to determine access charges. The introduction of liberalization in the telecommunications sector will move tariff structures toward underlying costs. It is anticipated that operators will use the period prior to liberalization to adjust and improve their pricing and cost structures. The maintenance and development of universal service must go hand-in-hand with this process of tariff adjustment, requiring a re-examination of the current methods of financing universal service and the establishment of clear guidelines to manage the transition from monopoly to a competitive environment.

The changeover to a system of access charges, and the necessity of providing a sound financial base to support the provision of universal service, imply the need for transparent principles of cost determination. In the context of the liberalization of services, the national regulatory authorities and the operators, on the basis of consultation, must agree upon numerous principles concerning access charges and universal service financing. The interplay between tariff rebalancing, improved efficiency, transfers from more profitable service areas and access charges will determine the speed with which member states and operators can adjust as they prepare for full liberalization.

At the same time, internal transfers and access charges must not be seen as alternatives to tariff rebalancing, which remains a fundamental imperative. Nor should they become a means of affecting competitors' cost structures. Internal transfers and access charges must, also, be appropriately structured, so that they cannot be used to delay or limit the effects of general improvements in cost efficiency or of productivity gains, which should also permit real competition.

Regarding the Community's peripheral regions with their less-developed networks, the network investment required to develop and maintain universal service may qualify for funding from the Community's Structural Funds, in partnership with national financial resources.

In preparation for the liberalization of voice telephony services, national regulatory authorities and national operators will have to rapidly establish, implement and monitor the necessary adjustment programs, in order to achieve a new equilibrium concerning the financing of universal service from direct subscriber revenues and transfers. In the transitional period, clearly, it will be necessary to regulate the different tariffs. Where required, the member states should establish the principles and basis for determining a fair and transparent system of access charges, to establish such a balance. The main objectives of the adjustment programs should be:

- The development of adjustment targets for tariff structures on the basis of recognized common principles governing the future balance between direct subscriber revenue and revenue from transfers. In doing so, tariffs must be based on the principles of cost orientation, while insuring reasonable and affordable charges to all users. Tariffs must promote an open competitive environment founded on transparency, non-discrimination and proportionality. The latter term means that service providers with small market shares should not suffer excessive or undue regulatory burdens.

- The determination of access charges according to common principles. As markets open and liberalize, effective competition occurs on the national, Community-wide and international levels. Thus, it is important that all the markets calculate charges on the same basis.

Privatization allows operators to successfully position themselves for the competitive race. For regulators to create a truly balanced and competitive environment in Europe, where each operator has traditionally dominated its own market, is difficult. Europe needs to facilitate the privatization process, which can play a large role in helping to accelerate structural adjustments in the Community's industry. The need to entrust the creation of the information society in Europe to the private sector and to market forces is an even more important reason to do so.

The Privatization Process

The Delors White Paper on growth, competitiveness and employment (issued in 1994) reaffirmed that one of the key supply side elements of global competitiveness is:

> to encourage continuing structural adjustment in the Community's industry. This means facilitating the privatization process, which can play a large role in helping to accelerate such adjustment.

The key issues for privatization in Europe are:

- Europe must make a break from public policies based on principles predating the information revolution. Only the private sector will be able to move as quickly as required in the new international environment. The Community is convinced that in this arena, private management will be more efficient than bureaucracies, which are saddled with strong unions and a weak sense of strategic imagination.

- In order for the telecommunications operators to be active in international competition, they require the capacity to raise the private capital needed for innovation, growth and development. This can be achieved through privatization.

- To retain their positions in the global market, the operators must be able to offer global integrated services to their major clients. Joint projects are vital to accomplishing this goal. Examples include: BT/MCI, France Telecom/Deutsche Telekom/Sprint, and AT&T/Unisource (a consortium of Swedish, Dutch, Swiss, and Spanish telecommunications firms). Most of the players in this field are reluctant to join with a public sector firm.

What is the current status of operator privatization in the European countries? In most countries, privatization represents, primarily, an administrative change in the state enterprises. At least initially, it does not call into question state control over the newly established companies (British Telecommunications, or BT, is the exception, a fully privately owned firm.) Privatization is characterized by a separation from the traditionally connected post and telegraph (P&T) and financial services activities. In some cases (Italy and Portugal), privatization has also constituted an opportunity for industrial restructuring by bringing together dispersed assets of public enterprises in the same sector.

In general, as companies are opened to capital investment, ownership opportunities should be spread as widely as possible, in order to benefit the public (and to a lesser extent the employees) and to prevent small groups in leadership positions from exercising undue control. However, it could be worthwhile to consider reserving sizeable blocks of stock for strategic alliances, including some oriented toward establishing international partnerships and others taking the form of vertical alliances of the operator-manufacturer type. Other options involve the techniques of putting capital on the market (the timetable for various tranches and their amount, the fixing of share value, and the quantity of shares reserved for international investors, golden shares, etc.). Finally, those techniques must be viewed in the context of weighing the interest of the state (improving public finances with funds received from the sale, and getting new investment requirements out of the state budget) and those of the operator (using funds to reduce debt or reduce the debt ratio).

For the governments, the driving forces behind privatization are the need to implement modern infrastructures, obligation to provide basic services, value maximization, and a belief in the virtues of competition. Objectives include protecting employment, the creation of broad ownership and currency for international alliances, and cash proceeds.

For the operators, the driving force behind privatization is competitiveness, which requires organizational restructuring and network investment. Objectives include long-term corporate strengthening through efficiency and internationalization, access to capital markets, high market valuation, and the creation of employee incentives through the issuance of shares.

For customers, the objectives are lower tariffs, improved service quality and product offering, increased choice, responsiveness, and innovation in a growing multimedia market. In Europe, this is far more true for corporate as opposed to residential customers.

Investors are concerned with breaking down national boundaries, cross subsidization, the impact of competition, multimedia positioning, and capital availability.

The European Timetable
Where are the Europeans in the current process? What are the consequences for alliances? In addition to the political timetable, the European operators have to take four other parameters into account:

- The condition of financial markets

- The changes in the status of other European operators

- The calendar for European deregulation with its intensification of competition policy

- The need to progressively reduce debt.

France—Seemingly, the dates for action are being postponed until after the presidential election. In a report by its chairman, France Telecom has already expressed concern that it be given the same status as that of its main competitors and partners, through the establishment of a company with a state holding of at least 51 percent, with additional capital reserved primarily for employees and for strategic alliances. (The latter point, of course, refers to cross-holding operations such as those expected with Deutsche Telekom.) France Telecom is adapting its structures, little by little, in order to meet the challenges of the new, liberalized, competitive environment. Privatization should help France Telecom's emerging strategy of realizing 10 percent of its activity in international markets by the year 2000. For France Telecom, the restructuring and internationalization truly constitute a cultural revolution.

France Telecom Strategic Alliances

1990—purchase jointly with STET (a subsidiary of IRI, the Instituto per la recostruzione Industriale, a government holding company) (Italy) of control of Telecom Argentina

   —purchase jointly with Southwestern Bell and a local group of Telmex

   —More recently, France Telecom has taken operating control of a GSM cellular operator in Greece (35 percent of Panaon), is purchasing 11 percent of the Moscow mobile telephone system, and, jointly with Ameritech, is operating a cellular network in Poland.

   —In the realm of private networks, since 1992 France Telecom has participated in an alliance with Deutsche Telekom to create Eunetcom for the management of large international networks. In 1995, this alliance will include "Atlas," a new structure for the international activities of the French Transpac and the German Datex.

United Kingdom—Ten years after privatization (the last tranche of BT shares was put on the market in 1993), British Telecom's competitor, Mercury, has only 10 percent of the market. Notably, privatization has already had a social impact: A reduction of more than 40,000 employees over the past two years, with 50,000 more scheduled for layoff in the coming five years. BT's new approach to accounting separation (starting in fiscal 1994–1995), separates its access, network and retail businesses, in order to provide additional transparency and to assure that BT's business segments pay for access (and access deficits) on the same terms as interconnecting operators. BT must confront an extremely vigilant regulatory authority, Oftel, with an enormous, unresolved problem concerning the status of its civil service employees.

BT Strategic Alliances

1993—alliance with MCI (BT took a 20 percent equity stake in MCI for $4.3 billion)

Belgium—The government transformed the ex-RTT into an "entreprise Autonome de Droit Public," and renamed it Belgacom. That company is scheduled to be privatized to the tune of 49 percent of the capital. A 25 percent stake is likely to be sold to a foreign operator and 24 percent put on the stock exchange through a public offering.

Belgacom Strategic Alliances

—In the GSM field, an alliance with Airtouch (USA) which owns 25 percent of Belgacom Mobile

—Belgacom is a 7.2 percent shareowner of Infonet

—Joint arrangement with Alcatel to modernize Moscow network

Italy—Privatization is expected in 1995. Meanwhile, STET decided to merge its five telecommunications subsidiaries (SIP, Italcable, Telespazio, Iritel, and Sirm) in August 1994, in order to become more efficient on an international level. The new company is called Telecom Italia. The problem of privatization in Italy is completely dominated by the difficult political context and the state's need to raise its revenues.

STET Strategic Alliances

—Joint ownership with France Telecom of controlling interest in Telecom Argentina

—GSM network in Greece

—Shareholder in Motorola's Iridium project

—Owns 51 percent of STREAM, a multimedia company (Bell Atlantic is the other shareholder)

Germany—Partial privatization has been confirmed for 1996. The "how" has yet to be decided. Almost certainly, however, there will be a 40 percent limit placed on foreign holdings during the initial sale of capital shares. As currently planned, the first tranche, 25 percent of shares, will go on sale in 1996, with the second following in 1998. The German operator's priority is to harmonize its networks between the East and the West, requiring an investment of 50 billion DM between 1990 and 1997. Germany does, however, have some international projects. There is a social impact to restructuring: Deutsche Telekom wants to fire 30,000 employees in the near future. The context is somewhat similar to the opening in France, and the unions are extremely vigilant. At least, though, the rhythm is more accelerated in Germany than in France.

Deutsche Telekom Strategic Alliances

—Atlas with France Telecom and SPRINT

—Fiber optic network between Germany and Moscow

—Mobile phones in the Ukraine

—Satellites with Intersputnik

Netherlands—PTT Nederlands was a monopoly. In 1989, PTT was transformed into a limited share company, with 100 percent of the capital stock owned by the state (Koninklijke PTT Nederlands or KPN). In June 1994, the company was partly privatized (30 percent of the capital stock was publicly offered).

KPN Strategic Alliances

—KPN is a 25 percent partner in Unisource

—Company also owns 7.2 percent of Infonet

Spain—Telefónica de España has been a semipublic company since 1924. The Spanish government has scheduled the complete liberalization of services for 1998. In the meantime, Telefónica is rapidly modernizing its network and investing in mobile telephony. The Spanish Ministry of Transport has agreed to a detailed rebalancing program concerning pricing adjustments, to be implemented by Telefónica before the end of 1996. One objective of this program is to restructure the tariffs for leased lines, moving from a system of three fixed rate bands (local, regional, and national) to a distance-related scheme. Under the new structure, the projected results would be a 45 percent global reduction in tariffs for leased lines.

Telefónica Strategic Alliances

—In Latin America, Telefónica owns 43.8 percent of the capital of the Chilean operator (CTC), and 29 percent of Telefónica de Argentina. The company also has properties in Peru, Puerto Rico and Venezuela

—In addition, it has a 7.2 percent interest in Infonet, 25 percent in Unisource, 5.8 percent in ATT-NSI, 15.3 percent in Amper, 100 percent in SINTEL, 25 percent of Hispasat Satellite System

Sweden—The operating company, Televerket, was transformed into a limited share company in July 1993, and its name changed to Telia. Telia has a competitor, Tele 2, which is owned 60 percent by Kinnevik and 40 percent by Cable & Wireless (UK). Telia is very competitive, having dismissed 8,000 employees since 1991, and shows excellent results in the mobile sector.

Telia Strategic Alliances

—In 1991, the company joined Unisource in order to offer international private networks and it owns 25 percent of that joint effort now

—Telia owns 7.2 percent of Infonet

Table 10-1 presents additional data about European carriers.

Today, competition policy has become a key element of Europe's strategy of positioning itself to successfully operate in and fully benefit from the global market. This represents a revolutionary approach for Europe. The competition rules also will be applied to cooperative agreements, and to mergers and joint ventures between telecommunications operations, such as some of the most recent strategic alliances.

Multi-company Strategic Alliances

—Global European Network (GEN) was set up by the French, Italian, Spanish, and German telephone operators and BT to coordinate the provision of pan-European broadband capacity.

—Financial Network Association (FNA) was founded by twelve telephone operators (eight European firms plus Stentor of Canada, KDD of Japan, and MCI of the USA) to offer services to the global financial industry.

—Unisource.

—Nordic Teleholding was formed by the Danish, Finnish and Norwegian telephone operators.

—France Telecom and Deutsche Telekom formed Eunetcom and are setting up a joint venture with SPRINT.

—In December 1994, AT&T and Unisource announced the creation of Uniworld to offer certain pan-European telecommunications services.

Table 10-1: The European Timetable

	Sales 1993 (MM$)	Net earnings 1993 (MM$)	Debt 1993 (MM$)	Personnel 1993	Opening up of capital	Comments
Belgacom **Belgium**	3207	279	3003	25643		Project for the sale of 49% of the capital. Government choice of partner for Belgacom soon.
BT **United Kingdom**	20576	2659	6017	156000		Privatization on 1st April 1984. Last tranche put on the market in 1993.
DBP Telekom **Germany**	35679	-1738	37878	231000	1st tranche of 25% (mid-96) 2nd tranche of 25% (98)	Privatization of DBP Telekom along with DBP Postdienst and DBP Postbank, 1st January 95. 40% limit on foreign holdings during initial sale of capital.
France Télécom **France**	22426	848	18736	155548		Report submitted to the government by the chairman of France Télécom during summer 94. Declaration in principle by the government for the partial privatization of the operator but decisions to be postponed until after the presidential elections in May 95?
KPN (P&T) **Netherlands**	8747 (5944 Telecom)	966	2964	94314	1st tranche of 30% on 6 June 94. A further 36% in 3 or 4 subsequent tranches	"Private" company since 1st January 89 (with State as sole shareholder until 1993). 22.9 billion Florin capitalisation. Capital available to all national and foreign investor (banking syndicate's right of option on 20.7 M shares, i.e. about 4.5% of the capital, limited to 30 days.)
OTE **Greece**	1453	281	1946	26716	1st tranche of 25% in Nov. 94.	Expected income from 1st tranche: $1 billion.

continued on next page

Table 10-1: The European Timetable (*continued*)

	Sales 1993 (MM$)	Net earnings 1993 (MM$)	Debt 1993 (MM$)	Personnel 1993	Opening up of capital	Comments
Portugal Telecom **Portugal**	n/a	n/a	n/a	22000	1st tranche of 25–30% in mid-95.	Merger of telecoms: TLP (Telefones de Lisbo e Porto), TDP (Telediffusao de Portugal) and Telecom Portugal, in July 94 into a public company: Portugal Telecom. Capilalization estimated at 1000 billion Escudos.
STET **Italy**	18925 (of which 15539 telecom operations)	978	12114	136184		Privatization in 95.
Telecom Italia	17028	651	n/a	101338	1st tranche 16 August 94	Merger to Italcable, Telespazio, Iritel, Sirm and Sip (IRI group) STET subsidiaries. 28000 billion Lira capitalization.
Telecom Eireann **Ireland**	1256	97	1454	13069		Discussions in progress.
Teledanmark **Denmark**	2513	241	1310	17064	1st tranche of 48.3% of the capital (B shares) in April 94.	Creation of TeleDenmark on 1st January through a regrouping of regional operators (State sole shareholder until 1993). Expected income from 1st tranche: $3 billion.
Telefonica **Spain**	10193	747	14364	74340		Private company since 1924: State still holds 32.3% of the capital and controls the operator.

Conclusion

As the Bangemann report emphasized, a critical question remains: whether this policy will be a Union-wide strategic creation or a more fragmented and less effective amalgam of individual initiatives by the member states. The answer to that question will have profound repercussions on every area of this policy.

A competitive environment, with liberalization and privatization, requires that telecommunications operators be relieved of political constraints, such as subsidizing public functions, external R&D activities, and sole responsibility for universal service. Therefore, in order to achieve competition, it is essential that a proper regulatory framework be designed. The framework will lead to a predictable environment, thereby making possible orderly investment and strategic planning. A competitive environment also requires the downward adjustment of international long distance and leased tariffs to bring those rates in line with those practiced in other advanced industrialized regions.

The European market is now truly opening. Governments need to support liberalization by working together with the European Commission to draw up clear timetables and deadlines, with practical measures to realize this goal. Furthermore, care must be taken to avoid overly rigorous enforcement, which would jeopardize these operations without yielding tangible benefits for community users. This openness must be matched in markets and networks throughout the world, to guarantee equal access.

Chapter 11

Competition, Privatization and Renewables: Wind as the Test Case

Gerald R. Alderson

What will happen to renewable energy sources as the global energy economy shifts from a regulated, command-and-control structure to one that features competition and privatization? The prevailing view is that renewables will whither away in these new, open markets—unable to compete.

Once again the conventional wisdom is often-stated, widely accepted—and wrong. We see the move to privatization and an open, competitive energy economy as reasons for optimism, not pessimism. Rather than becoming victims of change, renewables will benefit from the move to an economically competitive market. Indeed, rather than shrinking from open competition, renewables can actively embrace it as an agent of growth.

Renewable energy sources need an environment of progress and change to prosper. But the bureaucracies that run regulated utilities look for the future in the rearview mirror of conventional wisdom. They assume the status quo. With the exception of hydroelectric, renewables are not yet part of their conventional wisdom. Because these conservative organizations are so risk averse, they are, in themselves, significant barriers to widespread commercialization of renewables.

Yet the winds of change—in the form of open, competitive markets—are beginning to blow. And they are picking up speed.

Competition and Privatization Drive Wind Power

We see convincing evidence that wind power is on the verge of widespread commercialization driven by emerging competition. In fact, wind can be used as a case study of how privatization can affect renewables.

Of all the nonconventional, renewable technologies, wind power is the only one that is currently capable of cost-competitive, broad-based development. Wind is available throughout the world and, because of recent technological improvements, it is economically competitive with electricity produced by fossil fuel central generating stations. By contrast, direct solar and biomass are not yet economically competitive.

What stands in the way of successful, widespread commercialization of wind power? Simply put, it is the institutional inertia of the traditional electric utility bureaucracies—the same set of forces that have held back many types of change for many decades. Their line of thinking goes this way: since wind is not currently part of the accepted electric generating equation, this places it outside the circle of mainstream solutions (irrespective of its economics and technical advantages). Given this inward, self-referencing view, it's not surprising to find that, where wind power is in use, it has been "commanded into being." Typically, these command-driven policies have taken years to evolve and implement.

However, the emerging private, competitive electric power industry is challenging conventional wisdom. The status quo is under intense pressure to change. Below, we'll examine the factors which led to the evolution of the modern wind power industry. By comparing wind's potential acceptance in an open, competitive market—versus a state-owned monopoly—we can judge which environment is better for its commercialization. This analysis should hold true for any renewable technology at that point in the future when it has achieved commercial competitiveness.

The key to change is privatization combined with competition. It is not enough just to privatize electric utilities, i.e., raise funds for the state by selling a state-owned enterprise to private interests. If the activities of this new entity are still controlled by comprehensive regulation—again the heavy hand of bureaucracy—then the move to privatization does little to help renewables. Privatization can improve the odds that the enterprise will implement more crisply—but, in and of itself, it does not create a fertile environment where renewables can flourish.

Privatization *plus* competition will significantly affect the future of renewables. To flourish in open, competitive markets, electric utilities must adopt a portfolio management approach to generation. The utility companies will need to embrace a range of technologies—each with its own operating advantages. In this mix of generating resources, alternative technologies have a role to play. Because the marketplace already has established wind power's economic and technical viability, the shift to privatization and competition will speed its widespread commercialization.

Companies within a privatized, competitive electric utility sector will find it necessary to practice effective risk management as a matter of economic optimization. In virtually all "private, highly competitive" industries, the key to risk management lies in portfolio theory. Thus, in response to competitive pressures, those companies will hedge their risks by developing a portfolio of generation sources. In an increasing number of cases, cost/benefit analysis will lead utility companies to wind as a component of their generation portfolio.

A Brief History

A brief look at the history of the modern wind power industry is a good example of an open, competitive marketplace in action. The current industry owes its existence to two factors: (1) the rapidly escalating electricity prices of the late 1970s—which made the risks of the development of sophisticated, cost-effective wind turbines worthwhile; and (2) the creation of an open market for electricity in the United States.

These two sets of events—acting in concert—launched the industry. Many of the technology innovations that produced today's sophisticated wind turbines came from start-up companies funded by risk capital. However, if the only factor at work had been the run-up in electricity prices, this capital would not have been invested in these start-up companies. Venture capitalists knew that the sway of conventional wisdom and the conservatism of traditional utilities posed unacceptable risks to the commercialization of wind power. The prospect of success stemming from economic competitiveness achieved through technological innovation was not sufficient, in itself, to attract risk capital.

But when PURPA, the Public Utility Policies Regulatory Act, introduced competition into electric markets in 1978, the risk/reward balance tilted toward action. PURPA laid the groundwork for an open market—freed from archaic command-and-control processes. In this new market, nontraditional generation technologies could succeed on their own merits—unencumbered by bureaucratic decision making. As a result of these two conditions—the cost effectiveness of sophisticated wind turbines and open, competitive markets—capital flowed into a burgeoning wind turbine industry.

More than a billion dollars and 15 years later, the wind power industry met its original, mid-1970s objective: to produce equipment (such as the KENETECH 56-100 constant speed wind turbine) that could compete with fossil plants fueled by $30 per barrel oil. However, during this 15-year period, the price of a barrel of oil plummeted—seemingly undercutting wind power's chance of success. Because the development momentum was strong, though, technology continued to improve. The end result is that a variable speed, advanced wind turbine (the KENETECH Windpower model 33M-VS) is fully competitive in today's utility price environment. (See Fig. 11-1)

Wind Power: The Advantages

The argument for Windplants™ begins with cost neutrality; that is, wind is equally cost effective with virtually every other utility-scale electric generation option. Advances in technology have made wind turbines more efficient while simultaneously reducing their initial capital cost. New installations cost $750 or less per

Figure 11-1. Cost Comparison: 33M-VS vs. Other Technologies

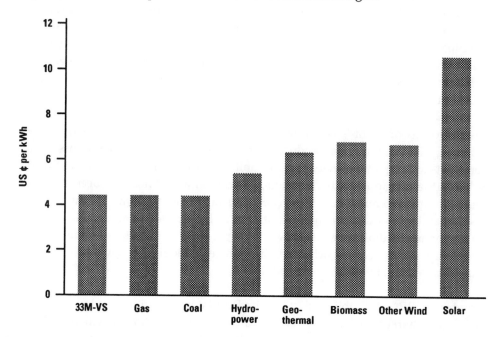

installed kilowatt. With zero fuel costs and modest operating costs, these facilities produce electricity at 5 per kilowatt/hour or less. Finally, the operating life of Windplants is consistent with that of other utility generating facilities.

Wind power is cost effective and therefore economically competitive. A close look at its advantages and disadvantages follows.

Managing Fuel Price Risk. Wind power, by its very nature, eliminates the risk that fuel prices will drastically escalate during the operating life of the plant. For the same cost of energy as from a newly constructed fossil plant, a Windplant provides a virtually perfect hedge against the risk of rising fuel costs.

In contrast, building a fossil plant creates long-term fuel price risk because the purchase of fuel for the entire operating life of the plant is required. In an increasingly dynamic, global geopolitical environment, exposure to this risk, lasting several decades, looms very large. State-owned and/or regulated utilities are often not required to manage fuel risks. Ratepayers and taxpayers—not utilities—have borne the risk of increased fuel prices. Utilities made decisions about their generation plants emphasizing factors other than fuel price risk.

However, in an open, competitive market, customer choice will tend to make the electric supplier responsible for fuel risks. To manage this risk, electric suppliers will adopt hedging strategies, including the rapid development of broad-based portfolios of generation technologies. Renewables, with their natural advantage as a fuel risk hedge, will take on greater value than they commanded in regulated electric markets.

Alleviating Hard Currency Constraints: Another fuel-based advantage of wind is the elimination of hard currency requirements for fuel purchases. In developing countries, where the availability of hard currency is often a crucial consideration, the cost of imported fossil fuel can slow or stop the widespread development of the electric sector. To the extent that wind power is part of the generation portfolio, hard currency requirements for fuel purchase are eliminated.

Segmenting Generation: A Windplant consists of a large number of quasi-independent operating units. By contrast, a fossil plant is typically an integrated operating unit. This distinction—called segmentability—gives wind power several distinct advantages.

The first advantage of segmentability is in the use of capital. Let's say a 500 MW power plant is the goal. Both a fossil plant and a Windplant of this size may take four to five years to build. During this construction cycle, all of the invested capital in the fossil plant is unproductive; the first kilowatt/hour is available only at the end of the long construction cycle. On the other hand, a 500 MW Windplant can come on line one wind turbine at a time and add new electrical capacity early in the construction process while continuing to produce ever-increasing quantities of power as construction progresses. If advantageous, smaller amounts of capital can be raised year-by-year to continue the construction of portions of the Windplant. Segmentation of capital formation reduces interest costs and segmentation of generation accelerates revenue and, hence, the return on invested capital.

A second advantage of segmentability concerns overall power plant availability. Because a Windplant has a large number of discrete generators, you never lose the whole plant. Wind's predictability will be covered later—but when the wind is blowing, the plant produces electricity at or near its capacity with virtually no risk of losing power. Historically, equipment problems affect only 1 percent to 2 percent of a Windplant at any one time. These few units are off-line without affecting the rest of the plant.

A third advantage is that scheduled maintenance can occur on a rolling timetable that maximizes the efficiency of maintenance people and equipment. Maintenance can also be scheduled to avoid the typical high wind season of each location.

Distributing Generation: Placing generation capacity closer to electrical users can produce significant reductions in overall system cost. Consider that half of the invested capital typically necessary to build a conventional electrical system is in the central generating plant itself. The other 50 percent is in the transmission infrastructure necessary to distribute the electricity. Distributed technologies such as wind reduce or eliminate the capital costs required to build the bulk transmission system. Thus, while the cost per unit of energy generated is approximately equal for fossil plants and Windplants, the costs to transmit that power are frequently less—sometimes much less—with a Windplant.

Maximizing Local Content: Much of the cost of a Windplant is from labor or material available locally. Civil works such as roads, foundations, and the electrical collection system; and electromechanical components, such as towers and transformers, represent a large portion of the cost. This can be a boon to a local economy. In addition, in areas where hard currency is a problem, local content can be a crucial issue in choosing one generation option over another.

Managing Development Risks: The development risk for Windplants is markedly lower than for fossil plants because it is a more benign technology. The designs are simpler; the environmental impacts more modest; the engineering and design costs lower and the integration with other uses of land in the area easier, especially when the primary use is agriculture. All these factors decrease planning and permitting time and increase the probability of ultimate success.

Decreasing Environmental Impacts: While the environmental benefits of wind are dramatic when compared to the fossil fuel alternative, we prefer to consider the environmental benefits of wind power to be a bonus. The most productive way to evaluate wind power is on the basis of its cost effectiveness—not its political correctness. With the economics right, the environmental benefits are free.

Wind Power: The Disadvantages
As with any electric power generating source, wind has its disadvantages. The two that are most commonly mentioned are its variability and its land use requirements.

Variability: Obviously, the wind does not blow all the time. However, the modern Windplant is not the rural windmill of 75 years ago—one generator connected to one user. Instead, a Windplant is a utility scale power plant that uses wind as its fuel.

Wind is not, nor will it be, a primary generating source. A reasonable intermediate-term objective for wind power is 5 percent of generation. So the growth expectancy for the widespread use of wind power is to move from 0 percent today to nearer 5 percent in the not-too-distant future. From this perspective, the key issue in evaluating wind's role in generation lies in the question, "How does wind integrate into a specific utility's portfolio of generating options?" Wind, while not constant, is quite predictable. Its daily and seasonable variability occur in known patterns. When you combine the factors of predictability and a small percentage of total generation, you can begin to see how wind power can effectively play its role in the portfolio. For example, a utility may schedule maintenance of a fossil facility during the peak wind season knowing it can rely on wind to produce a lot of energy during that period of the year.

A thorough analysis of a utility's generating sources is important in crafting the most cost-effective role for wind power. For instance, a developing country may use hydroelectric as its primary generating source. Assuming that the flow of water can be reduced when the wind blows, wind energy can, in effect, be "stored" in the form of greater hydroelectric capacity achieved through reduced outflows during windy periods.

Land Use: A common perception is that wind power takes a lot of land. In practice, it takes almost none. In a typical installation, the Windplant is built in an existing agricultural area. On average, 1 percent of the land is no longer availability for its previous agricultural use. As such, it becomes an added or secondary use of the land rather than a competing use.

Summary
The modern wind turbine is now cost effective when compared to virtually every other utility-scale electric generation option. Wind is a perfect hedge against future fuel cost increases. Wind power eliminates hard currency requirements of fossil fuels. The wind turbine's construction can be segmented and phased. The benign nature of wind power reduces development risks, and carries the lower costs associated with distributed generation. Environmental benefits are a bonus.

Wind power's advantages can be exploited to their fullest when it is an integrated part of a portfolio of generating plants. As a primary source, wind power's use is limited. At 1 percent or 3 percent or 5 percent of total generation, however, the advantages of wind power are significant. In the future, as utilities compile lessons learned with wind representing 5 percent of their generation, they may then make prudent decisions about further expanding its use based upon operating experience.

How will wind power fare as the electric energy economy changes from the old, regulated, command-and-control model to a system of open, competitive markets? The good news is that these restructured markets can properly value wind power's advantages in ways that old, regulated markets were never motivated to do. We strongly believe that wind power will truly come into its own in the emerging future of privatization and open, competitive electric energy markets.

PART III
Doing the Private Deal

➢

Chapter 12

Developing Power Projects in Developing Countries: Special Issues

David L. Haug*

(Note: The following is transcribed from a speech given by Mr. Haug at the conference, "Developing and Financing International Power Generation Projects," which was held April 27–28, 1993.)

This chapter focuses on the development of power projects in Latin America and other developing countries from the perspective of a developer. First, let me introduce you to Enron, a developer, owner, operator, and builder of independent power projects, with more than 4,000 megawatts in operation or under construction, and projects under development on six continents. We focus on projects fired with natural gas, where it is available, or, if not, on projects run on fuel oil. Our parent company has the largest gas transmission and pipeline in the United States (US), is the largest marketer of natural gas in terms of volume in the US, owns a large, independent oil and gas exploration company, has a gas liquids division, and has expertise in transporting and trading liquid fuels. Enron Development's areas of gas and liquid fuels are the same ones that the parent company focuses on in a diversified way.

What is going on outside the US and why do people like us want to play around in foreign places? Capital infrastructure problems exist all over the world, and power is one of the areas where problems exist. All countries need more energy. There is not enough money, even with international help and direct loans, to fund these projects.

What we are seeing, that maybe has had the most dramatic effect in the last two or three years around the world, is a result of what happened during the 1970s and 1980s. The US received a lot of people from various countries from around the world and trained them at some of our business schools and graduate schools. Those people learned the lessons they were taught at those schools, went back to their own countries, and are implementing them much better in our view than a lot of people from the US.

*Managing Director of Enron Development Corp. and President of Enron Global Capital.

The so-called Chicago School economic theory, taught at the University of Chicago and several other places, has taken hold in a lot of places in Latin America, Southeast Asian countries, and a lot of other places as well, for example, in Eastern Europe. Free markets are very popular. Privatization and foreign investments are also very popular. Rules on keeping currency in and not letting currency out have been easing or, in some cases, eliminated. Not only is lip service paid to these principles, but there are people who are running the show who actually believe them, accept them, and are implementing them—and are succeeding with them.

Different Models
Privatization is happening. Developers need to recognize that there is no fixed model for privatization. There are different strategies in different places. As my Czech cousin puts it, "Different countries, different customs." That's what we are seeing all over.

The basic models are:

• all facilities privatized at the same time: generation, transmission, distribution

• just generation only, not transmission

• only new generation

• sell electricity on wholesale versus retail level.

In our view, you do not need an extensive regulatory structure for an independent power producer (IPP) developer such as ourselves, to play in the privatization game. We believe that whatever is lacking in the regulatory structure can be implemented through contracts. Basically what we need is a creditworthy entity willing to buy our power that has a way to get it physically from us to them. We can creatively structure around a lot of the other issues, if not all other issues. As long as there is a judicial system that has a history of enforcing contracts and a judicial structure for that, then we will probably at least look seriously at a country that needs energy and that has privatization and fits that model.

The examples are:

• Argentina: radical restructure—privatize everything

• United Kingdom (UK): moderate—privatized via share offering. Keep various parts within the government, such as nuclear generation. Allow new entrants for new generation

- a number of countries are adopting the gradual approach—privatizing new generation only. Guatemala, the Philippines, and the Dominican Republic, where we are operating, are some of these. The projects in Southeast Asia, Central America, and Eastern European countries will probably go that way.

It is interesting to hear people from the US say that the easiest thing to privatize is distribution. In a lot of countries, distribution is viewed as the hardest thing to privatize because it is so difficult to price transmission. Another difficulty is figuring out how much to charge to move electricity from one place to the other if the company that owns the distribution assets is different from the one that owns the generation assets. The UK and some Latin American countries are experiencing that particular difficulty. In addition, the Colombian model that would privatize everything and allow wholesale and retail wheeling is still trying to determine exactly how to price that wheeling. This same debate is now beginning in the US. The key for developers is to be flexible and to make sure that you do not get set on any one kind of structure that really is not necessary for you to do business.

Target Markets

Target markets for us have features that are critical for a developer to get in. They must have a commitment to privatization. It has to be more than lip service. It has to be a deep understanding, as well as a commitment. We like to go in and talk to all the ministers and find out, "Are you really committed to this? Do you really understand and like how it works?" After two or three drinks, will they still say the same nice things about it as when they presented the slide show?

In addition, it is very important in our view to have the president, or whoever the chief executive officer of the country is, the energy minister, and the utility head all on board—all three. Our experience, after learning the hard way, is that if the utility head is not on board and not genuinely committed, you may get letters of intent, you may have nice dinners, and you may get awards, but at the end of the day, you are unlikely to get a contract that works and, if you are looking at a long-term project that has to be financed through international agencies where it takes a long time to recover your equity, you must make sure that the utility is as committed as you are and motivated as you are to make privatization work.

A legal structure for private property must be in place. We like to focus on places where the primary commercial language is English, German, or Spanish. Another very important factor to us is the absence of corruption at the highest levels of government.

There also must be a sensitivity to problems of fragile democracies. This is a significant distinction between doing projects in some parts of Latin America, for example, or some parts of Southeast Asia, where the government model is somewhat different. Because of a revolving door issue, the person who is agreeing to sign your letter today may not be in the government tomorrow. Depending on how the government changes, he might not even be alive tomorrow, so you have to be very ready for changes. That is why it is important to see the entire structure of the country committed to privatization since you may have a different person the next day to deal with.

In many of the new democracies, there is a multi-party system. Sometimes it can be four or five, sometimes ten or eleven, parties. You can have legislative paralysis since it is difficult to come up with majorities in the legislature to get anything done, not only because there are a lot of different political philosophies, but because the incentive is for everyone to be fighting against each other to try to increase their majority in the next election.

One last factor is particularly prevalent in Latin America and the Philippines: what is termed in the US as yellow journalism. Some countries have as much or more interest in what happens in business affairs—in Latin America and in the Philippines, for examples—as the US has in finding out which entertainment or rock star is sleeping with whom. That mentality is brought to bear on business. Any little scandal or any little story where one person is accusing the other of doing something wrong, or where someone can get a story about pricing or invalidity in a contract or corruption, the mere allegation can launch a front-page story in any one of five or six competing dailies whose principal goal is to increase circulation, not necessarily to worry about whether the story is accurate or not.

The bottom line for us is that it is important to look for a champion in the government, someone who is as committed as you are for his own political, or philosophy of government, kind of reasons, to make sure privatization happens. Secondly, it is important to get very good advisors. There are a number of excellent firms today in the international IPP market. It is important to us when we go to a country to have competent legal advisors—US legal advisors who are capable of structuring international projects, and local legal advisors, and to have both local and US accounting advisors. Given the tax and accounting structures in these countries, to actually make a deal happen and bring the money home and the income home, if you are a public company, is extremely tricky. The company ends up having to structure the project from a tax and accounting standpoint in at least two countries. There are a lot of hidden costs in developing a project that aren't automatically seen when a company is just thinking about signing a power contract.

Many competitors—Enron, Mission, AES, Hopewell in Asia, Cogentrix, Duke—run around in the same parts of the world. Now, especially since the Public Utility Holding Company Act (PUHCA) has been reformed, there is going to be a big entry of US utility subs. Entergy is already active in this, as is CMS, Utilicorp

United, and others will enter the market. These entities are going to be very difficult to compete with due to their protected home markets and low cost of capital, especially tough competitors once they staff up.

Foreign, state-owned utilities have been invited to Argentina and other countries to participate in privatization, resulting in a so-called "un-private" privatization. What the country, such as Argentine, is doing is substituting its own state-owned entity for the state-owned entity of Belgium or France or Spain, or, in the case of Chile, a private company that has a monopoly or concession that effectively functions as a government entity. Why Argentina would want to replace its own state-owned utility that it controls with a state-owned utility that France or Spain controls is not completely clear to us. However, those companies do bid a lot of money for assets in order to establish market share. It has not been demonstrated yet how this will work with US utility subs, but we are concerned that the same thing will happen. If you are in a regulated business in the US, and your regulated rate of return is 11 percent to 13 percent, you may go to a place such as Argentina or Peru or Brazil and think 15 percent or 16 percent looks just fine. For IPPs that do not have that sort of regulated base and cannot bring those assets to bear in terms of guarantees and financing, those kinds of returns in risky markets are not going to work.

Enron's Niche

What is Enron's niche? We try to be the first or second into a country. We enjoy the frontier, and agree with the World Bank executive who says you have to be in there on the front end of the project. If you wait until the third or fourth round, there will be too many competitors. The returns will be too low, and all the fun stuff has already happened. We look for places where a power shortage is either there right now or is imminent, so fast-track players who can move quickly, who can package a deal quickly, have an advantage. We believe that it helps us to have a big balance sheet that we are willing to put on the line to commit equity, experience, and a reputation for getting tough projects done. We try to be a full-service provider, and will develop, construct, take the construction risk, finance, invest long term in a project, and operate it. We don't have to operate in big (what we consider to be unwieldy) consortiums that can sometimes take days to make decisions that a single company could make in hours or minutes.

Enron is able to begin construction often before financing is in place. We go in and do some macro and micro economic studies of the system, of the financing sources, what the markets are, and we sometimes can make a bet that the financing that ought to be available will be available, so we start building without the financing in place. If that means that we bet wrong, we can have significant exposure or we could be strung out longer than we want to be. On the other hand, that gives us an advantage and helps us get in places before other people. This has worked especially well on our smaller "fast track" projects.

We try to be very flexible to fit the other countries' legal and regulatory structures. We do not necessarily believe that the US has anything to brag about in terms of its utility regulatory structure. We certainly would not want to export that to anybody else. So we are very happy to learn along with other people about what utility structures and what regulatory structures fit other places best.

We think what has been done in the UK is very innovative. It is unbelievable how the UK ever got such overwhelming and comprehensive change in place. Other countries are going to do similar things, and that innovation is going to be beneficial, not something that should be blocked by people wedded to the outdated US model.

Special Issues

There are certain special issues in foreign development. First of all, you have to learn a lot of new acronyms:

- **BOT** Build Operate Transfer

- **BTO** Build Transfer Own

- **BTL** Build Transfer Lease

- **BTL** Better to Leave

Once you get any more complicated that the first three acronyms, we are tempted to leap on the fourth.

An interesting thing goes on in some countries: they want to privatize on one hand, but they want to do it under a BOT structure, where after 10 or 12 or 15 years, the asset transfers right back to them, which means it is not privatized any more. Not only is that philosophically inconsistent, but it forces the IPP company to depreciate a project over a shorter period of time, thus driving up the cost of power. Some of the multilateral agencies are strongly encouraging the developing countries to move away from BOT model since it really does not benefit anybody except politicians.

Bids. The problem with bids is that many are called but few are chosen. Often countries will let everybody in, have dinners, have meetings, even invite you to come to participate in a bid. You have to be very careful, as we learned in one Far Western European country, not to be a stalking horse or a legitimizer of a deal that is basically already cut. Learning by experience has more impact than just hearing people tell war stories, but it is cheaper if you can learn just from the stories.

Pre-arranged deals. Make sure there is nothing going on behind the scenes. If there is a huge subjective element to the bid, be very careful. A few years ago the Atlantic Monthly had an article about poker. One of the things it mentioned was when you go to a poker game and sit down, look around, because at every poker game there is a sucker. The first thing you do is sit down and look around and find the sucker. If you don't see one, get up, because it's you. The same model happens in these bidding arrangements.

Competition with subsidized entities. Again, you have to be very careful who you are bidding against. You might spend a lot of money to bid, and you have someone else with a lower cost of capital or who sees the market differently or who has an incentive other than profit on one project to get in. It can really smack you.

Strange bid terms. Sometimes you see a country where the engineers know exactly what they are doing, but the people who put together documents for the bid present marked-up construction contracts that they have tried to turn into a long-term power contract. You quickly find out, if you have experience in financing, that such a document does not work. If the country has allowed you to make recommendations for changes to the contract as part of your bid, you can at least bid the deal and go in and negotiate the changes. However, if the country has said basically to bid you must sign the contract the way it is, and put up a bid bond, then you can have a problem.

This leads to bid and switch strategies. In some countries there has been some feeling that some of the players have known that if they must go in and sign an unacceptable contract, a few months later, there will be a quiet re-negotiation once they have gotten the deal, and all the problems will be fixed. There is a side understanding that that will happen. You must be very careful about that. If you see a bunch of people bidding on a deal that you know does not work, chances are that a bid and switch is going on.

Valuation. Existing projects are very difficult to value. How do you evaluate the tariffs? How do you evaluate the possibility of new generation coming on line? If you cannot value your project in a way that it beats new generation, if you cannot buy used assets and refurbish them at a lower cost than new generation, you should not be playing, because you will get beaten by new generation, which is almost certain to come in from an economic standpoint.

Local partners. This is a very tough issue. Everyone wants local partners; everyone needs them. In a lot of countries, they can be as much of a disadvantage as an advantage because, again for the political reasons noted above, one prominent local family or company is your local partner, then several other families are jealous and want a piece of the deal. Ultimately, when one gets awarded, political factions get jealous. A visible and influential local partner often has as many enemies as friends, and can be as much of a harm as a good.

That raises the question of whether to bring partners in early or late. If local partners are brought in, what kind of role will they play? Are they on the supply side of the project? Do they build it? Are they the power purchaser, or are they an equity partner? If they are an equity partner, at what stage do they get a full vote, a veto over the decisions you are making where you are bringing the money? How do they get paid? Do they get commissions based on either the gross or net revenues from the project, like a carried interest? Sometimes they cannot afford to put in equity, so do they just buy equity straight up? Or do you loan them their buying price? Obviously, the best partners are ones who win when you win, pay when you pay, lose when you lose.

Financing. We also see that commercial banks are mostly AWOL in developing countries' project financing. They are becoming AWOL even in power projects in developed countries, such as in Europe. In the absence of the commercial banks, you must look to other players. The International Finance Corp. (IFC), the Asian Development Bank, the African Development Bank, the Overseas Private Investment Corp. (OPIC), and the various Export-Import (Ex-Im) banks and the World Bank are going to be the key players for projects in developing countries until the capital markets come in, which we predict they soon will.

An issue with some of these agencies other than the World Bank—as well as with commercial banks—is, are they an advisor or an arranger? Commercial banks are all very willing to represent you as your advisor, and they are happy to take fees, but what they usually will not do is commit to put money in your deal. What the bank proposes is a unique paradox of having a commercial bank running around suggesting that it will be your financial advisor, but then when someone asks that bank, "Are you going to lend to the project?", they say, "We haven't made that decision yet," or "That's a separate section of the bank." This looks bad and is not a good deal.

When the IFC is your arranger, it has implicitly committed to do your deal. The commercial banks are going to have to catch up on that strategy or they are going to lose out. A company will find that it is going to have to pay fees when it gets someone with money to be its advisor, in addition to just arranging the financing. Extra fees can be worth it, because it is more of a motivator, and the advisor becomes eager to get the deal done.

We find in dealing with these multi-national agencies and international banks that they are more sensitive on technology than is the case in the US market. Furthermore, the borrower has to deal with 75/25 leverage or worse, which is difficult from an equity standpoint. The company must effectively raise the power price to get the same returns.

Environmental concerns. These agencies have their own environmental rules. From Enron's standpoint, environmental rules are good. Whenever we are in a country, our internal policy is to try to comply with the country's environmental rules, the World Bank environmental guidelines, whether the World Bank or the IFC are in the deal or not, and also the US ambient air quality standards that would prevail if the project were located in the US.

Most people know that the US Environmental Protection Agency (EPA) guidelines do two things. First, they look at the overall air quality in an area, and say, "Could you add a new project here without screwing up the air to the extent that people couldn't breathe it?" The EPA also has a single-source requirement which says, "Even if the air quality is OK overall, any one source cannot pollute more than X amount." The US has decided, in effect, to permit lots of little polluters, or a little industrial park with a lot of people who can contribute a little bit to the pollution. Many other countries have made a different decision: they would be happy to have one large power plant. What we look at there is, if we had our own people living in that location versus in the city where they live in the US, would the project prevent the ambient air quality in that location from passing the EPA guidelines? If not, we will do the project; if so, we would try to enhance it environmentally to make it work.

Regulatory and tax structures. These structures are big problems since they are often undefined and in flux. One response to that is to say, "Do not go into the country until all that stuff is settled." The other response, which we obviously have adopted, is to work with your power contracts, to include regulatory and tax pass-throughs, so that any change in the regulatory laws, any change in taxes can get passed through as an additional cost to the local utility who is the power purchaser. The purchaser absorbs the risk, and not you. In our view, that risk is not absorbable by the developer from a financing standpoint. You cannot get a project financed that way; even if you could, it would not be a smart equity investment.

Financing issues. Financing is the greatest challenge. Contract issues that are routine in the US are a big problem in emerging markets. You have the normal US issue of matching revenues and costs, and the special problem of regulatory and tax changes that were mentioned previously. Governing law is also an issue. Where is the contract going to be enforced, and under what law? We typically become happy if there is some international forum, even if the law that is applied is the law of the local jurisdiction.

Each emerging market is perceived differently by lenders. All are risky. We believe the Ex-Im banks and multilaterals need to, and will, move to broaden political and country risk coverage to enable private sector lenders to lend in emerging markets.

Payment issues. A company needs dollars or dollar-denominated contracts. If you do not have that, our view is that you are not going to be financed.

Currency conversion issues. OPIC will give insurance, but not necessarily guarantee the rate, so you must have a way to get your cash out of the country. You also must ask the question of where the utility gets the money to pay. Even if you hedged the dollar denomination issue, if there is a big swing in the exchange rate between the US and the local currency, where does the utility physically get the money to pay you? If, because of devaluation, the electricity price is now three times as many pesos as it was before, have they raised local rates enough to get that many pesos to pay you? Dollar indexing is something to look for; it is a trend that we believe is catching on. Dollar indexing has been done in certain Central American countries. It basically recognizes that for certain utilities, such as telecommunications and electricity, a bulk of the costs, such as capital costs and fuel, are denominated in dollars. The utility gets a law passed that says that not only can it index rates to inflation, but it can index utility rates in the country to the exchange rate that that country has. To make that deal, the country must have gotten over the patrimony and national pride issue about linking its currency to the dollar. Once it works through that issue, however, it finds that the currency becomes much more stable.

Emerging Techniques to Facilitate Financing of Projects in Developing Countries

Here is what a bank sees when it evaluates a national electric utility company that needs to borrow money for new projects, if the utility wants to go out and borrow the money itself. The utility is a government entity, and perhaps has no need to show a profit. The utility has very large revenues, very large costs, but potentially small or negative margins. The utility has a mandate to serve the people, but perhaps a lack of capital. Those things together may be more of a priority in that country than efficiency. Rate increases are decided by politics, not economics.

A former company may be divided up into privatization of smaller pieces. One of the things that is happening in privatization is that people are deciding that not only should we make things private, we should also subdivide them and make them smaller. That makes the entity a lot harder to finance. Sometimes a company might have no international borrowing or repayment history, and finds it very difficult to mortgage utility assets to secure payments. As everyone who has done a US project knows, you go to these banks, and you get stacks of security documents that secure your assets. That is of questionable value in real life in the US, and of almost no value in a foreign country. If those who develop the project cannot make money from it, the chance of a bank taking it over and making money are extremely slim. And there's typically no one else to sell the project or the power to.

Different accounting systems in emerging market countries make it difficult sometimes for the banks to evaluate what the revenues of the utility are and thus its ability to pay. Often times, countries do not want to provide parent or government guarantees of utility obligations, and they want these entities to be self-financing.

Why Emerging Market Utilities Need Project Finance

Even if you privatize a utility, what happens when it goes to the bank to try to build a big, new project? What does the bank decide? First of all, it decides that a very small change in the utility's revenues or costs could cause losses or diminish the ability to meet obligations. The bank is unlikely to give a good credit rating to this utility company until it proves it can perform over time. The bank also will not give it general purpose loans without government guarantees for the same reason, so each new project a utility does will need separate financing. However, lending secured by assets does not really work, or is limited, if there is no practical way to resell the asset, and no one to sell it to who can operate it any differently from the way the utility did. Furthermore, the utility may have no track record of completing projects on time or on budget. In fact, the utility may have the totally opposite track record. In a lot of countries where capital projects are undertaken by the same utility that has the mandate to serve, whenever you have customers that are coming off the system or you need new lines, you allocate capital to spread the electricity distribution system, and you sometimes delay other projects or put them on hold, and they run over instead of getting completed.

The result is lenders don't want to lend money to state-owned utilities. You usually need to use project financing and private developers to do big, new electricity projects.

However, project financing for private developers is also a problem. First of all, the sponsors (such as our parent company) cannot afford to go out and guarantee $1.5 billion of debt on Teesside, for example, let alone in a developing country. The government that owns the utility is big enough to provide guarantees, but it does not want to use up the market capacity to borrow by guaranteeing private projects.

The government says, "Now that we are privatizing these projects, why should we support them? Why should we be supporting private companies?" The exception we are finding to this is that countries are typically willing to give a partial guarantee to parts of the power contract in order to get the World Bank or other development banks involved.

We see the World Bank as potentially being an extremely important player in projects, particularly in difficult-to-finance countries, in that they can provide a layer of guarantees of host country obligations that gets them in the deal, maybe that is re-guaranteed by the government. The World Bank does not take all the project risk, but the mere presence of the World Bank in a deal—and it can take various roles (the Hab River project in Pakistan is fascinating from this standpoint)—lends a substantial level of credibility to the project. That's good and bad news for the World Bank, since what that means is that everyone is going to be knocking at their door wanting to do projects with the World Bank. Some will be very legitimate, strong developers with strong projects, and some will be developers of flaky projects that never should have gotten off the ground, who are going to walk into the World Bank and say, "Please, make our project go."

For the same reason that the utility is not a good credit risk, a company walks in with a power contract with that utility, and the lender asks the same questions. "How is the utility going to make these IPP power contract payments?" The utility has a limited payment history, and limited ability, perhaps, to increase revenues or control costs. Again, a small change in revenues or costs could mean the inability to pay the IPP.

One Financing Solution

One answer to this is what we call "senioritization" of the utility's obligations to the IPP. The Spanish translation of that word is *"mejorarizado"*—moving the obligation level up higher in the payment chain. Here is how this works. One thing that is true across almost all utilities, regardless of whether they are weak or strong, is they have a lot of customers and the customers pay them a lot of money. The utility also has very high costs, however, so if you look at Figure 12-1, the national electric company maybe gets $100 from its customers; maybe there is $90 in operating costs, fuel, labor, supplies, maintenance, taxes; its IPP payment is maybe just a small fraction of that; and it has a small positive net cash flow at the end of the day. The problem is that the banks look at those high overall costs and say, "How do we know that the IPP is ever going to get paid?" The bank is going to want to know that there is a multiple of cash flows above what the IPP is owed before it will want to invest.

Figure 12-1. Seniorization

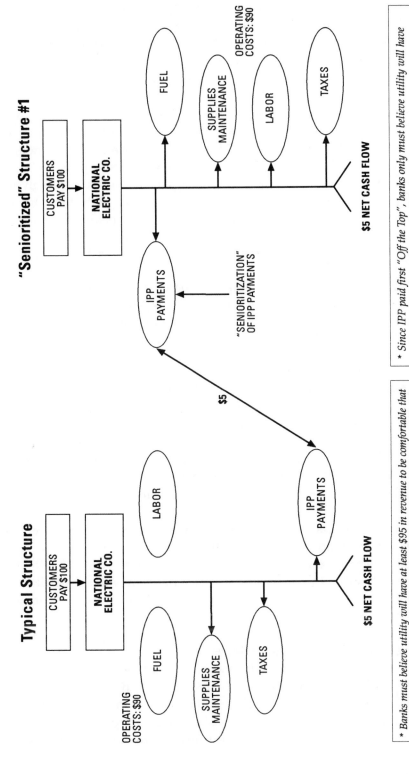

A solution to that is to "senioritize" the IPP payment so that it gets paid, from a legal standpoint, off the top, before any of the utility company's other costs are paid. The bank can then look at that and see not $5 of $90 costs getting paid out, but the first $5 out of the $100 revenues getting paid to the IPP. It remains the utility's problem, frankly, of how to pay the rest of its costs.

That is the way it looks. How do you structure it legally? First of all, you can set up a trust or a separate bank account so that all of the national electric company revenues go into that bank account, or that they only collect revenues from certain groups of customers. They may have much more revenues than you really need for the IPP. You can set it up so that that bank pays the IPP first and then gives all the rest of the money to the utility, which can happen either all the time, or only on a contingent basis if problems occur, such as the IPP is not paid or the letter of credit securing payments is not renewed, or the national electric company is broken up or privatized in a way that damages its credit rating or reduces its cash flows.

There are two pictures of this. Figure 12-2 shows the one we had before, and the one where all the money basically goes into a bank, $100. The bank makes the first payment to the IPP, $5, then pays over the rest of the money, in this case, $95, to the national electric utility, which then uses it to pay all its costs.

We see a modification of that in Figure 12-3 in which, instead of all the money from the utility's customers going into the bank account, only the money from the local distribution area, which we call *Ciudad Z* here, goes in the bank. Maybe it is three times as much money as is necessary to pay the IPP. After the IPP payment is made, it drops down to the national electric utility. All the other customers' money goes to the national electric utility. From the utility's standpoint, this really should be a harmless deal. At the end of the day, the customers are still paying the same amount of money; they are just paying you first.

This modification gets to be a problem when the utility already has a debt structure and lenders who are reluctant to subordinate, and even more so to an IPP. Typically there are still costs that you can move up in the structure in a partial way, or perhaps get the lenders, if they see a problem with capital allocation for that utility, to allow you to participate pari passu in the first series of payments that goes to them.

Why Fuel Supply Makes Financing Harder

The second tough issue is fuel. Why does fuel make financing so difficult? Utilities want to dispatch the generator hourly. You cannot buy fuel on an hourly basis. You have to get it monthly or on a longer-term basis to make a fuel contract work. You typically have minimum take provisions in fuel contracts, and it is very hard to match in a power contract, particularly on a day-to-day basis. The fuel contract

Figure 12-2. Two Senioritization Structures

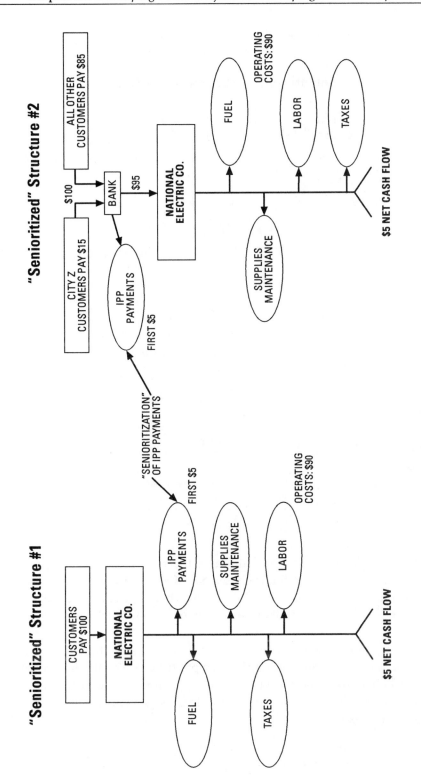

Figure 12-3. Modified Senioritization

"Senioritized" Structure #3 Partial

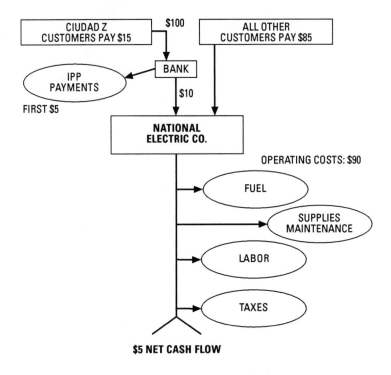

* In most cases, bank should require security from only a portion of National
Electric's customers. Can use Different group for each IPP.

escalation indexes need to match those in the power contract to get the predictability that lenders insist on. You must have fuel supply and transportation for
the entire life of the bank loan. In some countries that is just not possible. Also, you
must arrange back-up fuel facilities in case your primary fuel goes away.

For all those reasons, to get financing, the IPP must restrict the utility's dispatch
freedom in order to make fuel supply costs predictable. The IPP has to say to the
utility, "You have to dispatch us all the time," or "You have to dispatch us during
these hours," or "You have to dispatch at least X percent during these hours."
Utilities do not like that.

So the IPP is left with two choices, and they are both bad. One is to lock in the fuel delivery, storage, and backup it probably does not need to make sure it can deliver fuel any time it is dispatched. The problem with this method is that it creates high costs, therefore high electricity prices, and, if the IPP ends up not being able to take the fuel it has contracted for, there may be high penalties. The second choice is to leave the fuel arrangements flexible and not contract for fuel on a long-term basis. Then, however, it is hard to convince the banks that the IPP's fuel supply is certain, and it is very hard to finance. If the primary fuel expected is not available, the spot market price of fuel may be very, very high. The power price may be fixed, and not adjust to cover this. So the result is, under either scenario, higher electricity prices because of higher risks, the privatized project has a lower value, and the financing is difficult or impossible.

What is one good solution? We think it is a tolling contract. In this case, the national electric company is responsible for fuel. The IPP builds the project, runs the project, operates it, guarantees availability, but the electric company does what it is doing now, which is supplying all the fuel, for this plant and its other plants. The electric company pays what we call in the US a capacity charge. Whenever the company shows up at the IPP gate with fuel, it can dispatch the plant whenever it wants to. In this manner the IPP and the IPP's banks are completely unaffected by the dispatch decisions. The IPP's banks do not have to understand the fuel arrangements, and there is no greater risk to the national electric company than if it owned the plant itself. Again, you are not asking the electric company to assume any greater risk than it would assume if it owned the plant on its own. The national electric company can use nationwide fuel purchasing to achieve lower costs, and the financing is greatly simplified.

When we go through this and convince ourselves that these ideas are great, we may think, "If that is such a good idea, why isn't it happening already?" We think it is. Enron has a project in Massachusetts that has just converted to a tolling contract. Both of our projects in the Philippines have tolling contracts. We believe other US projects may convert to tolling contracts. We think that this is going to be the wave of the future. In our view, it has been an economic and regulatory anomaly that US utilities have signed up for IPPs and had each different IPP bring its own fuel. The cost of that is very expensive. We believe that the wave of the future is that utilities will start recognizing that if they are buying fuel anyway, they should buy fuel for all their projects, even the IPPs. It does not cost them any more money. They can probably save money. So we think that in the coming years, one of the things we are going to see with US utilities is that more and more of them heed the advice of their in-house fuel purchasing people—what they have been saying all along, "Why aren't we buying this IPP fuel?" Or, they could outsource all fuel acquisition to a private fuel manager.

Overcoming Corruption

One more topic of interest is corruption. A lot of people (including our board) ask us, "Why are you in these countries? Isn't there corruption? Aren't there a lot of problems with people asking for payoffs?" As was mentioned earlier, it is critical to us that we can be convinced that at the highest levels of the country, corruption is not an issue. There are different sources to go to for this comfort. Sometimes it has to be a gut feeling. In our view, if you find corruption at the highest levels of the country, you need to get out.

You may find, however, that corruption has been purged from the highest levels of the country, but because of institutional lethargy or custom, at the lower levels inside government bureaucracies, people are used to having grease payments made or little payments made; or people who really are not part of the process but threaten to hold it up, come to you and say, "We are going to hold Congressional hearings," or we are going to do this or that unless they get paid off. You typically hear this from a second or third tier source.

We learned the response to this question from Nancy Reagan, which is, "Just say no." We emphasized the concept, in the countries in which we operate, that certain projects are just too big to pay bribes. That concept is initially counter-intuitive, since in a lot of countries those are exactly the kind of projects that have been thought to pay the biggest bribes. If a project is really critical to the country and critical to infrastructure and you have honest leadership, the people at the top will make sure a company does not have this problem. That is why it is so important to have a political leadership structure that is committed to privatization and to your project.

We believe that paying bribes is bad for the host country. Bribes drive up costs and make business people not want to go there. Bribery is bad for the project because the price goes up and the requests never stop. Moreover, bribery is bad for a company because not only will it be penalized if it is caught, but bribery is a bad precedent. Anytime you go anywhere, people will have their hand out. It is bad for you personally, because you can go to jail.

That is our view of the world.

Chapter 13

Privatization of Utilities in Latin America

Roger D. Feldman, Partner
McDermott, Will & Emery[1]

Introduction

The privatization of utilities in Latin America reflects the intersection of two trends of historic stature:

- The global emergence of reliance on free market mechanisms as a tool for economic growth and resource allocation.

- The modification of the means and terms by which capital flows into investment in developing countries.

Each is a component of privatization.

Megatrends, however heralded, of course, do not just happen. They require initiative and interaction among those government officials willing to take risks to implement radical new policies; those multinational institutions with vision enough to assist them; and those, like myself, who seek to craft individual transactions. This chapter is designed to enable you to form an analytic framework to consider systematically the merits, mechanics, and implications of the two basic types of privatization that we are now seeing in the Latin American utility field:

- Asset spinoffs, reflecting the Argentine approach, of which, more recently, variations are being undertaken in Ecuador and Peru.

- Project finance-based development, reflecting, most recently, the proposed Mexican approach (where implementation has been stalled but may be expected to resume).

Key Questions on Privatization

Whatever our respective positions on the transactional chessboard, to evaluate these public-private ventures, we must take the longer view both of Latin American governments and of those being invited to assist in financing. From the governmental perspective, the issues in each case are:

• Optimal mechanics for each type of privatization transaction to optimize competition, price, market, and operational success.

• Understanding of how reliance on each type of transaction will affect the overall flow of capital into the national economy and its fit with the overall national economic program.

• Necessary additional steps in oversight or regulation of the utility sector to assure effective integration of privatization activities and the ability to attract additional capital into the utility sector.

From the private perspective, the issues are the obverse:

• Is the privatization program such that it offers private capital a sensible risk/reward profile?

• Is there multilateral agency capital capacity to sustain the number and type of utility privatization projects that are being sponsored by host governments?

• Is the regulatory environment that has been set up one that is likely to sustain the health of the investment and the availability of additional comparable investments (which will help to justify the private sector learning curve in structuring the first investment)?

The ultimate attractiveness of national markets to private investors depends on satisfactory reciprocal answers from a governmental and investor standpoint.

Let me illustrate the kinds of issues into which we hope to gain insights from this program by briefly using the contrasting application of the integrated United Kingdom (UK) approach, drawing on the Argentine example, with the project finance of independent power producers, drawing on the proposed Mexican approach and other examples.

Integrated System Reform

The integrated system approach being followed by Argentina and several other Latin American countries basically relates to the reassignment of roles between the public and the private sectors to remedy past problems caused by imbalanced public ownership. In Argentina, for example, as a result of public sector nationalization, prices lost their role as market signals, rates were used for internal economic management purposes, and fuel and other inputs from state-controlled entities were not fully priced. Remedy of this situation, from an Argentine public point of view, requires not only asset transfers, but also a satisfactory regulatory environment in which marginal cost pricing and indicative planning prevail. In other countries, state ownership has also had the effect of preserving economic inefficiencies, and attendant misallocation of foreign exchange.

Overall, therefore, Argentina has undertaken to simulate a version of the UK model, splitting generation, transmission, and distribution, and seeking to stimulate appropriate competition in each sector. It is contemplated that the deregulated generators will ultimately sell into a wholesale electric market, initiated on a transitional basis through a freely negotiated spot market, that is government-administered. The presence of an effectively regulated wholesale market should provide key economic information in projecting the cash flows that, in turn, can be used in valuation for asset spinoff. Ultimately, the government hopes that the wholesale electric market will be sufficiently all-source as to embody long-term wholesale contracts, stabilized-system prices for distributors, and spot market prices with hourly variable prices. Independent generators will be able to make forward market sales—the government's goal is to move away from spot sales. (Some Latin American countries propose to go further and split ownership of generation from the operation and maintenance thereof.

Furthermore, transmission will be effected by regulated open access carriers, holding concessions, that will not themselves engage in the purchase and sale of power.

Distribution will also be a regulated concession. Following a flexible schedule, and drawing upon World Bank assistance, Argentina hopes to achieve full private generation in the near term. The ultimate regulatory plan calls for the Secretariat of Energy to preside over a National Regulatory Entity, a National Dispatch Center, a Unified Fund, and a National Fund for Electric Energy.

Current needs for power have led both to pressure for privatization and to approaches and levels of pricing sufficient to induce investment in sufficient capacity. Spinoff of generation and of distribution in large generation centers has begun. SEGBA, which has been privatized, represents 36 percent of national demand.

This approach to privatization reflects a need for massive and immediate reform, given the condition of equipment, the high debts being carried, and the inadequacy of the already high rates either to meet industry requirements or to make a contribution to national competitiveness. Conceptually this model is ahead of where the United States (US) system seems to be progressing, albeit with much greater emphasis on the role of private utilities. At this point, however, the jury is still out on the question of whether the UK model, whether negotiated or based on a power pool reference price, ultimately is an optimal one. Particular concerns relate to the uncertainty of revenue streams—which affects project financeability— and the difficulty of installation of a sufficient regulatory framework—which tends to make cash flow projections uncertain.

In the course of our program, we hope to evaluate issues from the government perspective such as the following:

- Given the complexity of what is contemplated, is the accelerated approach the most efficient way to achieve implementation? Does it require an even greater concentration of government power in order to effect and preserve free markets? Even if implemented as planned, will it have short-term economic rate impacts that may not be politically acceptable?

- If the overall system works, power will represent an attractive credit support for long-term foreign debt. If foreign capital is drawn extensively to that sector, will this have the effect of reducing available capital to other sectors because of capital market concern with over-concentration in the risks attendant on investment in any one privatizing country?

- Given the likelihood of at least some delay in putting the entire integrated privatization program in place, (and setbacks experienced to date by private parties in operation of a portion of the system), what are the consequences for the government's ability to operate a hybrid regulatory system that includes elements of the old system as well as the new? Should multinational agency support be sought for overall system privatization?

- What are the implications of political and regulatory uncertainties for the valuation of power assets? How accurate can the forecast of rates be in this environment? What implicit obligations, if any, does a government actually or implicitly assume to assure that the forecasts of rates match with the prices for power actually established? Is this accentuated if a string of privatizations is anticipated?

The private perspective on the importance of these issues and the likely private strategies to be followed are also of great interest.

- Can an integrated system with assets of varying quality expect to be effectively, fully privatized? If not, how is the valuation of privatized assets affected? How are issues with respect to the effectiveness of central regulation to be handled in the asset valuation negotiation? What, if any, government guarantees should be sought and are likely to be provided?

- What is the nature of multilateral lending agency commitment to the efficacy of privatization of entire integrated utility systems, as opposed to the sale of particular assets? Is this necessary from the private perspective, given long-term system performance targets?

- How critical is the presence of the governmental regulatory environment to financing? For example, is there concern about the adequacy and timing of the wholesale market? Is there concern with the respective timing applicable, for example, to components of the system or the extent to which transmission rates may be set at a level that soaks up economic rents? How important is regulatory risk in pricing? What types of security do lenders look for? Are there other techniques that may be used to offset this risk?

- Is investment made with a view to future expansion opportunities with respect to concession in either the generation or transmission field? If so, what are the differences in pricing a bid for a concession and for a particular asset?

- Are regulatory concerns in a concession different from those in an asset context? What special terms must be sought in asset and concession transactions, respectively, in order to take into account the issues implicit in integrated system participation?

In sum, we must examine generic utility reform proposals not merely in terms of their objectives, but in terms of the difficult problems of timing, capital attraction, and use of political capital to provide regulatory attractiveness.

Project Finance

Several Latin American countries, notably Mexico, have chosen not to approach power privatization from the perspective of spinoff of their existing power system. Rather, those countries have, at least to this point, focused on a variety of techniques to attract private capital into particular projects and to interface the resulting investments with the national grid. In this respect, these nations have more resembled the US, where, until the recent Energy Policy Act, the only context (outside of certain quasi-public and cooperative ventures) in which any person could sell at wholesale were owners of cogeneration plants that met certain efficiency standards and certain renewable energy plants, in accordance with the Public Utilities Regulatory Policy Act (PURPA), and then only to regulated utilities.

Several countries have seen fit to enact some type of PURPA statute, in which the system "avoided cost" is paid to individual facilities. But it is important to recognize that the PURPA model works well only when:

- The purchasing utility knows its true, realistic cost of production.

- An impartial regulator has the power and administrative position to resolve disputes.

- The purchasing utility is willing to accommodate the profile of the system which it owns to independent power suppliers.

Frequently these situations do not obtain, if only because:

- The true cost of existing facilities is obscured by their finance with sovereign credit and multilateral agency debt.

- The agency charged with administration may also be the purchasing party.

The Mexican approach of mandated sales to state-owned utilities may be broadening. Currently there is a program in place that essentially provides for a private party to build equipment, lease it to CFE, the state-owned utility, operate the facility for a specific term, and then transfer the facility to CFE. The financeability of such transactions turns not on power rates, but on the creditworthiness of the CFE lease over the ten-year term.

The recent liberalization of the law would allow private ownership of facilities and export of excess power to CFE. (It is focused on the development of baseload facilities which complement the operation of the existing CFE system.) Previously only generation for self-use was allowed. No longer will an industrial firm have to establish, as was previously required under the law, before private generation was permitted, that CFE could not provide sufficient energy if called upon to do so. Foreign developers would, however, still be required to have Mexican partners.

A key issue in privatization in this new manner would be the level at which buy-back rates are set. Mexico has established a system of competitive bidding analogous to that currently utilized under the requirements of some, but not all, US states. Selection of the reference plant on which the marginal cost is based is thus of critical importance.

Facilities developed by private capital in the context of this type of regulatory system are likely to project financed, on a non-recourse basis with project cash flow (directly or via a lease) and the asset as the only security. This approach can be used with respect to acquisition of existing assets as well. Project financing of new facilities is more vulnerable to short-term interruptions in cash flow than finance based upon the overall balance sheet of a developer. From a host government's perspective, several issues are presented:

- Is a project financing an optimal means of new facility development since it must be priced to absorb the risk that it entails and the high cost of private venture equity? If governments are prepared to accept limited recourse for project financing, to make tax or other benefits available, or to obviate potential environmental and siting problems, the cost of project financing can be reduced. Are these likely developments? Can competitive bidding be structured to provide a more attractive market for private capital?

- Multilateral credit frequently may be necessary to effect project financing. Depending on the size of the particular project, it is possible that it may use up available multilateral credit otherwise available to transaction development of other power projects. What techniques can be used to minimize the extent to which project financings use up multilateral credit or to enlarge the available credit pool?

- Project-financed projects in countries which also continue to provide subsidized public power may encounter opposition because of the level of their non-subsidized rates, their impact on the position of and perhaps the reliability of the state-owned utility, and their relationship to existing state-owned plants that may subsequently be privatized (and whose economics therefore have to be preserved). There are also dangers that the interface between the state utility and the project may reflect these concerns and the project's economics may be harmed. What legislative protections, power purchase clauses, multilateral agency requirements, or implementation agreement terms may be provided by a government to reduce concern with the long-term impacts of these potential problems?

- From the private perspective, project financing in a Build/Lease/Transfer, or Build/Operate/Transfer, or Build/Own/Operate environment presents all of the same issues as are presented domestically, plus market risk-type issues related to price fluctuation, the risk of government-initiated reduction or impairment of market, and the risk of shifts in exchange ratios. Can arrangements be structured to provide for governmental credit enhancement or governmental measures to reduce currency convertibility risk to improve the risk/reward profile to private capital investors?

- Project financing proceeds under the cloud of the possibility of learning late in transaction development of the insufficiency of available credit from multinational agencies. Are there techniques in dealing with international insurance or credit agencies to reduce these risks? What (if any) cooperation is required from host governments in order to do so?

• What types of other legislative measures would facilitate project financing? For example, are there measures to be recommended to facilitate debt-equity or debt-debt swaps, to facilitate countertrade measures to deal with currency risks and to clarify the mechanics of creation of security interests in contracts and their enforcement (essential elements of project financing) that would facilitate the closing on a more regularized basis of more energy projects?

Conclusions

In sum, the discussion in this chapter can leave us with a framework for bridging the policy requirements and national objectives that Latin American nations bring to power privatization—capital, efficiency, debt relief, competitiveness, equity—and the clear requirements of the private sector in all financing projects, particularly when keyed to the acquisition or development of particular assets—certainty of regulatory environment, firmness of cash flow, ancillary support in dealing with credit risks. We need to clarify how these bridges can be crossed in a dynamic environment, where economic and political factors outside the energy filed must be taken into account.

By focusing on the dual national and transactional nature of privatization, and trying to answer the hard questions that it presents, we can assist ourselves in the important and exciting process of participating in Latin America's utility and economic development.

Part IV

The Public Offering and Beyond

➢

Chapter 14

Investment Bankers, Advisors, and Selling the Deal

Leonard S. Hyman

Privatization, by definition, means the transfer of ownership of the utility to private hands. Making the sale is not as simple as selling a house or a car. It involves huge sums of money, buyers from all over the world, legal and accounting requirements, and endless complications. Most governments do not have the expertise to do the job, and none have the hundreds or thousands of salespeople needed to sell the new company to investors. Thus, governments hire investment bankers to handle the work.

The investment banker combines the roles of orchestra conductor, circus ringmaster, travel agent, trusted advisor, strategist, psychiatrist and salesman. The banker helps sellers find buyers and helps buyers find sellers. Few large transactions take place without the services of bankers.

The Advisor
In the beginning, the government that wishes to sell the utility hires an advisor, usually an investment banking firm that has previously worked on privatizations. The government may hold a "beauty contest" to select the advisor. To do so, the government examines the qualifications of those firms that wish to serve as advisor, culls from the applicants a "short list" of the firms that appear most qualified, and then interviews the finalists, after which it chooses the winner. Most of the finalists have similar qualifications. The beauty contest has multiple benefits. The first is to give the government the maximum amount of information in order to help it choose the ablest and most compatible advisor. The second is to derive as much free advice as possible from the contestants. The third purpose—when the government has decided in advance upon the choice of an advisor—is to pretend that the choice was made after careful consideration of the capabilities of all contenders, in order to protect the government from criticism that it gives business to friends. The government's advisor usually works for a predetermined fee.

The government may sort out the candidates and get substantial free advice by asking questions of the candidates. The British Government did so, and other governments have shamelessly copied the British model. The questions would include:

1. **Do you believe that the shares in the new company will be attractive to investors? How would the shares be valued? What regulatory, capital structure, or other issues would affect the stock's valuation?**—No candidate will say that the shares will be unattractive. That would be a sure way of not getting the job. But the candidates' evaluation of the shares should tell a lot about his views. Beware of evaluations that are far above the others. That candidate may be trying to get the job by making promises that cannot be kept. On the other side, the government should ask many questions of the firm with the low evaluation, to get insights into what looks bad about the offering. One should be prepared for the worst. Moreover, the government must understand how decisions on capitalization, regulation and other issues can affect the valuation of the shares.

2. **How would investors react to the method by which the shares are placed, and whether they will be listed on the stock exchange, traded on the over-the-counter (unlisted) market, and whether ownership will be limited to large investors?**—Some investors want to buy shares that are listed on the big exchanges. Others care little. Some stock offerings are made in such a way that only large investing institutions may buy them, a method of offering that saves time and expense but limits the number of buyers. Furthermore, stock trading rules differ for offerings that go directly to large investors, and those offerings may be harder to trade, which deters many investors from buying the shares in the first place.

3. **What are the legal considerations associated with the type of offering being proposed?**—When selling shares in several countries, one must know the rules. Perhaps as a result of legal restrictions, the offering will not be made in certain markets.

4. **Must the shares be registered with the securities commission in the place of sale, and, if so, what are the requirements for registration?**—Rules of registration can be onerous, expensive and time-consuming. At the same time, registration and compliance with the rules by the seller may give greater confidence to buyers, thereby increasing the chances of success of the offering.

5. **How much preparatory work must the company's management do for the offering, and what must they do on a continuing basis after the offering?**—The management of the newly privatized utility will be busy enough just running the company. Investors, though, need to meet the management in order to decide whether or not to buy the shares. Bankers and advisors must have access to management, but not so much that they will impede the running of the business.

6. **Should the shares be listed on the major stock exchanges? What are the costs and obligations incurred by listing the shares?**—Many companies do not wish to pay the cost of listing or make the disclosures that are required for listing. Governments prefer to sell the shares quickly and with little bother and expense, which may preclude listing the shares. Yet listing brings the advantages of a highly liquid, well-publicized market, something that may not exist in the country of origin of the shares.

7. **What can be done to prevent flowback?**—Flowback is the return of shares placed abroad back to the country of origin. If the local market could have absorbed the offering in the first place, the government would have sold the shares locally. Foreign investors constitute an additional market. The utilization of which helps to raise the price of the stock. Ability to trade the shares in foreign markets increases the liquidity of the stock, makes it easier to buy and sell shares without causing major price changes, and opens up large markets for additional stock offerings in the future. There is no point in going to the trouble of selling the stock abroad if the foreign investors are going to turn around and sell all their shares, and the only buyers turn out to be local buyers. The local markets will have trouble absorbing the shares. The stock price will fall, and the company will lose all the advantages of foreign ownership and stock trading. To prevent flowback, the offering has to be designed to attract and retain foreign investors. The government and the privatized utility need to work with the bankers to construct policies that prevent flowback. (The British government, which made such a fuss about preventing flowback, made their offerings in a way that led to massive flowback.)

8. **What experience and expertise does the banking firm have in privatizations and in placing large stock offerings?**—Obviously, the government does not want to deal with amateurs, but the fact is that most of the large investment banking firms have experience in privatization, and most can place large offerings.

9. **Give the names, positions, and qualifications of those who will serve on the advisory team?**—Investment bankers like to bring out their top executives to impress future clients. The top executives, though, have other things to do than to spend a year advising a foreign government. The government should know who will work on the job, why they are qualified to do so, and how much time they will put into the project. (Most of them have other things to do, too. The junior people do most of the work.)

10. **Would the appointment as advisor create conflicts of interest?**—Several privatization projects may be underway at one time, for instance. Will they require the time of the advisors? Do they involve rival companies? Governments need advisors that are not busy elsewhere.

11. **What are the fees for the advisory role? If the government subsequently appoints the advisor as an underwriter who participates in selling the stock, would the firm deduct the advisory fees from any underwriting commission that the firm earns?**—Governments want advice for as little money as possible. One way to get that advice for a small fee is to imply that the advisor will be picked as an underwriter (a firm that sells the shares to the investors, with payment that is a percentage of the offering price). If the advising firm agrees, it will, in effect, advise for nothing by taking an underwriting fee that has been reduced by the advisory fee.

12. **Are any regulatory or judicial inquiries pending that could lead to adverse publicity for the firm?**—Governments do not want to pick as advisors firms that are in trouble, legally. That does not look good.

During the advisory period, which could last for a year, the government and the advisor work to get the company ready for sale. The government has to develop regulatory rules and tax policies, and may have to change the management and directors of the company that it plans to sell. Government-owned companies often have capital structures inappropriate for the private sector, so the government may have to reapportion its ownership between debt and equity.

The management of the company must prepare its books of accounts so that they follow the accounting rules of the private sector. In order to sell the company's shares in international markets, accountants need to prepare a set of financial reports using internationally-accepted accounting principles. Managements must determine whether the books of account properly value assets and liabilities, and if not, make adjustments before the privatization. The company to be privatized, incidentally, may select its own advisor during the process. The government's advisor, after all, will concentrate on how to sell the company for the best price. The company's advisor instead might help the company plan for its future as a private firm.

Private Sale vs. Public Sale

The government can sell the company to a small group of investors (a private sale) or to a large number of investors (a public sale). The government may sell part of its shares to a small group of investors who will control and manage the company, and then, later, sell the balance of the shares to many investors through a public offering.

In a number of instances, the government sells a part of its holdings in a public offering, but keeps control of the company by remaining the largest shareholder.

For a private sale, the government and its advisor will design a procedure to sell the company (or the controlling bloc of shares). They will draft the terms of the offering, determine qualifications for bidders, and then ask for bids. Usually during this process, potential bidders will talk to the government and to the utility to be privatized. Those discussions will help the government and its advisor formulate realistic offering terms, and will enable the potential buyers to judge whether they want to bid, and if so, how much they wish to pay.

The government must set terms that involve more than price. The government must decide whether it wants control of the company to remain in local hands; whether it wants an international operator as a shareholder; whether it wants many small, local shareholders; or whether it wants many international shareholders. In private, it may decide to sell control of the company to a group consisting of political friends, but will never acknowledge that decision in public. In addition, the government needs to set standards for service levels, goals for expansion of service, and even require minimum requirements for capital expenditures. Potential bidders have to know not only what they will pay for the existing assets, but also what they have to invest in the future.

Once the bids are received, the government and the advisor have to determine which bidding group has the best combination of operating expertise and financial capability, as well as which group offers the highest price. Sometimes the bidders make their offers based on terms different than what the government wants. Also, the government and its advisor may have doubts about whether the highest bidder can meet the standards set. Once in a while, the highest bidder cannot raise the money needed to pay for the property. Picking the winner involves more than price.

Choosing the Managers (Underwriters) of the Public Offering

Selling shares to thousands of investors is a massive undertaking, especially on a worldwide basis. In many instances, though, an international sale is required because the local stock market is too small to absorb the offering. Only a small number of investment banking firms have that capability. Rarely does any firm have the capability or willingness to do the job by itself. The government, then, must select the firm to lead the offering, and the other investment banking firms that will aid in the effort. The government's advisor may help the government choose the banking group, and continue to advise the government during the offering period, if the terms of its contract prohibit it from competing for the job of lead banker. In another case, the advisor may take the role of lead banker automatically, or it may be the leading candidate for role of lead banker by virtue of the knowledge and relationships developed during the advisory period. The question of the role of advisor *vis-a'-vis* the role of lead manager of the investment banking syndicate that sells the securities is a sticky one. The payment to the advisor is small compared to the payment to the lead manager. Some banking firms will try to avoid serving in an advisory role if doing so prohibits them from serving as lead manager. But how can an advisor provide impartial advice on the choice of a manager if it is one of the contenders for the job? And, how can the government get the best firms to compete for the job of lead manager if they believe that the advisor is almost certain to get the job, anyway? Most of the time, the government assures all candidates that the position really is open, and that all candidates stand an equal chance in selection. Most of the time, when that happens, the other candidates do not believe the government.

Before selecting the bankers, though, the government must decide what sort of an offering that it wants. Does it want shares sold domestically and internationally? Does it want large or small shareholders? Does it want the shares listed on stock exchanges? Does it have time to prepare the documents required for listing? Does it want the shares sold in some markets and not others? Each investment banking firm has strengths and weaknesses. The government should pick those firms with the greatest ability to do what the government wants. (As an example: if the government wants most of the shares sold in Japan, it will choose a Japanese banker. If it wants to sell the shares to American small investors who like to buy utility stocks, it will choose an American firm that has numerous small investors as customers.) The government will also make sure that the group of firms managing the deal have complementary talents. (There is no need, for instance, to have three co-managers who deal only with large institutional investors in the United States. Of the three, perhaps one should have a small investor clientele in the United States, and another might do most of its business in Europe.)

Often, the government chooses the lead banker and the co-managers of the offering by means of a "beauty contest". Again, a group of government officials, the advisors, and, perhaps, the management of the company to be privatized, meet to hear presentations from the bankers who are competing for the role. They ask questions similar to those asked potential advisors before.

The government needs a clear understanding of not only the firms' capabilities, but also of who in the firm will work on the offering. Investment bankers often bring their top executives to the table, in order to impress the potential client. Yet the top executives go back to their offices afterwards, and other people do all the work. Who are the other people? What is their level of expertise and commitment? What are their reputations? Governments should do what potential employers should do: talk to previous clients.

One can measure the banking firms in various ways. If this will be a big offering, requiring the ability to place large numbers of shares throughout the world, the government should make sure that the bankers are among the top underwriters in the world. Every banking firm has a way of calculating the rankings to make it look best, while some rankings are calculated by impartial observers, such as corporate finance journals. For the firm to appear as number one on every list is less important than for it to appear consistently on all the lists. You do not want an amateur in charge of a major securities offering.

The next step is to determine if the firm has experience in underwriting offerings for the particular industry. If it does, it will understand better how to market the shares, and who likes to buy those shares. The government should ask to see lists of previous offerings.

Does the firm know how to sell offerings from that region of the world? Does it have knowledge of the region, and does it know which investors like to buy shares of companies in the region? For that matter, can it sell the shares within the region, too?

Large, institutional clients, such as pension and mutual funds, buy large percentages of any offering. Does the firm do business with a broad range of institutional customers, or with only a small number of institutions? For that matter, small investors can buy large numbers of utility shares, but not all investment banking firms have small investors as customers. The offering should be made to a mix of small and large investors.

Has the investment banker been successful in its past offerings? If so, other questions may be asked, such as: Did the stock have to be sold at a price below the price at which it was supposed to be offered? Did it have to be sold much below the market price? Did the bankers sell more or fewer shares than they planned to sell?

Finally, the government has to consider what happens after the stock offering, after the investment bankers have collected their fees. Do the bankers trade the securities? Do they make markets for those securities? Do they provide investment research on the company, so that investors have sources of information? Without proper follow-up by the bankers, trading could fall and the stock price could decline, creating ill-will toward the new company as well as toward the government.

A number of the bankers will, undoubtedly, paint a rosy picture for the offering, and will compete with each other in offering to sell the most shares at the highest price. The government may be tempted to choose the most optimistic banker as the lead manager, dismissing more realistic firms as not enthusiastic enough. Governments should remember that "bait and switch" is an old game. Bankers playing that game get the business by making unrealistic promises. Then, as the offering process moves forward, they tell the seller that market conditions have changed, and the deal must be reduced in size and price in order to sell.

On occasion the choice of lead manager becomes even more complicated. The government might want a global lead manager to supervise the entire offering, and regional managers in each of the major markets. The government has to consider that some important firms will not participate in the offering unless they are the lead managers, and, some lead managers operate in a way to neutralize the efforts of co-managers that might be beneficial to the offering but not to the lead manager. Sometimes co-managers work well together and sometimes they do not.

After seeing all the potential lead managers during the beauty contest, the government selects the lead manager, and confers with the lead manager in order to pick the co-managers and the other investment banking firms that will play key roles in the offering of shares. The fee for the sale of the shares is usually a percentage of the total amount of money raised. The fee will differ, depending on the size and the expected difficulty of the offering. The lead manager walks off with the biggest fee, which is why banking firms fight so hard to get that role.

Making the Sale

Selling the stock is a complicated transaction that requires the cooperation of the government (as seller), the management of the corporation that is to be sold, and the banking group, over a period of many months.

The process begins when the lawyers arrive to do their due diligence investigatory work (lawyers and bankers are required to exercise "due diligence" which means that they cannot take the seller's word for everything, but must investigate the company, ask questions, and get answers that satisfy themselves that the information is correct), and then to begin drafting the offering circular or prospectus that will eventually go to prospective investors. The investment bankers begin their due diligence work, too. After all, when the investors buy the shares, they depend on the information in the prospectus. The lawyers and bankers who have helped to prepare the prospectus that sells the shares have their names on the document. If the document is not truthful, those who have helped to prepare the selling document will be held responsible. Thus, those people must satisfy their responsibility by exercising due diligence before taking part in the offering. Meanwhile, the accountants are preparing the financial statements that go into the prospectus.

If the process goes smoothly, within several months, the auditors, lawyers, bankers, and the company have solved all the problems, put together the prospectus, and furnished whatever other legal information that is required in the country of the offering.

With all the information at hand, the bankers and the seller have to value the stock to be sold. The government may want the highest price for its shares. The bankers want a price that is low enough to attract investors, and give those investors a profit as the stock price rises to its true value. After all, the buyers of the stock are the bankers' customers, and bankers like to have happy customers, who come back to buy when the banker has another stock to sell. Customers do not like to buy from bankers who overprice the stock that they sell. Overpriced stock goes down after the offering. The management of the company to be sold, in theory, has nothing to say about the price. They represent neither buyer nor seller. But they have to live with the results of the sale. The buyers of the stock become their shareholders. Presumably, the managements want shareholders who are pleased with the purchase. Generally, the bankers try to price the shares in a way that makes everyone moderately happy. That means they want the stock to go up after the offering, maybe up 10 percent. In that way, the investors are happy because they have made a profit, the seller is happy, because it collected almost the full value for the shares, and the company is happy, because its shareholders are happy. It sounds simple, but it is not. Sometimes, during the offering, the market changes abruptly, making the offering price too high or too low in relation to new market conditions. An unexpected news event may affect investors' perceptions about the stock. Also, bankers, at times, just plain miscalculate. Whatever the reason, disasters do occur. If the offering price was too high, the stock falls. The government may be happy, because it collected more than the stock was worth, but investors are likely to be furious. On the other hand, if the stock jumps way above the offering price, the government will feel that it got far less than the stock was worth, but investors will be thrilled.

How do investment bankers select a price? Generally, they look at the market valuations of similar companies, and then try to determine how the company being sold differs from that list. For instance, if stocks in the host country sell at prices that range between 10 and 15 times earnings, the bankers will try to price the offering within that range, but where within the range will depend on how good the company is relative to the others in the market. The bankers, too, will compare the company's stock with shares of companies in the same industry throughout the world. They will look at the predictability of income, prospects for growth, strength of the balance sheet, rules for regulation, competence of the management, size of firm, and stability of the country. The procedure looks scientific, but it is inexact. In the end the bankers will set the price based on their experience and a feel for the market.

Then comes the road show. The company's management must travel to major investment centers to present information to and answer the questions of potential investors. Management will visit large investors individually ("one-on-one" visits), make presentations to groups of investors at breakfasts, lunches and dinners, and speak to the salespeople of the investment banking houses. A typical road show could include visits to at least four European cities in one week and eight-to-ten North American cities in the following week. Add another week for Asia or Latin America.

While the management is travelling, the investment bankers are talking to customers, and their salesmen call clients to get indications of interest. Salesmen ask how many shares the client would buy if the price were within the indicated price range, and give that information to their syndicate desk which coordinates the selling effort. The salesmen continue to ask during the offering period, gather reactions to the road show presentations, and keep careful track of buying interest, especially when some big events in the marketplace might affect the price of the offering or the demand for the offering. The process of gathering indications of buying interest, keeping in touch with prospective purchasers, and encouraging them to put in orders is called "building the book." If the demand is strong, the bankers might raise the price of the stock and increase the number of shares offered. If demand is weak or market conditions are poor, the bankers may decrease the size of the offering, lower the price, or even delay the offering until market conditions have improved.

Finally, after the conclusion of the road show, taking into account all the intelligence gathered by the sales forces, the bankers price the deal and decide on number of shares to sell. The stock is then sold. Possibly a week later, the deal is closed and the seller is paid. After that, the bankers and executives celebrate at a closing dinner.

After the Sale

There is more to come. Just selling the stock is the beginning. The banking firms and the company must take steps to assure success for the stock in the future. To do so, the banking firm must dedicate resources to making markets in the shares. The bankers will buy shares when someone wants to sell them, and sell shares when someone wants to buy them. That activity assures investors that a liquid market exists for the stock. (A liquid market is one in which traders can buy or sell large numbers of shares with ease, without causing big changes in the stock price.) In addition, the banker must institute research coverage on the stock. Investors want to know what is going on. They want to be able to call a research analyst to ask for information and advice, and to see periodic research reports about the company. All the banking firms involved in the offering should provide research coverage.

The company that was privatized must now act like a corporation in the private sector. The company must furnish timely information to the public and to investors. In addition, management must, periodically, visit the large investors. Management must also run the company in a way that benefits its owners. Accomplishing these goals requires a major change in attitude from the time when the company was an agency of the government.

Conclusion

Selling a company means just that. The government that wants the best price must find the most eager buyers, encourage them, and also know what the property is really worth. If the government has more than one company to sell, it must assure that each deal is handled well, so that buyers come to the next deal with high expectations of success. Governments throughout the world are competing to sell assets, to lure private investors to their countries. Doing the job effectively and profitably may require help from outside firms. That help is expensive, but failure is more expensive.

Chapter 15

The Strategic Employment of Investor Relations in the Privatization Process

Angel García Cordero

(Translated by Leonard S. Hyman)

Privatizing the large, state-controlled enterprises of Spain has become a means of providing the government with much needed funds. Sale of shares of Repsol, the oil company, Argentaria, the bank, and of Endesa, the electric utility, have taken place, and in the future the government may reduce its holdings in Telefónica Internacional, the international telecommunications holding company, in Tabacalera, the tobacco firm, and in Repsol. (See Table 15-1.)

Two reasons are frequently cited to explain the phenomenon of Spanish privatization. The first is to correct the budgetary deficit, which has become one of the economy's major problems. The second is the trend toward privatization so prominent now in European thinking, which began a number of years ago in Great Britain, and which has now spread over the European continent and into Latin America.

The success achieved in the majority of the privatizations realized in Great Britain during the past decade has made it clear that strategic employment of communications contributes to reaching the objectives of the process of privatization. In fact, investor relations, in that situation, as well as in other instances, is becoming a basic tool in every privatization program.

Although just about every privatization process involves a number of economic, political and social variables, we can affirm that it would not be possible to assure a successful sale of shares without establishing a network of communications with channels to employees, investors, the media, and opinion leaders. In fact, it would not be possible to achieve any success in this process without involving the public. The clearest demonstration of this rule can be found in the recent privatization of Argentaria.

Table 15-1. State Controlled Corporations in Spain (a)

Company	State Shareholding (%)	Expected Privatization (%)	Net Income (Billions of Pesetas) 1992	Net Income (Billions of Pesetas) 1993
Argentaria (b)	51.7	—	56.2	64.8
Repsol (c)	40.5	20	71.9	80.1
Endesa (d)	65.6	—	106.3	116.8
Telefónica (e)(1)	32.3	—	80.8	96.4
Tabacalera (f)	52.4	—	12.6	4.4
Aldeasa (g)	100.0	33 (k)	3.8	NA
Trans-mediterranea (h)	95.2	40 (k)	3.0	NA
Teneo (i)	100.0	25	21.1	3.0
Telefónica Internacional (j)	23.4	23.4 (k)	9.4	21.3

(a) Information as of September 1994.
(b) Major bank.
(c) Oil, gas and petrochemicals.
(d) Largest electric utility.
(e) National telephone company.
(f) Tobacco.
(g) Duty free shops.
(h) Maritime ferry service.
(i) Holding company for state enterprises.
(j) Holding company for Telefónica's international ventures.
(k) Private placement expected.
(1) Possible sale of part of state position to Spanish banks is contemplated.

Communication and Relations with Investors

In order to mobilize and motivate the target audiences, it is absolutely necessary that they understand the purposes of the privatization, and that the potential investors are fully satisfied as far as information is concerned. While the social and economic needs and circumstances of each company vary from privatization to privatization and from country to country, two fundamental principles of the process remain constant.

The first is the necessity of reaching a widespread public acceptance of the concept of privatization. If the government does not obtain the backing and active participation of the public in the process of privatization, the process will be undermined and never reach its full potential. General support for the concept of privatization creates an environment in which each transaction succeeds. Experience shows that people tend to defend the ideas that they are familiar with and understand.

The second principle is that it is essential to provide as much information as possible about the nature of the enterprise being privatized, its line of business, and its operations. Experience shows that the propensity to invest increases with knowledge and comprehension not only of the company, but also of the privatization process.

Thus, it is necessary to elaborate a careful strategy of marketing and communication that transmits the purposes of the privatization. A simple explanation to investors of the benefits of the privatization is not enough: the benefits must be effectively communicated to a wide range of audiences, such as all those involved in the process in one way or another, including the employees of the company and the general public. We will elaborate on those ideas to demonstrate the role that investor relations plays in the privatization process.

Privatizations: First Steps

Perhaps the basic problem within the process of privatization lies in what the state should and should not do. "It is very important," according to Oscar Fanjul, president of Repsol, "to establish a policy of where the state wants to be and where it does not want to be, and to transmit a clear message to society, to company executives, and to the different agencies of the government." Of equal importance is for a government not to set up a rigid calendar of privatizations, but rather to maintain a flexible program, to set the general direction and long term objectives, and when executing the program, to take advantage of the possibilities created by social and political circumstances and by market conditions.

What one has to do, as a matter of priority, is to quickly begin the programs to communicate with investors. Doing so is necessary for several reasons: the planning of the timing of the process is essential; perceptions have to be directed in a consistent form from the beginning; the interest of the media is strong and stories about the deal emerge rapidly from all directions.

Distinct Audiences: Different Demands

A privatization program will not succeed without the *strategic* employment of communications programs. Among those, investor relations stand out as a key element in the privatization. One must satisfy the objectives of the government, while taking into account the objectives—sometimes wholly different—of the diverse groups involved in the process: the management of the company, employees, individual shareholders and institutional investors, mass media and opinion leaders. Each situation requires a specific strategy, with a different communications component designed to reach each of the audiences involved in the process.

When institutional investors are to play a major role, one needs to offer them complete and in-depth information about finances, business strategies, and growth potential. Communication with financial analysts and with the press, the customary sources of information for institutional investors, then requires special attention, given that in the future those sources will contribute to the success of financings over the long run in the capital markets.

If individual investors constitute the target market for the privatization, then the information aimed at them has to be managed to attract their loyalty and interest. Doing so requires the use of massive publicity, the creation of an efficient and broad system of distribution, and the furnishing of clear and concise information, as much about the company as about the offering itself. Thus, in the case of the Argentaria offering, the selling effort included a major, widespread publicity and direct marketing campaign with the objective of bringing about the maximum awareness for all aspects of the offering.

Investors tend to put their money in companies that offer a clear vision of where they are going, and avoid those that lack a clear definition of their position in the market and of their corporate strategies for the future. What is difficult is to design a program of investor relations that satisfies the information needs of the investors, and to provide suitable information to each investor (whether individual or institutional): complete information about the company's finances, business strategies, and the potential for growth of the market that the company serves and of the company itself.

The employees, too, need to be involved from the beginning. They must acquire a new sense of competitiveness. In order to motivate employees, the company must design a program of internal communications.

Relations with the press, as well, are essential to the process. The company must gain the confidence of the press through a professional and ongoing information program.

In sum, one must communicate the future benefits of privatizations to investors, to employees, and to the general public. In fact, one should try to incorporate investor relations into the management of the privatization, inasmuch as the relationships between all the groups in the process are as complex as the financial technicalities and no less important. The fundamental part of that process is to identify, understand and respond to the perceptions and preoccupations of all shareholders and to send them the right messages.

The Spanish Model: Repsol and Argentaria

When carrying out the process previously discussed, we occasionally come across some unexpected results. In the instance of the Spanish offerings, the massive placements of Repsol and Argentaria laid to rest two misperceptions: the supposed lack of individual shareholders, and concentration of stock market activity in the hands of large institutions. Now it is possible to think in terms of a strong potential for development of the Spanish stock market that might have remained hidden. If this potential is not appreciated by the financial community, perhaps that is because the would-be shareholder may have little faith in a market that is disregarded by the companies listed on it. The examples set by Repsol and Argentaria were surprising, not only because of the volume of funds absorbed by the market, but also by the number of orders, all of which lead us to conclude that there is an important and untapped market for shares in Spain. There is no shortage of potential shareholders, who want investment bankers and company managements that want to sell to them, and worthwhile offerings.

The need to privatize, in the case of Repsol, was carefully explained over an extended period of time, in 1989, thereby muting all criticism of the offering. Equally, the company ran a special information program for the employees, and designated for them a parcel of shares which they could buy at a discount and on credit. The company tried to encourage in its employees a commitment to the firm by inviting them to become shareholders. The publicity campaign was important and developed in two phases. The first, in the period before the flotation began, had as its objective to introduce the company. The second had as its objective to induce the public to buy the shares. As a result of this campaign, Repsol not only became better known but also admired for the quality of its management.

The offer of incentives—which improves the profitability for individual and institutional investors—also contributes to the success of privatizations. For the first time in Spain, in order to facilitate the sale of an international secondary offering, Argentaria 2, in 1994, two important incentives were introduced that made the offering more profitable: a 4 percent discount off the price for those who requested shares at the Information and Registration Office, and one free share for every ten purchased and then retained for 18 months. The objectives were clearly to sell to stable shareholders and to limit the sale of shares on the market after the offering. Above all, what those incentives achieved was the essential goal in every privatization: to promote the purchase of the securities. Since prices are set late in the process, it is advantageous to create an environment favorable to the offering. That requires the communication of "investment ideas" to institutions and an effort to educate and motivate individual investors. (See Table 15-2.)

In effect, those two programs of flotation of shares on the stock market succeeded in doing more than just placing the shares: they also consolidated the positions of the companies in the market, and improved their relations with the general public.

Table 15-2. Timetable of Argentaria's April 1993 Public Offering

Book Building

From March 24 up through the last work day before the commencement of Public Offering.

For General Public: minimum ESP 25,000, maximum ESP 8,000,000.

For Institutions: minimum ESP 8,000,000, no maximum.

Public Offering Period

Once the Selling Price is determined, the Public Offering Period commences, which will last a maximum of 15 working days (three weeks) and a minimum of five working days (one week).

Settlement, Clearing and Transfer

The Definitive Settlement takes place five days after the end of the Public Offering.

The number of shares finally settled is communicated one working day after the Definitive Settlement.

To seek out—by means of a carefully tailored program of investor relations—the right timing and the best way to carry through a process of privatization ought to be, in every case, a key objective of the managements of those state-controlled companies.

The work of those managements, however, does not end with the privatization. Beyond the share placement, managements will have to understand that communications are useful in dealing with the consequences of the privatization process, which has a major impact on the public; that, on privatization, the company ought to improve the quality of its product and services offered; and that investors may cease to invest in the firm if the shares of the privatized firm do poorly on the market, all of which means that the need for investor relations continues.

Chapter 16

What Do Investors Want from the New Company after Privatization?

Richard C. Toole

The answer to the question, "What do investors want from a new company after privatization?" is easy—SUPERIOR INVESTMENT RETURN. The answer is no different from what is expected of any Initial Public Offering, or for that matter, any investment. Before a decision can be made, timely and accurate information is needed: What are we getting into, and how does it compare with other uses for our funds? Most investors do not go outside the United States (US) merely to sport a global portfolio. If that is the objective, one can purchase one of a number of global mutual funds professionally managed and geographically diversified. By choosing a single entity, investors assess prospects relative to cost and see how profitable the proposed move is in total return compared with other options. Let us discuss the general information needed to make a good judgement about an investment after privatization takes place and then examine an example, Telecom of New Zealand, a successful post-privatization investor relations effort.

The ABC'S of Investing
An investor once insisted on buying only listed stocks with names starting with the letters A through C, i.e, American Telephone, British Telecom, and Chrysler. When asked the reason for this unusual approach, the investor replied, "I don't have to turn the page." Most of us share a variation of this trait; we want to keep track of investments in the easiest way possible and still get a superior return. Whether we go "by the alphabet" or "by the numbers" we need access to basic information that is not only reliable but easy to obtain, starting with something as obvious as the quote. Of course, the p,rice of the security is just the starting point, albeit an important one. The price determines the initial cost of an investment but is also a somewhat imperfect daily report card, measuring the progress or lack of it by the company. Market price is not only an indication of the perceived value but also acts as a news signal—good or bad, perhaps to prompt investors to revisit the original investment premise. A frequent objection to international investing has been, "I can't get a price when I want it." Not knowing the current market valuation of an investment is like watching a horse race blindfolded; it is fun to bet on a winner, but we would like to see how the race is run. Therefore, the security

price should be posted, if not on the same page, at least in one reliable source. This explains why we now have a subscription to the *Financial Times* of London as well as the *Wall Street Journal* and *The New York Times*.

The Tip of the Iceberg

The market price action of a security is only the tip of the iceberg. To make the right investment moves, especially involving international companies, one needs easy access to timely, complete and accurate company specific and country specific information. COUNTRY INFORMATION can be obtained from a variety of government and independent economic and political sources. Investment banks have investment rankings for each country. Economists track and project data for a number of countries and regions. Strategists weigh risks, political and other, against potential returns on investment. National sources of information are developed, including employees and branch offices on foreign soil. In addition, local banks and in country investment companies can provide valuable information on which to draw conclusions and base opinions. Company information is made available through financial reporting and an investor relations program. The reporting of results (income statements), flow of funds (cash flow statements), and financial standing (balance sheets) should be supported with detailed background information and commentary as well as by notes to financial statements. Investor relations should be two-way; of course, responding to questions, but also anticipating and volunteering information. A real fear, frequently-voiced, is that foreign investors will be the "last to know" the information needed to make informed, timely decisions.

Telecom of New Zealand: An Example

Telecom of New Zealand represents a model for how to deal with investors post-privatization. Early on, the company recognized the benefits of having well-informed stockholders. Obviously, the common English language simplify matters, but when a company starts with a "How can I help?" attitude, success is more likely. Some international companies are reluctant to part with information because that is the norm in their country. The attitude of "Why should I tell them?" is a turn-off to investors. In addition to the incentive of a superior return, potential investors will go with the company who makes it easy for them to understand what they are investing in. Some companies literally act as though their foreign investors are the enemy. A "caveat emptor" approach breeds suspicion and is not the fabric of a long term relationship. The New Zealand government initiated privatization to raise funds but also to improve the telecommunications infrastructure in the country. The company has continued this approach by appointing a solid investor relations manager, conducting periodic meetings with holders, providing financial reporting and providing access to needed information. The effort has been both active and pro-active. The results have been positive not only from standpoint of market performance but also from pleasing the important constituents or stockholders, the owners.

Background

A former Postal Telephone & Telegraph (PTT) entity with all the inefficiencies the name implies, Telecom of New Zealand (NZT) became an actual company when it was privatized in 1987. New Zealand set up a free and open entry competitive market and sold the entire company to Ameritech and Bell Atlantic, two US regional Bell Holding Companies, for $2.4 billion US, with a time schedule for the American companies to sell more than 50 percent of their holdings. This has occurred and Telecom, in the interim, has become a more modern company (close to 100 percent digitally switched) using up-to-date management systems and techniques. The employee count which started at 26,000 is now under 11,000 and is scheduled to drop to 7,500 by 1997. The company serves more than 1.6 million access lines and more than 200,000 cellular subscribers in a country with a total population of 3.5 million and 65 million sheep. NZT provides every form of telecommunications services, local, national and international long distance, enhanced services, including data, cellular, and directory.

NZT's appeal to investors is easy to explain. Most people believed it was a safe way to invest in a sound economy. Logically, it was assumed that the New Zealand government had an interest in keeping the telecommunications company healthy, especially with the goal of ensuring access to world-wide financial markets. The story was rather uncomplicated and NZT's large US holders were two Regional Bells. An investment in New Zealand was less exciting than speculating in Mexico, but the dividend yield and likely stability was attractive to many investors. Price appreciation is a pleasant additive.

The Initial Public Offering

To ensure worldwide diversity of share ownership, the selling effort occurred in three tranches: one for the home New Zealand market, one for the United States, and one for international markets. Bell Atlantic, Ameritech, and the investment banks (including co-leads Merrill Lynch and Goldman Sachs) put together a series of road shows featuring NZT's chief executive and chief financial officer. Using audio-visual support, management clearly described the company, its market, current position and potential. Nuances such as the "Kiwi" plan were explained. Ample time was allotted to questions and answers. The Manager of Investor Relations was kept in the forefront in order that investors, especially large institutions, and security analysts gained some degree of confidence and familiarity with the financial spokesperson for the company. Road shows were held in London and other European and Asian main cities as well as in the United States.

The security offering had to be priced and offered simultaneously in the currency where offered. Different time zones and market hours were obstacles but were surmounted. Despite the large size of the IPO, investor demand was strong. Ordinary shares in New Zealand dollars are listed on the New Zealand exchange where they account for 24 percent of total market value. In comparison, American Depository Receipts in US dollars represent 16 ordinary shares and are listed on the New York Stock Exchange. Finally, NZT shares are also listed on other major stock exchanges, including the Australian stock exchange.

Financial Reporting

Telecom issues quarterly and annual reports similar to US companies. Dividends are declared and paid twice a year. The timing of earnings releases is somewhat complicated by the fact that New Zealand's time zone is a number of hours ahead of New York. When the company (March fiscal year) released second quarter 1994 results at 8:00 a.m. (New Zealand time) on Tuesday, November 2, 1993, the New York financial community received the news at 4:00 p.m. on the previous day November 1, 1993. Following release of results to the various wire services, the company faxed copies of the release to analysts who have a standing interest. Less than 24 hours later, the company held a Conference Call covering results with a live two-way question-and-answer period following. In the United States, Telecom uses an investor relations firm to schedule meetings and conferences.

New Zealand Telecom's earnings reports are detailed and complete. They provide the usual required financial tables and footnotes, as well as worthwhile commentary on each revenue and expense category. There is a helpful outlook section as well as comments on particular subjects such as capitalization restructuring and dividend taxability. Background information is provided. The financial and other information is more than is absolutely required but makes for better informed analysis.

With Telecom's quarterly Conference Call, the company takes the time to thoroughly and patiently cover results for all levels of analysts, including those less familiar with Telecom. This approach is difficult to fault because it results in minimum confusion and more detail is certainly better than less.

We applaud the timing of the Telecom Conference Call, close to the time of the earnings release. Company conference calls held up to one week after the release of earnings can miss the mark. These calls almost appear to be an after thought and by the time the call is held, the information is already stale. New Zealand Telecom also does a good notification job. We are told well in advance when earnings will be announced and when the Conference Call will be held. There is plenty of time to mark the calendar and plan for the process.

Telecom's hard copy explanations of quarterly and annual results and commentary on a variety of topics are very worthwhile. The reports facilitate an understanding of conditions in the New Zealand market not easily attainable without detailed explanation. For example, one of the leading investor concerns in respect to Telecom is the competition the company is facing in the national and international long distance markets (CLEAR) and to a lesser extent, in cellular (BELL-SOUTH). Hearing how the company stacks up with competitors as well as its plan to retain market share and grow revenues provides valuable insights. Detailed accounts of marketing approaches, rate rebalancing and litigative efforts by the principal competitors are required reading to better assess company prospects. Of course, an analyst should not rely solely on a company view which may be more sanguine than warranted. Checking with other sources is a requisite.

United States and New Zealand Generally Applied Accounting Principles (GAAP) accounting are quite similar, which makes for ease of coverage. A footnote in the Annual Report covers the differences and demonstrates that results under New Zealand GAAP actually are more conservatively stated than under US GAAP.

Investor Relations Program

Telecom's investor relations program has been successfully supervised by an individual with a solid understanding of the company, its industry, and its service area. Perhaps of equal importance, the Investor Relations Program appears to have the full support of top management. This type of involvement is critical since a program left out of the loop is often a failure. At some companies, people have the impression that investor relations is the "last to know." The Director or Manager of Investor Relations needs to be on top of developments and cannot be caught off balance lest credibility be lost. The Manager or Director acts as would an official Press Secretary, espousing company rather than personal views, but at times can give clearly defined opinions. Telecom's, as well any good investor relations program, works on the basis that truthful information serves all parties better in the long run as opposed to those in which spokespersons adopt a "see no evil" attitude.

A successful investor relations program provides accurate information on a timely basis. Availability of a spokesperson is second only to integrity. This is especially critical because time differences exist between the company headquarters and major trading markets for the company's securities. Initially, some comfort was taken that the two largest Telecom investors, Ameritech, in Chicago, and Bell Atlantic, in Philadelphia, could be counted upon to provide solid information to US securities analysts at critical times. We have found this not to be the case. The Bell Regionals defer questions where they belong, back to the New Zealand company, but, it is comforting to know that one can turn to very large holders to ensure that information flow continues at the current high level.

When we have needed to be in touch with Telecom, we have found a way to get the information required. By use of facsimile wireless and voice mail, we have been able to schedule calls with the Manager of Investor Relations, who responds, answers the question and/or gets back with the information as quickly as possible. The Manager has shown common sense in gauging the degree of urgency and is quite capable of arranging contact with the right individuals when specific or particular information is required.

Obviously, field trips to New Zealand are not always convenient and can be quite expensive involving a twenty-hour flight from the New York area. However, on a recent visit, a full schedule of meetings in Wellington and Auckland with the right people was arranged. A tour of facilities and of the two principal cities was quite worthwhile.

Telecom of New Zealand also takes the time and makes the effort to keep investors informed by scheduling visits with analysts in their home country. Obviously, this is a tricky process and can represent a sacrifice on the part of the management. However, the effort has been more than rewarded with happier holders who are pleased to meet personally rather than simply hear a detached voice with a pleasant New Zealand accent. In 1993 and 1994, the Managing Director, followed by the Chief Investment Officer, have come to New York and other major cities in two separate trips, again accompanied by the Investor Relations Manager. In addition to verbal presentations and responses, informative chart and graph supplements were made available. Examples of these charts appear at the end of this chapter.

Also important, the program is a two-way street. At times, we-have received a call from the Company to alert us to developments, such as tax issues and political trends, to promote our understanding of a subject or a situation hard to follow half a world away. On some occasions, we have been asked by the company for information, mostly related to how the company is perceived or what topics are in vogue and, also, to find out if we are getting the information needed to do the analysis. This is a change from companies who are reticent when it comes to releasing information and sometimes seem to view the analyst as the enemy.

Conclusion

Gerald M. Loeb, the "wily wizard of Wall Street" often spoke of the "Battle for Investment Survival." He believed that the key to successful investing had to do with keeping informed and getting the best available information. We concur and also believe that investors will gravitate to investments which can be easily researched and monitored. All else being equal, and it never is, investors don't want to have to "turn the page." Finally, a solid investor relations program is a company's "window to the world" and critical to establishing credentials to potential owners.

Figure 16-1. New Zealand Price Performance

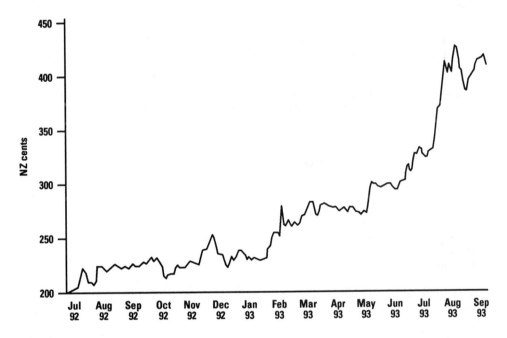

Source:
Telecom Corporation of New Zealand Limited

Figure 16-2. US Price Performance

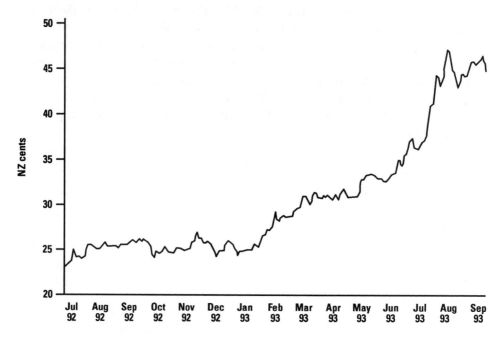

Source:
Telecom Corporation of New Zealand Limited

Table 16-1. Ordinary Shares

Ordinary Shares on issue	2.362m
ADR ratio	1:20
Market capitalisation at $45½	US$5.374m
12 month price range	$23¼–$46¾
Market capitalisation at $4.00	NZ$9.448m
12 month high/low	$2.19–$4.21

Source:
Telecom Corporation of New Zealand Limited

Table 16-2. Key Ratios

	94-Q1	93-Q1
Operating earnings*/Operating revenue	33.6%	27.7%
Operating revenue*/Ave total assets	50.3%	48.8%
Debt/Debt+equity	33.4%	35.9%
Return on average shareholders' equity**	18.9%	14.2%

* *Earnings exclude abnormal charges*
** *Annualised*

Source:
Telecom Corporation of New Zealand Limited

Table 16-3. New Zealand Economic Environment

	Mar-93	Mar-94	Mar-95
Inflation	1.3%	1.3%	0.7%
GDP	3.1%	2.5%	3.2%
Deficit as a % of GDP	-4.0%	-3.2%	-2.6%
5 yr bonds	7.5%	5.7%	6.0%
NZD/USD	52.0	56.5	58.0
Unemployment	11.0%	11.2%	11.8%

Sources:
Reserve Bank of New Zealand, Bank of New Zealand
Telecom Corporation of New Zealand Limited

Chapter 17

Privatization: An Investors' Perspective
or
"Will they still love us after the sale?"

L.Y. Rathnam and V. Khaitan

Imagine a world in which regions and sovereign states, through their designated representatives, and with the support of politicians of the dominant parties, cast aside their customary desire to get for consumers the lowest possible price no matter what the consequences; who soften their customary sternness with people who are not broke; who strive to assure providers of capital, both foreign and domestic, of the highest possible returns on investment at the lowest possible level of risk (entrepreneurial returns at government bond risk levels, they say), and one grasps the world described, or imagined by, the sponsors of electrical, gas, telephone, and the other grand international privatizations that so mark the global investment scene today. The careworn investor, accustomed to scratching out his meager performance numbers from the hard, infertile soil of uncertain and competitive markets, cannot help but be attracted by this promised land of abundant returns easily obtained, and wants to believe that it exists. "Pennies on the dollar—we guarantee it" How can you lose?

The process of communication and seduction that is a major global offering generally culminates with governments and their placement agents having had their way with a sufficient number of investors to close the deal. These investors are now presumably among a select group allowed entrance to the land of milk and honey that this government and its agents have promised. But when the music stops, the books are closed, the money has been transferred, and the dignitaries have gone home, what really remains for these investors? What remains is the ordinary world, not that of the illusion, a world where, as recently occurred, a government arrested the foreign general manager of a recently privatized electrical utility who cut off the power of those who had illegally tapped into power lines in order to steal electricity. (How could he be so depraved as to deprive people of electricity in the name of profit?) It is a world of expediency, where returns are risky and hard to come by and where the ability to capture the promised returns depends solely upon the perceived inconvenience that might be caused by the investors' exercise of his only clear prerogative, the ability to refuse additional capital. Meanwhile, the friendly finance minister you met on the road show is not returning your calls.

Sooner or later, investors will have to deal with the fact that the companies that they have acquired through privatization were in government hands because they were, at some point, and perhaps still, seen much more as instruments of public policy than as vehicles for creating investor wealth. The extent to which investors will be able to make good on their expectations will depend upon an interplay of conditions that can be grouped into three broad areas:

1. Politics

2. Law and regulation

3. Business practices and conditions

Investors often begin with some degree of understanding about how these conditions affect similar investments in their home countries, particularly as no business is wholly unregulated. In the United States, Canada, Germany, Japan, Norway, Venezuela, Hong Kong, and a few other countries, however, investors also have the additional benefit of considerable historical experience with privately-owned, publicly-traded utility companies. Conditions for such companies have ranged from benign, in countries like Germany and Hong Kong, to confiscatory, in the United States, producing a wide spectrum of investor sentiment, running from enthusiasm to wariness. Investors in the United States, for example, have, in recent decades, become used to a "heads you win, tails I lose" relationship between utility companies and regulators, where the cost savings from advances in efficiency are passed on to consumers in the form of lower rates while increased costs are borne by investors in the form of reduced profits and dividends.

This is because public utility commissions, when not directly elected, as is often the case, are at least appointed by people who must stand for election. Utility customers vastly outnumber utility investors at the polls, with predictable consequences for regulatory behavior. This situation is exacerbated by the fact that utility regulatory work pays poorly, and there is little glory or advancement from raising the prices of public utility services, all of which makes it difficult to attract and keep highly-qualified and experienced professionals. (True, there are admirable exceptions.) This situation is well illustrated by a single exemplary incident, in which a utility company teetering on the verge of bankruptcy, with a stock price so low that the yield was in the double digits, was deemed by one official as not requiring any increase in revenues as only a very profitable company could afford to pay such a high yield.

The antics of the regulatory commissions of selected states over the years have long been a source of both despair and hilarity in financial circles, where the virtuous know that, in the absence of compelling cheapness, "thou shalt not commit a utility."

In general, then, knowledgeable people in countries that already have privately-owned utilities understand that they should not pay a lot for one. Profit levels and growth are likely to be low, and they do not see why the regulatory situation should, in the long run, differ for newly-privatized companies in uncertain environments.

The greatest enthusiasm for a utility privatization usually appears among investors in the country of the utility in question. This is particularly true if there is little experience with private utility companies locally. The utility, as a government-owned corporation, is viewed as a powerful monolith, able to thumb its nose at the public with poor service and arrogant, uncooperative employees. (One of the authors remembers an incident in the United Kingdom in the 1970s in which a telephone operator refused to put through a collect call to the United States because, in her view, to make such an expensive call in the absence of an emergency must constitute a hoax and, as such, was an abuse of the time of a valuable civil servant, herself. She threatened to send the police when the caller persisted in his request. Until fairly recently, the French telephone company refused to go to the expense of providing customers with itemized bills—you either paid the invoiced amount, however outlandish, or had your service cut off.) The power of the utility was also seen in its flouting of normal business practices; suppliers were paid when convenient, in the amounts that the utility deemed convenient, or not at all. It is understandable that local investors, having experienced such conduct for years, would want a piece of the action. What they often fail to realize is that, with privatization, the tables are turned on the utility, which becomes the object rather than the source of abuse.

But let us not, as the Bard has said, "to the marriage of true minds admit impediments." The investor has talked to his analyst (securities analyst, that is), heard the presentation, and read the "prospectus." (It is curious that this document, the name of which means "a look forward," can, under United States securities law, as interpreted, make no representations as to the future but must be wholly backward looking.) The investor's desire to own this monopoly has been stirred. He invests, and therefore he owns. And his action has not been wholly illogical. Utilities, in the right environment, have great wealth-creating potential, if the politics, laws and regulation, and business conditions are right.

Utility companies are instruments of public policy. They are privately owned to the extent that private ownership is viewed as the most efficacious way to achieve public ends. These ends include economic and social objectives. When the primary public goal is providing infrastructure for growth, then regulation tends to make utilities profitable so that they can generate, both internally and through securities issuance and borrowing, additional funds for expansion. The present high level of profitability of the Mexican telephone company, for example, is the result of massive rate increases intended to permit the company to generate enough cash flow to fund a rapid expansion of the system. When public policy emphasizes growth, and such growth depends upon rapid development of the infrastructure, utilities tend to be quite profitable.

When policy is preoccupied with other issues, however, such as inflation, recession, or social reform, then utilities can suffer. It has been a common practice in both developed and emerging countries to use utility rates to mitigate the impact on consumers of rising prices. In order to control inflation, rates are allowed to decline in real terms and earnings plummet. Following the disturbances in Venezuela in 1992, for example, the government caused the rates of the privately-owned Electricidad de Caracas to fall precipitously in real terms to placate a restive population squeezed by inflation. Similar thinking guided regulators in many parts of the United States as well during the high inflation period of the 1970s and 1980s, with disastrous results for investors.

State-owned utility companies are often used as employment agencies in times of high unemployment. A program to increase jobs can often include "make work" at government-controlled corporations. And, of course, there is the need to provide work, or at least salaries, for the friends and relatives of the politically powerful. Rate structures often do not reflect the cost of service to various markets but rather social goals. Electricity is sold to farmers to run irrigation pumps in Mexico at a loss because keeping the price of food low is an important government policy goal. "Lifeline" rates have been established in various American states in order to assure that even the very poorest can have access to essential public services like electricity, water, telephones, and (coming soon) 500-channel cable television.

Because of their roles as instruments of public policy, state-owned utility companies tend to be extremely inefficient. They tend to be heavily overstaffed with "no show" employees, those who appear at their presumed place of business only on payday to collect their salaries. Projects tend to be poorly organized and overly costly. Maintenance is poor and facilities are underused compared with their potential. Inventories are poorly managed and excessive in terms of the results produced. Graft is often rampant. The cost of installed generating capacity may vary by a factor of 10x for the least efficient, state-owned companies compared to the most efficient private companies; staffing may vary by a factor of 5x or more. The greater the inefficiency and waste, the greater the potential for reduction in costs.

Of the privatizations that have occurred to date, the implications of the natural tendencies of policymakers and the highly inefficient operations of state-owned utilities have dramatically played themselves out: The promises of public authorities to maintain certain rate and regulatory regimes have been swiftly broken in ways to limit the profitability of the newly-private utilities. Rate regimes and franchises that were billed as commitments of as long as forty years or as brief as seven years lasted as little as a few months before the authorities swept in to prevent the economic potential of these companies from achieving the levels that were promised in their prospectuses. (Of course, if a private party behaved as these governments, he might be accused of fraud, misrepresentation, and breach of contract, but public parties are protected by the concept of sovereign immunity.) In evaluating a utility privatization, therefore, the investor should take into account the selling party's ability to lie with impunity and the likelihood that this ability will be employed.

Despite the mendacity of some public officials, privatizations have, in general, worked out well for investors, due to the extreme levels of mismanagement and inefficiency that these same officials and their colleagues had developed in the operations of these companies. Improvements in profitability from better management has generally exceeded the advertised level, which has been an effective offset for the breaking of regulatory commitments. This is understandable, as public officials, even as they tout the privatization play, do not feel comfortable in fully describing the full extent to which they had mismanaged the affairs of the government-owned corporations. Overselling regulation has approximately equalled underselling of efficiency gains.

Privatized utilities present exceptional investment opportunities. These opportunities are greatest in countries experiencing rapid economic growth and therefore a need for new investment that will contain the predatory tendencies of regulatory authorities. The ability of the investor to refuse additional investment is his only defense against confiscatory government policies. If new investment is not a pressing necessity, this defense is ineffective, while if such investment is of critical importance, it is powerful. Exceptional returns for investors in privatized utilities in mature economies, such as those of the United Kingdom, France, and the United States, relate to efficiency gains, while returns to investors in rapidly-growing economies come from both efficiency gains and growth. Both cases are interesting, but in the latter the music goes on longer.

Another advantage of privatized utilities in the emerging countries is their ability to arbitrage local and international capital markets to generate additional profits for shareholders. Due to their size and stability, such companies are generally among the very few in an emerging economy that are able to access the local real interest costs of the First World. If a company can borrow at 5 percent real per year and invest at 20 percent real per year, or even carry cash balances at 1 percent or 2 percent real per month, an unusually wide spread between the cost of capital and the return on capital exists.

Finally, while environmentalism and consumerism exists everywhere in the world today, they tend to be healthier and more constructive in emerging countries and have not yet developed to the more pathological form of pure obstructionism that we sometimes find in the United States and other developed countries today. In the United States, there are a great many people who make a living, and in many cases an excellent living, opposing all forms of infrastructure growth and the payment by consumers of the fair cost of the services they are consuming. Paid "intervenors" (usually lawyers paid by involuntary fees on utilities and from public and private funds), presumably acting on behalf of the public, can tie up in lengthy and expensive court and regulatory proceedings any action undertaken by anyone, for any reason. They add enormous costs and inefficiency to the system, to the detriment of service and profitability. Since newly-privatized utilities have until recently been government agencies and therefore immune from such challenges, the process of obstructionism has not been institutionalized to the extent that it has in the United States. This is a good thing.

In conclusion, the authors' experience suggests that investors are better off, generally, with offerings where (a) the government continues to own a majority of the shares (i.e. Endesa in Spain, KEPCO in Korea); (b) new management runs the business as a business (PowerGen in the United Kingdom); (c) strong growth in power demand continues (i.e. China Light & Power in Hong Kong); (d) regulatory and competitive policies are well established and in place (i.e. investors are not sandbagged). Unfortunately, many of these privatization offerings have not lived up to the expectations beyond the initial premium. Buyers beware! This is not a happy ending, but nevertheless, rewarding if you can differentiate from one to another.

Investing in privatized utilities can provide exceptional rewards from profitability improvement through greater efficiency and growth. In general, however, high prices should not be paid for mature utility properties, either directly or indirectly. Entry prices should be low in relation to the profitability level that is likely to be achieved through cost cutting. Growth utilities can reasonably be expected to maintain higher levels of profitability because of the regulators' desire to attract additional capital. As far as any other assurance that may be given by managements and government officials at the time of the road show, they should be disregarded, and regulatory behavior should be forecast solely in terms of political expediency. They may have promised an investment opportunity made in paradise, and they may have even "enshrined" it in legislation, but when the sweet talking has stopped and the music has ended, and they have the investor's money in their pockets, value is the only contract that looks good in the bright light of day. When Androcles came across the injured lion, the legend says he earned the thanks and protection of that fierce beast by removing a thorn from its paw; this story is a fairy tale: the lion really ate him.

Chapter 18

Preparing for Industry Upheaval: Why Electric Utilities Must Reengineer

Michael Weiner, Jeffrey Walker, and Huard Smith

Throughout the world, electric utilities face upheaval caused by new technologies, the move from strict regulation to the encouragement of competition, and the change in ownership from subsidized, government-controlled organizations to stand-alone, privately-owned entities. Although the speed and shape of change varies from country to country, there is one constant theme throughout: The utility must run as an efficient, market-oriented business in order to survive.

The newly privatizing utilities which often ran as government bureaucracies are losing the government support that allowed them to run with minimal thought to costs or markets. They, more than others, must make a rapid transition, rethinking and reengineering their operations to assure success.

Amid industry restructuring and bankruptcies, new niche players will proliferate. New or reamalgamated companies will compete in focused arenas such as energy management services, electricity brokerage and beyond-the-meter services. Selling off other traditional accouterments of the integrated company, others will devote themselves to a single business such as power generation.

Just how many utilities will become the Braniffs, Eastern Airlines and other casualties of deregulation is unclear. However, by analyzing the restructurings that followed the deregulation of airlines, trucking, telecommunications and other industries, we can predict the discontinuities all electric utilities will face:

- fierce competition on price and service. In a competitive market, price levels established by regulators will become irrelevant.

- a rush to dramatically reduce costs and increase productivity. Burdened with huge cost structures and inefficient business practices, utilities will zealously attempt to streamline themselves.

- rapid market segmentation. Niche players and new entrants will pick off lucrative customer segments.

- consolidation and rampant restructuring of the industry. Those with high cost structures and unresponsive operations will be gobbled up by competitors seeking greater market access.

How can utilities survive—and thrive? What strategies will win amid so much uncertainty? In this chapter, we will examine the forces of change in the utility industry and discuss why the most popular strategy of the day—modest cost-cutting—is grossly insufficient. We will describe how utilities, long protected by regulation and a protective rate structure, can meet the future needs of their most sophisticated and demanding customers in the deregulated environment.

We will then show how utilities can prepare for the future by looking through the lens of "customer value" and by reengineering operations that deliver the most value to customers. We will describe the core business processes of a utility and how they would look post-reengineering. Finally, we will outline the skills utilities need to make this wrenching transition.

The Forces of Change

Many assume that deregulation is driving the industry restructuring. In fact, a confluence of forces is the cause:

The end of ever-increasing demand and price inelasticity. Since the first oil well was drilled, unit costs of oil declined all the way through 1973. Then the Arab embargo ended the era of cheap energy. Later, Three Mile Island extinguished the hope that the nuclear industry could bring lower cost energy. Together these events dashed the prevalent belief that energy prices were inelastic. Over the last 20 years, consumers have reduced consumption or brought in technology to drive down energy costs.

The end of scale economies in generation. As eventually happens with every technology, the utility industry ran up against the curve of scale economies. Power generation, which comprises most of utilities' capital assets, is basic technology that has changed little in the past 100 years. What did change was the scale of the industry. To meet burgeoning demand for electricity, utilities built bigger and bigger power plants. That drove the cost of power down until the late 1960s, when unit costs of the incremental kilowatt of electricity began increasing. So adding a unit of capacity to a traditional power plant raised the average cost of power, rather than lowered it.

Large customers asserted choice. In contrast, independent power producers (IPPs) emerged as an anomaly of regulation and exploited the economics of small-scale technology. In the United States (US) in the late 1970s, federal regulation permitted cogeneration facilities (owned by large industrial companies) to sell excess power back to the utilities. These facilities proved the economics of smaller-scale generation technology. They also spawned a power-generation sector independent from the investor-owned utilities. In the 1980s, IPPs built the majority of new power capacity. That has created competition in the wholesale market. It also has pushed customers and legislators to seek true competition, and thus choice, in the retail market. In other countries, too, smaller producers entered the market, taking business that would have gone to the incumbent utility. And even more so than in the US, large consumers of electricity gained access to their chosen electricity supplier.

The interconnection of regional power pools has created the possibility of customer choice. The impact of this critical technological change was not understood until the system emerged. Designed as a backup, not a transmission system, regional grids were built in the 1950s and 1960s to move power in peak periods. Now these regional power pools are wired together. The national grid makes electricity markets and retail wheeling feasible. Now, expanded interconnection between national grids makes possible the wheeling of power on a continental and even intercontinental basis. Customers have far wider choices than ever envisioned before.

The globalization of business. Though utilities are largely local, they nonetheless have felt the impact of the globalization of many industries. As an example, from World War II until the mid-1970s, the US was in a growth economy. Then with unit volumes plateauing or declining, companies looked to world markets to fill the gap. Seeking savings to compete in global markets, American companies are now demanding lower energy costs and look to regulators to allow greater flexibility and supply alternatives. At the same time, manufacturers in the export-driven economies of other parts of the world have sought the lowest possible energy costs. Global companies can shift production to places where costs of production (including energy) are lowest. In a sense, utilities now not only face local but also worldwide competitive pressures.

The pressure on the electricity industry will force consolidations, divestitures, new types of regulation, changes in operational processes, and the internationalization of the market. When the aftershocks of this restructuring are over, regional differences will fade away, and the cost of energy will slide throughout all sectors of the electricity market.

Amid the Uncertainty, Utilities Are Making Only Minor Changes

Are utility executives responding strongly enough to these conditions? We think not. In October 1993 (one year after the passage of the US's national Energy Policy Act), CSC Index surveyed 32 American electric and gas utility executives. Some 65 percent said large structural change was advancing on the industry. They saw regulators moving to dismantle the regulatory model to favor competition. Few believed that pricing would continue to be guided by the traditional rate-of-return basis. Having already lost customers to cogeneration, executives said commercial and industrial customers would soon be able to select their generating company. They saw widespread competition just around the corner with significant structural change, disaggregation, and consolidation to follow.

Despite these dramatic expectations, management's most common strategy was reducing costs gradually. Even the most aggressive utilities had targeted cost reductions of a mere 10-15 percent of their non-fuel costs. Few were taking measures to dramatically improve their core business operations.

The study showed that utility executives, heavily invested in the current industry structure, were reluctant to make significant changes. With customer choice and competition looming, we believe that this incrementalist strategy has become risky. The strategic and operational changes utilities must make are so substantial that they must begin making them now.

While a number of countries have moved beyond the American model into the competitive framework, others still retain the integrated, monopolistic structure common in the US. We can only hypothesize whether integrated utilities outside the US favor the same risky strategy as their brethren in the US. However, we believe that many of the same attitudes prevail.

The New Strategic Planning Model

So how should utilities guide themselves amid all the market and regulatory uncertainty? We argue that today's planning methods must be a radical departure from the past. The reason is that prior utility business strategies have been driven by such factors as regulation, economic changes, new technology, and load-growth projections. In an era of customer choice, these factors are grossly insufficient. A new planning model is needed, one that puts the customer at the center.

CSC Index developed a new model for business and operational strategy after a three-year study in the early 1990s of 50 premier companies. The study assessed how companies attained and maintained market leadership. Many of them had gone through the same regulatory-driven metamorphosis that utilities are facing.

A key finding was that the strategies of market leaders were not largely driven by the conventional elements of business strategy—the actions of competitors within an industry, the actions of regulators, what customers were asking for today, and so on. Instead, market leaders in industry after industry focused first and foremost on providing extraordinary value to their customers—in many cases, value that their customers weren't aware they could get. They then delivered this value in three primary ways:

1. through rock-bottom prices and the highest levels of convenience, a strategy we refer to as "operational excellence." The operationally excellent companies (organizations such as Wal-Mart and Dell Computer) relentlessly minimize overhead, pare intermediate production steps, reduce transaction costs, and limit functional and organizational boundaries.

2. by addressing a much broader set of customer needs for a select group of customers. This is a strategy we call "customer intimacy." Customer intimacy entails narrowly targeting customer groups and matching products and services to meet exactly the demands of those niches. Leaders (such as the USAA insurance company) are flexible enough to respond immediately to almost any customer need. They invest in satisfying their customers and in return achieve high levels of loyalty.

3. by developing products and services that addressed untapped (and often unrealized) customer needs. This strategy, called "product leadership," is employed by companies like Microsoft, Sony, and Johnson & Johnson. They develop a continuous stream of state-of-the-art products and services. Creativity is the byword of this value discipline. These firms pursue innovation, seeking new ideas both inside and outside the company. They run at full speed to commercialize their concepts and move on to the next new product or service. They prefer to make their own products obsolete, rather than let competitors do it.

It is important to note that the 50 market leaders were not good at all three of these attributes, which we call "value disciplines." In fact, typically they were good at only one or, at most, two. The reason is that a company that excels at operational excellence is far different in business processes, corporate culture, incentive and other management systems, and information systems than a product leader or customer-intimate company.

In other words, market leaders excel at a single value discipline. They decide on which of the three they want to compete. Then they build their processes, culture, jobs and reward systems, and information systems accordingly. Knowing that customer value is a perpetually moving target, market leaders increase the value they provide every year.

Because of their history as regulated monopolies, utilities have not had to focus themselves this way, beyond ensuring that the utility could meet the collective needs of present and future power users in their protected territories. Now many utilities assume that they can realize higher prices by doing everything well. As the industry restructures and customers have choice, utilities will have to focus themselves to deliver superior value to customers, be they commercial, industrial, or residential.

The New Focus of Utilities
Our notion of focus is one of concentrating a utility's resources on the key business processes that deliver one of the three sets of customer value: operational excellence, customer intimacy, or product leadership. After analyzing the inherent value an electric utility provides its customers, we found there to be at least six major components of the business, each of which requires focus if a utility is to be excellent. They are: power generation, electric transmission, electric distribution, information and information-based products and services, electricity markets, and energy management services.

Operationally excellent utilities will concentrate on power generation, transmission, and distribution. They must be low-cost, capital efficient, and financially sound producers, as airline deregulation demonstrates. Southwest Airlines thrives not only because of its lower labor costs, but also because it keeps its planes in the air more hours of the day than its competitors. If utilization rates on plants and systems are uncompetitive, the deregulated market will quickly signal the need for closures.

Like the telecommunications business, the utility industry has had little historic or regulatory incentive to use capital efficiently. The more capital invested, the higher the utilities' rates and revenues are. Normally, it takes many years to unravel the accumulated capital decisions that determine the typical utility's rates. Deregulation will accelerate this process, leaving little margin for error. The components of the industry will largely operate independently as follows:

- power generation will deregulate, consolidate dramatically and be separated from the rest of the business. With an increasingly large share of new capacity in the unregulated sector, prices will fall, forcing utilities to consolidate. A commodity business largely independent of local conditions, power generation still retains potential economies of scale for companies that want to design, engineer, and run plants. Utilities will form consortia to focus on the generating end of the business. New competitors will include construction companies, power systems manufacturers, and petrochemical companies. Companies focusing on generation must be operationally excellent, low-cost providers, with assured supply availability.

- electric transmission will consolidate into regional, national and transnational groups, with parts of this sector remaining a natural monopoly. Transmission groups will secure power to provide trouble-free access to the grid and flawless transmission. This sector will remain regulated where there is insufficient competition between transmission groups.

- distribution companies (which may be either privately or government owned) will form this sector of the industry. They will offer hassle-free connection, maintenance and service, and reliable power at the lowest possible cost. Down the road, fuel cells and home generators could minimize distribution. Other businesses may be combined with a distribution company to create a home services company providing both before-the-meter and after-the-meter services. While the distribution business will require operational excellence, these other businesses will have to excel in product leadership and customer intimacy as described below.

Beyond-the-Meter Services: A New Arena

To flourish, some utilities will embark on customer-intimacy or product-leadership strategies. By doing so, they will address more of their customers' needs or create entirely new needs, which they will then uniquely fill. As a result, they will offer what we call beyond-the-meter services. Some examples:

Electricity markets. Utilities, investment houses, and a variety of other companies will position themselves in the traditional financial markets arena as traders and brokers. Already, in the US, companies such as investment powerhouse Morgan Stanley Group and utility pioneer Louisville (Ky.) Gas & Electric are applying for broker licenses. If utilities want to compete effectively against those who have brokered commodities for years, they must rapidly develop their skills as risk managers who can deliver hedges, options, and other futures.

Energy management services. Some utilities will parlay their expertise in managing energy into consulting services. For commercial and industrial customers, they will tailor strategies and process improvements to reduce energy costs. Success in this business demands deep knowledge of customer segments and individual customers. Already some companies are seizing the opportunity to develop underutilized assets such as the right-of-ways they hold across private properties. Utilities will form home services companies to package and market these assets to other businesses, such as phone, water, cable, and security alarm companies.

Information-based services. The information-based tools and skills a utility uses to run its business will be marketable in the new environment. Energy monitoring technology and brokerage tools are examples. Electronic meters will replace the mechanical versions. Eventually, fiber wires will be connected to homes instead of copper, letting utilities monitor energy-consuming appliances and perform sophisticated pricing mechanisms such as real-time pricing.

With deregulation and technology changes, services like the above will provide new opportunities for utilities. However, these businesses require very different management skills and corporate culture than those of a utility. Utilities will have to operate these businesses as independent units within their holding companies.

In the US, we believe, as many as 90 percent of the 200-plus investor-owned, integrated utilities will be broken up into one or more of these six businesses. Some survivors (like American Airlines in the airline business) will be national, while others will be regional. At the end of the shake-out, we predict, about half of the investor-owned utilities will remain.

Conversely, in some countries the single supplier could be replaced by numerous companies that focus on those aspects of the business in which they have the greatest expertise.

Reengineering for Customer Value

Once a utility has chosen the "value discipline" on which to compete, the next step is to rethink the core business processes in that value discipline. Given the magnitude of restructuring facing the industry, we believe that reengineering—the fundamental redesign of work—is required for dramatic improvements in operating performance.

Both our consulting experience and research studies in reengineering show the need for targeting dramatic improvements. A recent research study CSC Index conducted with 344 North American companies (including 25 utilities) found that their reengineering goals were usually too modest. For instance, the utility companies were aiming for an average 26 percent reduction in costs and 54 percent decrease in "cycle time," i.e., the time it takes to fill an order, respond to a customer, and so on. While laudable, these goals are actually not aggressive enough. The research found those who get big results set big goals at the outset, and much more often attain those goals than those who set low goals.

In reengineering, a big challenge for utilities is breaking from the traditional engineering mind-set of rigorous analysis and precision. The key to tackling reengineering or any other major change initiative is setting the aggressive goals necessary for tomorrow's competitive world.

Other Key Ideas in Reengineering

There are very few core processes in a utility, or any other company for that matter. At best, there are about six core processes, including order fulfillment, customer acquisition and retention, and energy delivery. If an analysis of the business produces 20 or even 100 different business processes, management runs the risk of scoping the pieces too narrowly. Changing narrowly defined processes yields a much smaller benefit than changing a broad process crossing functional and departmental boundaries.

Business reengineering doesn't end with process redesign. We prefer the term business reengineering because it connotes the redesign of all aspects of the business, not just process work steps. Although analyzing a process is an important step in uncovering the truths about how things really operate, the breakthroughs in performance may not come from simply streamlining the work. Reengineering requires changes in four other aspects of what we call a "business system": jobs and organizational structure; management systems; values, beliefs, and behaviors; and information systems.

For example, a reengineered customer-service process will organize work into caseworkers or case teams that can handle most of any one customer's needs. The new jobs, however, require more than new job descriptions. People must be trained to take on a much wider set of tasks and to work in teams. They must have information technology that enables them to see the customer's total relationship with the utility, as well as technology that facilitates teamwork. And they must have new measurement systems that gauge and reward how well they took care of customers, rather than how they performed some narrow task in the past.

A reengineered utility will be organized very differently from the vast majority of organizations today. The business of the utility, the customers it serves and the business processes—not the functions—will define the organizing principles of the company. The reengineered utility will be flatter and leaner. It will deploy teams aggressively. More important, it will demand new leadership styles.

We recently worked with one utility that has redesigned all transmission and distribution construction from five management layers to just two. Work is performed by resource teams or pools of multi-skilled workers previously deployed functionally, i.e., in customer-service planning, survey, right-to-way, bluestake, engineering, etc. For each construction job, the resource team now creates "virtual" project teams comprising only the necessary resources. All teams are self-managed, which means that the group leader is selected by team, not by senior management.

Different customer segments may require different business processes, particularly after the customer-value proposition is reevaluated. Because utilities have customer groups with very different needs (notably large industrial and residential), applying the "value disciplines" may require a different approach to each customer segment.

In addition to those processes close to the customer, processes in the plants present great reengineering opportunities. Utilities, however, are often reluctant to radically change how they run the plants. They usually focus on the distribution business. While this will yield benefits, they may not achieve the cost improvements from reengineering fossil or nuclear operations. We can point to successful reengineering projects that transformed plant operations, yielding dramatically lower costs, high quality and, in the case of a nuclear plant, improved safety. The redesigns have eliminated multiple handoffs among operations, engineering, maintenance, and a variety of support groups. They call for production teams with a cross section of skills and responsibilities.

The Skills Required for a New Utility

The reengineered utility of the future will demand a culture change among employees and management alike. With a different organization structure, utilities will adopt a new mind-set: "It's not my job" will not wash at any level of the organization. An adaptable, "learning organization" will flourish—receptive to change, willing to take risks, cost-conscious, and driven by market forces and transactions. A sense of urgency to win and re-win customers will prevail. Underpinned by a knowledge of what it takes to succeed, a clear vision, and capacity to develop new capabilities, management will adopt a style of mobilize and enable. Empowered by management, new processes, and technologies, workers will be able to satisfy the much more demanding utility customers of the future.

We see three major sets of skills for the utility of the future:

1. leadership skills

2. customer skills

3. strategic thinking skills.

Leadership Skills

The most difficult task will be shifting from traditional "command and control" management styles to leadership behaviors that allow employees to function more productively. When a company moves to a flatter structure, decisions will be pushed down the organization. While employees become more adept and productive at working in teams, as one example, they will expect little supervision in the traditional sense.

So what skills must senior management possess to lead utilities out of their regulated, static past and into the deregulated, dynamic future? We see at least four major types:

Setting and sustaining a compelling direction. Using strategic frameworks like the one mentioned earlier in this article, leaders must be able to create and communicate a clear picture of how the marketplace is evolving and how the company plans to pursue its opportunities. They must show the organization's various "stakeholders"—shareholders, key executives, unions, and others—what's in it for them. Leaders then must drive, not delegate, the change process. By the way, building effective partnerships with union leaders will be a key task for utility leaders if they are to successfully implement reengineering. In fact, our experience is that labor leaders must become part of the reengineering team.

Aligning people. This involves resolving conflicts at the top and building coalitions among people who for years have been defending their turf.

Motivating and inspiring. Key tasks include expressing consistent direction, delegating critical outcomes to demonstrate trust, showing courage in making hard decisions, and asking questions.

Stabilizing and supporting. With so much change going on in their organizations, utility leaders will have to demonstrate their resolve in moving away from old business processes to new ones. They will have to reinforce the use of new processes, make fast fixes to troublesome areas and stay the course.

Examining the leadership skills of the organization needs to happen early in a major change program. The behavior—not the words—of utility leaders sets the style for middle management on down. To lead their organizations through wrenching change, senior management must first change their own behavior to get the rest to follow.

Customer Skills

First and foremost, utilities must develop the ability to profitably segment customer groups and market to both specific consumers and groups. Once deregulation comes, power suppliers will begin offering unlimited ways of creating and marketing products. Pricing, packaging, and promotional options will proliferate. Electric utilities can make money by selling electricity in a multitude of packages that allow customers to trade off risks, benefits, and price with the supplier.

Selling to large target customers will require an agility at deal-making to which utilities are unaccustomed. Crafting a highly specialized package to meet General Motors' worldwide energy needs will demand sophistication, planning, and customer intimacy. The model for this will be engineering companies such as Bechtel. Another critical dimension of "deal-making" is selling to the masses—packaging concepts and products to meet the needs of large blocks of customers. Just as in the telecommunications industry, utilities will rely on importing expertise from the best consumer goods marketing companies.

Strategic Thinking Skills
Throughout the organization, employees and management must operate with a new level of business literacy and see their work through the lens of competition. They will have to ask, how do we deliver value to customers and increase that value year after year? Employees will have to think in terms of process and business outcome, not function.

Acquiring competence in these three areas requires training existing employees and hiring from outside. Relying strictly on internal training and development will limit utilities' ability to make the transition fast enough. We contend that utilities cannot afford the time to rely solely on internal development. The rationale for looking outside the industry is based on our view that utilities have largely been insular and, understandably, due to the dynamics of the industry. Injecting new thinking styles and leadership behaviors from more competitive businesses will help make the cultural shift to a restructured industry. Utilities that fail to look outside the world they live in today will miss a critical opportunity.

The Call for Change
Following the pattern set by other deregulating industries, the playing field in the utility industry and the rules of the game are undergoing radical change. With the bankruptcies, encroachment from outside the industry, mergers and acquisitions, the winners and losers are already emerging. The coming competitive market will accelerate consolidation and reaggregation.

Who will survive? We believe only one out of every two utilities. A handful of utilities, no longer bounded by local lines, will offer geographic reach on a national or international scale. Others will become profitable niche players concentrating on different parts of the business, some segments of which may not even exist today.

Recognizing they don't have enough scale to compete, others will cut costs to sell out at an attractive price. A high-performing small company can be the building block for a larger organization. A poorly run company will be bought cheaply, leaving shareholders shortchanged.

What kind of utility will continue to exist? The survivors will lay out a vision of how to function in the world of free-market energy. In doing so, they will deeply examine their value to consumers. They will stay ahead of the regulators by anticipating new demands and meeting the needs of their leading-edge customers.

Recognizing that new market leadership may come just as easily from outside the industry as within, leaders will come to grips with focus. They will build organizations that excel at one of the three value disciplines. Those in the business of electric generation, transmission, and distribution will have to become operationally excellent—providing low-cost, hassle-free service. Those venturing into beyond-the-meter services will have to excel in product leadership and customer intimacy.

To take control of the future, utilities must begin charting their futures and making significant operational changes today. They must not wait for deregulation to play itself out, competition to heat up, or customers to revolt.

Chapter 19

Financial Strategy in an Increasingly Competitive Marketplace

James T. Doudiet

The movement to competition changes the foundation principle on which the financial structure and strategy of the electric utility industry is built. The principle is that in a regulated monopoly the product is priced to recover its cost, including the financial cost. Because in a competitive market the product's price is not related to its cost, the recovery of the financial cost is not assured. That one change alters everything else.

Throughout the world the electric utility business is changing. After many decades of relative structural stability, the industry in the 1990s is rapidly moving toward significant changes in ownership driven by the concept of competition. Where utilities have previously been government owned, privatization is the order of the day. Where investor owned, competition will require the attraction of new types of investors with an appetite for different types of financial risk than current owners. Yet there is no model to follow or experience to show how to combine the concepts of electric operations with competition.

That electric operations and competition are considered compatible is interesting. We will explore the financial significance of the changes occurring in the electric utility industry and suggest strategies that will be appropriate for electric companies to pursue in a competitive market.

The Financial Significance of the Monopoly
The electric utility that has operated with a territorial franchise has enjoyed an assured capital-market access. As we will see, this access has had a fundamental influence on the financial structure and management habits that have evolved. Therefore, we should expect the decline of the monopoly to bring about a major change in financial structure and management habits.

There is nothing more secure for an investor than lending to or owning the equity of a monopolist where that monopoly also serves a critically important or essential product and provides service within a defined market or geographical area. This describes the circumstances of investors (and public owners) in the electric utility industry for the last 60 years or more. Investors gained confidence that whatever else happened, the utility would recover enough of its costs from its secure customer base to remain financially viable. Because of this, utilities had very little difficulty in raising capital and certain habits of financial management grew up in the industry. Some of the more significant habits are:

1) reliance on external sources of capital rather than internal cash generation

2) use of a large proportion of debt in the capital structure

3) payout of a large proportion of earnings in cash as dividends even when such cash was not available from operations

4) use of deferred accounting to delay recognition of expenses to the time of recovery from customers.

5) No requirement for generation of cash by operations

6) increasing the asset base to provide financial growth, creating a strong tendency toward the ownership of assets

7) accepting long-term, fixed-price contracts for all sorts of goods and services as a means of reducing supply risk

8) valuing external financial management skills (e.g., capital raising and investor relations) over internal skills (e.g., budgeting, pricing strategy, cost accounting, and cash management)

By combining these habits of financial management we can begin to see a picture of the financial strategy of electric utilities in a monopoly environment. In a monopoly environment, the financial goal is to increase the wealth of the common shareholders by earning a market return on an increasing book value base. This is done by using debt leverage and cost recovery to support added investment in the asset base and earning a return greater that the amount paid out in dividends. Market share (at 100 percent) is assured by the monopoly franchise. This is a viable financial growth strategy because the monopoly provides assured capital access. With the product (kilowatt hours) priced to recover the cost, the investor is confident his return will be earned and he is eager to invest ever greater amounts of capital.

Considering cash flow as part of the financial strategy is unnecessary because of excellent capital access. It is therefore appropriate for high dividends to take most of the cash net income. Similarly, depreciation is spread over a very long time to keep rates to customers low; and plant is kept running for a very long time. These practices keep the earning asset base high. Investment in new plant is not determined on a cash payback basis. Regulatory clauses are used to pass through certain costs, such as fuel. The accounting of many costs is bundled together because only the total cost of service counts. The financial size of inventories and the relationship between receivables and payables are not tightly managed. There is no strategy for the use of excess cash. These habits are all a result of easy capital access.

Financial Strategies and Structures in a Competitive Framework

The movement to competition changes the foundation principle on which the financial structure and strategy of the electric industry is built. What is that principle? In a regulated monopoly the product is priced to recover its cost, including the financial cost. In a competitive market the product's price is not related to its cost. Therefore, the recovery of the financial cost is not assured. That one change alters everything else.

The following sections will present thoughts on how financial and other supporting strategies must change in the electric industry as competition takes hold. Note that the primary objective of financial growth will not change, but the means to provide that growth will change. Also note that this chapter, in addressing strategies and structure, does not deal deeply with the financial consequences of failure to manage well the transition from monopoly to competition for electric companies. There is the potential for the consequences for many electric operations to be severe.

Having described the financial management strategies for a monopolistic electric franchise, we will now turn to how those strategies should change under a competitive framework and seek the strategy for financial growth.

If, under competition, product price is not related to cost, then recovery of any cost including financial cost is not a part of the pricing formula. Therefore, capital recovery is not assured and the investor has less confidence in financial returns. Furthermore, electricity is a commodity. We can study other industries to see how investors react to the attractiveness of competitive commodity businesses.

The high debt levels of the monopoly must be replaced with equity because without assured cost recovery lenders will be less willing to invest and because debt service is a fixed cost. A competitive commodity business tries to diminish all fixed costs. With poorer capital access, cash flow must become the central theme of the financial strategy. As a guiding principle for dividend policy, for example, this means that although the competitive electric company will have a greater percentage of common equity, the total amount of cash it is willing to devote to paying financial costs (including dividends) should decline. Cash will be strategically more valuable for other uses than to pay out in dividends.

Similarly, depreciation periods will be shortened so investments in plant can be written off more quickly. Companies will replace old facilities with new, lower cost technologies as quickly as they can. New investments will be determined on a cash payback basis with appropriate recognition of contribution of an operation to fixed or variable costs. Once costs have been diminished, substituting variable costs for fixed costs will take on strategic importance. Similarly, long term, fixed price contracts will be replaced with a series of short term contracts to try to make fixed costs mimic variable costs as much as possible. From these actions will come the need for new cost accounting systems so costs can be unbundled and matched with pricing strategies.

The financial management skills that will be highly valued will tend to be internal (e.g., budgeting, pricing strategy, cost accounting and cash management) and the external skills (e.g., capital raising and investor relations), while still important, will diminish in value.

What is done with "excess" cash? The competitive electric company will invest cash to lower costs and either increase profits or position itself to reduce its prices and capture greater market share.

In providing less capital market access competition will significantly alter financial strategy. Electric companies must increasingly look like competitive, commodity businesses in their financial structure and activities. Since this transition is likely to create financial stress for most electric operations, we can make the following list of financial concepts for a financially stressed company with less capital access selling a commodity product in a competitive market:

1) Costs must be reduced.

2) Cash flow is important, but one must have a strategy to use it wisely.

3) Fixed costs are not desirable.

4) Long-term commitments should be avoided.

Traditionally both the electric company and its suppliers have taken advantage of the security and stability afforded by the monopoly. In exploring financial strategies we recognize the capital markets as being made up of suppliers of financial goods and services. Utilities that have easy access to capital have developed long-term relationships with their suppliers of capital. The types of common stockholders attracted to electric utilities are an example of this. Suppliers of goods and services, such as fuel and capital equipment, have also benefited from a long-term relationship with electric companies. As electric companies enter the competitive era and capital access is diminished, their relationship with all of their suppliers will change because of the need to spread the increased business risk upstream. It will be recognized that supplier relationships will need to be rethought as part of a new financial strategy. New types of suppliers may be needed.

An example of changes in supplier relationships is just-in-time inventory. To make the supplier finance inventory, companies in competitive industries increasingly require delivery schedules more in tune with usage than in the past. There are also other techniques that can be developed that require greater cooperation between suppliers and users of goods and services. With cost and cash flow becoming major issues for the competitive electric company it is probable that the inflexibility of long-term, fixed-price contracts will be unattractive. Shorter-term contracts will reduce the risk of product prices being different than competitors' prices. The choice electric companies will have in dealing with suppliers ranges from increasing cooperative ventures with suppliers to increasing pressure on them by going to competitive sourcing (i.e., bidding) techniques. Whichever approach is taken, it is certain a complete strategic rethinking of supplier relationships will become a part of financial strategy in the future.

For the foreseeable future, regulation will continue to play a central role in the financial strategy of the electric utility. The objective should be to develop regulatory and legislative initiatives to influence regulatory changes that will maximize the financial benefits to the utility during the transition to competition. Regulation of generating assets will likely be replaced by market pricing. Stranded investment will be recovered only as the market pricing allows. Exit fees will be generally unworkable because the most mobile customers will have multiple alternative service options. Transmission will become a common carrier and as such will be strictly price regulated with no particular strategic advantage for the owner. Regulation of the distribution function will evolve into price-cap or performance- based regulation. These will give the utility incentives to manage costs carefully.

The regulatory changes needed by most utilities during the transition will be those that will allow utilities pricing flexibility to retain key customers, the ability to accelerate depreciation to recover their investments in certain assets before they become stranded and the option to retain at least some of the economic benefits of cost reduction actions. Since under competition the customers' market power will grow, regulation in the long run is likely to become increasingly irrelevant to the economic result companies achieve even though regulation will continue and may even increase in complexity and intrusiveness.

The replacement of earning a return on a growing asset base as a strategy for growth in shareholder value with other sources of earnings will be a key element of financial success in an increasingly competitive marketplace. To accomplish this in a competitive, commodity business the focus is on profit margin and market share. Since neither is directly related to return on assets, which is the key financial concept of the regulated monopoly, a whole new financial business culture will evolve needing new measures of financial success and new accounting concepts.

Cost reduction alone will not be the key to increasing shareholder value. Actions to increase revenues, although increasing the risk of the enterprise for shareholders, must take the place of monopoly services. While getting the most out of the core business, management must develop supplemental non-regulated income streams. As cash flow grows in volume and value, internal competition should increase between investments in cost reduction opportunities and investments in non-regulated ventures.

Because of increased financial risk and less cash dividends the traditional conservative investors will be replaced by investors with a higher risk tolerance who seek market appreciation. Because such investors may not at first consider utilities rewarding investments, it is probable that during the transition to competition the market value of some utilities will be driven to low levels. It will take time for a new set of financial parameters, objectives, and results to be understood and appreciated by investors and financial analysts.

Study after study of financial strategy in commodity businesses reveals that attention to an individual customer's wants and needs is the only way to differentiate a commodity product from that of its competitors. Historically, in the electric utility business, except for large industrial or wholesale loads, customers have been viewed in the aggregate as a result of lack of customer choice. The exclusive franchise has given the utility very little incentive to solve customers' electricity problems on the customers' terms. Services being priced on a bundled basis also prevent utilities from being specifically paid for unique services.

Customers don't want to buy anything from a monopoly. Choice of supplier implies lowest price and best service. Utilities themselves want multiple suppliers and are skilled at driving prices, particularly fuel prices, down by creating competition for their service among suppliers. Market based pricing, retail wheeling, competitive sourcing, and direct access all describe the recent move to electric competition that the largest customers view as essential to reducing their costs and improving their service. This customer receptivity to electric supplier choice will give low-cost, service-oriented utilities the opportunity to expand market share, which will become a key financial growth strategy.

New entities are emerging to facilitate these new business relationships with electric customers. Marketers, who will take future delivery positions of electricity, and brokers, who put buyers together with sellers without taking positions themselves, will play an important role in the future electric industry. A key strategy for electric companies will be to learn to use such services extensively, even though this will require a change in thinking. Having been deregulated earlier in the United States, the natural gas industry will serve as a model. Therefore, combination electric and gas companies should have a head start over straight electric companies.

Large energy users will continue to push hard for changes in the law at the national and local levels. Acceptance will take the form of an S-shaped curve, with first a few states making key changes, then many states will follow and finally the few stragglers will comply. "Locking in," "acquiring," or "owning" the customer will be critically important for the utility distribution company. We can see early attempts at this with the discounts given to large energy users in exchange for signing exclusive, multi-year contracts. Ignorance of the growing competitiveness of the electric market will keep many customers immobile for awhile, but eventually all customers will become aware of the opportunities to improve electric price and service. Form and length of customer contracts will help determine how long this transition takes. Other customer retention strategies that will be tried are to create brand loyalty, to assure the customer the best price and to price electricity based on either the cost of other goods or an index. It will be essential to survey customer satisfaction and then respond to the findings because research on customer attitudes indicates that 50 percent of customers would switch electric suppliers for as little as a five percent reduction in price. At the moment customers have little loyalty to their monopoly supplier.

In the future the price of electricity will reflect the customer's willingness to pay and not the cost of the product. Therefore, the concept of charging a price based on the cost of service will no longer be relevant. Since most electric utility accounting has been based on recording the cost of service to support the regulatory pricing process, this will require a profound change in thinking about accounting and other forms of data gathering. In fact, many utility information systems will have to be revised to support the new pricing needs under competition.

One critical pricing concept that this change threatens is deferred accounting. Many expenses have been incurred by electric utilities with the idea that regulators will allow them to be charged in future rates. Perhaps they will, but only if the market will allow such price levels. This is such a different concept that a new strategy is required to deal with deferred accounting. Managements and regulators must recognize now that their most important asset is the time left in transition from monopoly to full competition. The time remaining must be used to charge the currently price-insensitive customers enough to amortize the deferred assets.

Current accounting systems are also deficient in that they have not been designed to record unbundled costs or spread overhead. An accurate knowledge of costs will enable the electric company to price remaining monopoly services for full recovery and to customize prices to fit customer needs. Profitable pricing strategies must be developed. Splitting the company into business segments should ensure knowledge of full cost of activities and reveal hidden costs. Management must track the business segments profitability now as if the market was already deregulated.

Financial strategy will also require an assessment of the assets, systems, and activities controlled by the company through ownership. Monopolies have exercised control by owning everything they can. This tendency to vertical integration was reinforced by the financial growth strategy of earning asset growth. Electric resource management has focused on optimizing capital substitution decisions to provide the highest level of reliability. In the competitive future, more will be expected of the assets of the business. If operating an asset or performing a function does not in a short time increase revenue, reduce costs, or satisfy a customer, it must be sold, out-sourced, or eliminated. Competition will force utilities to reduce reserve margins, reduce costs, and increase availability.

Separation of the natural business functions will dictate some future resource management issues. Traditional approaches to planning, staffing, and supplier relationships will have to be redesigned. Making long-term decisions under uncertainty will be increasingly difficult. Finding and eliminating noneconomic activity and capacity will be a must. Similarly, identifying and enhancing high value assets will be critically important in managing toward a low-cost, high-reliability system.

Traditional utility functional organization structures with significant autonomy are evolving into strategic business units, but they still represent vertically-integrated organizations. The move to competition will require a transition to a more "enterprise" type unit structure that will be organized around customer needs, process teams, and internal service centers. This will shift operational focus to view the organization in terms of business processes that are wrapped around customer needs not just customers. The organization must devote more resources to performing activities most vital to its competitiveness.

Increased use of technology will provide critical capabilities. Support must be gained for investment in technology-based services. This will allow for increased outsourcing of functions previously considered necessary to manage in-house as a part of the creation of a horizontal structure. Such a structure should encourage and support the flow of information and responsibilities for delivering results and being responsive to the customer on the lowest possible cost basis. These capabilities will be essential when defending a current customer base or when seeking to increase market share at the expense of some less able electric supplier.

The only unifying force that can institute the changes necessary to transform a regulated monopoly into competitive organization is management.

In the long run, it is the human side of the organization that will determine the success or failure of the transition to competition. Current operating systems, cost levels, regulatory forms, customer relationships, contracts, and stranded costs will not have as much to do with the result as vision, understanding, willingness to champion change, and that most rare commodity, accountability.

An early and thorough understanding by the whole management team of the many changes described above, which together make up a new financial strategy, will be necessary to build a successful competitive electric company.

Chapter 20

Accessing the US Bond Markets

Rosemary Avellis Abrams

We are approaching an era of market globalization that has been made evident by United States (US) companies investing abroad and many foreign companies looking to the US markets. Thus far, a number of overseas companies have tapped the US marketplace by successfully selling equities and fixed income securities. Over the next several years, we will see a great number of companies become private entities. This investment revolution can be exciting for investors seeking to widen their portfolios and for the new companies being given the opportunity to raise funds worldwide. However, in most cases companies that have been owned by their governments have not had the guidance or experience to raise funds in the public marketplace. This chapter takes a step-by-step look at what a company needs to know when a decision has been made to privatize and sell securities to the public sector.

A company that has become public has several ways it can raise funds. Initially, management will sell common stock of the company. Once an equity base has been set, the company can then raise funds through the sale of additional equity or debt securities. An initial stock offering price would apply to a sale of debt securities. Somewhat similar to the pricing of a common equity issue, which is determined by various financial ratios, the pricing of debt securities is dependent upon the financial strength of the company. Newly privatized companies seeking to raise funds through the sale of fixed income instruments should seek a credit rating for those issues.

The Purpose of a Credit Rating
Foreign companies considering privatization should have a good understanding of the United States credit markets and the importance of credit ratings for the sale of corporate bonds. A credit rating will establish a meaningful pricing level and an appropriate coupon for those securities. In addition, in attaining a credit rating the company will insure the investor buying the securities that there will be ongoing surveillance by the rating agency of the securities sold.

While the rating agency assigns a credit rating, this is not a recommendation to buy or sell the security. The rating agency only assigns the rating, and the investment banker managing the offering of the debt will make the decision as to the price of that security based on the rating.

Prospective issuers should be aware that the ratings of their securities cannot be higher than the sovereign rating of their country. Normally, rating agencies will first study the credit rating of the country to establish the economic and political stability. For instance, if the sovereign rating is considered to be below investment grade, the credit rating of the issuing company would not be awarded an investment grade rating, although its financial measures would appear to be strong. Moreover, credit ratings are reviewed periodically by the rating agencies, and changed upward or downward depending on the ongoing developments of the company. Ratings assigned to sovereign governments, as of October 1994, are shown in Table 20-1.

Opening the Dialogue

The entity desiring to meet with a rating agency should be prepared to submit financial statements of the parent company and its subsidiaries. An investment banker may be of assistance in preparing a package of relevant information to be presented to the rating agency and in contacting the rating agency on behalf of the company. The banker will inform the rating agency as to the purpose of the meeting and the desire of the issuer to establish a credit rating. A credit rating is very important if the company plans to sell securities to the investment community. Investors interested in purchasing a debt security will always look at the credit rating of the issue and/or the company. This facilitates the investment decision. Furthermore, the investment banker will be able to price the issue and the coupon depending on the rating of the particular issue.

Meeting with the Rating Agency

The investment banker will contact the rating agency and schedule a meeting date convenient for both parties. Management should prepare an information booklet, and, if possible, send it to the agency a few days before the scheduled meeting. A meeting between the company and the rating agency could last several hours, depending on the complexity of the issues or the company. In its presentation, management should identify the purpose of the rating, and what type of security it plans to bring to the marketplace. The booklet should contain information on:

- management's objectives for the corporation

- the past, present, and future operating performance of the company

Table 20-1. Sovereign Ratings as of October 1994

Country	Long-term Rating	Short-term Rating
Austria	AAA	A-1+
France	AAA	A-1+
Germany	AAA	A-1+
Japan	AAA	A-1+
Luxembourg	AAA	A-1+
Netherlands	AAA	A-1+
Norway	AAA	A-1+
Switzerland	AAA	A-1+
United Kingdom	AAA	A-1+
Belgium	AA+	A-1+
Canada	AA+	A-1+
Denmark	AA+	A-1+
Singapore	AA+	A-1+
Sweden	AA+	A-1+
Taiwan	AA+	A-1+
Australia	AA	A-1+
Italy	AA	A-1
Spain	AA	A-1+
Cyprus	AA-	A-1+
Finland	AA-	A-1+
Ireland	AA-	A-1+
Portugal	AA-	A-1+
New Zealand	AA-	A-1+
Korea	A+	A-1+
Hong Kong	A	A-1
Iceland	A	A-1
Malaysia	A	A-1
Malta	A	N.R.
Thailand	A-	A-1
Chile	BBB+	N.R.
Czech Republic	BBB+	N.R.
Israel	BBB+	A-2
China	BBB	A-2
Turkey	BBB	N.R.
Columbia	BBB-	N.R.
Greece	BBB-	A-3
Indonesia	BBB-	N.R.
Hungary	BB+	N.R.
India	BB+	B
Mexico	BB+	N.R.
Venezuela	BB	N.R.
Slovakia	BB-	N.R.
Philippines	BB-	N.R.

N.R. – Not relevant
Source:
Standard & Poor's

- how the company will grow (from acquisitions or internal growth)

- how will acquisitions be financed (with cash on hand, issuance of common equity, or issuance of debt securities, or a combination of all three financing vehicles)

- management must provide the rating agency with information regarding the markets it is in and what its position is versus other companies in its industry.

Other very important documents are the company's financials. Management must make available its historical financial data, which will include the profit and loss statements, cash flow statements, and balance sheet. In addition, management should present financial projections, for two to five years out. By doing this, the rating agency will have a better indication as to the company's financial performance going forward, since a credit rating takes into effect the company's future operating and financial position.

What the Issuer Should Expect

Rating agencies are as bureaucratic as many foreign governments. The rating process could take two to six weeks to determine the applicable support for credit, depending on the complexity of the company. After reviewing the financial data and operating performance, the analyst assigned to perform the company analysis may have a series of unanswered questions. Therefore, it is important that the top management of the company is present at a rating agency meeting so that all pertinent questions and concerns can be discussed in detail. The analyst assigned to formulate a credit rating must then make a presentation to the rating committee, where he/she will discuss in detail why the issuer is seeking a credit rating, explore the company's operations and financial performance, and conclude with a rating recommendation.

In formulating the potential rating of the issue, the analyst must evaluate the business risk and the financial risk of the company. For example, a utility company with a monopoly on its service territory would have a lower business risk than a utility company that has been deregulated and has potential competitors selling similar service in that service territory. The financial risk is measured by the company's profitability, capital structure, cash flow protection, and financial policy. When the analyst has done a thorough analysis of the company's risk factor, the analyst will then organize a committee and set a date convenient to all committee members. At times, the analyst may encounter difficulties in scheduling a date and time convenient to all parties, in which case the rating agency could take as long as six weeks to reach a decision on the credit rating.

The Rating Process has Several Stages

The rating process can be summarized as follows:

1. The company requests a credit rating.

2. The rating agency assigns an analyst or a team of analysts to conduct the research.

3. The rating agency meets with the issuer.

4. The analyst prepares the material to be presented to a rating committee.

5. The rating committee meets and makes a rating decision.

6. The analyst informs the company of the outcome.

7. The company accepts or rejects the decision.

    7a. The rating is accepted by the company.

    7b. The company appeals the rating decision and schedules a second meeting with the rating agency.

    7c. The rating committee schedules a second rating meeting and informs the company as to the outcome of the appeal rating meeting.

8. The rating is made public.

9. The rating agency monitors the company's ongoing performance.

Stage One

Before meeting with management, those in the rating agency who will attend the management meeting hold a pre-meeting meeting, where the parties will discuss the upcoming meeting with the company management and, if they have the presentation material on hand, discuss their concerns associated with the issue or the company in question. Next, the rating agency meets with the management of the company in question.

Stage Two

Soon after the management meeting, the analyst assigned to the company prepares a rating recommendation. A date is set, and the committee meets to vote on the analyst's recommendation. Similar to a management meeting, the rating meeting could last several hours, again depending on the complexity of the issues. When all the questions of the committee members have been answered and all pertinent issues discussed, the committee votes for or against the recommendation. The committee is usually made up of an odd number of people so as not to have a split vote, because the vote is not usually unanimous. The greater number of votes determine what the rating should be.

Stage Three
When a decision has been reached, the analyst will contact the company to deliver the outcome of the rating committee. The company then has the prerogative of accepting the rating recommendation, or if it disagrees with the outcome, the company may appeal the rating. If the company accepts the recommendation, the analyst may then make the credit rating public, via a press release, at the company's request. If on the other hand, the company is disappointed with the rating and wishers to appeal, a new date is set for an appeal meeting.

The Appeal Process
The company normally has a few days (or a week) to appeal the rating to the rating committee, or a higher body at the rating agency. At the appeal meeting, the company is expected to present new information that would convince the rating committee to revisit the credit rating. This new information must have positive financial measures and/or improvements in both operational and financial performance. This could include an increase in equity infusions, better than expected cash flow measures, curtailed expansion projects, or a change in the type of security to be sold (i.e. first mortgage bonds instead of subordinated debentures). Following the appeal meeting, the analyst will schedule a second rating committee meeting shortly thereafter to determine the rating. The appeal meeting is in many instances successful, especially if the company can provide new information that would have a positive impact on the rating. If, on the other hand, there has been no change in the company's financial and operational goals, the issuer should accept the initial rating recommendation.

Ongoing Dialogue
It is very important for the company to be accessible to the rating agency for periodic company visits. On balance, a rating agency will meet with the management of the issuing company at least once a year. In addition, the company must keep the analyst abreast of the company's financial and operational performance and issues that could be detrimental to the rating. The company must keep an open dialogue with the analyst and inform the analyst of any developments be they positive or negative. The issuer must understand that many factors go into determining a credit rating. Although the securities may have an initial acceptance in the marketplace at an attractive price to the company, the price of the securities

may fluctuate depending on the ongoing performance of the company, management's credibility, and its ability to meet financial objectives. Normally, a rating is assigned taking into account the future financial and operational performance of the company over the next two years. However, the rating could be placed on positive or negative watch by the rating agency if unexpected circumstances arise. When a company is placed on a watch list, the rating agency will review the credit and make the necessary changes.

Type of Security

A company may sell an array of fixed income securities, depending on its needs. Here is where the investment banker will be of great assistance to the issuer. The company may sell long- term debt secured by a lien, unsecured, or subordinated to other debt outstanding. Most long-term debt would have a maturity date of more than seven years; while commercial paper would mature in less than one year. The company normally informs the rating agency which type of debt security it plans to bring to market. A commercial paper rating is determined depending on the overall credit rating of the company. Therefore, regardless of whether the company plans to sell long- or short-term debt, management must be prepared to provide the same financial and operational information to the rating agency.

Is One Rating Agency Sufficient?

There are four major rating agencies in the United States, three located in New York City and one in Chicago. The three rating agencies in New York are all in walking proximity from each other. The largest of these agencies is Standard & Poor's, followed by Moody's and Fitch Investors. Duff & Phelps is located in Chicago. It is important to meet with at least two, preferably three, rating agencies, when seeking a credit rating. All of these agencies have an analytical staff with extensive knowledge of industry issues and developments. However, the larger rating agencies tend to be more bureaucratic in the rating process. While it may take the larger agency three to six weeks to reach a rating determination, the smaller agency may reach the same conclusion in a more expeditious fashion. The sale process of the issue is facilitated when the company has a credit rating from more than one agency, since the buyer of the security will place more credibility on the rating if more than one rating agency assigns the same credit rating. In some instances the ratings may differ, in which case the company and the investment banker may discuss those differences with the prospective buyer of the security and the rating agency. The costs for obtaining a credit rating are normally set by the rating agency and in many cases these fees are competitive. However, the cost is minimal compared to the importance of the credit rating in the marketplace.

Financial Information Required

As mentioned previously, it is very important to supply the rating agency with as much financial information as possible. The issuer of the securities should keep in mind that historical financial data is as important as projected financial data. While a historical financial statement gives a good indication as to where the company has been and what it has done over the years, financial projections give the rating agency an indication of where the company will be in two to five years from the time the rating is assigned. The company should be very open both in its dialogue with the rating agency and about its financial strengths and/or weaknesses. The rating agency must feel comfortable with the data provided and the credibility of management.

Financial information should include a profit and loss statement, a cash flow statement, and a balance sheet. In this article we do not discuss the different accounting practices used by foreign entities. However, a rating agency will make adjustments to the company's accounting data as is deemed necessary in assessing a credit rating.

Financial ratios that are often used to determine a credit rating are:

$$\text{Total debt ratio} = \frac{\text{Long-term debt} + \text{short-term debt}}{\text{Long-term debt} + \text{short-term debt} + \text{shareholder equity}}$$

$$\text{Short-term debt ratio} = \frac{\text{Short-term debt}}{\text{Long-term debt} + \text{short-term debt} + \text{shareholder equity}}$$

$$\text{Pretax interest coverage} = \frac{\text{Income before interest} + \text{income taxes}}{\text{Interest expense}}$$

$$\text{Funds from operations interest coverage} = \frac{\text{Net income} + \text{depreciation} + \text{deferred taxes} + \text{other adjustments}}{\text{Interest expense}}$$

$$\text{Net cash flow interest coverage} = \frac{\text{Net income} + \text{depreciation} + \text{deferred taxes} + \text{other adjustments} - \text{dividends paid}}{\text{Interest expense}}$$

$$\text{Cash flow to total debt} = \frac{\text{Net income} + \text{depreciation} + \text{deferred taxes} + \text{other adjustments} - \text{dividends paid}}{\text{Total debt}}$$

$$\text{Dividend payout ratio} = \frac{\text{Total dividends paid}}{\text{Net income}}$$

Internally generated funds as a % of capital expenditures =

$$\frac{\text{Net income + depreciation + deferred taxes + other adjustments - dividends paid}}{\text{Total capital expenditures}}$$

$$\text{Operating income margin} = \frac{\text{Operating income}}{\text{Revenues}}$$

Conclusion

As companies privatize, many decisions must be made as to how, when, and where to raise funds. By understanding the mechanics of the credit markets, a company will be better prepared in accessing the capital markets in the United States and abroad. The credit rating is a very important factor for a company wishing to sell corporate bonds. Therefore, the company should consider obtaining a credit rating when the decision has been made to raise those funds through the public markets.

Chapter 21

Long-term Power Purchases

David H. Spencer

Power purchases from independent generators are a common feature of privatized power systems. Even state-owned systems are negotiating power purchases from private generators.

Every utility is concerned about the effect of generators it does not control on the safety and reliability of its system. State-owned or privatizing utilities are faced with other issues. The seller's demand for adequate returns and financeable terms will be novel to a system that has been financed from the state treasury. If the country has no recent experience of large-scale private-sector enterprise, the buyer may be unfamiliar with the seller's basic business assumptions, such as recovery of investment over time, risk-weighted returns, and capital budgeting.

The standard structure for long-term power purchases from reliable generating units provides the seller a reasonably secure stream of payments to service its financing and reward it for risking its time and capital. In return, the buyer receives a reasonably secure long-term source of power.

Price
The price formula for a long-term purchase of reliable power commonly has two components: a capacity charge and an energy charge. The capacity charge will be paid on the kilowatts reliably available, and the energy charge will be paid on the kilowatt hours actually delivered.

In theory, the capacity charge will cover the seller's fixed costs, amortize its development and construction costs, and cover its financing costs. The energy charge will pay the variable costs of generating the delivered energy. The seller's willingness to deviate from theory will depend on its and the financiers' analysis of the economics of the contract as a whole. For example, if the buyer is willing to commit to minimum purchases at an attractive energy charge, the seller may be willing to forego a capacity charge.

Capacity Charge

A capacity charge formula is typically the capacity of the plant (in kilowatts) reliably available to buyer, times a per-kilowatt factor. The per-kilowatt factor may vary from month-to-month or year-to-year.

Even in low-inflation environments, the capacity charge will be indexed against the exchange rate for a hard currency. If there are identifiable classes of fixed charges that have recognized price indices (for example, labor to perform periodic maintenance), they may be separately indexed.

Capacity may be determined in a number of ways, such as testing under controlled conditions, experience in meeting buyer demand, or sustained deliveries over a test period. Any test must be normalized for environmental factors such as temperature. The choice of test will depend on the type of plant, the type of demand, and the preferences of the parties.

Energy Charge

An energy charge formula is typically the amount of energy in kilowatt-hours delivered in the billing period multiplied by the sum of a number of factors indexed to the seller's principal expected costs. These factors typically include proxies for labor, fuel, transport, consumables, and general inflation. The factors reflecting imported items are also likely to be further indexed to the exchange rate.

If the buyer is satisfied with the economic characteristics of the seller's plant, the buyer will accept a formula reflecting the seller's anticipated costs. However, if the plant has costs different from those common to the buyer's system, such as a natural gas plant in an area supplied by the hydroelectric plants, the buyer may want a formula providing a price similar to what it would pay for competitive power that is either self-generated or purchased. This can be difficult for the seller, as it will have no assurance that its revenues will correlate with its costs. Even if the seller will accept the risk, its financiers generally will not.

If demand on the buyer's system has daily or seasonal peaks, the buyer may offer a premium for deliveries at peak times. Similarly, the buyer may offer incentives to offset seasonal declines in supply, for example, declines in hydropower supply in the dry season.

Payment

Formulas that rely on published indices require that some factors be estimated, with a refund or extra payment when the exact amount is known. The parties will need to agree how often bills will be sent, how soon bills must be paid, whether late payments require interest, who will read the meters and prepare statements, and whether estimated bills are allowed.

Demand

The level of a buyer's commitment to demand power will depend on the nature of its needs, the nature of the seller's plant, and the seller's analysis of whether the buyer's commitment is sufficiently strong to secure financing and recover its investment.

For a base load plant, the buyer may commit to take the entire output of the plant or to make a minimum demand. If the plant must run at a steady, high load to be efficient, the seller is likely to insist on commitment to steady, high demand. Commitments for minimum demand over a period can be complicated by seasonality and by need to avoid inefficient, or impossible, bunching of demand.

A buyer may offer no demand commitment if the plant is designed to meet peak loads or if the buyer expects ample sources of competitive power. A seller may find this acceptable if its plant can efficiently meet varying demand and the buyer offers an attractive capacity charge or other economic terms that assure recovery of its costs. However, most plants have significant startup, shutdown, rampup and rampdown costs, and unpredictable demand requires either substantial fuel storage costs or spot market purchases. Most sellers will consequently want protection against too much variability in demand.

The strength of the buyer's commitment to demand power will affect the price it must pay. Unless the buyer offers either a minimum demand commitment or a substantial capacity charge payable "come hell or high water," the seller must finance the plant with equity. The high return required for equity will require a high price for the power. On the other hand, the seller may be willing to forego a capacity charge if the buyer commits to buy all the output or to make a substantial minimum demand.

In any event, the parties must agree on procedures to coordinate demand and delivery. The seller must periodically advise the buyer of the capacity it has available, and the buyer must be able to communicate demand for the energy it needs. The procedures can usually be arranged quickly between the parties' technical personnel.

If legally possible, the buyer may seek to have the plant dedicated to the contract, so that the plant can only be used to perform the contract. A dedication may assure the buyer that it will not lose the plant's capacity regardless of sale, insolvency, or foreclosure. Even if dedication is not possible, the buyer should restrict transfers of the plant, changes in control, or changes in operator if the identities of the operator and owner are important to it. For the same reasons, the buyer may wish to negotiate a first refusal over sale of the plant.

Capacity and Reliability Damages

The contract for power from a base load will normally have liquidated damages if capacity falls below a minimum. Above the minimum, the buyer is compensated for a reduction in capacity by paying the capacity charge on a smaller number of kilowatts. However, once reliable capacity falls below the level expected in the buyer's generation plan, replacing the capacity entails substantial delay and additional cost.

The damages for reduced or unreliable capacity may also have an element reflecting recovery of overpayment in early years. Although the buyer may not need the capacity in the early years of the contract, it may nevertheless agree to pay a high capacity charge in those early years to ensure that the project is on line when needed. The buyer expects to recoup the overpayment (with interest) through a lower capacity charge in the later years of the contract. If the buyer overpays for capacity in the early years, but the capacity later proves unavailable or unreliable, the buyer should expect to have the overpayment returned as damages.

Specifications

The buyer must supply detailed specifications to assure that the energy will be sagely delivered in the form anticipated. Specifications should cover the basic characteristics of the buyer's system, such as phase, voltage (nominal, maximum, and minimum), and frequency. They should define acceptable operating limits, such as load pickup, stability, voltage flicker, reactive power, availability, and forced outage rates. They should be as detailed as the buyer requires to assure safe and reliable operation.

Much detail can be provided by reference to national, international, or foreign standards. The International Standards Organization, the American National Standards Institute, and the North American Electric Reliability Council, for example, have standards relating to electrical equipment and electrical systems. Even where these are not official national standards, they can be used by reference to establish contractual standards.

The buyer should also prepare a manual of standards for equipment connected to its system. This manual should be kept current and distributed to all generators. Any contract should refer to it, and permit it to evolve as the buyer's system evolves.

Most sellers will allow the buyer to set the specifications, as long as they are within reasonable industry standards. A financier will regard this as an operational matter between the buyer and the seller, so long as the financier has an opportunity to rectify problems before the contract is canceled.

The penalty for failure to conform to a specification depends on the specification. If a seller is unable to provide power conforming to the basic characteristics of the buyer's system—such as failure to deliver at the correct phase, voltage, or frequency—the buyer should be permitted to disconnect until the seller can demonstrate an ability to deliver conforming power. On the other hand, a damage provision (perhaps liquidated in accordance with a formula) may be appropriate to compensate buyer for such failings as slow load pickup or excessive forced outages.

A disclaimer of consequential damages is common in commercial contracts. The consequential damages to the buyer and it customers from a system failure are so enormous that this seems appropriate for a power purchase contract. However, either party may wish explicit indemnity against damages or third party claims resulting from the other party's negligent actions.

The specifications for the meters and protective devices, and the standards for maintaining them, are particularly important. Typically these require both parties to be present for inspection, testing, and repairs. The parties may wish to provide for backup meters and may provide elaborate procedures for adjusting erroneous payments resulting from faulty meters.

Construction and Operations

If the buyer is required by law to accept power tendered from any qualifying generator, it will ordinarily demand the right to review the seller's construction and operations to protect itself against poorly built or operated plants. In addition to the usual obligation to construct, operate, and maintain the plant in accordance with prudent utility practice, the buyer may wish to review and make changes to the seller's plans and to participate in testing. The buyer may also wish to review fuel contracts, to assure itself that the seller has provided for adequate supplies.

Developers do not like these review rights. Financiers strongly disfavor them, particularly if they permit the buyer to cancel the contract after the financier has advanced money. Financiers may be satisfied if the buyer has approved seller's plans before the financiers make their first advance, and the buyer has the right thereafter only to disapprove changes to the plans. Sellers and their financiers are also comforted if the buyer's objections must be reasonable, or if the buyer's objections must be submitted to an engineer for resolution.

The buyer may not need these rights if the project has a reputable developer, contractor, and operator. However, if the seller is a special-purpose entity, the buyer may wish to reserve rights of review if there is a change of control.

In any event, the parties should agree on a procedure for coordinating and limiting scheduled outages, such as those for periodic maintenance. These procedures can usually be arranged quickly between the parties' technical personnel.

Power purchase contracts often require the seller to reconstruct a destroyed plant. However, these provisions are of limited effect where the seller is a special-purpose entity and the proceeds of the casualty insurance are paid directly to the financiers. Insurance adequate to cover the buyer's expectation that the plant will be rebuilt—in addition to the insurance for the financiers—is likely to be prohibitively expensive if it is available at all.

Force Majeure

Long-term commercial contracts typically contain a force majeure clause, excusing a party if its performance is prevented by forces beyond it reasonable control. The general principle is normally accompanied by a "parade of horribles" describing specific acts of God that will excuse the parties.

There is a standard set of issues in force majeure clauses. Should strikes, lockouts, and other labor disturbances that interfere with performance be force majeure, regardless of the reasonableness of managements positions? Should general economic conditions, or a grossly inadequate or excessive price, ever be force majeure? Should the "parade of horribles" be qualified by the general requirement that the cause be beyond the party's control, or are they force majeure regardless of the party's actions? Should force majeure indefinitely extend the date the seller has committed to have the plant on line?

In the electric industry—with its history of comprehensive government interest—an important issue is whether acts of regulatory bodies should affect the parties' obligations. A recurring issue is whether the contract should be terminated or the price formula modified if the buyer is unable to pass the cost through to its customers. Similarly, should a party be excused for failure to obtain or keep necessary permits, regardless of the reasonableness of its positions or actions in seeking them? Conversely, should a party be excused if a permit is obtained, but has unacceptable conditions? This can become complicated; the outcome depends on the nature of the local regulatory scheme and the parties need for certainty.

In addition to general force majeure, the buyer will demand carte blanche to deal with an emergency threatening the safety or reliability of its system. The seller may wish to mitigate the effect of the emergency clause by limiting its effects on the capacity charge. Normally, the buyer will also demand that the seller take any action that the buyer reasonably requests to deal with the emergency, such as interrupting scheduled maintenance or running the plant in a manner that might otherwise not be prudent.

Termination

Long-term contracts typically allow a party to terminate the contract if the other party becomes insolvent, repeatedly breaches the contract in a material way, or fails to promptly cure breaches of the contract. The seller's financier is likely to request that the buyer provide the financier the opportunity to cure the seller's breach or assume the seller's obligations. The buyer should require the financier to act quickly, and should not let cumulation of the seller's and the financier's cure periods become substantial.

As a practical matter, if a default occurs the buyer is likely to accommodate any reasonable solution that will keep the plant delivering power on terms similar to those it negotiated.

Disputes

Arbitration is common in long-term commercial contracts, although major international contracts sometimes refer disputes to a foreign court respected for its commercial expertise. A foreign developer or financier is likely to insist on arbitration by an international body or consent to (possibly exclusive) jurisdiction in London or New York. The enforceability of these provisions may be restricted by local law, particularly if the buyer is state controlled.

The law to govern the purchase may be problematic. Local commercial law may not be sufficiently developed to give predictable answers to complicated commercial issues. On the other hand, an Asian buyer may consider it peculiar to apply New York or English law to a contract to sell power generated and consumed in Asia.

Referring technical disputes to an independent engineer rather than to a court or arbitral body may save substantial time and money. Typical commercial contracts require the parties to pay amounts not in dispute, and pay the disputed amounts on settlement of the dispute (with interest from the date originally due).

Change In Law

Sellers and their financiers like payments to be increased to reflect tax increases. They also seek adjustments to the capacity charge to reflect capital expenditures required by changes in law (such as environmental law) or adjustments to the energy charge to reflect increased operating costs.

A buyer will naturally feel that these are risks of doing business, which the seller should bear. Unless the taxing and regulatory regime is very predictable, however, the buyer may not be able to attract developers—particularly foreign developers—without these protections. Moreover, the buyer may find that assuming these risks is less expensive than paying a price high enough to induce sellers to assume them.

A foreign seller may assume that the buyer will have more influence over these matters than it will, and will argue that the buyer would have to pay these costs (directly or indirectly) if the buyer generated the power itself or bought it on the spot market.

A buyer that assumes these costs will want extensive protections and it should have the right to audit the seller's asserted costs. A buyer should not bear costs caused by the seller's own actions.

OTHER ISSUES
Cost of Service Tariffs

A cost-of-service price formula gives the buyer the economic benefits and burdens of ownership. The formula exactly covers all the seller's costs and provides the seller an agreed return on capital. A cost-of-service tariff consists of a depreciation component that amortizes the construction and development cost of the plant over its useful life, a return on capital component (which may be an assumed rate or the actual cost of the capital), and an operating cost component that reimburses actual operating costs. This is the traditional method of utility rate regulation in the United States, and requires detailed accounting and audit procedures to assure that costs are properly classified and are properly chargeable to the service.

A buyer that does not control the project's costs is unlikely to agree to pay a cost-of-service price formula. Moreover, most developers are entrepreneurial, not seeking the limited return implied by a cost-of-service price formula.

Avoided Cost Formulas

United States regulation requiring utilities to purchase power from independent developers sets the price of the power at the buyer's avoided cost. In theory, avoided cost is the price the utility would have to pay if it generated the power itself. In practice, the meaning of avoided cost is open to interpretation, and does not provide sufficient comfort to financiers. Consequently, it is a basis for discussion of price, rather than a price formula commonly used for long-term purchases of reliable power.

Transmission and Interconnection Facilities

New facilities (such as transmission lines) may be necessary to connect the plant to the buyer's system. Regulation or condemnation law may make it easier for the buyer to own these facilities. If so, the buyer will need to recover the cost of these facilities by directly billing the seller, or paying a lower price.

General Contracting Issues

A power purchase will raise all the usual issues of commercial contracts. Is the other party creditworthy, or should it post security for its obligations? Are representations necessary? Who is responsible for permits?

In addition, the privatization context raises the host of issues associated with development projects. Is the host country stable, or is political risk insurance appropriate? Will the seller or its financier require a government guaranty? Can one obtain government agreement on critical issues such as exportation, taxation, and regulation? What are the local restrictions on payments in or conversion to foreign currency? Will the buyer pay in hard currency in a foreign money center? What are the local restrictions on capital repatriation? Who bears responsibility for these issues?

A buyer will only attract developers if it can convince them that these are not issues or it bears these risks itself. Even where sellers will bear these risks, the buyer may find it less expensive to itself undertake the risks than to compensate the seller for undertaking them.

Chapter 22

The Restructuring and Privatization of the Electricity Supply Industry in England and Wales

Alex Henney

THE BACKGROUND TO PRIVATIZATION[1]

The electricity supply industry in England & Wales was nationalized in 1947, and restructured in 1957 to create the Central Electricity Generation Board (CEGB), which was a generation and high voltage (275 kilovolts [kV] and 400kV) transmission organization that had a virtual monopoly of generation for public supply. When the CEGB was dissolved in 1990 it owned 55 gigawatts (GW) generating capacity, which made it the second largest generation organization in the western world after Electricité de France. Apart from supplying five very large customers directly, the CEGB sold its power on a "Bulk Supply Tariff" to twelve Area Boards, which were retail distribution organizations that owned the distribution network (132kV to low voltage) and supplied 22 million customers with 226 terawatt-hours (TWh) of electricity in 1988/89.

There were many criticisms of the performance of the electricity supply industry, particularly of the CEGB. Planning within the CEGB started not from the market, but from what it wished to build, which was large conventional coal and nuclear plants that cost about 50 percent more than international prices and took far too long to construct. The CEGB was over manned (as were the Area Boards) and politically manipulated, particularly in being forced to buy expensive coal from state owned British Coal and in promoting an expensive nuclear program. Few would now dispute those claims, which I set out at length in 1987.

Mrs. Thatcher had a clear belief that "private equals good—public equals bad." Her government began privatizing state-owned undertakings in 1980, commencing with "normal" commercial companies such as Britoil, the state owned oil company. In 1985 the government privatized British Telecom as a monopoly, and in 1986 British Gas as a monopoly.

---

[1] *This paper draws extensively on my book "A study of the privatization of the electricity supply industry in England & Wales" published in 1994 by EEE Limited, 38 Swains Lane, London N6 6QR (Telephone +4471 284 4217; Fax +4471 284 4331).*

Following the election in June 1987, the government started work on privatizing the electricity supply industry. During that summer the chickens came home to roost on the monopoly privatizations. British Telecom's performance was widely criticized, and *The Times* conducted an unparalleled campaign which led to the chairman retiring earlier than he intended. British Gas was criticized for discriminatory pricing to industrial customers who had no alternative fuel source. The CEGB vainly strove to persuade anyone who would listen that it should remain intact.

In February 1988 the government published a White Paper "Privatizing Electricity", which proposed to divide the CEGB into a grid company (along with 2GW of short cycle pumped storage capacity) that would be owned by the distribution companies, and two generation companies. The larger company (which became National Power) would own fossil plant and all of the nuclear power plant, and the smaller company (which became PowerGen) would only own fossil plant. The Area Boards were to be privatized as twelve independent companies. The White Paper referred to competition both in generation, and to supply customers.

At the end of July 1989 the Electricity Act passed through Parliament, and also the government decided that it was impossible to privatize the older gas cooled magnox nuclear reactors. In November the government announced that it would not be possible to privatize the other reactors, and would create Nuclear Electric as a publicly owned company.

On 1 April 1990 the industry was "vested." All the legal changes took place to create not only the new companies, but also a new trading regime, which is the radical aspect of the restructuring. More specifically, the industry has been "unbundled" into four components:

- generation, with sale of virtually all output to a wholesale Pool

- high voltage transmission as a common carrier

- medium to low voltage distribution as a common carrier

- wholesale purchase of virtually all electricity from the Pool by "suppliers" for "supply" to customers.

Customers with premises where the load is above 1 megawatt (MW) had a choice from which supplier they buy—about 5000 such premises exist; from 1 April 1994 choice was extended to premises with loads above 100kW of which there are a further 47,000; and from 1 April 1998 all 23 million customers are supposed to have a choice.

In November 1990 the twelve distribution companies—now called Regional Electricity Companies (RECs)—along with the National Grid Company (NGC) were sold to the public, and in February 1991 the government sold National Power and PowerGen. The whole process was at least as complex as the break up of the Bell telephone system.

The following section outlines the key parameters of what was done, and is followed by sections explaining how various facets of the industry function, namely:

- the National Grid Company

- the Regional Electricity Companies (RECs)

- generators

- the Pool and contracts for differences

- regulation.

The final sections assess the benefits and mistakes of privatization.

UNDERSTANDING WHAT WAS DONE

There are many lessons that one can learn from the restructuring that can help people in the United States think their way through some of the implications of liberalizing the electric system, and help policy makers elsewhere in designing privatization plans. To make sense of what was done and to draw out lessons that might be useful it is important to appreciate the key parameters of the process. The government was doing four things:

- restructuring the organization of the industry

- introducing competition

- privatizing it

- pursuing a number of political objectives.

Because the government owned the industry it could redistribute value and restructure finances as it wished without regard for private property rights (e.g. value was shifted from generation into the wires), and the finances of the companies could be structured to meet the requirements of the new—and untried—market that was devised. The fact that the industry was being privatized imposed a discipline on what was done. The government had to ensure that for several years the companies would be financially viable.

Furthermore, since the wires part of the industry is a monopoly and customers would continue to be supplied on a franchise for up to eight years, the government was in the position to determine the division of benefit between itself from the sale, future shareholders, and customers. To this end the government determined that the sales income to the industry would remain constant in real terms for three years. The consequence of this decision, coupled with the decision to introduce a competitive market initially for customers over 1MW, meant that prices for tariff customers would increase. Finally the government had a number of political objectives:

- to support British Coal for three years, which it achieved by requiring National Power and PowerGen to enter into contracts to take 70 million tonnes in 1990 and 1991, and 65 million tonnes in 1992 at well above world coal prices. In turn these contracts were backed by three year contracts for the RECs' tariff markets

- to levy what is effectively a tax to pay for the disposal of radwaste and the decommissioning of reactors

- to ensure that large customers did not lose the benefit of their special agreements (which competitively subsidized energy intensive industries) until after the industry had been privatized

- to "widen share ownership" by selling the industry to the public who were voters. Consequently the government had to sell the shares cheaply and ensure that profits would increase.

To achieve the economic and political objective, the government undertook a complex financial modeling of the industry to divide its added value between generation, transmission, distribution and supply. The objectives determined both the pricing in the initial three year contracts that were put in place between the major generators and the RECs, and the price control regulation of the RECs. They also distorted the behavior of the major generators in the Pool.

THE NATIONAL GRID COMPANY

The Electricity Act 1989 imposes two main requirements on NGC:

- to develop and maintain an efficient coordinated and economical transmission system

- to facilitate competition in supply and generation.

246

NGC has been created not as a market maker—it does not buy and sell electricity—but as a neutral transmission agency which also manages despatch and provides an agency service operating a Pool.

The transmission license, which is the basis of the award to NGC of the de facto monopoly of providing the system, defines its rights, its obligations, and imposes conditions upon how it performs. The license is also the basis for regulating NGC. The license divides NGC's operations for regulatory purposes into five ring-fenced "separate businesses":

- owning and maintaining the transmission system

- operating the interconnectors with Scotland (AC) and France (DC)

- purchasing and providing "ancillary services" (voltage and frequency control) to ensure the stability and security of the system

- administering the Pool settlement system

- generating from pumped storage.

Each separate business must prepare separate accounts, is separately regulated, and may not be cross subsidized.

The license conditions include the requirements that NGC:

- must provide access to the system on a non-discriminatory basis

- should not increase the average level of unit charges for the "use of system" more rapidly than the Retail Price Index (RPI, in US parlance CPI) less 1.9 percent (i.e., its income in real terms reduces by 1.9 percent per annum, or p.a.), which is the so called "RPI-X" British approach to price control where X is the efficiency gain in real terms

- must schedule and issue direct instructions for despatch in accordance with a (price) merit order all plant with a capacity in excess of 100MW.

NGC has a two part pricing structure:

- "entry" and "exit charges," which are the annualized costs of the equipment necessary to connect particular generators and suppliers into the grid

- an "infrastructure charge," which varies by fourteen zones, and is supposed to reflect the long run marginal cost of providing the system to move bulk power. The charge is lower for generators in zones where there is a deficit of generation compared with consumption and higher where there is a surplus, and conversely for suppliers—the charge is intended to convey a locational message.

To ensure that the NGC is operated in an independent manner the grid has been organizationally structured in two tiers. National Grid Holding is a company whose sole purpose is to own NGC. The directors of the owning RECs appoint the directors of National Grid Holding, but no director or employee of a REC may be a director of NGC. The respective memoranda and articles of association define the relationship between the companies in such a way as to prevent the owners influencing the operation of the grid. Effectively, the owners are passive investors, and most are prepared to sell out a significant part of their shareholdings.

The Financial Structure of NGC

NGC's finances and its initial price control formula were devised to ensure that it would be financially viable and could undertake a much larger capital program than the CEGB (capital spending increased from $120 million in 1988/89 to an average of $650 million annually from 1991/92 to 1993/94 without recourse to any loans or guarantees from its owners. NGC's profit and loss accounts and balance sheet for 1990/91 to 1993/94 are shown in Table 22-1.

In historic cost terms NGC's pre-interest pre-tax return was 38 percent in 1993/94. When NGC was initially financed by the government it had a debt/equity ratio of 89 percent; despite undertaking a very large capital program its debt/equity ratio had reduced to 19 percent by 31 March 1994. NGC is a money machine.

THE REGIONAL ELECTRICITY COMPANIES (RECs)

The activities of the RECs divide into three regulated separate businesses:

- distribution of electricity over the network in their "authorized area"

- the supply of electricity to customers. "Supply" is a legal term which involves purchasing electricity from the Pool—all suppliers must buy all of their electricity from the Pool—and generally hedging the risks of volatility in the Pool with contracts for differences, which are explained below

- generation, which is limited to their equity participation in capacity equivalent to about fifteen percent of maximum demand in their authorized area.

In addition they can undertake any other businesses, which are not regulated.

Table 22-1. NGC's profit and loss accounts for 1990/91 and 1993/94 and summary balance sheets at the year ends

	1990/91	1993/94
Profit and Loss	($ millions)	
turnover	1,716	2,138
operating profit	698	945
interest payment	118	76
pre-tax profit	579	869
tax	189	210
post-tax profit	390	660
dividends	158	223
Balance Sheet		
fixed assets	2,889	3,996
current assets	628	965
creditors due within 1 year	928	1,213
creditors due after 1 year	1,125	975
provisions	-63	-231
net assets	9,481	12,501

Sources:
The National Grid Company Annual Reports.
 *Note all £ figures have been converted to US$ at £=1.5$.
**Note all accounting figures are on a historic cost basis except where they are stated to be on a current
  cost basis.

The RECs have been granted "Public Electricity Supply Licenses" for their authorized areas which provide them with the right to provide a distribution system (but this is not an exclusive right), and an automatic entitlement to supply customers with electricity. The license requires them:

- to connect up customers requiring connection

- to offer non-discriminatory use of system charges

- to offer tariffs to customers up to 10MW

- to provide own-generators with top-up and stand-by power on a cost-reflective basis.

The RECs' distribution business is a monopoly, and is regulated with a price cap formula that (in simplified terms) allows them for five years to increase their charge per kWh distributed through their system by RPI + X, where X varies from 0 to 2.5 percent depending on the REC. In August 1994 the regulator announced his proposals for modifying the formulae from April 1995, with initial reductions varying between 11 percent and 17 percent in real terms with subsequent annual real price reductions of 2 percent annually.

The RECs' supply business divides its service between the franchise and the competitive markets. The supply to the franchise market is essentially regulated by allowing a modest amount for the costs involved in supply together with pass through of the costs of purchasing electricity, of using the grid, and of using the REC's own distribution system. Competition in supply is achieved by other suppliers obtaining a "second tier license" to buy from the Pool to supply specified customers or classes of customers who have a load in excess of the franchise limit. These licenses are readily given, and have been obtained by RECs wishing to supply customers outside their authorized areas; by generators wishing to supply customers directly; and by a few customers wishing to supply themselves.

The key discovery from the process of unbundling the supply from the distribution of electricity is that the big money is in the wires, not in supply, see Table 22-2.

Table 22-2. The consolidated results for the twelve RECs for 1993/94

	Sales turnover capital at end year	Operating profit employed	
	($ millions)		
distribution	5,884	9,175	2,341
supply	20,584	*	334

The figure was distorted by pre-payments to avoid a new tax, but should have been about $1500–1600 million.

The message is clear: the RECs' monopoly of the wires comprises most of their added value and there is at best modest profit in the business of supply, which is a high turnover, low margin, merchanting business. This should not be surprising. There is clearly added value in transporting electricity from a generator through a grid and distribution network to a customer (and also providing system stability, etc.). But stripped to its essentials, electricity in a developed system is basically a non-differentiated commodity. The business of supply is little more than providing financial hedging between the varying cost of generation and a (quasi) fixed price tariff or contract, together with an invoicing and debt collection service. The added costs in the business are small, and apart from the computer system the only capital is the working capital from the difference in timing between suppliers paying for electricity from the Pool and receiving payment from customers. That said, there is some money to be made, and supplying customers can be part of a package which involves additional services that can be sold such as security systems, shared energy saving schemes, power quality, etc. Yet these services are small change compared with the return from actually distributing electricity.

The consequences of competition have been profound. For example it does not pay to discriminate in the way that so many utilities do—or are required to do—in favor of one group of customers or another. Next, lacking a franchise, the company has to devise a business and marketing strategy to determine which customers to target based on identifying their competitive advantages and disadvantages. The RECs and generators are now much more customer responsive—no longer do they say "take it or take it" because the customers can walk away. No longer can they conduct their business knowing little about their customers; now they have to know how to price to customers; now they have to be nice to customers. Most critically, the private company has to determine how to buy electricity against customers' demands from the wholesale market— it has to manage risk. Now the utility managers have to behave like normal business people.

The Financial Structure of the RECs

The basis for constructing the RECs' finances was a modeling exercise of the forecast performance of their businesses for five years from vesting. The government was aiming to sell the RECs on the basis of real earnings and dividend growth of about 4–5 percent p.a. Assuming inflation at 5 percent p.a. and an initial yield of 7 percent such a figure would be equivalent to a pre-tax equity return of 16 percent in nominal terms. Because it was not possible to make much more than a guess about the downside risks of the supply business, the focus of the work was on the distribution business. From the computer modeling, guesses, and gaming emerged a deal on the X factors for distribution that would make the sums add up. In the event, as Table 22-3 shows, two plus two equalled much more than four.

Table 22-3. The operating profits of the Area Boards and RECs from the year before their incorporation and sale to 1993/94

	1989/90	1991/92 ($ millions)	1993/94
current money (£m)	1236	2236	2715
constant 1992/93 prices (£m)	1464	2305	2668

Not surprisingly, a City analyst called the 1991 results an "electricity profits bonanza," a comment that could apply almost as well to subsequent years.

The phenomenon of substantially increased profits is similar to the experience of other privatized utilities, but the magnitude of the increases (and the increases in the value of the shares, see below) embarrassed the government. Much of the increase was due to the conservatism with which it was necessary to prepare the business forecasts and the particular risks of their flotation. The government cannot afford companies sold to the general public to fail—the majority of investors are voters— and thus in constructing the finances and agreeing the X factors for distribution it had to allow generously for downside risks including the uncertainties of the new trading market, the fear that the Pool might collapse, and the prospect in the autumn of 1991 of war in the Gulf upsetting both the oil market and the stock market. The distribution X factors were very slack, and in five years the RECs will have made about $2 billion more than the government anticipated.

The Flotation of the RECs

The flotation of the RECs and NGC was planned like a military operation. Preparatory work began in the spring of 1988 leading to drafting the massive prospectus in the summer and autumn of 1990. At exactly 800 closely-printed A4 pages it was the largest ever written in Britain.

The program to market the RECs to financial institutions in the UK and overseas started in June, and the program to market the RECs to the British public commenced on 12 September with letters to all householders, and an advertising campaign that cost $23 million. A share information office was set up to register people's interest in the sale and to provide them with information. At peak the office employed 400 telephone operators; over two months it registered 7.3 million people. "Impact day" was Wednesday 21 November with the price announcement at 10:00 o'clock, and mini prospectuses were mailed off to be available by 28 November at latest; completed application forms were due by 5 December; the basis of allocation was announced on 10 December and dealing in the shares commenced on Tuesday 11 December.

The shares were priced at a notional dividend yield averaging 8.4 percent. The minimum offer was for 100 shares at $3.4 each. To further the policy of 'widening share ownership', 55 percent of the shares were available to the British public along with a choice of either electricity vouchers worth $30 off electricity bills for every 100 shares allocated, or a bonus of one share for every ten shares held until 1994. Employees and pensioners of the RECs and NGC were offered an allocation of up to $24,000 worth of shares on preferential terms including some free shares and shares at a discount of 20 percent. Thirty percent of the stock was offered in a portfolio package of all 12 RECs to UK institutional investors, and 15 percent of the stock was placed as a portfolio package with financial institutions in Europe, the United States, Japan, and Canada. Two-hundred and thrity thousand copies of the main prospectus and 12½ million copies of the mini-prospectus were distributed to institutional investors and stockbrokers and financial advisers in the UK, and (along with mini prospectuses) to 25,000 bank branches, 21,000 post offices, and 4,500 libraries, and the application form was also published in most national newspapers.

A total of 12.7 million applications were made for shares and the issue was subscribed 10.7 times over. The sale raised $11.6 billion net of sale costs. With the massive oversubscription the institutions were short of stock, and to the government's considerable embarrassment, the RECs' shares increased rapidly in value, and have continued to increase so that on 22 September 1994 they were valued on average at 3.2 times their flotation price and had increased by 120 percent compared to the average increase in the stock market as a whole.[2]

THE GENERATORS

When the system was created on 1 April 1990 National Power owned 29GW, PowerGen 19GW, Nuclear Electric 9GW, NGC Pumped Storage 2GW, EDF had an interconnector with a capacity of 2GW and Scottish companies an interconnector of 1GW. National Power and PowerGen had a more dominant position than the simple numbers indicate because they owned virtually all of the plant which runs at the margin and determines the Pool price.

Like the RECs, the generators received a very favorable financial deal. To get themselves in shape for the new world they were allowed to charge $1.4 billion as exceptional and extraordinary items in the two years preceding their flotation (of which half was for "rationalization and restructuring"), and they were sold with provisions totalling $1.4 billion. The generators were valued on a residual basis, working back from the level to which the government thought the wholesale market would move, namely the price of a new entrant combined cycle gas turbine (CCGT). Given the uncertainties of the new market; that the two generators would have to install flue gas desulphurization scrubbers; and that they would have to build CCGTs from their own resources and without offtake contracts, National Power was sold with a debt/equity ratio of 13 percent and PowerGen was sold in a net cash position. However, with the benefit of the three year vesting contracts, massive demanning, and some use of their generous provisions, operating profits increased by about three quarters in three years.

---

[2] *The pattern of increasing share prices in the early years after flotation has been common in all major utility privatizations, but over time tightening price controls have reigned the stock price down. As at 22 September 1994, after substantial early increases, the share price of British Telecom (privatized in 1984) had increased by only 4 percent compared to the stock market as a whole, while British Gas (privatized in 1986) had increased by only 21 percent.*

Table 22-4. National Power's and PowerGen's operating profit

	National Power		PowerGen	
	1990/91	1993/94	1990/91	1993/94
		($ millions)		
	640	1101	400	715

The government decided to sell 60 percent of the stock in the two generators, again offering a substantial proportion of their stock to the British public at a yield of 6.3 percent, but using the US book building approach to selling to the institutions coupled with an international back-end tender for 15 percent of the stock. The government realized $4.3 billion from the sale of equity and debt. Again, the share prices increased rapidly, and by 22 September 1994 they were an average of 2.8 times the offer price.

National Power and PowerGen will not have an easy market because the privatization coincided with a "gas bubble" in the North Sea. In consequence, after only ordering one plant since 1979, over the period 1989–94 there was a flood of orders for new plant. Seven GW of "independent power projects" are either completed or under construction. These schemes are project financed with non-recourse debt on the back of 15-year must-take gas purchase contracts and matching 15 year power offtake contracts with RECs, and all have equity investment by the RECs. A particularly notable scheme is the development by Enron in conjunction with Imperial Chemical Industries and four RECs of an 1850MW CCGT cogenerator, which is thought to be the largest such scheme in the world. Responding to the threat of loss of market share National Power and PowerGen are currently constructing plants with a capacity of 6GW, which are being built on their balance sheets with no offtake contracts.

Whatever else may be said about the competitiveness of the system, there has been fierce competition to build new plant. The earlier schemes got cheaper gas and were better placed to get offtake contracts for baseload power for which there is a limited capacity on the system. Consequently there was a race to get the schemes together called "the dash for gas."

The burst of new construction, together with the greatly improved performance of Nuclear Electric, which increased the output of its existing plant from 45TWh in 1990 to 61TWh in 1993, plus the forthcoming completion of the Sizewell B Pressurized Water Reactor and the upgrade of the interconnector with Scotland, will result in either a massive surplus of capacity and/or premature retirement of plant, and is significantly changing the pattern of generation, see Tables 22-5 and 22-6.

Table 22-5. Scenario forecast of pattern of production to 1999/2000

	1990/91 (TWh)	(%)	1996/97 (TWh)	(%)	1999/2000 (TWh)	(%)
total market	268	100	287	100	291	100
National Power	122	46	78	28	90	31
PowerGen	76	28	64	23	61	21
Nuclear Electric	45	17	63	23	55	19
other	25	9	73	26	85	29

Table 22-6. Fuel source of generation in England and Wales

	1990/91 (%)	1999/2000 (%)
coal	76	40
oil and Orimulsion	6	2
nuclear	18	21
gas	0	37

The figures show:

- National Power and to a lesser extent PowerGen losing market share to other generators

- there will be a significant switch of fuel sourcing from the traditional dominance by coal to a diversified output based on coal, nuclear, and gas. The switch from coal has caused collapse of British Coal, which employed 221,000 people in March 1985 after the year long miners' strike, reduced to 85,000 in March 1990 at vesting, and to 14,000 by March 1994—this is "Thatcherism" in action.

THE POOL

As noted above (virtually) all generators commercially sell their electricity to the Pool, and all plants with a capacity in excess of 100MW are despatched by NGC. Every day by 10:00 o'clock the generators put in bids for each of their units which (in simplified terms) offer for the next day the price above which each unit will run and the output it will provide. NGC prepares a forecast of demand, and an unconstrained schedule which stacks the generators. The system marginal price (SMP, which is analogous in US parlance to the system lambda) is determined on a half hour by half hour basis by the bid price of the generator at the top of the stack. In addition there is a "capacity element" measured by the half hour loss of load probability (LOLP) multiplied by the value of lost load (VOLL) which is (in theory) the expected value at the margin to customers of losing load. In an optimal system this value should equal the cost at the margin of serving lost load, which is the cost of capacity plus the SMP. Again, in theory an optimal system pricing at the margin should recover the capital cost of all of the units. With some manipulation:

Pool Purchase Price = SMP + LOLP(VOLL-SMP)

VOLL was set at $3/kWh in 1990/91 and is indexed by CPI. All of the generators that are scheduled in a half hour are paid the Pool Purchase Price regardless of their bid price.

The real system is of course constrained, and some units are constrained-off and others constrained-on and run out of merit order. Some units run for voltage and frequency support ("ancillary services"), thus incurring additional costs. The forecast will not be precisely accurate, and some plant will not run as bid in. Also there are losses on the system. The costs of constraints, ancillary services, discrepancies and losses are currently averaged across the system on a half hour basis and effectively added to the Pool Selling Price to derive the Pool Purchase Price, which is what the suppliers pay for power from the Pool.

The Pool has been the focus of a great deal of attention and some excitement over the four years of its operation. The Pool's mechanics are very complicated. Pricing behavior has on some occasions been odd because of the consequences of must-take coal contracts, and anomalies in the software. During the early days, prices were increased by PowerGen manipulating its bidding, which the regulator termed "an abuse of the company's dominant position," and later according to the regulator, National Power price led and PowerGen followed. The regulator produced five reports on various aspects of behavior in the Pool, before threatening in 1993 to refer National Power and PowerGen to the anti-trust authority unless they modified their behavior. The issue was temporarily resolved in February 1994 by an undertaking that the companies would use their best endeavors to sell 4GW and 2GW of plant respectively, and in addition would in effect collude to keep the price down to a specified level—it is an odd market indeed!

Pope wrote "A little learning is a dangerous thing; drink deep or taste not the Pierian spring." A discussion of either the Pool's pseudo problems, or its marginal problems, let alone its real problems is not possible in a paper of this length. We have found—as have the Norwegians—that the successful operation of a competitive pool is more complex than we thought it was. That said, the surprise is not that the Pool has shortcomings. Rather, given that the Pool was created in a very short time, it is a tribute to those involved that it works as well as it does.

Contracts for Differences

Pool prices are volatile and RECs selling electricity on tariffs that are fixed for a year in advance would be exposed to considerable risk if they were to buy all their electricity at Pool prices. RECs might make a great deal of money if the level of Pool prices were lower than the estimate they had used for constructing tariffs or contracts. If Pool prices were much higher than anticipated, REC's costs would be higher and would quickly eliminate the margin in the supply business. The generators do not want their income to depend entirely on the vagaries of the Pool price. Thus, both sides have an interest in hedging their Pool risk, which they can do with "contracts for differences." There are two basic types of contract: "one-way" contracts and "two-way" contracts (see Figure 22-1). One-way contracts are like an interest rate cap—namely for payment of an option fee by a REC, a generator agrees to pay the difference between the Pool Purchase Price and a "strike price." Two-way contracts involve the generator paying the REC when the Pool Purchase Price is above the strike price, and the REC paying the generator when the Pool price is below the strike price.

Notwithstanding the attention that has been focused on the Pool, the wholesale electricity market will be predominantly a contract market because:

• independent power projects must have contracts to procure financing

• the RECs need contracts to hedge against the risks of the Pool

• PowerGen, National Power, and Nuclear Electric want substantial contract cover to provide financial stability to enable them to plan their operations and profits. To the extent that they are uncovered they can be considered to be speculating on the Pool price

• many medium size customers prefer simple and reasonably fixed prices to fluctuating Pool prices.

Contracts for differences provide a very flexible means of trading between parties. Contracts can be very simple offering cover for particular short term periods; they can be constructed in complex ways with indexing, minimum-take requirements, and apply during certain time slots; they can be written to have the same form as an independent power project contract and used for raising finance.

In the short term, Pool prices and contract cover interact in a complex manner on a day to day basis. The type, quantity, and strike price of the contracts which a generator has for a particular day will affect its bidding pattern and its interest in whether the Pool price is high or low. When the generators contract forward, then

Figure 22-1. One and two way contracts

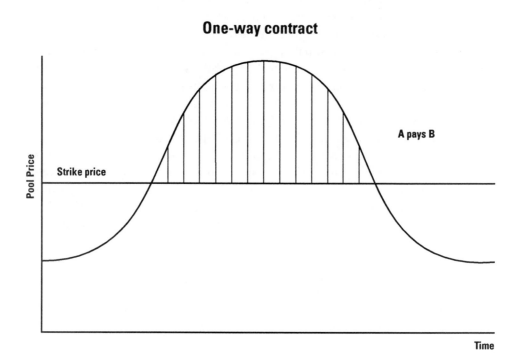

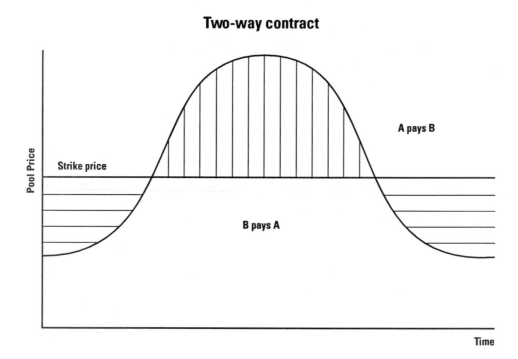

their immediate benefit from high Pool prices diminishes until they are exactly covered, at which point they are indifferent to the short term level of Pool price. When generators are over-covered they have a short-term interest in the Pool price being low. Contracting forward thus reduces the generators' market power in the Pool, but does give them financial stability. Thus the generators joint strategic interest is in being slightly under-contracted compared with their assessment of output in a year with an average winter.

When the system has settled down, year on year Pool and contract prices should converge towards each other. If (say) contract prices were consistently significantly much higher than equivalent Pool prices, then demand for contracts would decrease and drive contract prices down, and conversely if contract prices were consistently lower. The contract price should be based on the expectation of Pool price plus or minus an 'insurance factor' reflecting the relative risk averseness of the parties.

The shorter term contract market has been distorted first by the initial three-year contracts which the government put in place at vesting, and then by the five-year contracts which were negotiated from April 1993 to further support British Coal and were secured against the RECs' franchise market. Ironically, the effect has been to make the market for shorter-term contracts more competitive because by removing about half of National Power's and PowerGen's contracting capacity from the market, the two generators are no longer so dominant in the residual contract market.

THE CUSTOMER PERSPECTIVE

Prices

The real price changes for industrial and domestic customers for the five financial years before vesting and the four years after are shown in Table 22-7, and the change in the prices for different sizes of industrial customers are shown in Table 22-8. The tariff customers financed the privatization. The pattern of price changes up to April 1993 was largely determined by government policies, and the way it set up the vesting contracts, the price controls for transmission and distribution and the subsidies for British Coal. Subsequently domestic tariffs reduced in real terms in April 1993 by an average of 5 percent and by 2 percent in April 1994, reflecting the terms of the new five year coal contracts.

Table 22-7. Index at constant prices for domestic and industrial customers (1990–100)

	Domestic	Industrial
1985/86	105.1	117.5
1986/87	103.5	113.3
1987/88	97.7	105.6
1988/89	98.5	106.0
1989/90	98.4	106.7
1990/91	100.6	77.3
1991/92	104.6	97.2
1992/93	103.8	99.2
1993/94	98.9	95.2

Source: Department of Trade and Industry.

Table 22-8. Price for different sizes of industrial customers in constant 1992/93 prices (c/kWh)

	small	medium	moderately large	extra large
1988/89	9.90	8.07	6.66	4.68
1989/90	10.06	7.99	6.72	4.91
1990/91	10.19	7.17	5.73	4.55
1991/92	10.73	7.01	5.60	4.22
1992/93	10.55	7.27	5.55	5.03
1993/94	9.95	6.98	5.94	5.01
	<0.88	0.88–8.8	8.8–150	>150
	GWh p.a.	GWh p.a.	GWh p.a.	GWh p.a.

Source: Department of Trade and Industry.

Prices to medium size and moderately large industrial and commercial customers over 1MW reduced significantly in 1990/91 because they were freed from paying a subsidy to British Coal. In 1992/93 and again in 1993/94 prices increased mainly because the generators increased contract and Pool prices and transmission and distribution prices increased. Prices to very large industrial customers were protected in 1990/91, but subsequently some customers suffered significant increases in 1991/92 when the special agreements were withdrawn.

Small customers do not appear to have complained much about the increases in prices. Indeed, according to a customer survey in late 1992, more customers thought that electricity prices were reasonable (56 percent) than considered them unreasonable (a third), which is comparable with the perceptions of prices of other utilities. Very large customers, however, have complained vigorously that their prices had increased more in recent years than, and were not generally competitive with, prices for similar loads on the Continent.

Competition in Supply

Customers in the competitive market have a choice of buying either on Pool price terms (about a third of 1MW+ customers buy on Pool price terms) or on a contract which will be fixed price if it is for a year or indexed if it is for longer. Some customers will prefer a contract because they want to budget the cost of their electricity purchases with reasonable certainty, and others because they prefer a simple method of payment. Competent buyers put out tenders inviting suppliers to bid, and contract prices for electricity vary about 10 percent. In 1993/94 31 percent of the sites over 1MW, consuming 57 percent (40TWh) of the power in the competitive market bought from a supplier other than their local REC.

The competitive supply market is still in an embryo state, with the participants feeling their way. PowerGen has been consistently aggressive in pursuing direct sales, supplying about 20TWh in 1993/94 which is more than most RECs supply in total, while in contrast National Power's enthusiasm was blunted by substantial losses in 1991/92, and it now emphasizes selling to RECs. The policies of the RECs range from one or two who have more or less withdrawn from the 1MW+ market to several who wish to be serious national players.

UK-STYLE REGULATION

The regulatory framework created by the Electricity Act 1989 follows that created for telecoms, gas and water. The Electricity Act:

- requires that undertakings which generate, transmit, and supply customers directly must also have a license for their activities

- creates a Director General of Electricity Supply as a "statutory appointment." The Act defines the Director General's broad powers and duties, including those of enforcing license conditions and modifying them, sets the period of appointment as five years and provides that the Director can only be removed "on the grounds of incapacity or misbehavior"

- the Director General exercises some of the Director General of Fair Trading's powers under the Fair Trading Act 1973 and the Competition Act 1980, which are explained below

- the Secretary of State has various powers including that of issuing licenses (a power which is used for defining the initial licenses which are set for privatization), and issuing general directions to the Directors General.

The regulator is intended to be reasonably independent of Parliament and the government, and to have fairly extensive powers of discretion, but the government still retains considerable formal and informal regulatory powers over the industry.

The general duties of the Director are to promote competition, of which one major aspect is to regulate access to the market, and another is to curb anti-competitive behavior and to protect customers from potential monopoly abuse. In exercising those duties he or she, in this case he, also has to ensure that the licensees are financially viable. His main powers can be grouped into those:

- **relating to licenses.** The licenses provide a critical part of the regulatory framework defining what a licensee must do, may do, and may not do, thus setting constraints on its business activities. Subject to a general authority given by the Secretary of State, the Director may grant licenses and in granting the licenses he may attach conditions that are consistent with his general duties. The Director is also responsible for ensuring that the licensee complies with the conditions of the license, and may modify conditions of licenses with the agreement of the licensee. But if the parties cannot agree then he may make a 'license reference' for arbitration to the Monopolies and Mergers Commission (MMC), whose prime role is that of competition agency. Of particular significance, the Director proposes modifications to the price conditions

- **relating directly to individual customers and customer service standards.** The Director has a number of duties and powers specifically dealing with customers including establishing consumers' committees for each REC which can investigate complaints, and resolving certain types of disputes between customers and RECs. He can also make regulations prescribing standards of service for supply to individual tariff customers

- **anti-competition powers.**

The Director's anti-competitive powers broadly empower him to try to persuade a person engaged in a course of conduct which he considers is detrimental to the interests of, or unfair to, customers to give undertakings to desist. If the Director is unsuccessful in the attempt he may make a 'monopoly reference' to the Monopolies and Mergers Commission (MMC) to determine whether a monopoly situation exists and if so whether it acts against the public interest in any respects. The MMC prepares a report to the Secretary of State for Trade and Industry, and the Secretary of State may then request the Director to seek legally binding undertakings to prevent adverse effects. The potential power of these provisions is shown by how they have been applied to British Gas. Namely following an MMC report in 1987 it was required to offer supply to industrial customers on tariffs, not to purchase more than 90 percent of a gas field, and to reduce its share of the industrial market from 95 percent to 40 percent by disposing of gas supplies to competitors. Following another report in 1993 it was required to separate its gas supply business from its transportation business. The Director used the threat of a referral to gain undertakings by National Power and PowerGen to keep Pool prices down and to offer 6GW of plant for sale.

The Principles and Application of Price Control Regulation

Price control originated with the MMC price controlling condoms. The government adopted the approach for the regulation of British Telecom on the advice of Professor Stephen Littlechild, now the electricity regulator. He argued that "US experience of regulation is not encouraging, and suggests that regulation should not be too ambitious...investment has been distorted and efficiency and innovation discouraged...[price] controls are easy to understand, relatively cheap and simple to monitor, they preserve the incentives to efficiency, and they can be focused precisely on the areas of concern so as not to restrict the operation of the business in other respects."

The initial values of the Xs for privatized regulated companies are set by the government in a bargaining process with the directors of the companies, and have been consistently lax. Subsequently on review by the regulators the Xs have invariably been tightened. Thus the Director tightened NGC's X from 0 percent to -3 percent, the RECs' supply business from 0 percent to -2 percent, and the RECs' distribution business by an initial reduction of between 11 percent and 17 percent followed by 2 percent annually in real terms thereafter. The review process involves modeling the business over a period of generally five years, then instead of arguing cost elements line by line, agreeing an all in figure. The process is really equivalent to incentive rate of return in that the licensee is enabled to retain the benefit of productivity gains by beating the control. On review the past gains are taken away, as they would be competed away in a competitive market, and the process starts again.

Customer Service Standards

During 1993/94 the regulator received, investigated and resolved 11,684 complaints, which was a reduction of 30 percent on the previous year. The total number of domestic customers disconnected by the RECs was 2,535, a reduction by 93 percent from 35,675 in 1991/92. The RECs have to meet customer performance standards set by the regulator, and to comply with codes of practice for serving elderly and disabled people. The regulator also specifies 'overall standards of performance', such as performance connecting new domestic customers within 30 days of application (there were 1600 failures in 64,000 requests). Also, ten areas of individual customer service are now covered by legally binding minimum 'guaranteed standards' against which a REC pays a penalty when it fails to meet the standard. For example, if a REC does not provide and supply a domestic customer a meter within three working days it pays the customer $60, and if it misses an appointment it pays the customer $30. During 1993/94 the RECs made just over 8000 penalty payments totalling $220,000 on 13 million services. Although the penalties are negligible financially, they act as a shame factor and the media and some City analysts take an interest in the ranking of customer performance.

An Assessment

UK style regulation has a number of advantages compared with US style regulation, notably:

- relative speed, minimal legalism, and cheapness

- price control is simpler, provides a greater incentive to improve performance, and avoids the economic distortions (due to financial front-end loading) of rate of return regulation based on historic cost accounting

- it avoids second guessing management to the degree implicit in US style regulation

- it has been relatively distanced from politics compared with the United States. The regulators' independence and ability to exercise their discretion is a strength of the British approach

- it is more flexible in adapting to changing circumstances and helping to resolve the problems arising from flawed privatizations

- there are no complaints of gross technical incompetence, agency capture, or corruption. The success or failure of regulation is very dependent upon the quality and stature of the regulators. By British standards the appointments are well paid (about $130,000 p.a.), and they have attracted good people

- the regulator has a broader role than state public service commissions in having a responsibility to promote competition, and thus a significant part of his remit is to regulate access.

There are complaints that regulators are not sufficiently open and accountable, which is true and could easily be dealt with; they do deals behind closed doors, which is also true, but in some instances it is cheaper than negotiating in public; and they have been accused of moving the goal posts. IBM would surely prefer the chance of doing business on a playing field where the regulator moves the goal posts, to one where competition has changed the playing field.

The perception of the electricity regulator depends upon the perspective of the commentator—the City has been very happy; electricity companies have generally been content, particularly the RECs; while customers, British Coal, politicians, and the press have been less pleased. His price control reviews of both NGC and the RECs are widely thought to have been easy for the companies, and the *Financial Times* wrote an editorial titled "Littlechild underpowered" and the *Economist* a piece titled "Shocking leniency."

The idea behind price control is to give companies an incentive to cut costs by allowing the companies to retain the benefit for a period, and then (as in a competitive market) it is taken away and they start again. A cost of the incentive is an increase the cost of capital and the possibility of significant windfall gains. From a customer and public policy point of view, little is achieved by increasing the cost of capital substantially to achieve an annual rate of performance improvement similar to that which the RECs were achieving in public ownership, which has been the case. If one wants to provide an incentive, this could be done either directly to the management through a price target or by some sharing arrangement between customers and shareholders for improved performance, while providing shareholders with a guaranteed minimum rate of return.

AN ASSESSMENT OF PRIVATIZATION

"Sentence first, verdict afterwards."
— Alice in Wonderland

It is too early to draw up a definitive assessment of the pros and cons of the restructuring and privatization. The exercise was very complicated and in total cost at least $900 million for restructuring and privatization. In addition, due to lack of foresight by the government, Electricité de France will have benefitted by more than $900 million, making the total cost for Britain of the order of $1.8 billion. Offsetting the costs there have been many benefits, but mistakes were made and there are a number of areas where things might be done differently if the process were repeated.

The Benefits of the Privatization

The benefits of privatization can be grouped into four:

- political gains

- cost reductions

- greater commercialism in the industry

- modest customer gains so far.

Political gains: the privatization was a political act that was founded on the view that "the business of government is not the government of business." Now, although the industry remains politicized, privatization has distanced it from government and Parliament in a manner that would have been inconceivable if it had remained in the public sector. For a start privatization has freed generation from government fuel policies. If the industry had remained in public ownership, then instead of the 'dash for gas' there would have been lengthy political arguments about coal versus gas. Freeing the system from government planning means that the industry will have one of the most balanced and diverse fuel sourcing arrangements in Europe.

Next, privatization has virtually eliminated the political power of the ESI and its dependents:

- in place of a large and more or less unified industry, there are now sixteen separate companies which to varying degrees have different interests, and argue amongst each other. The dominating power of the CEGB has dissolved into four medium size companies which only employ between 4,000 and 9,000 people

- the power of both the nuclear industry and British Coal, twin incubi that fed off each other and poisoned the politics of energy for a quarter of a century, have been broken, as have the political power of the plant manufacturing industry and of large customers.

The foregoing does not imply that the industry is no longer politically sensitive—it is a political creation and is very important. But now the scope of the government to interfere has been limited, and it is much more difficult to use the industry to pursue 'energy policies' and impose surrogate taxes to redistribute income.

Cost reductions: privatization has:

- stopped the construction of three PWRs of 3½GW that would have produced about 22TWh p.a. at about 7½c/kWh (say $1650 million p.a.)

- stopped the construction of 4 x 900MW coal plants that would have produced 27TWh p.a. at about 5.2c/kWh (say $1400 million p.a.)

- eliminated the need to install 2GW of scrubbers at a cost of some $450 million capital expenditure incurring an increase in annual operating cost of some $45 million.

In place of the three PWRs and coal plants we thus far have 13GW of CCGTs that will produce 100TWh p.a. at about 4c/kWh. A 'back of the envelope' calculation is that the annual saving on the 50TWh output of the PWRs and large coal stations replaced by some of the CCGTs is about $1050 million p.a., and the savings on the scrubbers is about $115 million p.a. Some of this benefit has been lost by building CCGTs earlier than necessary—say 2–3GW costing of the order of $1½ billion has been built four years sooner than needs be, which represents an additional cost of the order of $225 million p.a. over those four years. The levelized net saving is thus of the order of $950 million p.a.

Privatization has forced down the cost of coal, and the coal contracts signed in 1993 represent a saving of the order of $2.5 billion in October 1992 prices over the five years compared with what the coal would have cost if the price had remained at the level of 1992/93.

Market pressures and regulatory incentives have motivated the companies to perform more efficiently, and resulted in significant cost reductions:

- the number of people employed by the National Power, PowerGen, NGC and Nuclear Electric divisions of the CEGB on vesting totalled 47,000; four years later they employed 25,000 people, and there are plans for further reductions

- the RECs have demanned by about 20 percent

- equipment costs have been reduced by inviting international turnkey tenders for CCGT plants, which are now built to international time and cost levels

- NGC and the RECs are now more careful in the investment plans, invite international tenders for equipment and believe costs have reduced by 10–20 percent.

Perhaps one of the more unexpected advantages of privatization has been the improvement in the operational performance of Nuclear Electric, which increased output from 43TWh in 1989/90 to 61TWh in 1993/94 and downsized by 35 percent.

Although there are distortions resulting from National Power's and PowerGen's market power and from the character of independent power projects, and consequently the market does not provide accurate economic signals, nonetheless planning of new generation capacity now starts more from an assessment of the prospects of the market than previously. Although shareholders will not bear all the costs of mistakes as they would in a truly competitive market, they are likely to bear some. And because of that discipline, there will hopefully be fewer really large and inexcusable mistakes than there were in the past.

Greater commercialism in the industry: competition in supply has had profound implications for how suppliers look at the market, such as they now have to really understand customers; to offer competitive prices; and to really be nice. The RECs and generators have come a long way in a short time in improving their knowledge of, and attitude to, customers. They now offer a range of price structures, have trained their staff to improve communication and negotiating skills, and generally improve care for customers.

One of the most important achievements of privatization has been to make people think and to strive to increase efficiency. The challenges have forced people to think of solutions to problems that were regarded in electricity circles as difficult, if not insoluble. The process liberated some bright people in the industry, and involved talented people from the civil service and from economic, accounting, merchant banking and legal firms. Throughout the industry, managers have had to learn to behave as real businessmen, rather than as administrators of a politicized bureaucracy. The process has forced a culture change at the top that will spread downwards over the next few years. There has been an infusion of people from outside the industry, especially from oil companies. No longer will the industry be dominated by an engineering ethos admixed with politics. While hopefully engineering excellence will continue to be valued, commercial and financial considerations now receive due weight.

Pandora's box is open, and a dynamic has started that will continue for a while at least. Although the industry will never be as dynamic as the information technology or consumer electronics industries, the change compared with what it was (indeed compared with electric industries in many other countries) has been remarkable. The 'law of unintended consequences' has already manifested itself and the industry— like the rest of the private sector—will have to learn to manage uncertainty, if not to manage chaos. The people in the industry are being converted from 'special (utility) people' who expect monopoly privileges to normal (commercial) people, which the successful find is a lot more fun.

THE FLAWS WITH THE PRIVATIZATION

The attempt to privatize nuclear power was responsible for two of the worst mistakes in the privatization, namely:

- the creation of a duopoly of major generators, which has:

  - stimulated overbuilding CCGTs and premature closure of plant

  - maintained prices higher than they would have been

  - distorted the Pool and contract market

- the payment of large sums of money to Electricité de France (EDF) which benefitted in two ways from the way the government privatized the industry. First, it has access to the market (while the French government refuses reciprocal access to British generators), which enabled it both to increase volume and prices compared with the former system to systems trading at avoided costs. Second, it benefitted by $900 million over eight years from the levy which the government imposed to pay for decommissioning nuclear plant. All in all, the British government tossed $300 million annually down the interconnector.

The other major mistake was that customers did not get a good deal because the government wanted to:

- raise a substantial sum from the flotation of the RECs and NGC, and so it set their use-of-system charges at levels that would produce substantial and increasing profits

- continue forcing tariff customers to subsidize British Coal

- ensure that Nuclear Electric imposed no burden on taxpayer's funds (the government also pocketed the $1½ billion that had been collected for decommissioning).

These were political choices, not economic necessities, and highlights the government's conflict of interest which has been at the heart of the sale of all of the monopoly undertakings.

In view of the speed of change and novelty of what was done it is not surprising that there are loose ends, notably some problems with the Pool and shortcomings in transmission pricing. Many of the problems emerged because the economic characteristics of an electric system are very complex. In a traditional integrated utility they are internalized and generally ignored, but in an unbundled and competitive system, the difficulties are exposed at contractual interfaces as a nexus of inter-related issues.

With the benefit of hindsight it is clear that on organizational grounds it would have been better to have created NGC's transmission business as an independent entity, owning no generation. Furthermore, in view of the complexity of the costs of the system and the problems of perverse incentives that have been created, it would have been better to have formed it as a non-profit oriented undertaking either state owned (supposing it were possible to protect it from political manipulation), or effectively 100 percent debt financed. The lack of profit motive should in principle allow it to more easily act in the public interest as a users' cooperative.

LESSONS FOR OTHERS

It is a mistake to look on the system in England & Wales as a model, whether then to criticize it or to applaud it. Rather the system should be regarded as a set of experiences from which one might learn some ideas that may be helpful and some that are to be avoided. Regulators and electric companies should look at what they can learn, take and adopt what might help them to improve their own system. Possible lessons cannot, however, be over-generalized and will depend upon the current circumstances of an industry; its generation mix; and the political framework within which it operates.

Perhaps the first and most important lesson is that one should not embark upon proposals for change without first identifying the problems with the existing system and having clear ideas as to why possible changes will remedy the problems within the particular political context of a country. The main lessons are:

- the industry is complicated and introducing competition is difficult and complex. Indeed, there are extensive areas of market power in electric systems, which can cause a variety of problems and in a small system, or one with many transmission constraints, there may be no point in trying to introduce competition. The industry is particularly complex where there are already private interests

- it is essential to look at the changes in an integrated manner and to devise a market where the economic incentives and financial structures will be efficient and stable. It is just not enough to open access—consideration has to be given as to how a market can function

- a competitive Pool or spot market may well be required—its design will be difficult

- competition reallocates the risk between customers and the industry, and between parts of the industry. The way in which competition is introduced should not unduly increase the total risk of any of the parts of the industry

- consideration must be given to the financial mechanisms and motivations for building new plant if the industry is privately owned

- competition involves changes in generating plant values up and down. Generators must either have strong balance sheets to absorb downside changes and possibly also the risks of financing the construction of new plant, or they must be able to find distribution companies who are willing absorb the risk through long term contracts

- it is unlikely to be possible to change from monopoly to competition in one step without financial difficulties, which will depend upon the prior distortions in the monopoly system compared with a market system. Incorporation of transitional arrangements may be necessary

- if the experience in England & Wales is any guide, there are likely to be significant possibilities for reducing manpower costs, and for improving marketing and customer service. Furthermore there are likely to be considerable benefits from opening up the industry to external talent

- ideally, for competition, the grid should be a separate entity and a common carrier. The design of transmission pricing is complicated, and the organizational and cost relationship between transmission, system support services, and a Pool are complex

- it is difficult to use a genuinely competitive electric system as a vehicle for implementing energy policies, whether of protecting indigenous plant manufacturing, fuel sourcing, subsidizing particular groups of customers or promoting energy efficiency.

The final lesson is that there will be surprises—the law of unintended consequences will come into play.

Markets break the political nexus—what happened to nuclear and coal is an example of the crumbling of political protection when confronted starkly by economic reality and legal constraints. The market provided solutions to arguments which otherwise would have dragged on for years at the expense of electricity customers. Churchill once observed:

"No one pretends that democracy is perfect or all-wise. Indeed, it has been said that democracy is the worst form of Government except all those other forms that have been tried from time to time."

So it is with markets—they are not perfect and they are often uncertain and messy, and sometimes chaotic and painful. But they are preferable to politicians, civil servants and supplicants for public patronage at public expense.

Chapter 23

The Successful Privatization of Britain's Electricity Industry

John Baker

The concept of privatization of state-owned industries is one of the big ideas of the 1980s, for which full credit must go to the Government of Mrs. Thatcher. Initially conceived as a means of relieving the public sector of financial burdens and raising money for the Exchequer, then as a vehicle for wider share ownership, the privatization concept has also proved to be a major stimulus to management innovation, efficiency and improved customer service.

There can be no doubt that privatization has already profoundly changed the face of British industry. We have transferred from Government to stockholders our gas and telecommunications industries, our major steel producer, our aerospace manufacturer, international airports, British Airways, our water and electricity supply industries, and British Coal. The success of this policy now makes it highly unlikely that the Labor administration, if it wins the next election, would seek to return these industries to state ownership.

Further transfers of industry from the public to the private sector are taking place, notably, British Rail. This latest transfer is more like the privatization of electricity than some of the earlier privatizations—that is to say, preceded by an industrial reconstruction to ensure a more competitive structure in the industry.

To my knowledge, there are few precedents for the wide-ranging structural changes that have been implemented in the United Kingdom's (UK's) electricity supply industry (ESI). Probably only the unbundling of the United States (US) telephone network of AT&T has presented the scale of challenges we have faced. There were certainly no precedents for the speed at which the transformation was made. And it was achieved during the Gulf War and in the middle of a recession. I believe such an accomplishment speaks volumes for the strength, stature, and soundness of our industry.

In looking at the privatization of the ESI in Britain, it is important to distinguish between three distinct but interconnected aspects:

1) we have restructured the industry to break up the old monopolies and facilitate new entrants joining the market, so that we now have competition in generation and supply of electricity;

2) we have privatized the new companies to emerge from this radical reconstruction;

3) we have changed the legislative rules so that new forms of technology and new fuels have been able to enter the market.

Restructuring the Old System

Let me start with structural and competitive issues and outline the previous structure—the situation as it was in England and Wales (E & W).

All the power stations and the transmission system were owned and operated by the Central Electricity Generating Board (CEGB), which had 55,000 megawatts (MW) of capacity, 35,000MW coal-fired, 10,000MW oil-fired, and 8,000MW nuclear. The CEGB planned the whole system on an integrated basis, and sold electricity in bulk to 12 Area Boards, who were each responsible for the distribution networks and supply of electricity to all the customers within their areas—50 million people in total. In effect, there were 13 monopolies who met together as the Electricity Council (EC), they were all Government-owned and financed, with no formal regulation of their activities or prices except insofar as the Government chose to exercise its ownership role to intervene in tariffs, choice of technology, or use of fuels—which it did.

Although the whole industry was profitable and had an excellent record in fulfilling its statutory duty to provide reliability of supplies and keep the lights on, it also suffered from being engineering rather than customer led, rather bureaucratic and hierarchical, and somewhat fat. The tariffs were cost plus and enabled the industry to be rather soft and feather-bedded, though powerful enough to cope with such difficult issues as the management of nuclear power programs and major environmental issues.

The key to the new structure is that the supply of electricity is competitive both at the wholesale and retail level. The twelve Area Boards have been converted into twelve Regional Electricity Companies (RECs), but with the crucial difference that their previous area monopolies or franchises are being progressively reduced. From the outset, very large customers, taking more than 1MW of capacity, were able to shop around for their electricity from either their local REC, another REC, any generator of electricity, or from the market itself. Large customers are also now no longer captive to their local supplier. Early in 1994, the boundary between the franchise market and the free market was reduced from 1MW to 100 kilowatts (kw), and in 1998, the franchise is to be abolished altogether and all customers will be able to shop around for supplies in a totally free market. (The regulator might even accelerate, for some customers, the 1998 deadline to 1996.) How far this is realistic probably depends on the continuing development of remote metering and control systems.

To make retail competition possible and realistic, there are two preconditions: first, there has to be open access to the transmission and distribution networks on a non-discriminatory basis by any generator, supplier, or customer. In other words, open access to all the wires must be available to all the users, the so-called common-carrier principle. This type of process is required, of course, because a transmission system or distribution network is a natural monopoly and it would be a waste of resources to duplicate or triplicate systems side-by-side. Second, there has to be total competition in generation, and the establishment of a whole-sale electricity commodity market—known as the Pool. All generators compete to sell their electricity into the Pool and all suppliers of electricity buy from it to sell to customers in the retail market. So we devised and put in place, in about one year, this new trading pool in which each generating unit has to declare its availability to the market, and the price at which it is prepared to generate, for every half-hour of the day, every 24 hours.

In practice, such a market will tend to produce volatility in prices which neither purchaser nor seller will welcome, and so it will tend to be overlaid with contracts, both short and long term, to make capacity and energy prices more predictable. Thus, much of the electricity being generated is covered by contracts.

Of course, this meant that the monolith of the old CEGB had to be broken up. It was divided into four parts:

- the National Grid Company, owning the transmission system, control centers and the pump-storage plant, responsible for providing electrical highways for all the electricity trades in the pool and the scheduling and dispatch of plant according to the price bids received;

- two fossil-based generating companies: National Power (NP), with 30,000MW of plant, and PowerGen (PG), with 20,000MW; and

- Nuclear Electric (NE), with all the nuclear plants (8,000MW), and which was to be retained in Government ownership and not privatized.

So, the new trading pool could be supplied by NP, PG, and NE, plus Scottish and French operators through their links to the market in England and Wales, and by the many new entrants who are entering, and are committed to enter, the market.

These new markets are based on the belief that competition provides the best spur both to customer service and to efficiency. Where there is a fully competitive structure, as in the case of generation, there is no need for regulation. Indeed, the primary role of regulation in these circumstances is simply to encourage competition. Where there are residual monopolies, as in the case of the transmission and distribution networks, and the franchise market, a regulator (Professor Littlechild) has been appointed to ensure transparency, equality of treatment and no discrimination, and to control the maximum tariffs that may be charged for using the networks and for the supply of energy in the franchise market. These price caps are set prospectively (initially for five years) on what is called the RPI-x formula, where x represents the gains expected to arise from improving efficiency, and which in effect limit annual increases in the charges to customers.

Comparison of the Old and New Regimes

Now we can compare the old and the new regimes. The relatively simple regime of the CEGB, twelve Area Boards and EC has given way to a much more complex but looser and market-driven structure, with twelve RECs, a Grid Company, three large generators and many new generators. The key features are that electricity can be bought and sold by any of the parties, customers can be supplied in a whole variety of ways, generators can sell direct to customers, the RECs can generate up to 15 percent of their own requirements, and auto-generation (and hence combined heat and power or CHP) are encouraged where they are economic.

Again, we can show the difference in character between the old and new regimes.

Old	New
state owned	shareholder owned
monopolistic	competitive
cost-plus	price-regulated
engineering-led	market-led
centrally planned	diversity of thinking
closed to new entrants	open to new entrants

These changes have been a great stimulus to new thinking, ways of doing things, and approaches to customer services. Productivity is rising sharply. Above all, great diversity in management thinking now exists.

Thus far, all these changes *could* have been made without privatizing the organizations involved. But, of course, the industry has also been privatized. The twelve RECs, who between them also own the Grid Company, were floated on the international stock exchanges in December 1990. The flotations raised £7.2 billion for the Exchequer comprising £5.2 billion of equity and £2 billion of debt. The shares were given a nominal value of 240p, of which 100p was to be paid on flotation, with two further installments of 70p each. The shares were sold on yields of between 8 and 9 percent. By March 1995, four years after privatization, the share prices stood at approximately two and a half times the fully-paid offering price of 240p, and their dividend yields ranged from 4.8 percent to 5.7 percent.

The two generators were floated in March 1991. The sale of 60 percent of their shares raised some £3 billion for the Exchequer, comprising £2.2 billion of equity and £800 million of debt. The shares were valued at £1.75p each, of which £1 was payable on flotation with a second installment of 75p payable in February 1992. In March 1995, the Government completed the sale of its remaining 40 percent shareholding in the two companies for a further £4 billion.

Since the two generators are in a fully competitive market and are to be regarded as more akin to heavy manufacturing businesses than to utilities, the markets are coming to rate them more on earnings. By March 1995, the price/earnings multiples were around 11x for National Power and around 10x for PowerGen, and the share prices were approximately two and a half times the fully-paid offering price of 175p.

The restructuring of Scotland was different from that in England and Wales. The nuclear stations were again kept in public ownership in a Scottish Nuclear Company, but all the other assets were divided between two companies, Scottish Power and Scottish Hydro, each being a vertically integrated company responsible for generation, transmission distribution and supply. These two companies were floated in June 1991, and realized almost £2 billion and £1 billion for the Exchequer respectively.

Looking at the privatization process as a whole shows the following:

- The aggregate money that will be raised by Her Majesty's Government by way of equity and loan when fully paid will be £17 billion.

- There were 17 million share applications.

- There are currently some three-to-four million shareholders on the combined registers, which include shareholders in the US, Canada, Europe and Japan as well as the UK.

- The shares have performed well in the market.

Transformation Developments

Another key aspect of Britain's electricity industry transformation is developments in technology and fuels that coincide with structural changes and privatization, and arguably have also been influential in shaping the way we will develop in the 1990s.

As part of the process, the Government itself decided, for strategic reasons, to provide support for nuclear energy and for renewable energies—in other words, to ensure their survival in an otherwise free market. For nuclear power, a levy equivalent to about 10 percent of the ultimate cost of electricity to the customer is raised annually to 1998 on every non-nuclear kWh generated to subsidize the nuclear plants. A small fraction of the levy is used to encourage the development of renewable energies, such as wind power and waste to energy schemes. To enforce this policy, each REC is required by law to purchase certain quantities of nuclear and renewable energy.

In the UK as under European Union (EU) law, it had been forbidden to use gas for power generation. Both in the UK and EU, that prohibition has been lifted. The result is that the power industry in the UK now has for the first time access to gas supplies from the United Kingdom Continental Shelf (UKCS). The supply is abundantly available at a competitive price. Used in combined cycle gas turbines (CCGTs), gas has become the fuel of choice in place of coal for all significant power plants likely to be built in Great Britain this decade. Gas has particular value for National Power and PowerGen as a means of enabling us to comply efficiently with European and British limits to sulphur emissions from existing coal plants. Without substituting gas for coal we would need to retrofit additional flue gas desulphurization (FGD) plants, a technology that is hugely expensive. The benefits of these plants compared with coal are well known.

CCGTs	Coal
low capital cost	twice cost of equivalent CCGT
2–3 year construction time	5–6 year construction time
54+% cycle efficiency	39% efficiency
low emissions	requires special control measures (FGD)
low staffing	high staffing
no materials handling	coal/ash handling

As a result, we expect to see some 13,000MW of CCGTs built in the UK by 2000. Importantly, the relative ease of this technology in operating terms, plus the relatively easy financeability of short lead time/low capital cost plant, eases the way for new entrants to come into power generation, and significantly aids the achievement of Government policies to secure increasing competition in generation. In fact, some ten or more independent power schemes—in prospect, commissioned, under construction, and in planning—will provide 6–7,000MW of the new capacity forecast for the decade.

System Development

What is the impact of all these changes, and how is the system likely to develop?

First, the new arrangements are undoubtedly working effectively. The computing software required for the operation of the pool and for settling the trades every half hour was without precedent and very sophisticated. The software has worked reliably and with surprisingly few problems. Britain has proved that a real-time trading market can work efficiently.

Second, no problems are found with reliability of supplies, and, as indicated, the novelty of the new arrangements is proving no barrier to new investment in power plant whether by the incumbent generators or new entrants.

Third, since 1990 in the non-franchise markets, i.e., the over 1MW market, customers have used their freedom aggressively to shop around for supplies. (More recently, the market has been opened successfully to 100kw customers.) For example, my own company now sells directly to customers on contracts tailored to their individual requirements.

Fourth, no significant problems are being experienced over the operation of open transmission and distribution networks.

In respect of important technical areas where many of us had serious doubts at the outset of this exercise, we can now say that these doubts have been resolved, and the experiment in that sense is clearly a success.

What about the wider implications of the changes, as competition in generation and supply continues to increase? What about the effect on customers, suppliers, and the environment? Perhaps I might illustrate what is happening by reference to my own company.

National Power now sells electricity at the factory gate into a real-time commodity market known as the Pool. To meet the burgeoning competition, we have transformed the company since its inception in 1990. We are now by no means a conventional monopoly utility. In that time, we have:

- cut wholesale prices by around 8 percent in real terms for domestic customers and around 20 percent on average for a typical industrial customer

- increased staff productivity by around 75 percent

- committed investment of more than £1.5 billion largely on new, cleaner generating plant, and on environmental improvements

- increased operating profits by around 60 percent

- invested more capital than our total post-tax profits

- achieved total returns for shareholders—measured as capital growth plus dividends—of some 200 percent, and the taxpayer has benefitted similarly through the Government's 40 percent shareholding in the Company

- improved availability and efficiency of existing plant

- made substantial progress in developing an international power business.

We believe we have demonstrated the success of privatization, and have delivered benefits for customers, shareholders, and the economy. We aim to continue to do so—by putting further downward pressure on our costs and through greater attention to customer service and business innovation.

Privatization, of course, has wider impacts—on National Power's plant suppliers on whom the Company is more and more demanding for performance. There are even wider impacts on other utilities. The world has been watching the British experiment. Now the EU Commission has prepared draft directives to apply the principles underlying the new British system to the electricity systems of the other 14 continental members of the European Communities—that is to say:

- the abolition of monopolies;

- segregation of generation, transmission, and distribution; and

- open access to the transmission networks.

The directives are being resisted by some European utilities. In the US, Independent Power Producers (IPPs) are taking a larger share of the power market, and the Federal Energy Regulatory Commission (FERC) is evaluating open transmission networks. American utilities resist the trend. Portugal, Australia, New Zealand, and many others are now looking at various approaches to competition, open networks and even privatization. I can say that, where there is resistance, our experience largely discredits the arguments on which resistance is based. I know that because we deployed them and we were wrong.

There are also decisive benefits in the sort of arrangements we have made—for customers, in more efficient services; for Government, in relief from public financing burdens; and for management in the stimulus it has given us to find better ways of doing things.

Where the market rules rather than Government controls, a virtuous chain emerges. Customers get cost-effective and rationally priced electricity on which to base their own expenditure decisions, whether in the home or for industry. Suppliers, whether of fuel or plant, know there can be no 'sweetheart' deals, because soft options lead to uncompetitive performance and hence to loss of market share and profitability.

Of course, all is not yet perfect, and our system will continue to develop.

- We can improve the scheduling and dispatch of plant under the new regime, where we need to overhaul the old algorithms that were based on a centrally planned system.

- We can improve the structure of charges for use of the grid which as yet is rather crude. The necessary transparency and non-discriminatory features are in place, but the allocation of costs needs fine-tuning. The principles of charging should be based on LRMC, with proper signals given for the siting of new power plants taking system losses fully into account.

- We need to establish markets for matters such as quick start capability, constrained-on running and voltage and frequency control, the prices of which are as yet fixed rather arbitrarily.

- We expect to see considerable development of a whole variety of contractual overlays to the spot market, as is normal in commodity markets, e.g. oil. Ultimately, we can expect an electricity futures market should develop. But, fundamentally, our market works.

- The regulator has shown concern with the pricing of electricity within the pool, as reflected in several reviews. In particular, he has shown concern about mid-merit plants which set the price of electricity, and the concentration of ownership of generating assets. This led to an agreement, in February 1994, between the regulator and National Power and PowerGen in which they agreed to use all reasonable endeavors to dispose of some 6000MW of generating plant. The generators also entered into a pricing undertaking for a period of two years. Significantly, the regulator's statement did not criticize either company for its market behavior.

As stated at the outset, privatization is a big idea that has global value. I hope that I have shown how radical its impact has been on the UK electricity industry.

I believe that it is a success story, and will continue to bring increasing benefits for the electricity consumer.

Chapter 24

Managing Change

I.M.H. Preston

In this chapter, I will identify some of the key issues that I, and the management and staff of ScottishPower, have had to face in meeting one of the classic challenges of the late nineties: reorganizing a company structure, its philosophy, and its methods of operation to meet new targets and demands—new targets and demands that are being set by new shareholders, a new market, and more demanding customers. Also, I will describe how ScottishPower has risen to the challenges of privatization, which is a traumatic change for any organization.

Most of you have faced the need to manage change, for there is only one thing that is certain in today's business world and that is uncertainty—change is inevitable and the pace of change is increasing. A business that does not adopt and apply a change- driven culture will not survive.

ScottishPower was created as a public limited company (PLC), out of the old state-owned South of Scotland Electricity Board (SSEB) in 1990. Cast your mind back to the electricity "Board" of a few years ago and imagine it being capable of, or willing to do, the things we at ScottishPower now do as a matter of course. Imagine it apologizing for mistakes and compensating customers for broken promises. Imagine it being able to provide a heating solution or an industrial process that best suited the customer's needs whether by gas or electricity. Imagine it being willing to bargain on price. And above all, imagine it thanking customers for their business. All of these things are now commonplace. These are some of the outward manifestations of the change that has taken place.

There has been revolution, not evolution, in the world of utilities, and I would like to share some of the experiences of an organization going through the pain barriers of change. I hope to demonstrate that our customers are the focus of change, and, in turn, the beneficiaries—financially and in quality of service—of the process of change that has transformed our business.

ScottishPower

To understand better how we have addressed the challenges of change I would like to describe what ScottishPower looks like today. We are a company with a market capitalization of some £3 billion and we have almost 700,000 shareholders. Our turnover is £1.5 billion, our profit before tax is £350 million and our gearing (leverage) is very low.

We are big; we are Scotland's largest industrial company and in the middle of the Financial Times Stock Exchange (FTSE) 100 index vying for position with the Royal Bank of Scotland, Scottish and Newcastle, the Rank Organization, Commercial Union, British Steel, and Whitbread.

ScottishPower is a vertically-integrated electricity business. This means that we generate, transmit, and supply electricity unlike England where two private companies generate electricity that is supplied to customers by 12 regional electricity companies after making its way along high voltage cables operated by a separate company, National Grid Company, which is jointly owned by the 12 supply companies.

If you think this is complicated, believe me you are just beginning to appreciate the utility industry's love of complexity.

ScottishPower's main franchise area is in the south of Scotland from a line north of Stirling and Fife south to the English borders. We have some 1.7 million customers. We are competing for business in England and Wales with a good measure of success. About 10 percent of our electricity goes south and we expect this to increase to around 30 percent within the next 2 to 3 years.

Almost 5,500 of our 8,000 employees are engaged in our electricity businesses – some 2,500 fewer than we inherited at privatization. But, in our developing businesses we have been creating jobs, particularly retail, which has doubled its work force to 1,500.

We now have 10 separate businesses.

You should note that each of these 10 businesses, i.e., generation, transmission, distribution, supply, wholesale, gas, retail, technology, contracting and, most recently, telecoms, has been established as stand alone operations with full management accountability delegated for operations. Each is trading profitably, again with the appropriate management skills bought from outside and still has the appropriate manpower and salary infrastructure for the fields in which they are operating within the planning and financial policies established by a small corporate office.

The Electricity Board

The SSEB, our predecessor board, was a totally centralized functional structure. It was also completely dominated by the desires, intents, dare I say the whims, of the government of the day. So its strategic, tactical, and functional performance was ruled by myriad government departments, including:

The Department of Employment
(pay policy, wage freezes in the public sector, chairman paid less than directors)

The Department of Energy
(coal, nuclear, oil, renewables, gas)

The Department of the Environment
(ash, gases – so2 – nox, electro-magnetic fields)

The Department of Social Services
(the poor/disadvantaged, special cases, elderly, sick, etc.)

And, not forgetting the all-important Treasury.

It is not hard to appreciate that with so much of the organizations' objectives in life being controlled by third party influence; i.e., by government and not by commercial pressures; capital investment restrictions, wage freezes, price controls, etc. were introduced whenever political pressure dictated.

The SSEB was the subject of a Monopolies and Mergers Commission (MMC) investigation in 1986 on its efficiency and costs. The commission's report said that SSEB was well run and that it managed its core function, the generation, transmission, and distribution of electricity efficiently and skillfully.

That report continues, "the concentration of strategic decision-making in the hands of the Chairman, Deputy Chairman and the two Directors and the generally high control over the business exercised by head office, is well suited to an organization where electricity is produced from a small number of large generating units and the bulk of whose consumers lies within a narrowly confined geographical area. The board set itself high standards of technical and managerial efficiency and competence and monitors achievement against them. In the management of its main operations, we believe that these standards have been met."

The commission expressed some concern that in industrial relations and with its consumers, the management ought to have devoted more time and adopted the same rigorous approach that they had in planning and building Torness Power Station, a project that dominated the company at that time.

What I am trying to point out here is that this good performance was against a set of standards totally different from those in the private sector and that it is this major shift in targets that drove the change process and the culture shock.

Becoming a PLC

When ScottishPower was launched in 1990, its management structure was forced into a PLC format by government advisers, but there was no real appreciation of the scale of commitment to changing custom and practice that would be required for the era ahead. Even in the aftermath of a major transformation in the shape of privatization, there were managers who could not, or would not, accept that the change they began to witness around them would require a change of themselves. They believed that competition was something that affected others in different industries. It was true that the technical facilities in SSEB were well engineered but the consumer (not the customer) was treated in an impersonal manner.

It was extremely difficult to convince a reluctant management that the world they were entering was totally different from the one they had lived in all their days. Their performance had, after all, already been endorsed by the MMC. What they didn't realize was that the criteria for performance and values were now to be completely different.

The scale and nature of the change required was significant. The organization had to move quickly from an engineering-orientated culture to one that was commercially focused. The new company needed accountability and ownership from all of it's employees rather than the diffused responsibility of the SSEB.

I want to stress accountability. It is the key to establishing a management structure that can be devolved and that can release all the talents of the core business managers.

The emphasis had to be shifted from maintaining supply to serving customers and from being large and centralized to being lean and de-centralized. From being risk averse it had to move to become entrepreneurial in attitude and from electricity only, the commercial base of the company had to be broadened.

Another facet of the inherited culture was the lack of decision-making, even at senior management level. Everything was pushed upwards to either the Managing Directors (MDs) or the small executive team. The industrial society once reported that SSEB were the best example they had found of delegating upwards!

Most challenging of all was the fact that a large proportion of the management believed that things did not need to change. As has been found elsewhere, industrial and lower level staff did recognize the need, and the road block, as it were, was among the middle management population.

As I said earlier, full accountability for the operation of each business was placed with its MD. I ensured that corporate directors did not interfere with the operations within divisions and equally ensured that MDs of divisions did not develop policies at variance with those of the company.

Later, as the need for more strategic thinking and development became pressing, and with the MD Structure working well, we created Chief Operating Officers to relieve me as CEO of some of my duties and free me for the more strategic role. More recently we have had to redistribute the portfolios of executive directors as personnel have changed—top management have had to change each year. This constantly evolving process requires the recruitment of top-flight management in order that structure changes made in response to changing circumstances can be undertaken without difficulty. Today ScottishPower's success is built on this top-class management team that has been built up since privatization. It is of fundamental significance that this team only contains two out of the top twenty who have long-term SSEB experience like myself. All the rest have been recruited from outside—a critical requirement in my experience if you wish to really drive the change process.

Further recruitment at more junior levels is continuing to inject the necessary PLC culture into the business while we train up the company talent to fill the future management ranks.

This was a major testing period for the fledgling PLC and the lesson I learned was that to drive change, first test all options for clear accountability—I re-emphasize this part—then, clearly define the objectives. The objectives have to be backed up by the whole leadership team sharing the same vision of the company and its future. Those who do not believe should have no part in the culture change or they will be hindrances to progress.

In driving towards a results-focused culture, we needed to introduce a new set of values and establish new practices and business processes, stimulating more teamworking, cross-business, and multi-level activity in developing these. In such a time of transition, with a significant reduction in manning levels, it was imperative that we treated employees sympathetically and fairly. And we had to begin to work harder at improving our internal communications processes to establish more formal lines to counter the inevitable rumors and the tomtoms.

Some Lessons To Be Learned

The first lesson to be learned from changing from state ownership to private industry is that with dominant, successful top management, major change in organization and accountability cannot be achieved without the use of external agents of sufficient experience and standing and with appropriate authority to force the change process.

To break into a strong, established structure and culture from within is extremely difficult, particularly if the owners of the change process are numerically overwhelmed by the conservatives. Their credibility is difficult to establish unlike that of world-class external consultants that are brought in.

The second lesson is that change will not happen unless the executives of the company take on the driving role. You may think that is crashingly obvious, but consider how often initiatives are given a chief-executive's blessing and then die as they are left to others at lower management levels to implement.

The Process of Change in ScottishPower

There were several inhibitions to change. There was not enough management in depth to drive the culture change, and neither was there a management or career development program, or the organizational structure to match the pace of change. There was no performance based reward structure and no employee relations strategy. There was no balance between hard-drive management decisions and "winning the hearts and minds of employees" initiatives.

We learned that to help along the process of change, we needed to develop a strategy and work to it. Our strategy has been simple, but effective.

The strategy that we adopted to address the needs of the company and that we have followed religiously since our creation is as follows:

- we set out to improve the efficiency of the business and to cut costs

- we determined to make better use of our assets, such as power stations, and the skills of the management and work force

- we set a course prudently to broaden our utility base

- we set out to invest in, and develop, the full range of skills that would be required to permit the company to take advantage of any business opportunity that might present itself. We call this enablement.

Improving Efficiency

To tackle the efficiency drive we did the following:

- set focused plans for each business

- set objectives for each business

- reorganized to remove layers of management

- reviewed working practices to match them to the various markets

- reduced manpower

- conserved capital

- initiated improvements in service and maximized sales.

All of this was done to increase shareholder value. These actions were taken in the knowledge that a government regulator would have an extremely influential, and unknown, part to play in our progress where he controls our income and profit on our regulated electricity businesses and dictates the minimum customer service standards.

Put simply and ambitiously, we have set out to be the best in the world and have embarked on a program of benchmarking against companies recognized to be the best in many aspects of customer service or production processes. Teams, embracing many levels of our work force, have visited businesses—not just utilities—in America, Japan, Australia, and in mainland Europe to identify leading, world-class practices.

Results

We are looking, listening, learning; then adopting, adapting, and applying what we learn to achieve step changes in our practices and processes, and in making our assets—physical and human—and our money, work better for us.

One of the most tangible improvements has been in customer service. In privatization year, some 16,000 consumers were cut off supply for not paying bills. This year the number will be no more than a few dozen, and our bad debt situation has never been lower; this is because we are working with our customers, devising methods of helping them and us to meet their commitments.

Last year we won a government charter mark for customer service and we won the highest accolade in the electrical sector – the Electrical Review Customer Care Award. We are now regularly recognized for the speed and efficiency of our telephone answering. Recently our district offices gained seven of the top twenty places in an independent telephone service survey across the whole of British industry. And yes, we did claim the top spot.

We have made special arrangements to know more about our customers, particularly the elderly or immobile, and we work in partnership with community organizations and social services.

There is accountability all along the customer service line and much more front-end response and decision making on the customer's behalf.

We are investing in marketing, recruiting more specialists, and sharpening our competitive edge, internally and externally. We have opened offices in Birmingham and London to be nearer our national customers and we are aggressively pursuing new business.

Human Resources

I'd like to turn now to the all-important area of reward: salaries and conditions, organizational development and succession planning; and management recruitment, compensation and benefits planning, training, management and career development, and health and safety; all of these are being integrated into our Human Resource (HR) strategy for progress that will support our business plans.

The most significant terms and conditions development is a two-year wage agreement, signed last year, that is changing the flexibility of working patterns and extending working hours to suit customers. We now work six days a week, 8:00 a.m. to 8:00 p.m. We focus on customer service, such as customer enquiries and meter reading. We have introduced annualized working hours for power station workers to reduce overtime and improve efficiency. In addition, we have introduced business-unit bargaining, eliminating company-wide wage and conditions agreements. We believe we have introduced one of the most advanced and ambitious employee relations change agendas in the industry.

We are relating rewards to the competitive context of each business, so that for example retailing and electrical contracting rewards are relevant to their fields, not to those applying in the separate divisions of the energy businesses.

We will continue to be realistic and competitive in developing pay and conditions at all levels of the company. For senior management, we have introduced merit and performance-related pay against agreed company and personal objectives and have abandoned cost-of-living adjustments and incremental scales. We are cascading this through the management structure. We are investing heavily in training and development.

Open learning centers have been established across all of our locations and more than 1,300 employees are currently undertaking lecture- and computer-based training in their own time, in a wide range of courses. In the 15 months since we started this initiative, more than 1,900 staff have been involved in open learning courses, representing 25 percent of our work force.

We have developed a company-specific MBA course at Heriot Watt University in a consortium partnership with Dawson International. This part-time MBA will enable about 80 of our young, talented managers to work together at acquiring high level business education while still developing their business skills in full-time jobs.

We developed, with Strathclyde Graduate Business School, a Senior Management Development Programme to enable the executive directors and the key 100 senior managers from the divisions to share, in debate, the corporate vision and strategy. The program was also aimed at increasing commercial awareness, management skills, and leadership qualities.

As a follow up to the Senior Management Programme, cross divisional programs and assignments have been introduced to consider critical issues. One such programme is considering the interface between our customers and our businesses and will be developing systems to enhance the services we provide our customers.

We have improved our framework for graduate development and we have started competency-based training and vocational qualifications. Career development planning is being introduced progressively.

Also, we have introduced new health care services, including voluntary health screening and new on-site health services.

Our HR strategy, as exemplified by the activities I have just described, is a balance between the hard drive to introduce 'best-in-class' and cost effective employee relations practices and market driven reward systems with major employee development programs to ensure both the effectiveness and employability of our managers and staff.

The first phase of our benchmarking has moved us forward dramatically in efficiency and in cost effectiveness. We are now engaged on phase two, which will bring even more cost reductions and service improvements—with a view to positioning us at the top of the world's utility companies.

Employees are being encouraged to accept more individual responsibility. We are seeking even greater flexibility and merit pay at all levels of the company to achieve 'best-in-class' working practices.

We are also seeking to improve our internal communications, developing core values and sharing our strategy and vision and what it means at every level. And we are listening to people's concerns and priorities and trying to reflect this within our plans.

This year we completed a major communications exercise where our directors undertook many presentations to deliver our annual results eye-to-eye to all of our 8,000 employees and then conducted an open question and answer session (I did 19, myself, in one week).

Conclusion
Where in our developing businesses we consider that we require the addition of highly-professional partners to limit the company risk to acceptable levels, then we will seek them.

We will stick close to the knitting to ensure we have the skills, resources, and competencies to undertake and manage new ventures.

We will only invest in new businesses that will bring our shareholders more value than they would achieve through a direct investment. We have not rushed overseas. We have set out to make sure our present business is in its best possible shape before we divert management time and effort to some wider horizons; it is prudent diversification that we intend for the Company.

So we are being patient and we are being canny; but the city would expect that of us, of course, since we are Scots!

We do not profess to have all the answers, or to have gotten it all right, but our results, financially and in service to our customers, reflect the successful consequences of dramatic change within our company. We know that change will continue, because the demands of customers will continue to change, and the external pressures of competition, or legislation, or of regulation will continue to bear on us. We are developing a culture that embraces and relishes change for the challenges it brings; we want to anticipate change, not to react to it; that will be key to continuing to offer our customers the best service in the world, at the best prices.

Chapter 25

The British Experience:
The Pioneering Major, if Partial, Success

Allen Sykes

The Pre-privatization Culture

The general virtues of privatization (and its close cousin "deregulation") are now so widely accepted throughout most of the world that it is difficult to appreciate how major a political, social, economic, and business culture change has been pioneered in Britain over less than half a generation. Before examining the progress of privatization in Britain it is useful to consider briefly the circumstances and atmosphere that previously prevailed in the now successfully privatized companies, particularly in the major utilities, and in government departments.

Coal and Electricity: The Background

The most instructive industries to consider are the closely related coal and electricity industries, both nationalized shortly after the Second World War, and controlled by the large Department of Energy. More than 75 percent of electricity was generated from coal, more than 90 percent of which was supplied by British Coal, with small, almost token imports to a few coastal power stations. Of British Coal's output of just over 100 million tonnes per annum (m.t.p.a.), 75 percent was sold to the electricity supply companies, the Central Electricity Generating Board (CEGB) for England and Wales, and the South of Scotland Electricity Board (SSEB) for Scotland. In 1987 there were 110 underground mines producing 88 m.t.p.a. mainly at a loss despite charging at least 50 percent more than the cost of imported coal, and numerous open cast sites producing only 13 m.t.p.a. at a very large profit per tonne, with costs significantly below import costs.

British Coal

British Coal (BC) owned all the coal reserves in Britain. A few million tonnes (4 percent) of coal was produced each year by very small, private mines who licensed their reserves from BC at a large royalty, and who had to sell their output at a price determined by BC. BC further imposed controls on the number of men who could work in each underground mine (heavily restricted). Despite these onerous conditions, and working on only the smallest and lowest grade reserves, this tiny private sector consistently produced profits, an ironic commentary on the huge and largely unprofitable BC.

BC sold its coal mainly to the CEGB and SSEB under annual bulk contracts. Each pit manager and open cast site manager had volume and cost targets and in the case of deep mines a productivity target. But neither they nor anyone else either knew or needed to know the profit of the individual underground mines as the coal was accepted and transported in bulk and allocated to different power stations by central fiat.

BC dealt mainly with one all-powerful union, the National Union of Mineworkers (NUM). It was the received wisdom of successive governments that the demands of the NUM must always be accepted, more particularly after the disastrous strikes in the 1970s that had helped topple a Conservative government. So ingrained was political fear of the NUM that it continued almost unabated even after their resounding defeat in the one year 1984/85 strike.

Productivity in BC's underground pits was a mere fifth of that in comparable American pits. Overmanning was rife, redundancy payments and pensions were the highest per head in Britain, and higher than anything in Western Europe.

The producers, the management, the miners, and the unions, had captured the industry, as is common in any monopoly, but particularly nationalized ones.

The Electricity Supply Industry

The same lack of competition and disregard of costs, efficiency, and manning levels that characterized BC, applied equally in the electricity supply industry (ESI). As with pit managers so too with power station managers; none of them knew the real costs of their delivered coal, and hence their individual costs and profits.

The CEGB ran its own transmission grid, the "National Grid." The wholesale price of electricity to the distribution companies was the aggregate of total generation costs plus total grid costs to give the "Bulk Supply Tariff" (BST). The cost to customers was based on the BST plus the distribution costs that varied somewhat amongst the regional distribution companies. Total costs were allocated to different customers under a variety of tariffs depending on size and time of day, etc. The distribution companies like the CEGB and the SSEB were monopolies. While in theory company-owned private power plants (e.g., at chemical complexes and aluminum smelters) could sell any surplus output to third parties, in practice they were forced to sell at low prices to the CEGB and SSEB.

As for the 10 nuclear stations that supplied 16 percent of all electrical power, their accounting costs were included in the BST, but no one really knew their real costs. It was commonly represented that their aggregate costs were lower per unit of energy than for oil or coal. In the activity leading up to privatization, however, it emerged that their real costs were 2½ times those previously claimed, and more than double the cost of coal generation.

The CEGB and SSEB could have imported foreign coal at less than two-thirds of the price of imported coal, but were continuously discouraged from more than token imports by successive Labour and Conservative governments. Equally the two generating companies accepted government pressure to buy plant and equipment almost entirely from British manufacturers whose costs, not surprisingly, reflected the absence of serious competition. The same policy extended to power station construction by only British companies. Power stations cost much more and took much longer to build than in any other industrialized countries.

The Department of Energy
The Department of Energy, a very large and important government department, presided over these cozy, non-competitive conditions without ever seemingly questioning their desirability, or the large extra burden of higher than necessary electricity costs on Britain's overall competitiveness.

The Treasury
The Treasury was ultimately responsible for the financial supervision of coal and electricity. While it insisted on a real discounted cash flow rate of return of eight percent on capital expenditures, there was no serious checking of outturn profitability, and the overall rate of return achieved varied from two to three percent for electricity, and to negative returns on coal when all subsidies were taken into account. Capital funds were often limited because of government budgetary requirements. Conversely, electricity prices were often held down to suppress reported inflation. It was no one's responsibility to consider long-term national efficiency issues.

The Resulting Muddle
In sum, we see two basic industries, riddled with cross subsidies and uneconomic arrangements, with no real knowledge of costs, efficiency, and profit at individual pits and power stations, and hence at distribution company level. With the exception of coal strikes, it was a system the Soviet Union's energy planners would have recognized as similar to their own. It resulted in huge over capacity, and over manning, high costs, and major inefficiencies. Yet for forty years this situation was defended almost unanimously by politicians, civil servants, senior managers, and union leaders. To question the basic rationale was regarded at best as misguided and at worst as a blend of ignorance and national disloyalty. These attitudes prevailed in the ESI and at British Coal until the late 1980s when the privatization of the former was imminent and of the latter in clear prospect.

PRIVATIZATION ORIGINS
A British Invention

Britain has been the indisputable pioneer of privatization, one of the major successful ideas of the last 50 years. The process began gradually in 1982, with the first major utility privatization, that of British Telecommunications, in 1984 followed by British Gas in 1986, the water industry in 1991, and electricity in 1992, with coal and railways scheduled for 1994/5, the Post Office for late 1995/early 1996, and the National Health Service, apart from dentistry, perhaps not at all. Over the last 12 years the government has divested itself of a huge number of companies in diverse fields from hotels and "pubs" to ports and airports, from oil and steel to aerospace and airlines, from car companies and shipyards to buses and research companies, etc. The state ownership of national production has fallen from around a quarter to under a tenth, and within a few years will be virtually nonexistent. The scale has been all embracing, and the pace hectic. While there have been mistakes, even serious mistakes, as is inevitable in a pioneering process, there is no doubting the major beneficial effects on the British economy and spirits from this massive dose of liberalization. Without it Britain would not be a leading second rank world power.

Even the Western world was at first slow to copy the British experiment but now privatization has been taken up almost universally. Significantly it is the main force liberalizing the desperate economies of the ex-communist world that cannot wait for western economists to devise an efficient working model to transform wholly state-owned economies to largely market driven ones. What began as a minor shake-up of parts of the British economy has become a major beneficial force throughout most of the world. It can confidently be forecast to reach the rest of the world before ten years are past.

The Catalytic Events

The powerful and beneficial effects of privatization took even its originators by surprise, or surely it would have been implemented much earlier. It began because of the parlous state of the British economy when the Conservatives pushed a discredited Socialist party from office in 1979. By then around 45 percent of Gross Domestic Product was in the public sector, with public expenditure and the National Debt rising, despite high levels of taxation. The position was unsustainable: radical action followed. The government could no longer afford the large subsidies to the poorly performing nationalized industries, nor could it meet their heavy capital expenditure requirements. With the high marginal rates of income tax more than halved to restore personal incentives in business, with mounting unemployment and necessarily increased social expenditure, the government desperately needed to increase its revenues and reduce expenditure.

The sale of selected state-owned businesses, in particular those earning some profits, became attractive since it reduced the need for subsidies and brought in much needed capital sums. Further, it was the belief of at least Margaret Thatcher, the Prime Minister that the privatized businesses would be better run in the private sector removed from the unbusinesslike hands of Civil Servants and the political priorities of Ministers. Almost certainly there was also the attraction that the government would no longer suffer from the opprobrium of having to deal directly with difficult unions. Further union power would be diminished when facing managements who could no longer rely on government handouts. Their companies would either have to pay their way or go out of business.

There was another attractive feature to the emerging privatization process. Margaret Thatcher had begun the popular process of selling council (government-owned) housing on favorable terms to their largely working-class tenants. It soon became apparent that once tenants became owners, i.e., capitalists, many began to support the Conservative Party and to look more to their own efforts to raise their living standards rather than to the unions or the government. This led the government to wish to extend "peoples capitalism" by selling shares in privatizing companies on favorable terms, partly to the employees, but mainly to the general public. Companies and investment institutions were largely precluded from applying for shares. To the surprise and dismay of the opposition Labour Party, and the Unions, the policy proved very popular with employees and public alike. The typical take-up of employee share options was more than 90 percent, and the proportion of individuals owning shares rose from 7 percent to 25 percent, i.e., by nearly a fifth of the adult population. Both sets of figures came as a surprise to all shades of opinion. A permanent change in the political, social, and economic culture was taking place. Nowadays, when firms are being privatized, unions argue for more shares and on better terms for employees—a sea change from their earlier attitudes of opposing share purchases on grounds of "disloyalty." Further, after losing three General Elections in a row, by 1987 the Labour Party had given up its threats to renationalize privatized industries. The political and economic landscape had indeed changed fundamentally and permanently. Privatization was here to stay.

Applicable Equally to Loss-making Industries

The successes of the early privatization of profitable and marginally profitable industries, and the greatly improved economic performances that they all achieved, led the government to realize that loss-making companies could also be privatized because economic performance was transformed by the process. There followed a spate of such privatization, including the National Freight Corporation largely sold to its management and staff, and eventually the big loss-making

British Steel (the nationalized steel industry) and British Airways, now international models for service, efficiency, and profit as in state ownership they were once the reverse.

A Major Surprise

The growing success of privatization took the government as well as virtually everyone else by surprise. This determined the government to consider privatizing the huge nationalized utilities. As they were all national monopolies they earned profits even in state ownership, albeit usually modest ones. It was apparent that in private ownership they could be expected to be run much more efficiently and profitably while raising substantial revenue for the government—and so it proved. Thus out of economic desperation a remedy emerged that was to have far reaching and largely unforeseen major benefits. It was to help transform Britain's economy and to go on to become the justifiable received wisdom of most of the world.

THE PROCESS
Reducing State Activity

The British Prime Minister, Margaret Thatcher, began her 11-year period in government with a dislike amounting almost to a loathing of unnecessary state activity. She wanted to reduce taxes and government interference and to free businesses to face the realities of the marketplace. After 5 years she realized that there was no good case to retain the major utilities in government ownership and she set about privatizing them. There was no useful experience to draw upon anywhere in the world but she had a firm conviction that businesses would perform more effectively when subject to the disciplines of the marketplace, and, where appropriate (in particular for monopolies such as the main utilities), with a suitable degree of regulation. There was a general dislike and distrust of the American system of regulation that concentrated on not allowing excessive rates of return, but that at the time had little regard to the actual cost of the services provided. Instead the preference was for "light" regulation that concentrated on efficiency and the promotion of competition. This could permit higher returns on capital than would then be acceptable in the United States.

Promoting Competition: British Telecommunications

From the beginning, the intention was to introduce some competition. For the first two major utilities that were privatized, British Telecommunications (BT) and the British Gas Corporation (BGC) the importance of introducing serious competition received quite inadequate attention. The first large utility to be privatized was BT in 1984. As a nationalized industry it had a complete monopoly of the telephone system that was then virtually entirely cable based. It was not clear how another British competitor could be created and no consideration was given at the time to encouraging foreign competitors to come in to share the market with BT. Accordingly, it was decided to start with a single licensed competitor, Mercury, which could count upon only 5 percent of the initial market. To prevent so small a competitor being ineffective, considerable attention was given to the powers and appointment of the first regulator, Bryan Carsberg (later Sir Bryan). He bravely and persistently interpreted his brief to introduce the maximum of competition, the sharing of BT's cable system and an insistence upon common dialing numbers. Because of his persistent efforts, and the advent of highly efficient radio-based telephone services that have spawned a number of competitors to BT, competition has effectively been introduced to the telecommunications industry over a period of ten years.

British Gas Privatization: A Step Back

Sadly, the logic that led to setting up a new competitor for BT was not extended two years later to the privatization of BGC in 1986, which was just one year before a likely general election. The government had urgent need for additional revenue to finance tax cuts and therefore it was much easier to privatize BGC as a continuing monopoly since it would have taken a year or two longer to plan its break-up and the introduction of competitors. By this time, the main free market, economic and political institutions, academics and numerous financial journalists were all urging the merits of delaying privatization until a fully competitive form could be introduced. Government political and financial realities prevented this from happening in the case of BGC, which was regrettable but perhaps inevitable. It has to be said that the financial institutions (the City) much favored the monopoly form of privatization as it gave them a much easier job to market the shares, which led to higher receipts and hence larger fees. This was particularly true because, by government decision, most of the shares were to be sold to the general public. This was for two reasons: first, a wish to extend the increasingly popular "peoples capitalism" and, second the realization that to privatize a nationalized industry in separate pieces would be much harder to explain to the general public and would raise much smaller sums. It was written into the share prospectus that the structure of the industry would remain essentially unchanged for seven years, which meant that the greater efficiencies that could have accrued for the British economy were deferred for at least seven years. Now the period is over, BGC is being subjected, in effect, to breakup and major competition.

Again, as in the case of telecommunications, the government gave reasonably strong powers to the Gas Regulator, James McKinnon (later Sir James). He proved to be a very tough regulator indeed and, one can only suspect, far tougher than the government, and more particularly the Department of Energy, had intended. He loathed the existence as well as the abuse of monopoly power and believed in the virtues of promoting maximum competition in ways that were equalled only by the Prime Minister herself. BGC had first thought they could stand up to him and even ignore his requests for major change. They threatened to go either to the Courts or to the Monopolies and Mergers Commission (the MMC), but their attitude proved no match for the regulator. He is generally conceded to have done an outstanding job with a relatively unpromising form of privatization. Even so, the achievements of a doughty regulator have not justified the government in unnecessarily imposing higher costs and inefficiencies on the British economy for over seven years.

Electricity Privatization: An Improvement

Despite the efforts of the two regulators, much public hostility developed towards what was seen as the abuses of monopoly systems. In the next major utility privatization the government had to introduce more competition.

The next two utilities that were ripe for privatization were coal and electricity. In the run up to the May 1987 General Election no mention was made of privatizing either industry until one month before the General Election when the government announced its election manifesto. This included a few sentences to the effect that the electricity supply industry (ESI) was to be privatized, but in a form that would preserve the continuation of the nuclear power station program, then seen as an effective insurance against the dependence upon the coal supplies. (As mentioned above, the government hardly seemed to recognize that it had won the year long 1984/5 coal strikes and that the NUM had no stomach for either further strikes or for opposing the closing down of mines due to high cost and surplus capacity. It had become part of the folklore of British politics that the miners were never to be unnecessarily provoked.)

The suddenness of the ESI announcement just before the May 1987 election meant that no preparatory work had been done by politicians or the Department of Energy. Indeed, only a few of the political and economic institutions had done any work at all on the subject, but such work as had been done stressed the need to distinguish between the generating 75 percent of the ESI that was not an inherent monopoly from the 25 percent that was (the transmission and distribution). The obvious way forward would have been to break up the CEGB into six or 80 major companies that would compete with one another, plus imports from France and Scotland, to sell to the distribution companies. It was also clear that if the government were to encourage new power station competitors—a strongly stated intention—then the National Grid (i.e., the transmission system) had to be open to all comers on equal terms.

The CEGB strongly resisted an independent transmission system, arguing that only they could be guaranteed to ".... keep the lights on." They alleged a mystique beyond the reach of ordinary mortals, quite ignoring that the problem of safely matching power supplies to demand was daily encountered and daily overcome by all other electric power systems in the world whether competitive or monopoly.

The CEGB equally resisted the break up of the power stations. The political pressures on the government, however, absolutely required considerably more competition than the five percent in the case of BT and the zero in the case of BGC. The government were in something of a dilemma because they wanted to privatize the ten nuclear power stations as part of the privatization of power stations. It slowly emerged that the real costs and, even more, the contingent liabilities of making retired nuclear stations and waste fuel safe for centuries, were proving increasingly difficult to quantify even broadly, and hence for the City to accept. For a long time the government thought that this problem could be overcome by concealing the nuclear power stations in a much larger number of conventional power stations such that their costs and contingent liabilities would not appear to be very important. The first suggestion for splitting the CEGB was 90/10 but this was strongly criticized as was the next suggestion of 80/20. The government finally settled on a 70/30 formula with all the nuclear power stations in the 70 percent. This was the intention right up until legislation was about to go through Parliament. By then, however, the auditors had refused to agree on the contingent liabilities for retired nuclear stations and waste fuel. The existence of an open ended liability made the sale of shares impossible. Hence, at the last moment the government had to withdraw the nuclear power stations from the proposed 70 percent; they remain in government ownership to this day.

The two generating companies (National Power and Powergen) were then privatized, one with 50 percent of the non-nuclear power stations and the other with 30 percent. The nuclear component "Nuclear Electric" provided 16 percent of total power and because of its low operating costs this is always base load power. To overcome the criticism that a monopoly had been replaced by an oligopoly the government introduced a complicated power pool system whereby power is auctioned for every half hour for the next day. The system has not proved particularly satisfactory.

It is to be regretted that again the form of privatization that suited the short-term political imperatives of the government and the monopoly privatization instincts of the City has been at the expense of long-term national efficiency. The outcome has been mitigated in that the form of privatization has encouraged a large development of private gas-fired stations and this has introduced a major competitive element. It is also worth remembering that the Department of Energy thought that there was insufficient management capability in Britain to have more than two generating companies—an interesting commentary on the understanding of business by politicians and civil servants alike.

Neglecting the Consequences for British Coal

No attention was given to the effect of the ESI privatization upon its 75 percent supplier, British Coal. It was the government's announced intention also to privatize British Coal at some time. Most expert commentators argued strongly for either the simultaneous privatization of the two closely linked industries or at least planning the form of British Coal's privatization and announcing it at the same time as the ESI privatization. This virtually unanimous advice was completely ignored by the government, yet it has spelt disaster for the British coal industry. ESI privatization included arrangements that there should be initial three year contracts for coal at essentially the high nationalized prices. Had British Coal been privatized with the ESI this would have given its new owners time to modernize the mining practices and methods of development of the underground coal mines to international standards. As this was not done, and as gas powered stations were encouraged, the market for British Coal's output fell dramatically at the same time that it was trying to adjust itself on its own, while still nationalized, to the prospect of having to be fully import competitive, a task that needed 5 years involvement of world class private sector coal operators. Because no such requirement, or anything like it, had been laid on it for more than 40 years, BC's ability to become internationally competitive was sadly beyond it, despite the most gallant efforts to more than double productivity, while shedding huge numbers of jobs. Now that BC is very belatedly on the point of privatization, the delay in introducing world class mining companies has shrunk it beyond recognition. Accordingly, its chance to provide at least 30 percent to 40 percent of the fuel for British electricity generation has, quite unnecessarily, almost vanished.

THE LESSONS FROM THE BRITISH EXPERIENCE
Enormous Scope for Privatization

What is apparent from the British pioneering experience of privatization is that it is capable of being applied very widely. There are few business activities that most governments can expect to undertake anything like as well as the private sector. It is clear from the British experience that virtually all such businesses could and should be privatized with very considerable advantages to all parts of the nation. Government does, of course, have a legitimate interest in how business is conducted but these aims are best achieved by imaginative, light regulation rather than by ownership. Heavy regulation is nearly always at the expense of long-term efficiency.

The privatization that Britain has undertaken in the nationalized industry sector is now being successfully extended to major government departments. Here it has been found that all manner of special activities, often involving the majority of government employees in that department can, with considerable advantage, be hived off into separate government executive agencies run as businesses on suitable terms of accountability. It could well be that by the end of this decade the direct employment by British government departments will be perhaps only ten percent of what it was ten years ago. The Departments will largely confine themselves to policy making, strategic direction, and regulation. The energy and efficiency that this process can release when properly handled is too important a contribution to national efficiency for any nation to neglect.

Widespread Popularity

Prior to the privatization program being well established there was no significant popular demand for privatization. In practice, however, it has proved immensely popular. Consumers almost universally have benefitted from and praised the improved quality of products and services that result. The same people in their role as tax payers have equally been pleased as public expenditures have been transferred to the private sector with very considerable savings. The managements of privatized industries often opposed privatization in the early days but this position has now faded to be replaced by very considerable enthusiasm. The removal of interference from politicians and civil servants and no longer having business priorities subordinated to government priorities has been widely welcomed. Managements also found their pay, pensions, and opportunities to build up capital were all transformed by the process. The result of all this is that managements in still-to-be-privatized industries are almost universally impatient for the liberalizing and satisfying process.

Workers, like managements, at first opposed privatization, often very vigorously. They foresaw, correctly, that most nationalized industries were inefficient and seriously over staffed. The experience of privatization, however, has led to sensible redundancy and retraining programs to the point where serious opposition is now largely nonexistent. Further, as mentioned previously, employees have taken up over 90 percent of the share allocations made to them under privatization. All this has caused unions to drop their opposition to the process and they are now generally cooperative.

In sum, privatization has proved so popular that such criticism as there is amounts to the pace of the remaining privatization being, if anything, too slow.

Identifying and Prioritizing Privatization Aims

As is to be expected from a pioneering process, privatization began in an often confused way and was not well thought through. There are four main aims of privatization and they are in partial conflict. It is important, therefore, to think them through carefully in advance, prioritize them and resolve conflicts between them.

The first aim of privatization was to relieve the burden of government financing, which had become intolerable by 1979. The majority of nationalized industries needed subsidies of one kind or another, sometimes huge, and many of the industries had a voracious need for capital expenditure with much of the money being spent inefficiently. Privatization reduces both the call on government revenue receipts and capital funds, and in addition brings in both major capital receipts and eventually major taxable revenues as profits rise and subsidies disappear. These financial benefits are very considerable and indeed usually of national significance.

The second aim, and one that was a priority of Margaret Thatcher, was to free business activities from the political priorities of ministers and the financial and other objectives of civil servants. With a huge, nationalized industrial sector having major influences on jobs, incomes, prices, etc., the temptation to constant interference is well nigh irresistible. This seldom makes for long- term efficiency and indeed efficiency may easily become a very low priority of privatization. Freeing business to do its own job properly under well thought out arrangements confers very large benefits of international significance.

The third aim was to extend "people's capitalism" by encouraging widespread share ownership by selling privatizing industries mainly to the general public at a discount, which ensures an immediate capital profit. This aim is not one to be denigrated even though the majority of new shareholders have not gone on to buy shares in non-privatized concerns. That will take time. It has, however, encouraged ordinary consumers to think of themselves as owners in a spread of national industries and to take more interest in the general efficiency of private sector business.

The last, but by no means the least important aim of privatization was to raise the efficiency of the businesses concerned. Without exception all privatized businesses have raised their efficiency and profitability, often remarkably. However, this aim of privatization has nearly always been subordinated to the other aims, particularly maximizing government receipts by rushing the selling of privatized firms. Many nationalized industries were monopolies and quite insufficient attention was paid to introducing competitive structures. Yet it is undoubtedly true that the major contribution to long term national efficiency and growth comes from the careful planning of privatization to achieve that aim as the major priority. While bad privatization is better than no privatization, good privatization is very considerably better. It takes a badly-privatized industry with considerable monopoly elements something like seven to ten years before it can be restructured on more efficient and competitive lines.

It is much easier and quicker to privatize an industry as a monopoly and this has been strongly supported by management, employees and, of course, the financial institutions of the City, who have preferred the ease of privatizing a monopoly and the bigger resultant fees. Introducing more competitive structures raises less immediate capital for the government and hence involves lower advisory fees. The greatest privatization successes have undoubtedly been British Steel and British Airways. While these near national monopolies were privatized intact they both faced fierce international competition. They spent several years in state ownership preparing for privatization, which they did well, and they are the best British examples of what competitive privatization can achieve.

Government Failure to Ensure Experienced New Management

The most serious justified criticism of British privatization has been the relative neglect of ensuring optimal long-term efficiency. A neglected part of this process that deserves special comment has been the general failure to ensure that newly-privatized firms had the advantage of experienced private sector managements in the key positions, particularly in the utilities. Virtually all the large utilities were privatized with all their directors and senior managements intact, yet before privatization their tasks were far simpler and their responsibilities much less. This was reflected in the pay and calibre of those concerned. As a group they could not generally have expected to be recruited into the level of private sector positions, particularly the top positions, where most of them stayed, and where pay and pension levels are typically two to five times the levels prevalent in safe nationalized monopolies. It is of course true that with the liberating release of the privatization process many of them have grown in stature and effectiveness. This shows the importance of organizations and structures in either retarding or enhancing performance. That apart, it is nevertheless true that many, indeed most, privatization would have benefitted from the initial recruitment of top level private sector managements from competitive industries and preferably with wide international experience. This was done with conspicuous success both for British Steel by bringing in Sir Ian MacGregor and for British Airways by bringing in Lord King to help prepare them for privatization, but it was not the general rule. The introduction of high quality, experienced private sector management would have followed automatically if there had been "trade sales," i.e., selling privatized firms, broken up where appropriate, to major relevant companies. This is what is intended for British Coal because the company is and always was necessarily a risky and specialized business quite unsuited to direct ownership by the general public. Only world class mining companies are suitable purchasers for the larger underground mines, and smaller mining companies and contractors for the small mines and open cast mines. In principle, however, trade sales, or partial trade sales would have been appropriate for at least British Gas and the Electricity Supply Industry. Such sales, however, would have been at the expense of the aim of selling the industries only to the general public to encourage wider share ownership and to provide secure capital gains.

Long-term efficiency has undoubtedly suffered from the failure to bring in new private sector management either by special recruitment or trade sales, to the nation's detriment. It has also flouted the best international standards of corporate governance. Widespread public share ownership effectively hands power to boards of directors as individual shareholders are without significant power.

Eventually, many shares will of course become owned by investment institutions, but in Britain, as in America, they are not in practice effective shareholders either. What privatized firms needed was the discipline of some knowledgeable, committed, active, long-term shareholders to provide managements with the incentives and preconditions for long-term performance, and to ho]d them accountable. It is always worth bearing these points in mind.

Conclusions

From this brief survey of the British privatization experience it will be apparent that while significant mistakes were undoubtedly made in the process it can be judged only a partial, albeit major, success. Privatization, however, nevertheless represents one of the great, effective, liberating economic ideas since World War II, of general applicability as its widespread international popularity has proved. It is a process to be commended to every country since the benefits are huge and the eventual popularity is very widespread. Britain can be justifiably proud of its pioneering achievements.

PART VII
The Telefonica Experience

➤

Chapter 26

Privatization of Telecommunications

José Luis Martín de Bustamante

(Translated by Leonard S. Hyman)

Telecommunications today represents a challenge to our society as well as the vehicle for a great adventure. Without the perspective of time, however, it is difficult to appreciate the extent to which telecommunications has changed our lives. Whether we refer to what happens at work or during our leisure time, we can say without exaggeration that there was a "before" and an "after".

If we live in a global economy, that is due to telecommunications. If we live in a world without borders that inhibit the flow of information, where the news arrives instantly everywhere, permitting us to consider ourselves citizens of the world as much as of nations, we owe that to telecommunications. If our planet has its own nervous system through which information arises and circulates, the telecommunications network is that system. Progress, as rarely has been the case in history, is clearly and concretely related to telecommunications.

But this world of telecommunications—which during its years of birth, development and consolidation lived a repetitive, inward-looking and rigidly structured existence—has been forced, in the past decade, to confront dizzying changes caused by a series of circumstances that finally led to progressive liberalization and, in many cases, to the privatization of services.

When we refer to telecommunications, we mean, and will continue to mean for some time, the basic telephone service, that is the local, long distance and international calls. Those services now represent—and will continue to represent—over 80 percent of the total billings. Although value added services such as cellular telephony, data processing and transmission, paging, "party line," and others are expanding at an explosive pace, it will take years before those services in total surpass 20 percent of the market.

Until the mid 1970s, three characteristics were common to the provision of telecommunications services throughout the world. Putting aside a few exceptions such as the United States and Spain, the operator was the state itself. The market was firmly regulated. Finally, the business was run almost totally as a monopoly or near monopoly.

In the 1980s, a gradual process of breaking down the monopoly began, in parallel with gradual deregulation, which, for many of the large state operators such as those of Japan, the United Kingdom, New Zealand, Mexico, Chile and Argentina, led the way to privatization. Technical, economic and political factors influenced those changes.

1. Technical advances, like battering rams, broke through the walls around telecommunications. The globalization of satellites, the digitalization of the networks, the convergence of data processing and telecommunications, and the increasing integration of switching and transmission were so many spearheads that opened up the obsolete structure.

2. As for economic factors, sophisticated clients developed new needs which the existing suppliers clearly could not supply expeditiously. Additionally, new players—attracted by the growing telecommunications boom—appeared on the scene. The new players forced their way into the marketplace in order to reap the high profits that they expected to earn from providing telecommunications services despite the heavy investments required.

3. Finally, suppliers of telecommunications equipment exerted political pressure to break down the traditional monopoly situations that limited their access to markets. Also, the suppliers wanted governments to send clear signals on which technologies should be developed and on what constituted industrial policy. The telecommunications operators themselves fought to break out from local boundaries and to operate in other countries, taking advantage of whatever opportunities were offered by the laws of the respective countries.

Liberalization and Privatization
A number of state-owned telecommunications entities found themselves in difficult circumstances characterized by:

- Deterioration of service

- Decapitalization and chronic budget deficits

- Over staffing

- Obsolete internal structure incapable of dealing with competition

- Noncompensatory tariffs

- Corruption.

Facing such circumstances, some governments saw the possibility of improving the situation by selling all or part of the assets—privatizing—but reserving for themselves the control and supervision of the licensees or of the new owners, even as they sally forth into the competitive battles that will ensue during the irresistible process of liberalization.

Liberalization

In fact, on April 28, 1993, the European Commission proposed the total liberalization of telecommunications services, with the termination of all types of monopolies by January 1, 1998. The proposal of the Commission emphasizes the inevitability of the process thanks to the nature of technological development. At the same time, it takes the precaution of establishing periods of transition in various countries for realizing the objective. The United States, which has traditionally been a case apart, has been carrying on the liberalization for many years.

The situation in Latin America does not have the same characteristics. Many countries there have passed with hardly a transition from a state-run marketplace to an advanced stage of liberalization, despite poorly developed and highly obsolete networks. Economic circumstances—inflation, external debt, high taxes, etc—complicate the picture even more. At the same time, though, political conditions facilitate privatizations more than on other continents, especially because of the lack of backing for a democratic state-dominated economy, and the lack of opposition by the nationalist sector to the massive entry of foreign capital.

Steps in the Process

The privatization process must deal with three aspects of telecommunications:

- Regulation and control

- Operations

- Manufacture of equipment and terminals.

Regulation and Control

Independently of whether the telecommunications system is state or privately owned, governments always reserve for themselves and never privatize the functions of audit, regulation and control of communications. Thus, when privatization takes place, the state—without being the owner of the enterprises—may exercise power over them, often decisively, imposing goals, service quality standards, and at times, investment requirements.

The agencies of control differ from country to country. In the United States the dominant agency is the Federal Communications Commission, in France the PTT (Postes, Telegraphes et Telephones) ministry, in Spain the Dirección General de Telecomunicaciones, and in Argentina the Comisión Nacional de Comunicaciones. The common denominator is that all those agencies are governmental, with members appointed by their respective governments.

One of the most important responsibilities of those agencies is the approval of tariffs that permit a level of profitability within the limits compatible with the quality of service that one expects from a public service. In a sense, the less the telecommunications operator is a part of the government, the more arduous and complex become the negotiations for the revision of tariffs, unless—as took place in the United Kingdom—price cap regulation is instituted.

For a correct tariff system, one must refine the calculation of costs of each service, because in a free market, the infrastructure may be shared, and the firm must avoid a situation in which, thanks to cross subsidies, unprofitable services continue to exist, supported by overcharges on profitable services. The company has to justify its tariffs not only on the basis of costs but also on the basis of what customers would pay in a free market.

Operations
This is where privatization brings about the greatest changes. Usually the passage from government management to private enterprise is accompanied by a certain type of liberalization for the most profitable services as a result of competition. In fact, cellular (despite a limitation of frequencies) and data transmission are the first to operate under liberalized rules. Private networks grow, too. In every case, the old pattern of the unity of the network is jettisoned. Those who initiate competition have the advantage over the traditional operators because, from the beginning, they can utilize the newest technology without the weighty burden of old infrastructure and excess personnel. Prudence in granting new licenses may be required in order to avoid unfair competition.

Manufacture of Equipment and Terminals
Until now, where a single supplier of equipment controlled the market or where a few suppliers traditionally divided up the market into more or less pre-established quotas, many of the telecommunications operators took whatever plant and equipment that was imposed on them by the suppliers. Privatization, with its goal of making operations more profitable, encourages an expansion of the list of suppliers. Privatization forces all suppliers to lower costs, increase their capacity

and improve managerial efficiency, in order to offer the product the customer wants at the price the customer is willing to pay. Those pressures may force suppliers to merge or reorganize in order to attain economies of scale.

The private managements of some formerly state-owned operating companies have succeeded in lowering prices substantially by means of an exacting and competitive bidding process. In one case, the operator reduced the per line cost of switching equipment to one third of the previous purchased price. The beneficiary of these changes, ultimately, is the purchaser. Instead of having to take what is offered, the purchaser sees its needs considered more and more, to the point of being able to acquire the desired product, with acceptable quality at a reasonable price.

Advantages of Privatization

In general, the objectives—and advantages—of the privatization of telecommunications, defined as the disinvestment of the state in this business activity, can be categorized as either financial or of a public policy character.

Financial Objectives

The financial objectives involve both the government and the capital markets:

- As a minimum goal, reduce the government deficit, but do so in a manner linked to a much wider objective, which is to reduce the public sector's participation in telecommunications.

- Create well managed, solid, profitable corporations whose existence will entice new investment funds into the market.

- Widen and deepen the capital market by bringing in a large number of new investors.

- Stem the continuous flow of public funds that had to be made in order to upgrade existing plant to new technologies.

- Reduce the external debt of the country, where such debt exists, by means of debt-equity swaps (that is, sale of the government shares in the telecommunications company in return for payment in government debt).

Public Policy Objectives

Public policy objectives range from economic to technological:

- Strengthen popular capitalism by increasing the number of small investors including the employees of the enterprises.

- Improve efficiency, transforming a state monopoly into a competitive activity, not only creating the right conditions within the enterprise but also making it more responsive to the desires of its customers.

- Incorporate the most advanced technology by attracting world class operators to the enterprise.

- Establish national and international alliances with other service providers, thereby bringing the service offerings into the process of globalization of economic activity.

- Provide an impetus to growth throughout to economy by requiring the new franchisee to meet investment goals that will require substantial expenditures.

Difficulties of Privatization

The privatization process is not an easy one. For it to succeed, the state must:

- Aid the privatizing entity before, during and after the privatization in order to keep the process moving forward.

- Reorganize the enterprise before selling it, and assume the political responsibility for the restructuring in order to obtain the best possible price. The alternative is to sell the company as is, for less money, and let the buyer assume responsibility for the unpopular measures taken during the transition to private ownership.

- Establish a secure juridical framework, safe from future political changes of direction.

- Create the regulatory agency ahead of time, to involve it in the process from the beginning.

The Telefónica de Argentina (TASA) Experience

The privatization of the Argentine telephone system provides an excellent example of how the process works, and what it can accomplish.

Antecedents

The history of the privatization of the Empresa Nacional de Telecomunicaciones de Argentina (ENTEL) is in two stages. In 1988, the Radical government proposed to create a corporation whose owners were Telefónica de España and the Argentine state to own ENTEL but the project never got through Congress. The second stage began in 1989, after the inauguration of President Menem. It had its origin in the laws of August 1989 that called for the reform of the state. The government opted for a massive privatization of state enterprises, and ENTEL was first on the list.

In the case of ENTEL, the government had more in mind than the generic benefits of privatization. ENTEL's privatization would lead the pack, and it had to work out well in order to promote the prospects for succeeding privatizations. The economic setting in which the government had to make its decisions for this first effort could not have been worse. These are some of the highlights of 1989–1990:

• A post-hyperinflationary situation after price increases had reached a peak of 200 percent in July 1989

• A precarious fiscal situation

• The Bonex Plan: refinancing bank deposits with the emission of external bonds (Bonex 1989)

• Unstable foreign exchange rates

• High rates of interest

• A lethargic stock market

• Nonexistence of credit for all practical purposes.

In short: deep economic recession.

Within this framework, in January 1990 the government called for an International Public Bidding for the privatization of telecommunications services under the terms and conditions set forth in the bidding document. The rules for the privatization called for:

• Division of the network into two regions, North and South (today Telecom and Telefónica de Argentina)

• Granting to the licensee in each region the exclusive license to provide basic telephone service in the region

• Granting to Sociedad Prestadora del Servicio Internacional (today TELINTAR), an entity jointly owned by Telefónica and Telecom, a license to provide international telecommunications services

- Granting to Sociedad de Servicios en Competencia (today STARTEL), an entity jointly owned by the two basic service companies, a license to provide services such as national transmission of data and telex

- Transfer by ENTEL to the new companies of almost all its assets and personnel to provide services.

The bidding document established, furthermore, that the licenses to Telefónica de Argentina, Telecom and TELINTAR were exclusive, and the license to STARTEL would allow competition. The exclusivity was granted for a period of seven years, but could be extended for another three years if the companies met the goals set by the bidding document.

In May 1990, the consortium led by Telefónica de España obtained prequalification approval to bid, and in June it presented the highest bids to acquire 60 percent of the shares of both regions. On July 28, the government sold control of the southern region to the Telefónica consortium for $114 million cash plus $2720 million face value of external debt plus $202.4 million payable to ENTEL semiannually in six payments, with a three year grace period.

According to the terms of the bidding document, the 40 percent of the shares not sold to the consortium would be distributed:

- 10 percent to employees of the former ENTEL

- 30 percent in a public offering, which took place in December 1991.

After a period in which the role of the regulator was defined and the contract for transfer was discussed, on November 8, 1990, the Argentine president signed the decree of privatization of ENTEL, and Telefónica de Argentina began its life.

Point of Departure

The best word to explain what Telefónica de Argentina encountered upon acquiring its region is "chaos." In the 32 years of ENTEL's existence, the company had 25 administrators, or an average of one every 1.3 years, a significant indicator of the firm's lack of continuity in management and planning.

It would have been easier to start from scratch. Telefónica de Argentina had to fix a situation characterized by:

- Extremely old plant

- Deterioration of maintenance

- Lack of administrative control

- Lack of motivation on the part of personnel

- Operation losses.

Of the 1.9 million lines purchased, 25 percent were at least 43 years old, 59 percent were at least 14 years old, and the balance between three and eight years old. Only 14 percent of the lines were digitalized. Roughly 30 percent of the lines had been rendered useless and 20 percent had exceeded their useful lives. The company had no diagrams of the network, no parts inventories, no tools, and no measurement equipment. The median waiting time for installation of a line was over four years, and some requests had been pending for more than 20. There were more than 90,000 repair requests pending, some for over three years. The company had no audited books. Nonpayment of bills was high, organization confused, and control non-existent. This deterioration of organization and control facilitated the existence of irregular behavior such as solicitations of payments from customers, alterations of work verification documents, connivance with suppliers and contractors, and simple theft from warehouses.

As for the personnel, they were profoundly unmotivated as a result of the obsolescence of the internal organization, low salary levels, and insufficient training. The company was over staffed, with 22,000 employees, which worked out to 78 lines in service per employee, one of the lowest ratios in the world. The average age of the staff was high, too (49 percent of the employees were over 40 years old). Absenteeism attained excessive levels. The staff abused overtime, which they considered a normal part of their pay. The company promoted by seniority. Employees were categorized into 2000 specialties grouped in 32 levels.

In sum, the situation could be characterized by deficient quality of service, low saturation of the market, long delays in satisfying demand, scarce and poorly functioning public telephones, obsolescent technology and as a consequence little or no advanced services, and as far as personnel was concerned, complete lack of motivation and of loyalty to the firm.

Corrective Actions
The conditions of the purchase set objectives for the buyer involving improvement of service, investments,line installations, the growth of the system, and its modernization. From the beginning, the official goals were considered the minimum, and the company's objective was to exceed them.

Since taxes could change, the company worked out a plan in which new taxes would be passed on to customers directly through the tariff. At the same time, in February 1992 the company and the government signed an agreement which fixed the tariff on a dollar basis, revised semiannually in accord with variations of the Consumer Price Index of the United States.

A collective bargaining agreement, signed with the unions in May 1991, improved and rationalized salaries, regulated working conditions, and led to an improvement in productivity, so that in 1993 the lines per employee ratio reached 122. The company also sponsored a voluntary retirement plan. Four thousand employees took advantage of it.

The new management restructured the entire enterprise, improving administrative procedures and controls. They formulated an aggressive strategic plan that involved putting 1.8 million lines into service through 1997, thereby raising saturation from 12 to 20 lines per inhabitant, and increasing the level of digitalization to 72 percent by that year. The maximum time on the waiting list has fallen to 12 months.

Management prepared an urgent plan for the rehabilitation of the network which allowed it to reduce outages of service and to make repairs within normal limits of time. They attacked irregular practices, strengthening inspection procedures. The company installed three fiber optic rings in central Buenos Aires in order to furnish quality services to major customers. Cumulative investment in the first three years has exceeded $1700 million ($206 million in 1991, $610 million in 1992, and $925 million in 1993). Net profits reached $121 million in 1991, $219 million in 1992, and $300 million in 1993. Until now, the company has complied with all the standards imposed by the Comisión Nacional de Telecomunicaciones.

One should mention, too, that in March 1993, Telefónica and Telecom jointly began to operate the second cellular franchise in Buenos Aires, and by June it had more than 30,000 subscribers.

The accompanying table of Significant Variables (Table 26-1) shows the evolution of the most important measures of the progress of the enterprise from its beginning to the end of its third fiscal year in September 1993.

Explaining these accomplishments makes them appear simple, but there are no comparable situations in which the practically total rehabilitation of a plant took place while the company grew at a rate of over 10 percent per year, and at the same time succeeded in improving the quality of service spectacularly.

Table 26-1: Telefónica de Argentina

Fiscal year ended	Significant Variables			
	8 Nov 1990	30 Sept 1991	30 Sept 1992	30 Sep 1993
Installed lines (a)	1915.2	2023.1	2257.8	2666.5
Lines in service (a)	1695.5	1782.4	2008.4	2213.3
Public telephones (a)	12.7	14.6	20.7	24.0
Total employees (a)	21.8	18.1	19.3	18.1
Lines in service per employee	77.9	98.4	104.3	122.3
Lines in service per 100 inhabitants	12.0	12.6	12.6	14.1
Digitalization of the network (%)	14.6	18.1	24.0	38.2
Waiting list (lines)(a)	—	109.6	193.4	233.2
Repairs pending (lines)(a)	90.3	16.2	4.1	4.0
Megatel (plans pending) (a)(b)	90.8	38.9	12.3	0.0
Lines billed (a)(c)	1635.2	1714.4	1920.8	2103.9
Pulses billed over minimum (c)(d)	3110.9	3185.3	3804.5	4241.4
Investments (e)	—	206.9	610.3	925.3
Operating revenues (e)	—	1152.0	1584.6	1784.2
Gross profit (e)	—	452.8	618.0	736.6
Net profit (e)	—	121.3	219.3	300.5

(a) In thousands.
(b) Prepayment plan for connection to telephone system.
(c) Billing every two months.
(d) In millions.
(e) Millions of 30 Sept 93 pesos.

In the end, the practical results of the privatization of ENTEL of Argentina have included an important improvement in the quality of service, new investments to modernize plant, the direct and indirect creation of thousands of new jobs, development of a national industry, and the initiation of Argentina on the irreversible journey in which, through telecommunications, Argentina will before long join the group of countries that have advanced communications serving as the engine of their development.

Chapter 27

The Privatization of Telefónica Larga Distancia de Puerto Rico

by Jorge Robles

Eighteen years after Alexander Graham Bell invented the telephone, service was established in San Juan Puerto Rico, for the exclusive use of the government. A ten line system was installed at La Fortaleza, the seat of government. Public telephone service began in 1897, in the cities of San Juan, Ponce, and Mayaguez. Initially, the telephone company included some small central offices for the sugar mills and refineries. The Behn brothers, Hernand and Sosthenes, acquired the first system in 1905. In 1914, the government authorized the Behn brothers to expand their operations throughout the island, and the system was named Porto Rico Telephone Co. Expansion of telephone service, in the beginning, was very slow. The Behn brothers, in 1920, established International Telephone & Telegraph (ITT), and the Porto Rico Telephone Co. was its first property.

In 1936, telephone service between Puerto Rico and mainland United States was inaugurated using a radio link. During the Second World War, demand for service was very heavy and all systems were overloaded. Due to that situation, the system was programmed for conversion from manual to automatic operation. The first automatic central office was placed in operation in Santurce in 1945. In the 1960s, the number of telephones increased to 276,000 and automatic (direct) service between the principal cities (San Juan, Ponce and Mayaguez) was instituted. In this period, too, the first coaxial cable system between Puerto Rico and mainland U.S.A., and Direct Distance Dialing (DDD) were both put into service. By 1971, all the central offices on the island were connected by microwave or cable, giving the island a much better network.

Due to the poor telephone service being offered to subscribers, the government decided to acquire the telephone company from ITT, which it did in July 1974, through the recently created Telephone Authority. Since 1974, the telephone company has engaged in a broad expansion program for the telephone system. Telephone subscribers in Puerto Rico have benefitted from technological advancements.

Historically, the tariffs from Puerto Rico to the U.S.A. and vice versa have been much higher than for similar distances within the U.S.A. Due to transmission via satellite, the Federal Communications Commission (FCC) ordered that calls between Puerto Rico and the U.S.A. must be integrated into the domestic tariffs. That determination resulted in a lower cost per call to and from Puerto Rico. As a result of this FCC order, the Puerto Rico Telephone Co. made some carrier arrangements with various interexchange carriers and with some countries against the strong opposition of All America Cable and Radio (AAC&R), a subsidiary of ITT. Those arrangements started a prolonged legal dispute with AAC&R, and later with American Telephone & Telegraph (AT&T), which purchased AAC&R from ITT. The dispute ended in 1988, in an agreement between AT&T and the Puerto Rico Telephone Co. As a result of that agreement, Telefónica Larga Distancia (TLD) was created as a long distance carrier, and a subsidiary of the Puerto Rico Telephone Authority.

Telefónica Larga Distancia

Telefónica Larga Distancia (TLD) was organized as a public corporation wholly owned by the Puerto Rico Telephone Authority under the laws of Puerto Rico on June 9, 1988, and was licensed by the FCC on September 14, 1988.

The first interconnection agreement was entered with Telefónica de España on September 19, 1988. On October 10, 1988, an agreement was established with Codetel of the Dominican Republic. During that same period, interim access codes 135-10 and 135-01 were assigned for DDD and International Direct Distance Dialing (IDDD) services under National Exchange Carrier Association (NECA) tariff FCC # 5, effective February 16, 1988, commencing operations in March 1989. On October 24, 1989, TLD made an agreement for participation in the TCS-1 fiber optic submarine cable between Florida and Puerto Rico.

TLD's plant investment was around $50 million, including, principally, the computer center, two domestic general use earth stations; nine dedicated earth stations for private lines of big users such as Digital Corp. (two stations), Intel, G.D. Searle, the Federal Aviation Administration (FAA), Navieras de Puerto Rico, DuPont, Abbott Labs, and Sea Land Corporation; three transponders, one digital toll switch for domestic traffic, one international gateway switch, and the participation in the TCS-1 fiber optic cable.

During 1990, the FCC ordered equal access balloting in Puerto Rico, with participation by all the inter-exchange carriers (IXCs) recognized in Puerto Rico, including TLD and AT&T. Prior to the equal access process, AT&T handled approximately 95 percent of all long distance calls in Puerto Rico. The process of equal access was held in a gradual manner, and ended in late 1990, with the following results:

IXC	Equal Access Balloting Results		
	Commercial	**Residential**	**Pay Stations**
AT&T	26.5%	43.3%	5.7%
MCI	6.7	6.7	0.8
TLD	59.0	31.0	79.8
P.R. Telecom	5.7	17.2	1.3
Others*	2.1	1.8	12.4

* IDB, Call US, Sprint, No Pic, etc.

AT&T was successful in retaining 70 percent of the market share in similar balloting processes in the United States, but finished second to TLD in Puerto Rico.

The Process of Privatization

In 1990, the government of Puerto Rico offered to sell its ownership in the Puerto Rican telecommunications system, consisting of 100 percent of the local telephone exchange franchises (PRTC and PRCC), 100 percent of the wireline cellular system, the long distance company (TLD), and the telephone manufacturing and refurbishing company.

The telephone system was to be sold in order to endow public funds to be used for further direct investment in Puerto Rico's continued economic development. One of the funds, the Permanent Educational Endowment Trust, was to be established to construct educational facilities and to provide books and other educational materials for the Commonwealth's public education system. The other fund, for infrastructure, was to be used to expand Puerto Rico's roads, ports, bridges, and other related infrastructure necessary to expand and support the economy.

For purposes of the sale, the system was considered as four different businesses. The prospective buyers could place bids for one or more of the businesses. The telephone system was a unique asset, operating in a growing industry critical to economic prosperity. The government of Puerto Rico had fostered a very strong economy. (Today, Puerto Rico has the highest per capita income in Latin America and the Caribbean.) The purchaser of the telephone system would not need to make switching and transmission network capital investments due to the world class switches already in operation. The government of Puerto Rico adopted a regulatory regime creating the Telecommunications Regulatory Commission to provide the owner of the system the proper incentives to make it more efficient and to expand the telecommunications services.

In recent years, the system experienced rapid growth of around 12 percent per year in operating revenues. Also, penetration in the market increased to around 25 access lines per 100 persons by the year 1990, compared to 53 access lines per 100 persons on the U.S. mainland. The management organization strongly believed that ownership by a large private telecommunications company could provide the necessary technology and management to continue improving the telecommunication services, and to continue the expansion of the telecommunications system.

By 1990, the local exchange business consisted of about 1.0 million central office lines, state of the art, with approximately 87 percent digital transmission and 98 percent digital switching, all in a stored program control mode.

The PRTC cellular business, which commenced operations in September 1986, offers service similar to that of cellular companies on the mainland. By the time of the proposed sale of the PRTC (1990), the cellular business serviced approximately 17,200 subscribers, which was about 0.5 percent of Puerto Rico's total population. (By November 1994, the PRTC Cellular System had approximately 100,000 working lines.)

Telefónica Larga Distancia de Puerto Rico, which commenced operations in 1989, is a facilities based interexchange long distance carrier. TLD expected to achieve a significant share of outgoing interstate and international telecommunications traffic as a result of equal access balloting conducted at that time in Puerto Rico. Its competitive advantage consisted of being the only well known, locally-based interexchange carrier.

TLD was a relatively new entrant in the long distance business. It was staffed with a young, aggressive and entrepreneurial management team. The management saw opportunities for growth due to pending equal access balloting, an aggressive marketing effort, and recognition of Puerto Rico as a strategic geographic location and a hub for Latin America. TLD was licensed as a nondominant carrier by the Federal Communications Commission to provide interstate and international long distance service in September 1988. In March 1990, PRTC transferred all its assets related to the long distance market to TLD. Those assets included earth stations, satellite transponders, two toll switches, and an ownership interest in a submarine fiber optic cable (TCS-1).

TLD offered a wide variety of products and services similar to those offered by any U.S. interexchange carrier. TLD tariff policy was based on its analysis of market conditions, rates charged by competitors, and the need to maintain a competitive position in the market. TLD maintained a healthy balance between pricing and the cost of providing service.

As part of the privatization process, a series of presentations was made to the telephone companies interested in the system. Five to seven organizations participated in the process. BellSouth and Telefónica de España were among the most active players. Among the regulatory issues incorporated in the process were the following:

- Puerto Rico Law 5 of April 10, 1990, which provided for a Regulatory Commission, a rate freeze for three years for basic services, employee protection against dismissal, and the protection of pension rights

- Federal Communications Act of 1934 as amended

- Communications Satellite Act of 1962.

Due to the regulatory environment and to the high sale price, the privatization of the whole system could not be achieved.

At the last minute, when the privatization process had stalled and was about to be terminated, Telefónica de España made an offer for TLD, subject to the approval of the FCC.

After more than six months of consideration, on December 18, 1992, the FCC implemented the TLD order authorizing Telefónica de España to acquire the assets of TLD from Puerto Rico Telephone Authority subject to the following major considerations:

1) The public interest was served by permitting Telefónica de España to enter the market in Puerto Rico by the acquisition of TLD.

2) TLD would be regulated by specifically defined safeguards in addition to the applicable conditions imposed by its dominant carrier status for the international traffic in order to insure that TLD would not competitively benefit from its foreign affiliation to the detriment of U.S. competitors. (For domestic traffic, TLD is considered a nondominant carrier by the FCC.)

3) The adequacy of those safeguards to protect against anticompetitive activity by TLD would be reviewed when TLD was required to seek authority to expand its international service offerings and capability.

4) TLD facilities applications would be reviewed by the full FCC when necessary to prevent discrimination favoring TLD to the damage of its competitors.

5) The TLD interests acquired by Telefónica de España were limited in scope.

6) Social reasons favored the sale, including the use of the proceeds for educational reform in Puerto Rico.

7) Fifty eight other clauses were ordered by the FCC in order to approve the sale of TLD to Telefónica de España.

All of the above considerations were to be reviewed by the FCC in three years after the approval of the transaction.

Finally, the new TLD, acquired by Telefónica de España, was to manage the operations (engineering, marketing, international relations, and the administrative and staff functions) and the Telephone Authority would operate the technical side of the business (the earth stations, microwave links and cable heads).

Three companies were created as a result of the process:

- Telefónica Larga Distancia (80 percent owned by Telefónica de España, 18 percent by the telephone Authority, and 2 percent by employees of TLD)

- Telecomunicaciones Ultramarinas de Puerto Rico (85.1 percent owned by the Telephone Authority and 14.9 percent by Telefónica de España), which operates and maintains the earth stations and microwave systems

- Isla Verde Telecommunications (100 percent owned by the Telephone Authority), which operates the submarine fiber optic cable head at Isla Verde, Puerto Rico.

The final transaction, made between the government of Puerto Rico and Telefónica de España, for approximately $141 million, was made on December 22, 1992.

For Telefónica de España, the purchase of TLD was more of a strategic decision than an economic one. TLD represented the achievement of two important objectives for Telefónica de España: first, to enter the U.S. market, and second, to obtain a first hand experience with competition in the telecommunications market.

Telefónica de España's expansion into foreign countries, specifically Latin America, would provide it with access to underdeveloped monopolies which, when well managed, would prove very lucrative, especially in countries like Chile and Argentina, with stable and democratic governments. However, the most important telecommunications market in the world is that of the United States, of which Puerto Rico is part. TLD was an interexchange carrier authorized to originate traffic in Puerto and the U.S. Virgin Islands. Due to being classified by the

FCC as nondominant for domestic traffic, TLD can expand its operations into the continental U.S. without further authorizations. (To originate international traffic from the mainland, TLD needs to obtain previous authorization from the FCC due to its classification as dominant carrier for this type of traffic.)

Even though restrictions imposed by the Government of Puerto Rico for the sale of the Puerto Rico Telephone System seriously limited the profits to be generated from the operation of the local network, buying the long distance subsidiary, TLD, was still a good strategic decision, as a means of entering the U.S. market.

The second consideration for Telefónica de España was that TLD was operating in the most competitive telecommunications market in the world, that of the United States. Entering that market could provide Telefónica de España the experience necessary to understand and operate under the forces of competition in its own country and in other markets abroad.

Conclusion

The privatization of TLD was considered a good deal by both the buyer and seller. The seller, in this case the Government of Puerto Rico, fulfilled its promise to privatize (although partially) the telecommunications companies owned by it, and to improve service to subscribers while at the same time using the proceeds from the sale for the public interest (improvement of the public education system in Puerto Rico). Also, since TLD was a very small operation (300 employees), the government avoided the strong opposition of the employees of the local operators, PRTC and PRCC (approximately 8000 employees).

As for the buyer, Telefónica de España, purchasing TLD provided as entry into the U.S. market at a very low price, with the added benefit of using this new company as a model to gain experience in the field of competition in the telecommunications market.

Chapter 28

Strategic Alliances: the Case for the Telecommunications Sector

Francisco Blanco

(Translated by Leonard S. Hyman)

The proliferation of strategic alliances between business firms has characterized worldwide business activity since the beginning of the last decade. Those alliances, which encompass firms within a similar or different business sector, have different scopes of operation, ranging from lines of business to geographical regions of operation.

Those agreements, whose objectives may be to maintain a sustained rate of growth or simply to guarantee survival, are a response to three factors that have radically changed the context in which business activities are carried on.

First, the growing interdependence between countries, together with the globalization of the economy, has eliminated geographic borders for economic activity. Markets become increasingly internationalized. This trend has been intensified by the slow rates of growth of domestic markets in the industrialized nations, which encourages the firms in those markets to look elsewhere for business; the elimination of commercial barriers (European Union, NAFTA, Mercosur, etc.) and by the rise of emerging markets that offer new business opportunities. While this new picture means greater efficiency in the markets thanks to a higher level of competition, it also entails an increasing volatility in the foreign exchange markets, as well as a certain degree of protectionism on the part of some governments. All of those factors, undoubtedly, have favored the creation of collaborative agreements or strategic alliances whose purposes are to facilitate access to particular markets, and to reduce risks and obstacles (country and exchange rate risks, cultural and political barriers, etc.).

Second, the process of intense technological innovation, that has characterized some sectors of the economy in the past few years, has pushed the firm into making alliances. Worldwide research and development efforts have been translated into real strategic assets. Internal development work within the corporation improves its competitive position, because those developments are not often open to non-paying outsiders. The high cost of purchasing such new technologies—and in many cases the impossibility of doing so because of the strategic advantage to the owners of keeping the technology to themselves—has induced companies with complementary technologies to approach each other so that, working together, they can produce operating synergies and share fixed costs. In that way, corporations can avoid the major financial risk inherent in the alternative path, the direct acquisition of firms in order to gain access to a given technology.

Third, the sharp competition for capital in increasingly integrated financial markets has raised the standards of credit demanded of borrowers, many of whom, during the decade of the eighties, leaned heavily on the debt markets in order to finance expansion. In this context, cost rises and capital is scarce for investment projects which incorporate a certain degree of business and financial risk and do not have strong balance sheets behind them. Enterprises lacking financial capacity or seeking to share risks have turned to strategic alliances as an efficient means of undertaking new business opportunities while assuming a lower financial risk through sharing it.

This last element appears, repeatedly, as a component of the internationalization strategies of enterprises, especially when responding to privatization processes in countries with emerging economies. In those cases, the formation of a consortium constitutes the preferred route to penetrate the market, to become familiar with the socio-economic and political situation by means of partnership with local associates, and to limit exposure to the numerous risks inherent in foreign investment. (See Figure 1.)

Putting together an alliance agreement involves a long and rigorous process of analysis and negotiation between parties. One must first identify the opportunities involved in the possible alliances, not the least of which is the selection of the right partner, with whom one must afterward deal with the different issues (valuation, responsibilities of the partners, shareholder agreements, impact of taxation, etc.) that have to be settled in order to arrive at an agreement.

Every strategic alliance has the same objective: to maintain or improve the competitive position of the participating firms, not only in reference to direct competitors, but also to the largest customers and suppliers, giving the firm a greater power to negotiate on a global scale. Obviously, one can reach the final objective in different ways, as well as reach intermediate objectives that diverge or coincide from that goal, depending on the particular alliance. The most common strategic goals include the following:

- To participate in new markets, giving the business a more global dimension in order to meet the needs of multinational customers. Normally, one wishes to enter growing markets, but even in those with some degree of maturity, the

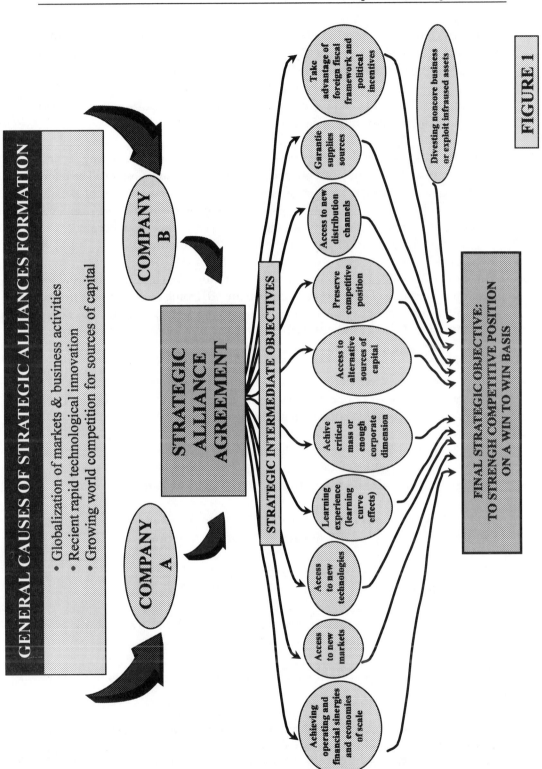

GENERAL CAUSES OF STRATEGIC ALLIANCES FORMATION

- Globalization of markets & business activities
- Recient rapid technological innovation
- Growing world competition for sources of capital

COMPANY A

COMPANY B

STRATEGIC ALLIANCE AGREEMENT

STRATEGIC INTERMEDIATE OBJECTIVES

- Achieving operating and financial synergies and economies of scale
- Access to new markets
- Access to new technologies
- Learning experience (learning curve effects)
- Achive critical mass or enough corporate dimension
- Access to alternative sources of capital
- Preserve competitive position
- Access to new distribution channels
- Garantie supplies sources
- Take advantage of foreign fiscal framework and political incentives
- Divesting noncore business or exploit infraused assets

FINAL STRATEGIC OBJECTIVE: TO STRENGH COMPETITIVE POSITION ON A WIN TO WIN BASIS

FIGURE 1

331

national competitors are able to maintain a good brand image that constitutes a considerable barrier to entry. The way to overcome that obstacle is to take as a strategic partner one of the principal local groups in the market.

- Gain access to specific complementary technologies or management systems that might allow operating synergies between partners.

- Take advantage of the learning curve that comes with sharing strengths and weaknesses with other organizations to improve competitive position. The information gained that improves the current position of the firm in terms of exploiting new lines of business or markets, improving productivity and personnel training, and consolidating or enlarging market share, ends up incorporated in all aspects of the firm, from physical plant to human resources.

- To reach a size sufficient to take on investment projects of a certain breadth, for example, purchase of enterprises being privatized. Doing so permits the firm to reduce the amount of capital committed and to reach the first of the objectives cited, sharing the costs and risks which, in the case of international operations, include exchange and country risk.

- To gain access to alternative sources of financing that permit the firm to take advantage of business opportunities even when the firm itself does not have the financing capacity to consummate the deals alone.

- To preserve local market share, as a defensive measure, from hostile competitors, while avoiding transactions such as acquisitions, mergers, or disinvestments, which normally are less cost-effective, as will be analyzed later.

- To obtain specific channels of distribution for products and services, and to assure sources of supply that are key to the production processes.

- To take advantage of favorable tax regimes or political incentives, most of all in third countries.

- To disinvest businesses with negative or marginal results, or to exploit resources hitherto under-utilized for various reasons.

- To undertake an internal restructuring of the organization and its production processes.

In short, many objectives provide a rationale for strategic alliances, in spite of the fact that success is not assured, a matter that will be discussed later. Clearly, many organizations are moving, strategically, in the direction of the business alliance.

The alliance, in this decade, may become a clear alternative to traditional mergers and acquisitions. These types of accords proliferated in the seventies, and were often erroneously identified only with the joint venture, which, as will be discussed in the second part of this chapter, is one of many forms of strategic alliance, although perhaps the most popular one. Between 1972 and 1979, 7,000 companies in the United States were involved in joint venture agreements, which were especially popular in the oil and gas industries.

Traditionally, capital intensive industries, such as petrochemicals, aerospace and construction, produced those accords. Without doubt, this strategic movement reached a point of inflection in the eighties, as it extended its scope into other sectors of the economy. The number of announcements of strategic alliances grew at a 15 percent compounded annually in the eighties. The rate of joint venture announcements exceeded five per day in the nineties. Alliances made by means of minority interests too, grew at a significant rate, although not as fast as that of joint ventures. (See Figure 2.) The automobile, chemical, semiconductor, pharmaceutical, metallurgical and telecommunications services led the pack in terms of closing alliance agreements in the past few years. The telecommunications sector shows the greatest dynamism, not only in number of transactions but also in their size.

In terms of geographic distribution, the location of accords has changed. Previously, in 1986, 63 percent of the "joint venture" agreements were signed in the U.S.A., and only 22 percent in Western Europe. In 1990, the percentages were 41 percent and 36 percent respectively. Similarly, 61 percent of alliances made by means of minority participation in 1986 were signed by American firms and the balance by Europeans. In 1990, Western Europeans made 55 percent of those agreements and Americans only 36 percent. (See Figure 3.)

Cross-border mergers and acquisitions, recently, have evolved in a similar fashion. Nevertheless, the volume of international transactions has fallen, especially in 1993, due to the fall in economic activity in the U.S.A. and in Europe, that induced a policy of paying greater attention to the home market and making sure of market position there.

These statistics reflect not only the real move toward agreements and alliances, but also provide evidence that merger and acquisition transactions have peaked, and other types of operations, such as joint ventures, minority stakes, and share exchanges are growing significantly, due to the great flexibility of means that they provide managements in reaching national and international objectives. That conclusion comes from an analysis of the evolution of completed privatizations, taking into account not only amounts paid but also the number of times in which companies formerly under state control have been sold to private consortia

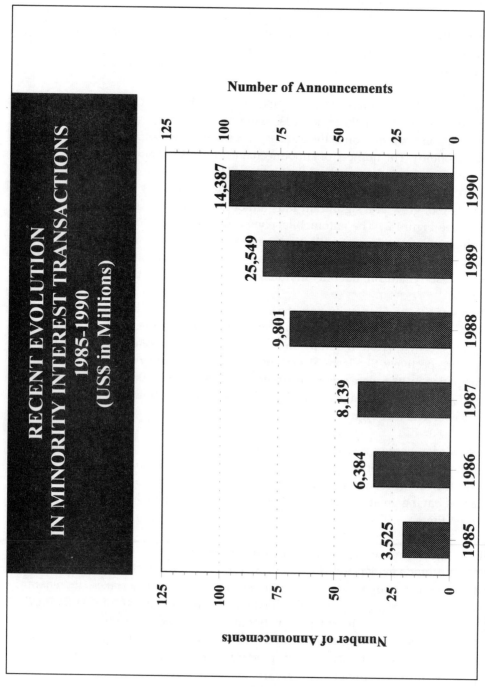

RECENT EVOLUTION IN MINORITY INTEREST TRANSACTIONS 1985-1990 (US$ in Millions)

Source: Securities Data Company

FIGURE 2

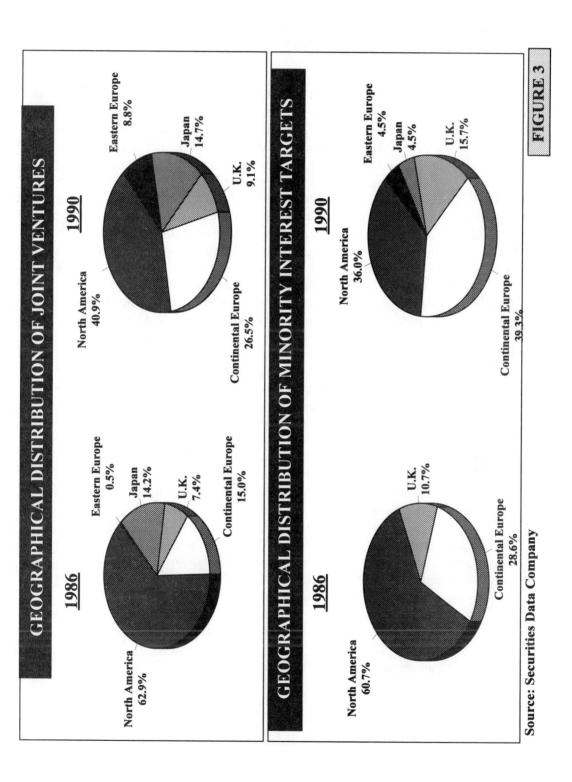

GEOGRAPHICAL DISTRIBUTION OF JOINT VENTURES

1986

North America 62.9%
Eastern Europe 0.5%
Japan 14.2%
U.K. 7.4%
Continental Europe 15.0%

1990

North America 40.9%
Eastern Europe 8.8%
Japan 14.7%
U.K. 9.1%
Continental Europe 26.5%

GEOGRAPHICAL DISTRIBUTION OF MINORITY INTEREST TARGETS

1986

North America 60.7%
U.K. 10.7%
Continental Europe 28.6%

1990

North America 36.0%
Eastern Europe 4.5%
Japan 4.5%
U.K. 15.7%
Continental Europe 39.3%

FIGURE 3

Source: Securities Data Company

constituted as joint ventures, as well as the number of licenses and concessions granted to private groups with foreign participation constituted as consortia. (See Figure 4.)

By and large, privatizations realized in the past decade have involved enterprises in developing countries. The privatizations have injected significant resources into those states, reestablishing confidence and encouraging the participation of private capital in productive activities. Privatizations have promoted exchange rate stability and the opening of the economy to the foreign sector, have stimulated competition and foreign investment, and have led many enterprises in developed countries to initiate international expansion. That strategy of expanding via privatizations, for some, may be the key to success in reaching a critical size internationally sufficient to position the firm to compete or to negotiate possible strategic alliances. If so, then the rash of strategic alliances, initiated in the eighties mainly to effect privatizations in emerging economies, may represent just the beginning of the trend. According to a 1994 study issued by Morgan Stanley, the governments of developed countries in Western Europe alone, in the next few years, have planned to transfer from public to private hands enterprises with a value exceeding $150 billion. If true, entrepreneurial activity in this sector has barely begun and every sign points to more activity in the immediate future. Nevertheless, no matter how clear the objectives and the benefits of the alliance appear, during the entire process of negotiation, the potential partners must weigh all the costs and risks implicit in the process itself. Among those risks are: the costs of the search for an adequate partner, the costs of coordination and management of the alliances put in place as well as the costs attributable to decisions taken to resolve the problems that arise during the life of the partnership, and the costs incurred upon dissolution of the alliance. In this sense, the statistics that recapitulate the historic evolution of this type of business accord are not yet conclusive as to whether alliances are or are not the best strategic solution to deal with the new scenario of global business activity.

In fact, according to several studies from McKinsey & Co. and Coopers & Lybrand made in 1986, of a sample of 895 joint ventures in 23 industrial sectors, approximately 70 percent failed either in the sense that did not meet the expectations raised by the business collaboration, or because they were dissolved. The lives of those alliances varied from a few months to 40 years, with an average life of three and a half years. Only 14 percent lasted more than a decade.

Among the reasons given to explain the failures are:

• The expected development and access to new technologies did not materialize

• Incorrect planning for the alliance

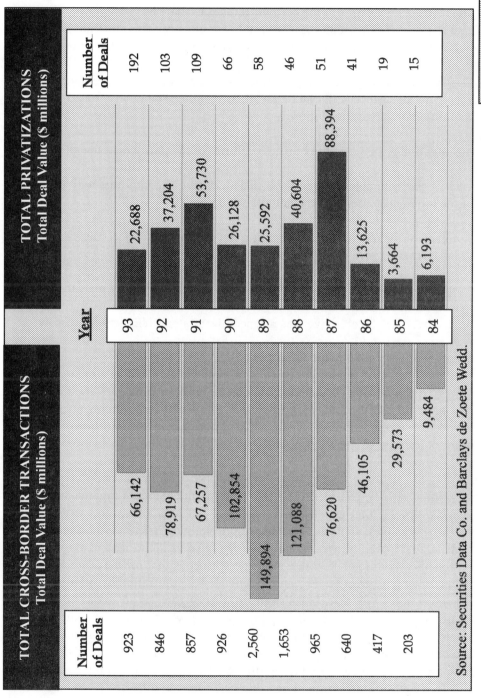

TOTAL CROSS-BORDER TRANSACTIONS
Total Deal Value ($ millions)

TOTAL PRIVATIZATIONS
Total Deal Value ($ millions)

Number of Deals		Year	Total Privatizations	Number of Deals
923	66,142	93	22,688	192
846	78,919	92	37,204	103
857	67,257	91	53,730	109
926	102,854	90	26,128	66
2,560	149,894	89	25,592	58
1,653	121,088	88	40,604	46
965	76,620	87	88,394	51
640	46,105	86	13,625	41
417	29,573	85	3,664	19
203	9,484	84	6,193	15

Source: Securities Data Co. and Barclays de Zoete Wedd.

FIGURE 4

337

- Lack of the necessary agreements to achieve the basic objectives of the alliance

- The management of one of the partners refused to share its know-how and managerial techniques with its counterparts in the alliance (This situation has been typical in alliances made by European or American firms with those in Japan.)

- The competitive position or the contribution to the alliance of one of the partners was so out of balance with that of the others that the alliance terminated with an acquisition or with a dissolution

- Incompatibility between the business cultures of the partners in the alliance

- Lack of clarity of objectives and insufficient degree of commitment on the part of the top managements of the enterprises involved

- Conflicts of interest and of competition not determined before the signing of the agreement.

Nevertheless, dwelling on the number of alliances dissolved may miss the point, in that on many occasions the alliances were formed with short term objectives in mind, so that once the objective was reached, the strategic alliance was dissolved.

Concepts and Types of Strategic Alliances

The existing literature commonly speaks of strategic alliances as similar to joint ventures. That, no doubt, is due to the fact that the strategic principles and functions of both are similar. One could say, furthermore, that a joint venture agreement is one of the possible forms of strategic alliance, in that two or more organizations establish a means of business cooperation that can be qualified as a strategic alliance.

According to a definition made by R. Porter in 1989, a joint venture is: "a cooperative business activity, constituted by two or more independent organizations for strategic purposes, that create an independent business entity, and that assign share ownership participation, operating responsibilities, risks and financial profits to each partner, while still preserving their own separate identities and autonomy." The fundamental difference with a strategic alliance is that for the latter, it is not strictly necessary to create a new and independent organization in order to bring about cooperation. We can define a strategic alliance, then, as an accord or cooperation between two or more companies by means of which they contribute, share, or interchange resources in order to reach one or more defined business objectives. Those resources may range from capital to properties, shareholder participations, know-how, management systems, production techniques or commercialization, channels of distribution, or other types of assets. One can differentiate the types of alliances depending on whether the agreement does or does not include a contribution of capital, or better said, an assignment of shareownership participations. (See Figure 5.) Among those that entail or maintain shareholder structures, we may distinguish the following:

1. **Joint venture:** this requires the creation of a new company, starting from the resources contributed by the partners, that maintains its independent identity as a joint venture. Normally, the partners maintain 50-50 or 60-40 ownership participation in the new entity. This type of organization may adopt, on one hand, the form of a corporation, with its respective shareholder agreements and possess the disadvantages of double taxation on dividends, and the fact that the tax benefits obtained by the joint venture cannot be utilized by the partners to reduce their own taxes. On the other hand, the joint venture may take the form of a partnership, which offers the disadvantage to the partners that they have unlimited liabilities to third parties for the liabilities of the partnership. Yet the partners gain the advantage that the partnership is a more efficient vehicle, from a taxation standpoint than is the corporation. That is because in the case of a partnership, the joint venture is not subject to corporate income tax and then because the partners avoid double taxation on profits.

2. **Partial merger:** could be considered as a case of a joint venture in which the partners merge divisions with similar characteristics or merge affiliates of the parent firms.

3. **Minority interest:** entails the establishment of a strategic alliance in a particular field (technology, supply, commercialization, exploration for new markets, etc.) based on the acquisition of a minority share ownership position, between 5 percent and 35 percent, of the capital of one of the corporations by the other.

4. **Cross-ownership:** the collaboration agreement is established on the basis of an interchange of participations in the shares of each of the corporations involved.

The alliance that does not entail a transfer of capital or creation of a new entity with its own shareownership structure usually has a shorter life and involves a lesser degree of commitment on the part of the organizations that signed the agreement. It may be no more than a commercial operation with little strategic content. One finds, among these types of transactions: distribution agreements, patent and license sharing, and franchising agreements that permit the acquisition of a technology or a product by means of payment for a license or use of a trademark. There are, also technological cooperation agreements, which, through joint research and development efforts, permit the development of a new product more efficiently, and thereby, share the high risk inherent in any research activity. For

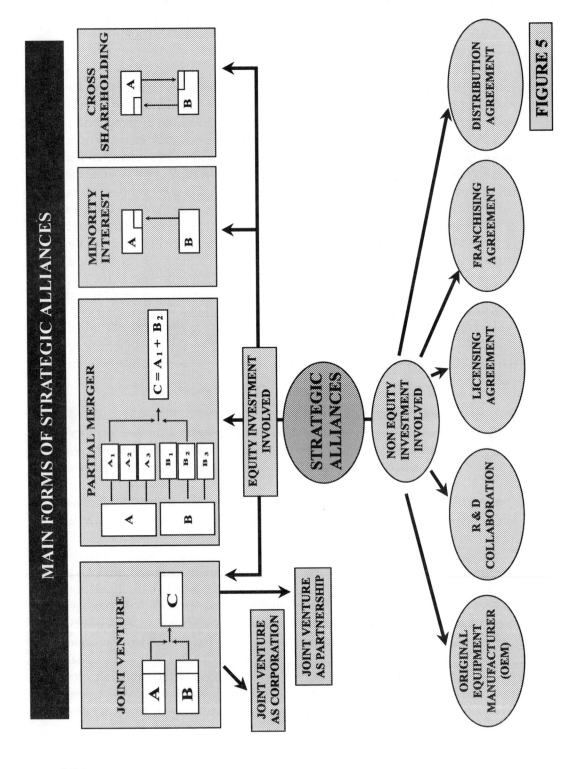

MAIN FORMS OF STRATEGIC ALLIANCES

JOINT VENTURE

JOINT VENTURE AS CORPORATION

JOINT VENTURE AS PARTNERSHIP

PARTIAL MERGER

$C = A_1 + B_2$

MINORITY INTEREST

CROSS SHAREHOLDING

EQUITY INVESTMENT INVOLVED

STRATEGIC ALLIANCES

NON EQUITY INVESTMENT INVOLVED

ORIGINAL EQUIPMENT MANUFACTURER (OEM)

R & D COLLABORATION

LICENSING AGREEMENT

FRANCHISING AGREEMENT

DISTRIBUTION AGREEMENT

FIGURE 5

the entity that provides the technology, this type of venture implies a tax payment on income derived from a royalty that will be higher than if the sharing of technology were in the form of a technological contribution to the joint venture.

Clearly, the diverse tax implications of each of the legal frameworks is not the only thing that differentiates them from each other. As one may appreciate from Figure 6, there are other important aspects of differentiation, such as: the degree of control or participation of each of the partners, the character of the contribution of each to the alliance, the different degrees of commitment ("corporate credibility") of the respective top managements of the participants, as well the degree to which the strategy of the alliance is determined in advance. For each participant in the alliance, all of these aspects will be conditioned, no doubt, by the strategic objectives being pursued, as much as by the priorities determined at the time when the participant analyzed the reasoning for arriving at an agreement of this type, as opposed to choosing other alternatives, such as borrowing money to launch a business, or a classic merger or acquisition.

In this sense, in recent years, the strategic alliances have proven to be a flexible instrument for the attainment of specified objectives, in cases when the partner seeks to commit limited resources and to limit the financial risk, as opposed to the major risk exposure inherent in an acquisition. Following are the significant advantages derived from an alliance as opposed to traditional mergers and acquisitions:

1. In terms of the structure and design of the operation, the merger of the two organizations may be more complex and less efficient than an agreement, such as a joint venture. This is especially the case when dealing with a contribution of determined resources to reach predefined objectives.

2. When the objective of the acquisition is to take control of a property, or in the case of a merger to absorb it, the price paid normally incorporates a premium for control whose size depends on diverse factors such as whether an existing market for the shares of the target company provides a reference price, the financial capacity of the acquiring firm, and the prospects for the target company. In strategic alliances, the valuation of assets contributed or acquired do not incorporate this premium on its own right. To the extent that this produces an imbalance in the aggregation of the contributions of both partners, there are mechanisms to alleviate the financial burden that the partner who contributes less must pay.

3. Although one should analyze transactions on a case by case basis, generally the initial tendency on the stock markets is to take an unenthusiastic view of purchase and merger announcements. Mergers are often viewed in the same light

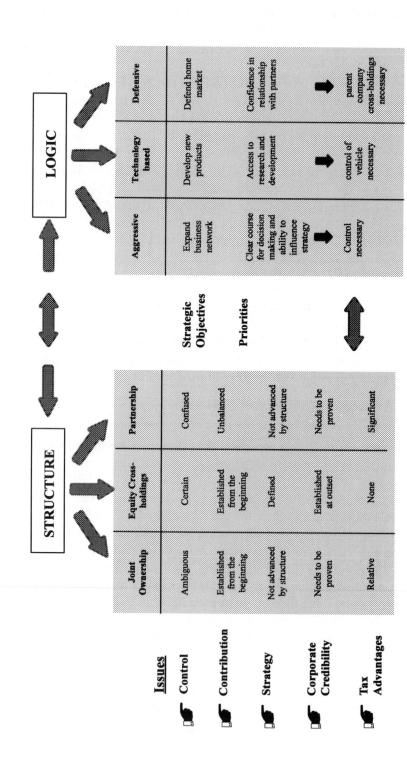

FIGURE 6

as acquisitions, in spite of supposedly being the integration of equals. This behavior of the market is most evident when investors do not view as realistic the synergies hoped for by the merging corporations—more so for the acquiring than for the acquired company. Normally the market reacts by dropping the price of the shares of the acquiring firm. That reaction becomes more pronounced when investors consider the premium paid as disproportionately high. That negative view translates into an unfavorable price for the shares of any acquiring corporation that does not know how to convey to the market the rationale for the transaction. On the other hand, announcements of strategic alliances usually are seen as positive steps by security analysts and investors.

4. Sometimes, the different sizes and business cultures of the respective entities involved in the acquisition process creates obstacles to retaining aspects of the acquired enterprise considered key to maintaining its value. Those at-risk elements include certain human resources, and management systems and procedures that are never internalized but are diffused or lost in an organization possibly too large, with slow decision-making processes and perhaps even less qualified staff. Dealing with these types of details requires a great deal of attention in alliances. Doing so is essential, first in the decision to make an alliance, and afterwards, in the management of the accord.

5. The joint venture has a certain advantage over acquisitions, from an accounting standpoint, in that the partner-owners do not consolidate the financial statements of the partnership into their own. That allows them to eliminate the need to amortize the goodwill that, almost always, is the accounting consequence of a merger or acquisition.

6. Last and by no means least, the acquisition process often produces an asymmetry of information flow that leads straight to bad acquisitions. At times, this risk of adverse selection is produced by an excessive overvaluation of synergies. That is nothing more than a problem of negotiation. It results from the opportunistic predisposition of one of the parties, that in the case of the seller, is translated into a lack of transparency or of skill at the time of transmitting to the buyer all negative or positive aspects of the object of the negotiation. That situation can be avoided through an agreement of alliance. Where both parties, through mutual interest, honestly provide all relevant information, the chances of purchasing or contributing "lemons" as opposed to "peaches" diminishes greatly compared to the chances incurred when making an acquisition.

Alliances however, not only have advantages but also present some risks or added costs not assumed with an acquisition. Disadvantages include the following:

1. The risk that one of the partners loses its interest in and hold on the day to day management of the alliance. When that happens, that the partner exposes itself to loss of market position instead of improving it, or transfers its know-how in management or technology to the other partner but cannot internalize any competitive advantages in return. Furthermore, the confidential information shared in this type of arrangement loses its character of confidentiality, something natural in this type of accord, which may have negative implications if the firm cannot realize offsetting benefits from the alliance.

2. As noted earlier, the process of negotiation can be complex and time consuming, with all the costs implicit in such a process, with no guarantee of reaching a final agreement. That process involves many aspects. Among the most important are: the identification of the potential partners, the definition of the strategy and the objectives of the alliance, the valuation of the contributions, the responsibilities of each of the founding partners, the participation in the capital and profits, choosing the organizational framework, the legal form, the definition of other agreements within the alliance (among which might be non-compete clauses), options to increase or decrease ownership participation, the physical location of the joint venture, and last, an array of taxation, accounting and legal matters that normally requires the advice of external experts.

3. One of the critical points for the success of all alliances centers on fluid communication between the managers responsible for the joint venture and those at the parent companies. The efforts and costs, in terms of human resources, needed to keep open those lines of communication are greater than those required in the case of an acquisition.

4. Another additional cost would be that associated with loss of sole control over business units contributed to the alliance, in return for representation on the board of directors of the alliance, and thus sharing decisions and the definition of strategy. Clearly, this cost will arise, depending on the type of alliance and on the position of each partner in it.

Some Considerations on Alliances

The factors determining strategic alliances, their objectives, the different forms that they take, and their advantages and disadvantages relative to traditional mergers and acquisitions have been described. Before going into a discussion of the telecommunications sector in general—and specifically the case of Telefónica de España as representative because of the company's formation of consortia and alliances derived from its policy of international expansion—perhaps it is worthwhile to make some points about this type of agreement.

Strategic alliances entail an agreement to collaborate with direct or indirect competitors within the industry. The agreements may incorporate different degrees of integration. At times, the sequential development of an integrative policy may be viewed by one of the partners as a test to visualize the rationality of a possible merger or acquisition. Furthermore, the competitive framework within which the allied companies operate may be changing so rapidly that they need greater integration in order to reach their objectives. Through the alliance, they can discover new opportunities for collaboration that may require the dissolution of the previous accord in order to launch a new and wider one, perhaps with the participation of additional partners. For those reasons, it is wrong to measure the success or failure of an alliance by its duration, rather than by whether the competitive position of each of the partners is better after the conclusion of the alliance than before its inception.

From an analysis of successful strategic alliances, one may distill some ideas about how the company positions itself toward the alliance itself, and toward the potential partner:

1. In a sense, collaboration between two enterprises involves competition in a way, because the privileged information and strategic resources that they share may be converted by one of the partners into decisive weapons to destroy the other, if the alliance fails. Therefore, it is fundamental to weigh how the aims of the other partner could affect the attainment of one's own goals.

2. One should not dramatize the conflicts that arise during the development and management of the alliances. They may be the best indicators that a collaboration with mutual benefits is succeeding. In the long term, though, it is difficult for both partners to win equally.

3. One can set limits to cooperation on paper, but in practice, these limits are often exceeded in the day to day management of the alliance. That is, the professional relations between the employees of the partners produce transfers of information or know-how that goes beyond what was set forth in the alliance agreement. Thus, in order to achieve the objectives set by each company, it is indispensable, on one hand, to make clear to the employees most directly involved in the accord, what type of technology, information, or skills, they may or may not share, and on the other hand, to follow up on the requests for information from the partner, as well as those made to the partner. This aspect is especially critical if we consider that the interaction of professionals from one side to the other of the agreement does not normally involve a balanced flow of information. That is, certain information transferred may have a great short term value, while that received may be generic and perhaps of more long term application. For this reason, it is desirable

that all alliances, on their operating sides, limit the channels of access to information and to other assets to a small circle of people who are concerned with the coordination of this aspect of the business in their respective organizations, with the object of avoiding possible abuses.

4. The most important reason for any alliance is to take maximum advantage of the strengths of the other partner to the agreement. If the other partner does not pay attention to the issues discussed in point 3, above, one could see a situation in which the first partner absorbs and internalizes skills from the second in areas that, in principle, have nothing to do with the agreement of alliance as signed.

5. In the case of joint ventures or alliance through minority participation, the majority partner should realize the importance of the role that the minority shareholder can play in bringing about success, whether the minority shareholder is a local partner in a country different from that of the majority partner, or a technological or strategic partner. The majority partner needs to avoid translating the management role conferred by ownership into an attitude of superiority, which is not effective in daily management. For this reason, it seems reasonable to confer some management responsibilities on the minority partner based on the qualities that it can lend (better knowledge of the functioning of the market, of the legal, tax or labor situations, of the socio-political environment, of specific technologies, or of the profile and preferences of the potential customers).

Often, the continuity of the alliance is threatened during the process of mutual internalization of the strengths of both partners. In this sense, experience seems to indicate that the most positive alliances have turned out to be those in which one of the partners assumes or desires to maintain a certain relationship of dependency in respect to the other as far as the possibilities for growth or improvement of competitive position. That does not signify that in order to assure the survival of the alliance it is necessary for one of the partners to give up more than it gets. Certain conditions exist under which it is possible to reach mutual benefit: for instance, although the competitive objectives of each partner may diverge, the strategic objectives converge, and somehow, these conditions can be made implicit in the non-compete clauses that are common in these types of agreements.

The risk produced by the situation described in point 3, above, in respect to the success of the alliance depends to a great extent on the type of information or know-how that is contributed, and to what degree its rapid internalization may be facilitated by one partner. To avoid this risk, the agreement should define clearly its scope in terms of what technology, markets, lines of business, and personnel, are shared. If doing so proves undesirable or creates an obstacle to the advancement of cooperation, one could get around the problem by defining a set of quantitative objectives for the alliance, so that whenever the alliance reaches a milestone, it passes to a greater phase of integration. For example, achieving: larger market share would lead to greater access to the technological developments of one of the partners, or vice versa.

Studies of alliances examine the implications for each of the partners when a particular partner's headquarters or research center is located close to that of the alliance. Without doubt, and paradoxically, that proximity reduces the learning opportunities for the nearby partner because of the distractions inherent in being able to take care of home office business as well, instead of concentrating on that of the alliance. That phenomenon seems more pronounced in the case of alliances made by means of minority positions or cross-ownership. On the other hand, though, the proximity reduces the risk of loss of control over assets and information that are transferred for the nearby partner.

The role played by personnel that is, on occasion, lent to the alliance, is of maximum relevance to the success of the alliance. Those employees may develop a loss of linkage to the company from whence they came, that can lead to lack of loyalty. Thus the selection of personnel is important. For, as noted previously, it is fundamental, on one hand, to learn as much and as soon as possible, everything worthwhile from the other partner, and, on the other hand, to contribute the right human resources so that the alliance can produce the maximum benefits from the integrated parts. The predisposition to learn has been, on occasion, absent in the cases of western companies that have signed agreements with Asian firms. That shows an arrogant attitude that is, perhaps, a consequence of a historic role of leadership. Therefore, it is important to make personnel involved in collaborative tasks aware of the advantages offered, for their respective organizations, of benefitting from the experience and knowledge of others, not only to improve the competitiveness—but also to assure survival—of their own organizations.

At times incorporation of the development work and know-how of the other partner into the framework of the alliance is not possible for a variety of reasons. Nevertheless, the mere fact that a comparative reference is available is a positive factor that permits the realization of an internal exercise involving the areas and processes that need improvement (benchmarking analysis). That, without doubt, produces an immediate advantage for every alliance as opposed to another type of operation.

Finally, as a consequence of the issues previously discussed, in many of the negotiations of alliances, the negotiators show an obsessive behavior in regard to the percentage ownership of their firm in the alliance. This is especially the case in the formation of joint ventures, where the fight for political control is obvious in the phases previous to the signing of the agreement.

Based on what has been discussed, it is clear that the purpose of collaboration is to better the competitive position of each of the partners. The partners should not worry about whether they control 60 percent or 40 percent of the capital of the joint venture, but rather whether each partner has the capacity and disposition to apply the principle of learning while doing and teaching while doing so that within a reasonable period of time, each may say that it is better positioned in the market than it was before the signing of the agreement, independently of whether its partner reaches the same conclusion. This attitude leads those companies that are conscious of their capacity to learn to prefer signing on to alliances with more ambiguous legal structures, in place of shareholder agreements and other types of excessively rigid legal documents that by protecting against specific risks or contingencies also create major obstacles that hinder one from exploiting the *a priori* advantages of every agreement of strategic alliance.

Alliances in the Telecommunications Sector

The telecommunications sector certainly is one that has caught the prevailing fever of signing strategic alliances. In fact, in the past few years, it has become the most dynamic sector in terms not only of the number of collaboration agreements signed between the most important global operators, but also of mergers and acquisitions. (See Figure 7.) A brief survey of the most recent transactions carried out show how important they are in this sector, and demonstrate that the proliferation of these activities, which are more and more taking on the character of the alliance and less that of M & A. This phenomenon is taking place in every line of business and in almost all regions of the world.

This new strategic behavior on the part of the principal telecommunications service companies is in response to changes in regulation and ownership that are taking place in the traditional framework of the sector, such as: privatizations of the state telephone administrations (the PTTs), breakdown of the natural monopolies under which the companies operated and, just as important, opening the offering of services and use of the network to competition, and the battle to reach a critical size internationally in order to position the firm better to compete or negotiate with other operators, with equipment suppliers, and with large corporate customers. In addition, other causational elements, similar to those previously discussed, have defined new strategies for the operators, in which alliances presently play an important role in confronting the future of the sector with some certainty of success.

In the third place, the incipient technological change in a capital intensive sector destines the deployment of great resources into the purchase and development of new technologies. That is especially important because of the role that the telecommunications sector plays, especially in developing countries, as an engine for economic growth, spurring economic activity in the balance of the economy.

LARGEST ANNOUNCED M&A DEALS IN 1993

Target Name	Acquiror Name	Value of Deal (Billion US$)	Industry
McCaw Cellular Commun. Inc.	American Telephone & Telegraph	17.6	Telecommunications
Paramount Communications	Viacom Inc.	10.0	Media
Midland Bank PLC	Lloyds Bank PLC	6.8	Finance
Volvo AB	Procordia AB	6.7	Manufacture
Medco Containment Services Inc.	Merck & Co.	6.0	Healthcare
HCA-Hospital Corp of America	Columbia Healthcare Corp.	5.5	Healthcare
MCI (20% stake)	British Telecom	5.3	Telecommunications
Galen Healthcare	Columbia Healthcare Corp.	4.2	Healthcare
Travelers Corp.	Primerica Corp.	4.0	Finance
Time Warner	US West	2.5	Media/CATV

FIGURE 7

Source: Goldman Sachs.

This third factor materializes in the introduction of digital and fiber optic technologies that substantially augment the quality and variety of services offered to customers who increasingly demand more sophisticated and global solutions.

This attractive picture, without doubt, attracts the entry of new competitors. That, in turn, is changing the profile of the traditional financial results of the operating company, which, up until recently, achieved economies of scale in the provision of services and networks with relative ease. In recent years, the appearance of new companies in the field of telecommunications has intensified. In fact, over the short term, all signs point to a proliferation of providers of service, linked to the convergence of telephone, television, cable and data processing technologies, which is going to furnish, first to business customers and later to homes, a wide menu of interactive telecommunications and entertainment services (multimedia) all transported on the same medium of communications.

The need to share the risks derived from the huge investments necessary to install and provide content offerings for the so-called Electronic Superhighways that will offer the multimedia services, to obtain the indispensable know-how to develop a wide catalog of services, and to achieve the critical mass necessary to compete in an increasingly globalized business, all constitute fundamental factors that have pushed the principal operators of basic telephony, cable television firms, movie producers, catalog merchandisers, those providing correspondence school education by wire or over the airwaves, etc., to start to take positions in this new business by means of alliances and acquisitions of blocs of shares that may represent minority or control interests. (See Figure 8, which appears at the end of the book.)

The growing globalization of economies has been another determining factor. In effect, the growing interrelationship of world economies has led to a significant enlargement of the demand for international telecommunications and services, not only at the level of the local market, but also on a supranational basis, mimicking the international expansion policies of the large customers. Services on an international basis can be achieved by means of alliances with other operators that permit the offering of global networks to multinational clients, or through an active policy of internationalization by means of physical presence in other countries. The decision to cross national frontiers responds not only to the objective of retaining customer loyalty of the large business clients no matter where they locate their facilities, but also to the necessity of compensating for loss of share of the national market as its rules are liberalized. In this sense, the processes of privatization and bidding for licenses to operate mobile services and data networks have become the principal routes by means of which the most advanced operators are configuring their international presence, with the ultimate object of achieving an optimal size to survive in the new global market.

Clearly, the factors discussed are conditioning the strategic decisions of the principal global operators. Among the distinct strategic approaches, three trends dominate:

1. **Vertical integration:** This strategy consists of developing new lines of business by means of firms or alliances that permit direct access to the new services, taking advantage of the more or less dominant position that the enterprise maintains in its traditional businesses. The policy of diversification of telecommunications businesses has reached its greatest intensity in the United States and the United Kingdom, for regulatory reasons. As just one example, in the United States the long distance operators are trying to incorporate cellular mobile telephony into their operations, as an intermediate step to penetrating the local telephone markets controlled by the Bell companies and the independents (GTE, Alltel, etc.). Those moves are typified by AT&T's takeover of McCaw, the largest cellular mobile operator or the plans of MCI, and the alliance of Sprint with cable TV companies (TCI and Cox Cable) to develop personal communications services (PCS), as well as its integration with Centel (local and cellular telephony). For their part, the local operators, while they insistently petition to have existing restrictions against their participation in the long distance market lifted, are forming alliances in cellular mobile telephony (a case in point being the joint venture between NYNEX, Bell Atlantic, US West and Air Touch, the spinoff from Pacific Telesis) with a defensive character in order to counter the movements, primarily, of AT&T. (See Figure 9.)

At the same time that basic services are evolving, new services are exploding, both in terms of supply and demand, propelled by technological innovation, liberalization of the rules for the offer of services, and the new demands of clients. In this area of discussion, one should examine the strategies of the principal basic telephone operators, addressing their participation in the promising market for multimedia services. Thanks to certain regulatory restraints in the U.S.A., the United Kingdom has become, for many American companies, the test market in which they may learn about offering such services. That, certainly, is the case for the TeleWest joint venture between TCI and US West, which operates various cable TV franchises in Britain. Recently, the restrictions have been lightened, thereby initiating a rush of alliances made with the principal cable TV operators (NYNEX—Viacom, US West—Time Warner, Southwestern Bell and Hauser), some of which never got off the ground, such as that proposed between Bell Atlantic and TCI, or that between Southwestern Bell and Cox Cable.

Aside from basic telephony, mobile and multimedia services, other types of services exist, such as data transmission and value added services. In spite of the fact that other services do not yet represent an important part of the business of the

MAJOR CELLULAR ALLIANCES-PCS (EE.UU)

ALLIANCE	EQUITY PARTNERS	SUBSCRIBERS	POPULATION INSIDE THE ZONE OF COVERAGE (Pop's)
ATT-McCaw- Lin Broadcasting	ATT acquire 100% of Mc Caw, Mc Caw owns 52% of Lin with a call option for the rest of the capital	3.097.000 cellular subscribers	66 millions
Sprint TCI Comcast Cox Cable Teleport(1)	40% 30% 15% 15% Associated	652.000(cellular) 16.289.000 (Cable TV)	85 millions
Bell Atlantic Air Touch NYNEX US West	Ownerships non defined	3.474.600 (total joined cellular subscribers)	175 millions

(1) Teleport, is a "Competitive Acces Provider" ("CAP") 100% own by TCI, Cox Cable, Comcast and Continental Cablevisión.

(*) During the last months several alliances and mergers have taken place in the U.S. to participate in the coming assigment of PCS licences, with the perspective for building up alternative movile networks.

FIGURE 9

traditional operators, they are predicted to be a principal activity of telecommunications in the future as well as a primal source of profits in the relatively stagnant future seen for the basic services which, thanks to a high level of penetration, have little potential for growth. Those are businesses with high margins and, due to their focus on large customers, they should generate significant volumes of traffic which will improve the utilization of the network. In this field, one would expect the rapid formation of alliances such as that already existing in Infonet (a company with the most internationally diversified data transmission network that is owned by eight international operators) in which companies like IBM, Reuters, EDS, Extel, and ICL, can transform themselves into appropriate partners for the traditional operators.

2. **Horizontal integration:** Some companies, at the same time that they are undertaking a policy of diversifying their lines of business, are carrying on a horizontal integration within the industry in order to extract the maximum yield from a strategy of segmentation of the market by the needs of specific groups of customers or by specific geographic regions. The object of rapidly reaching economies of scale is evident in the formation of alliances—within this strategic focus of the business—to share networks, client lists and market shares, in combination with a unified management in different markets. The segmentation between the necessities of the business and residential clients is the most immediate commercial action in this type of business. Furthermore, it is precisely to meet the needs of the major corporate customers that national and international alliances are being formed. (See Figure 10.)

Business clients, clearly, are keener to have global network services, which simplify in an effective manner the interchange of information between enterprises. The most significant alliance agreements that have centered on this segment of client base and on global network services for multinational services are those established between France Telecom (FT) and Deutsche Telekom (DT) by means of the formation of a 50-50 joint venture (Eunetcom). This agreement has been enlarged, recently, with the planned joint venture with Sprint. The two European operators would each take minority ownership positions (10 percent each) in Sprint. Another grand alliance in this field was formed between MCI and British Telecom (BT) through a similar process, that is, BT taking a minority position (20 percent) in MCI and after that, the two set up a joint venture, called Concert, of which BT owns 75 percent and MCI 25 percent). The lack of financial capacity to deal with important joint business opportunities often characterizes one of the partners, a factor that the latter partner takes advantage of by providing the needed capital through taking a minority position in the former. That is the case of BT in MCI, and of DT and FT in Sprint. Sprint, as a result of

MAJOR GLOBAL ALLIANCES

ALLIANCE	EQUITY PARTNERS	DISTRIBUTORS	OUTGOING MINUTES OF INTERNATIONAL TRAFFIC (million of minutes 1992)	OPERATING REVENUES (million US$ 1993)
Concert	75% BT 25% MCI (*) * BT acquired 20% of MCI by 4,300 Mill. US$	BT MCI Norway Telecom Nippon Information & Communications Telecom Finland Tele Danmark	BT: 2,188 MCI: 2,083 TOTAL: 4,271	BT: 21,588 MCI: 13,508 TOTAL: 64,400
Eunetcom-Sprint	50% France T. → Eunetcom 50% Deutsche T. ↗ FT+DT ——20%——→ Sprint	Deutsche Telekom France Telecom Sprint KDD (?)	Deutsche Telekom: 4,087 France Telecom: 2,449 Sprint: 940 TOTAL: 7,476	Deutsche Telekom: 30,000 France Telecom: 23,000 Sprint: 11,400 TOTAL: 64,400
Unisource	25% Telia 25% KPN Holland 25% Swiss PTT 25% Telefónica	KPN (Holland) Telia AB Swiss PTT Telefónica Helsinki Telecom World Partners	Telefónica: 804 PTT Suiza: 1,551 KPN Holland: 1,134 Telia: 691 TOTAL: 4,180	Telefónica: 11,060 KPN Holland: 10,431 Swiss PTT: 6,012 (92) Telia: 5,316 (92) TOTAL: 32,819
World Partners	40% AT&T 24% KDD 20% Unisource 16% Singapore Telecom	AT&T KDD Singapore Telecom Unisource Hong Kong Telecom Telstra Korea Telecom Unitel	AT&T: 6,984 KDD: 900 Singapore Telecom: 412 Unisource: 4,180 TOTAL: 12,476	AT&T: 71,732 KDD: 2,500 Singapore Telecom: 2,091 Unisource: 32,819 TOTAL: 109,142

FIGURE 10

the funds to be received from the European operators plans to join into additional alliances that, now, would seem to improve the competitive position of the American long distance operator.

The other two grand alliances have been formed to satisfy the international communications needs of the large customers. The first is Unisource, in which Telia (Sweden), KPN (Netherlands), the Swiss PTT and Telefónica de España are partners at 25 percent each. The second is World Partners, formed by AT&T (40 percent), KDD of Japan (24 percent), Unisource (20 percent), and Singapore Telecom (16 percent).

Emphasis of Unisource is important because of the extent of integration found in this alliance. At the present time, Unisource represents a single, unique, platform for the four partners in data transmission, and the development of all sorts of offerings, such as satellites, corporate networks and other services. In this manner, the harmonization of the commercial offering to clients with the infrastructure that supports those offerings will be coordinated and developed, all of which will facilitate international communications from end to end, by means of one contract that may be executed in the commercial offices of any of the associates (one stop shopping). Telefónica de España was the last partner to join this alliance. For it, the agreement signified, first, access to an important technological and commercial platform necessary to carry on a correct segmentation of the market; second, preserving its position providing those services in the national market; and, finally, a substantial advance in international strategy, augmenting in a notable manner its participation in the immense and strongly growing European telecommunications market. For its part, the incorporation of Telefónica into it allows Unisource to extend the reach of its service into the south of Europe, and given Spain's position as a bridge to Latin America, to tap into the possibilities of global growth represented by that position.

3. **Internationalization:** a third line of action that can be observed among the distinct strategies carried forward by the operators could be called productive internationalization, not only in terms of the operation of networks in other geographic markets but also in expanding the offer of services outside the national frontiers. These policies of international positioning in the telecommunications sector was preceded by a process of financial internationalization that characterized the activities of the American and European private operators during the seventies and eighties. In effect, many of the Bell companies, AT&T, British Telecom and Telefónica de España implemented a policy of diversification of sources of financing and sought listings on foreign stock exchanges, with the objective of improving access to international capital markets, and thus reducing their cost of capital. This presence in other financial markets was necessary in light of the new situation of an explosion of demand

for telecommunication services in the respective local markets, which required the execution of ambitious investment programs whose financing could not always be realized from funds raised in the national markets. During that period, the processes of deregulation were not even at their initial stages, as they were in the last years of the eighties. Furthermore, the telecommunications markets of the developed countries were still in an expansive stage. Observe the levels of telephone penetration measured in terms of lines per 100 inhabitants in those days compared to now.) Both factors, without doubt, favored the undertaking of financial internationalization in the first place, with the realization of productive internationalization later. At the end of the past decade, there was a rapid transformation of the sector, as regulatory changes adjusted to the new conditions of technology and demand.

In this new environment, the principal operating companies gave top priority to their international positioning which, at times was defensive in nature (compensating for the potential loss of national market share due to the appearance of new competitors in a market that had, until recently, been reserved by law for the regional or national operator) and at other times was offensive in nature, taking advantage of the new market opportunities present in other countries. This policy reflects an active enterprise strategy, as opposed to a passive behavior which, while it would permit the company to continue to receive the short term benefits inherent in its locally dominant position without making major investments at the international level, would have a negative impact on the value of the company in the long run. The international panorama offers new opportunities for investment, not only from growing international traffic, but also from the privatizations of basic telephony or of the licenses to operate mobile services and data networks in an industry whose new technologies permit the simultaneous reduction of unit costs and the widening of the quality and capacity of the networks.

As in the previous cases of vertical and horizontal integration, the final objective that underlies the policy of international expansion is none other than to arrive at size sufficient to strengthen the competitive position of the operator enterprises in a sector that, in coming years, will open up to competition in all its lines of business. The development of international business, while aimed at meeting more or less similar objectives for distinct operators (strengthening of competitive position, configuration as a multinational operator, a wide enough market, improvement of bargaining position vìs à vìs suppliers and large customers), takes on different focuses depending on the competitive advantages that each company offers. The advantages include: the degree of technological specialization, the capacity to manage large programs of investment, position and size in international traffic, financial and human resources capabilities needed for international expansion, cultural affinity with the country in which the investment will be made, recent experience in similar market cycles, and the compatibility of business cultures.

International expansion follows different strategies that can be distinguished by the following patterns:

- Geographic specialization with diversification of lines of business. This is the policy followed principally by GTE and Telefónica de España, with investments largely made in Latin America and participation in almost all possible lines of business (basic telephony, cellular, Yellow Pages, cable TV, data transmission, and private networks).

- Geographic and line-of-business diversification. Those elements characterize the international positioning of operators such as AT&T and France Telecom. They, like GTE and Telefónica, want to diversify their service offerings, but do not want to limit the geographic scope of their investments, and they already are present in different regions of the world, including Latin America, Western and Eastern Europe, and the Far East.

- Geographic diversification with concentration on one line of business. BellSouth provides the most obvious example of this form of international effort. Aside from operating in the basic telephony segment, the company is one of the leaders in cellular mobile services in the USA, in terms of size and knowledge of the market. That position of leadership has encouraged the company to base its international expansion on specialization in cellular mobile telephony, taking advantage of technological advances with a growing geographic presence, in order to try to capture part of the business that presently is served by the fixed wireline network. Basically, BellSouth's participation in foreign markets is localized in Latin America (Argentina, Venezuela, Chile, Uruguay) and in Europe (Germany, Denmark, France, and the U.K.).

- High degree of specialization both geographically and in terms of line of business. That is the situation represented by British Telecom in the U.S.A., in a business of global voice and data networks for multinational enterprises.

Determining which strategies will be most successful is difficult. As a matter of fact, the important changes that occur every year in this sector make one think that the existing positioning will not be definitive, and will not be sufficient to guarantee success. Nor have the stock markets given clear signs on the results of these processes of international investment and configuration of strategic alliances. That should be evident from the disparate valuations seen in Figure 11. That figure

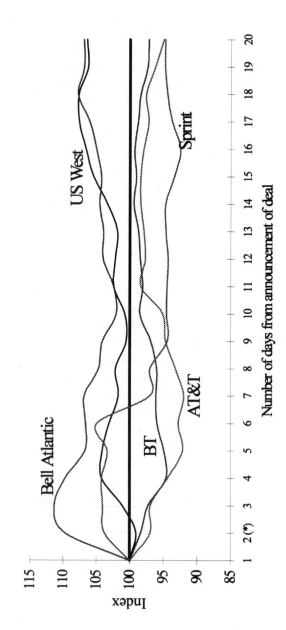

STOCK PERFORMANCE VS S&P 500

FIGURE 11

(*) Day of announcement of the deal.

summarizes the stock price movement relative to the New York Market (represented by the S & P 500) of five corporations that, in 1993 and 1994, launched some of the major alliance or acquisition efforts in the telecommunications sector. Specifically, the statistics compare the variation in price (off a base of 100) with that of the market in general, in order to show the reaction of investors to an announcement of alliance or acquisition in the 20 days after the announcement. As an example of what happened in this period, AT&T and BT shares performed 5 percent and 3 percent worse than the market, after announcing the acquisitions of share positions in McCaw (cellular telephony) and MCI (long distance) respectively. For their part, though, the multimedia alliances announced by US West (with Time Warner), and by Bell Atlantic (with TCI) were well received by investors. They were willing to pay up for the significant profits expected, despite the untried nature of the venture. The stocks of US West and Bell Atlantic rose 6 percent and 7 percent relative to the market. The other case analyzed in Figure 11 is that of Sprint, the long distance carrier. Despite the breakdown of negotiations with EDS, it reached an accord with France Telecom and Deutsche Telekom, in which those two companies will buy minority interests in Sprint and simultaneously set up a joint venture with that company. In this example, the stock market initially valued the transaction positively, but later began to look at it more negatively, because of the possibility that the Federal Communications Commission (FCC) would not approve the transaction due the opposition of AT&T.

Mercer Management Consulting recently (1993 and 1994) published some studies that pointed to three factors that provided signals to the possible success of the chosen strategy. Those factors are:

- The structural characteristics of the market to which the strategy of positioning is directed. Those characteristics are represented by expectations for growth, and by the degree of capital intensity required to be represented in the market.

- The comparative analysis between the point of departure of the operator (measured in terms of size, market share and technological leadership) and the necessary requisites to gain a competitive position.

- The valuation of the technical qualifications of the operator, understood to include: managerial capability in business, the degree of knowledge of the needs and profiles of the customers, the level of development and definition of product, the availability of advanced systems of billing and collection that can be utilized as commercial tools.

In accordance with those studies, the operating companies of the principal developed countries have begun to take different paths that correspond to the three strategies (vertical integration, horizontal integration and internationalization) defined previously. Nevertheless, few of the companies have undertaken an internal analysis that takes into account their strengths and weaknesses, in terms of choosing the market in which they could best develop their potential and obtain the highest returns. This situation is especially important in terms of negotiating an alliance, in that the internal analysis permits one to detect the complementaries needed from the potential partner in order to gain competitive advantage in the segments of the business at which the strategy is aimed.

In a way, the Mercer study identifies six strategies of development that, more or less, condition the positioning in the market of each company or alliance. They will also forecast the abandonment of certain lines of business by very diversified operators in the face of maintaining in every line the degree of competitiveness required in the current environment. Nevertheless, the position of departure of each traditional operator in the national market, normally one of leadership, will continue to constitute an essential factor for competitiveness in an increasingly global sector. The six lines of business that the new competitive environment makes possible, that are beginning to define the development strategies of the principal companies and alliances, are the following:

1. The global provider of telecommunications services, oriented mainly toward business clients (especially multinational enterprises).

2. The provider of multimedia services that, on the contrary, prioritizes the demands of residential customers.

3. The operator of mobile services with a policy of segmentation aimed at residential and commercial clientele.

4. The distributor of the signal or dial tone (the transporter) that bases its differentiation from other operators on its control of costs.

5. The operator specialized in medium-small size business customers, reflecting in part, a market ignored by the global providers, due to lack of economies of scale for those giant operators.

6. Finally, there is the operator of traditional services (the turnaround operator) that bases its growth on, and improves its competitive position from the acquisition of operators characterized by inefficient management of the network, absence of commercial strategy to sell services, inattention to the customer, and lack of financial resources to make necessary investments. Telefónica de España, has acted in this capacity of turnaround operator in the acquisitions made through privatizations. In those situations, considering that most of these

are one-time investment opportunities, what is especially relevant is the speed, certainty and success with which the operator can take advantage of the opportunity, as well as the existence (or not) of unique competitive advantages in certain local markets derived from the existence of economic or cultural links, including the sharing of a common language.

The identification of each operator or alliance with one of these six strategies of development should not be viewed as a static exercise in categorizing each company, but rather as a dynamic analysis. The analysis shows, on one hand, how each of the operators identifies with different lines of business, more or less, according to its capabilities, ambitions and plans. On the other hand, there exists the strategic option of jumping from one line of business to another once the firm's strategic objectives have been met, or because of the possibility of reaching agreements for alliances that permit the firm to launch new projects or businesses from a different competitive position, in accordance with the needs of the marketplace.

This situation is clearly seen in the sixth strategy (turnaround) defined above. Once the strategic operator has turned around the state in which it found the basic network and moved it toward a normal situation, as measured by indices of quality of service and market penetration appropriate to the socio-economic environment of the nation, the operator may then put into place more complex strategies aimed at furnishing advanced services. This policy makes a great deal of sense considering that, in many instances, the telecommunications networks of developing countries, at the time of privatization, show extremely low levels of penetration and digitalization. That permits rapid growth and modernization to take place simultaneously. If, in addition, the strategic operator enjoys a strong geographic position in the region, the possibilities of operating synergies are more feasible, permitting it to evolve from a mere operator of traditional services to a global provider of telecommunications; or to the position of a regional (more than one country) operator of cellular mobile telephony; and even a multimedia services provider, offering a network as well as information contents, with a geographic scope beyond the territory of one country.

All of these considerations are, no doubt, behind the alliances that have been formed recently, and will surely be taken into account when negotiating the next alliances. Thus, it is interesting to observe how, in nearly all the alliances made to date, at least one American partner participates, in part due to the technological and regulatory changes that have characterized the United States market in recent years. The American companies offer some complementarities important to the European operators. They may help the European operators to choose one of the development strategies discussed previously. The European operators have certain advantages such as size (control of their respective, somewhat mature networks), standing in the local market, and the best access to information about the local market and their own customers. Yet, they also show a certain vulnerability and deficiency, especially in terms of commercial culture (traditionally they operated a monopoly). That translates into a limited knowledge of the needs and reactions of the customer, and of the techniques of marketing, and of the commercialization of services in a competitive environment, all of which will hinder them in the competitive scenario that will characterize the telecommunications sector of the European Community beginning in 1998.

The point of departure of an operator with plans to negotiate an alliance is a critical element in reaching a satisfactory accord and in playing in active role in the daily management of the alliance. This reflection underlies, doubtlessly, the decision that Telefónica de España made at the time, to undertake its process of internationalization, which was one of the first realized by telecommunications companies, and which can be qualified as a success in operational and economic-financial terms.

The International Positioning of Telefónica

The international expansion of Telefónica, which began in earnest in 1989, is linked to the rapid transformation that occurred in the Spanish telecommunications sector since the late eighties, which combined the introduction of new technologies with an explosion of demand for telecommunications (basic and advanced) derived from the economic growth of the period. The investment and managerial effort expended by Telefónica in 1987–1992 translated into a total investment of more than $27 billion, with the installation of lines, in one year, exceeding one million. That effort to meet the elevated needs of the Spanish market in such a short space of time has been converted into know-how that, today, represents a competitive advantage in developing telecommunications services and networks abroad, which, in the majority of instances, require the implementation of investment programs designed to satisfy new demand and improve the quality of services. Taking into account those considerations, Telefónica has tilted its internationalization policy toward a position in Latin America, for a number of reasons:

- In the first place, it is a region with rapidly growing markets characterized by low measures of penetration for nearly all types of services (basic telephony, cellular, data transmission, and cable TV). (See Figure 12.)

- In the second place, presence in several Latin American countries makes it possible to realize operating synergies. To cite some examples, they are produced from the larger volume of international traffic carried (Telefónica is the third largest operator of submarine cables in the world), from the unification of network management systems, and from increased bargaining power when dealing with suppliers.

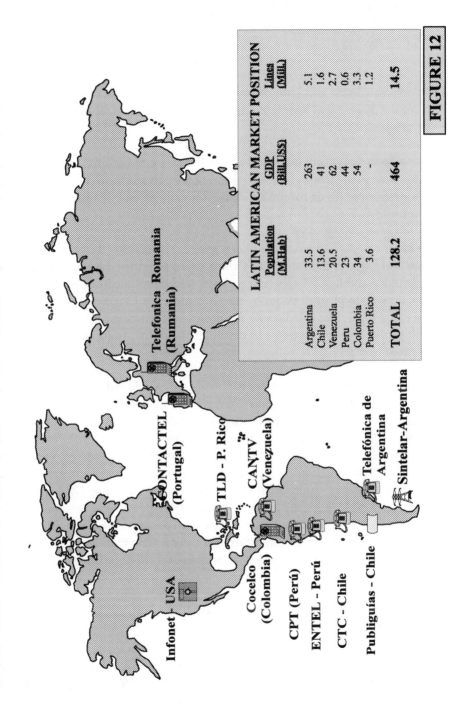

TELEFONICA'S INTERNATIONAL INVESTMENTS

Telefónica Romania (Rumania)

CONTACTEL (Portugal)

TLD – P. Rico

CANTV (Venezuela)

Telefónica de Argentina

Sintelar-Argentina

Infonet - USA

Cocelco (Colombia)

CPT (Perú)

ENTEL – Perú

CTC – Chile

Publiguías – Chile

LATIN AMERICAN MARKET POSITION

	Population (M.Hab)	GDP (Bill.US$)	Lines (Mill.)
Argentina	33.5	263	5.1
Chile	13.6	41	1.6
Venezuela	20.5	62	2.7
Peru	23	44	0.6
Colombia	34	54	3.3
Puerto Rico	3.6	-	1.2
TOTAL	**128.2**	**464**	**14.5**

FIGURE 12

363

- In the third place, because Telefónica has recently experienced market cycles similar to those presently taking place in Latin America, it can rapidly put into place the management techniques and programming of investments that it uses in Spain.

- Last, and by no means least, the shared affinities of language, culture and interests between Spain and Latin America enormously facilitate Telefónica's penetration of the market and adaptation to the local scene, done rapidly and with low costs of learning.

For all practical purposes, most of Telefónica's international investments, to date, have been made through participation in the privatization processes for basic telephone companies or through bidding for cellular mobile telephone licenses. (See Figure 13.)

In every case, the approach has been selective, executing those investment projects that add value to the Telefónica Group, that strengthen the competitive position of Telefónica and its affiliates in the global telecommunications sector. This creation of value has to be understood within a framework. On one hand each project must exceed a minimum hurdle rate for profitability, taking into account the different risk profile of each project. On the other hand, the project may realize synergies for the Group.

The internationalization policy of Telefónica is carried out by an affiliated company, Telefónica Internacional, owned 76.2 percent by Telefónica de España. Telefónica Internacional, as the vehicle for the international strategy of the Telefónica Group, analyzes, makes the transaction, and manages the international investments in the telecommunications sector. From an administrative point of view, Telefónica Internacional functions as a corporate headquarters of an integrated group that operates telecommunications enterprises, not as a mere holding company in which shareholdings are placed. Looking at investment results at the end of September 1994, the market value of the total assets of Telefónica Internacional has reached a notable size, more than $6.3 billion. The market value of shareholder equity at that same date, reached more than $4.3 billion, while the net profit in 1993 was $152 million.

As for the way Telefónica has localized its investments, the major ones are: (See Figure 14.)

- Active participation in the management of the Chilean basic telephony operator, Compañia de Teléfonos de Chile, (CTC), in which share ownership stands at 43.6 percent. Also in Chile, Telefónica is in the Yellow Pages business, through ownership of 51 percent of Publiguías.

LARGEST TELECOM PRIVATIZATIONS

YEAR	TARGET COMPANY	STRATEGIC PURCHASER	OWNERSHIP	PRICE (Million US$)	PUBLIC OFFERING
1984	British Telecom	-	50.2%	2.173	YES
1991	British Telecom	-	26%	3.462	YES
1993	British Telecom	-	21.1%	3.598	YES
1986	NTT (Japan)	-	13%	13.850	YES
1987	NTT (Japan)	-	12%	36.500	YES
1988	NTT (Japan)	-	9%	21.400	YES
1989	CTC (Chile)	Telefónica (Spain)	43.6%	(380	NO
1990	Telecom New Zealand	Bell Atlantic/ Ameritech	90%	2.460	NO
1992	Telecom New Zealand	-	26%	(818	YES
1990	Telekom Malaysia	-	24%	2.350	YES
1990	TELMEX (Méjico)	Southwestern Bell/ France Telecom	20.4%	1.757	NO
1991	TELMEX (Méjico)	-	15%	2.173	YES
1994	TELMEX (Méjico)	-	n.a.	3.731	YES

Source: Barclays de Zoete Wedd and Goldman Sachs.

FIGURE 13

LARGEST TELECOM PRIVATIZATIONS(II)

YEAR	TARGET COMPANY	STRATEGIC PURCHASER	OWNERSHIP	PRICE (Million US$)	PUBLIC OFFERING
1990	Telefónica de Argentina	Telefónica (Spain)	60%	1.207	NO
1991	Telefónica de Argentina	-	30%	637	YES
1990	Telecom Argentina	France Telecom / STET (Italy)	60%	(1,020)	NO
1992	Telecom Argentina	-	30%	1.227	YES
1991	CANTV (Venezuela)	GTE / AT&T / Telefónica (Spain)	40%	1.885	NO
1991	TLD (Puerto Rico)	Telefónica (Spain)	79%	141.6	NO
1993	Matav (Hungary)	Deutsche Telekom / Ameritech	30.2%	875	NO
1993	Singapore Telecom	-	11%	1.488	YES
1993	Korea Telecom	-	2%	200	YES
1994	CPT / ENTEL Perú	Telefónica (Spain)	35%	2.002	NO
1994	KPN (Holland)	-	30%	3.682	YES
1994	Tele Danmark	-	49%	2.974	YES
1994	Pakistan Telecom	-	10%	900	Private Placement

Source: Barclays de Zoete Wedd, Goldman Sachs.

FIGURE 13

ORGANIZATIONAL STRUCTURE

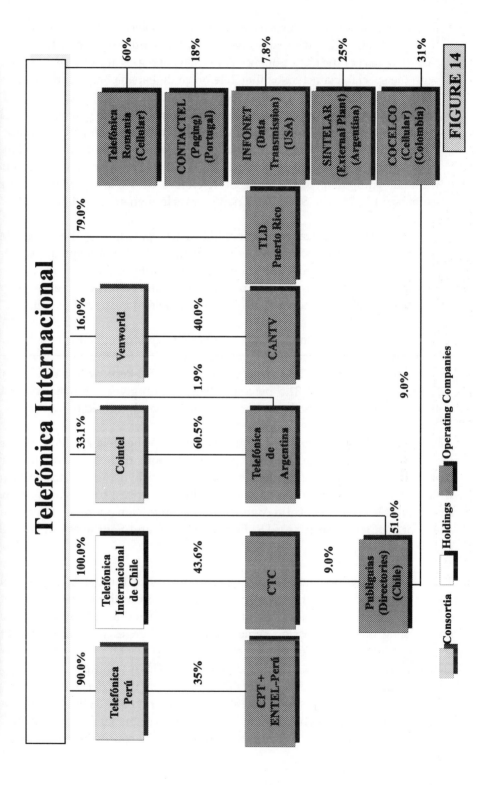

Telefónica Internacional

FIGURE 14

- The investment made, in successive phases, in Telefónica de Argentina stands out in the portfolio. That company operates in the southern zone of the country, including part of the city of Buenos Aires. Ownership is at 22 percent of capital, with the special characteristic that Telefónica de España has had the responsibility of managing the Argentine operator since its privatization at the end of 1990. In the same country, Telefónica Internacional owns 25 percent of Sintelar, which while it is far less important in size than the investment in Telefónica de Argentina, reflects a real case of synergies for the Group. Sintelar is a company in the business of construction of external plant and installation of telecommunications equipment. An affiliate of Telefónica de España, dedicated to the same business lines in Spain, also participates in ownership of Sintelar.

- In Venezuela, Telefónica Internacional has participated, since the end of 1991, as a minority shareholder (6.4 percent) in the capital of Compañía Anonima Nacional de Teléfonos de Venezuela. Telefonica Internacional shares management with the North American operators, GTE and AT&T, in an example of a strategic alliance for a concrete project of local telephone development.

- The most recent investment made in a basic telephone operator took place in Peru, where Telefónica now has responsibility for the management of Compañía Peruana de Teléfonos (CPT) and ENTEL-Perú, with a direct shareholder participation of 31.5 percent. That position gives it a majority on the boards of directors of both enterprises, which recently agreed to merge.

At present, those investments in Chile, Argentina, Venezuela and Peru together represent participation in the management of more than seven million lines (approximately half the size of the present Spanish network), which, when weighted by ownership position in each of the enterprises, confers on Telefónica a position of leadership in Latin America, as the top foreign operator of lines there, ahead of companies such as GTE, France Telecom and Southwestern Bell. (See Figure 15.)

This favored positioning acquires a greater relevance through the geographic diversification of the international presence. Aside from the investments in the operators already mentioned, that include not only fixed telephony, but also cellular, paging, data transmission, cable TV and Yellow Pages, take note, also, of the strategic value of Telefónica's 79 percent ownership position in Telefónica Larga Distancia, the operator of a domestic (within the U.S.A.) and international long distance network that has a leadership position in the Puerto Rican market. Telefónica is, also, paying special attention to cellular mobile telephony, as shown by its presence in Colombia, by means of 31 percent ownership in COCELCO, which obtained the license to operate a cellular mobile concession in the western part of the country.

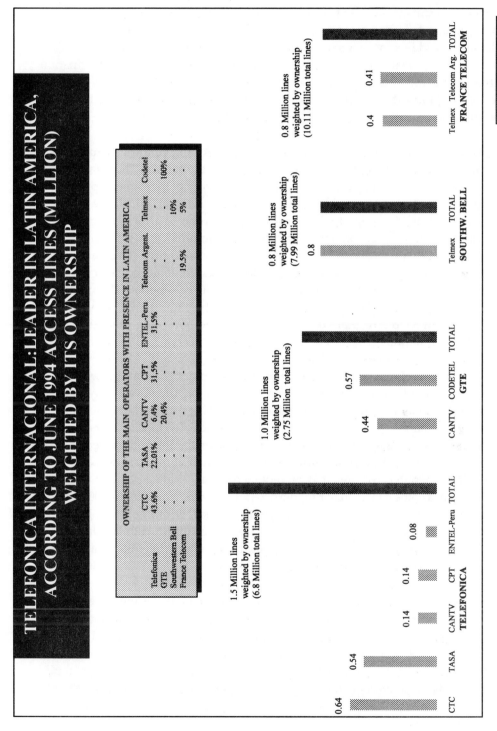

TELEFONICA INTERNACIONAL:LEADER IN LATIN AMERICA, ACCORDING TO JUNE 1994 ACCESS LINES (MILLION) WEIGHTED BY ITS OWNERSHIP

OWNERSHIP OF THE MAIN OPERATORS WITH PRESENCE IN LATIN AMERICA

	CTC	TASA	CANTV	CPT	ENTEL-Peru	Telecom Argent.	Telmex	Codetel
Telefonica	43.6%	22.01%	6.4%	31.5%	31.5%	-	-	-
GTE	-	-	20.4%	-	-	-	-	100%
Southwestern Bell	-	-	-	-	-	-	10%	-
France Telecom	-	-	-	-	-	19.5%	5%	-

1.5 Million lines weighted by ownership (6.8 Million total lines)

TELEFONICA

CTC	TASA	CANTV	CPT	ENTEL-Peru	TOTAL
0.64	0.54	0.14	0.14	0.08	

1.0 Million lines weighted by ownership (2.75 Million total lines)

GTE

CANTV	CODETEL	TOTAL
0.44	0.57	

0.8 Million lines weighted by ownership (7.99 Million total lines)

SOUTHW. BELL

Telmex	TOTAL
0.8	

0.8 Million lines weighted by ownership (10.11 Million total lines)

FRANCE TELECOM

Telmex	Telecom Arg.	TOTAL
0.4	0.41	

FIGURE 15

369

Although Latin America constitutes the preferred geographic region for its international investments, for the reasons explained, that has not prevented Telefónica from taking advantage of opportunities that arise in Europe. On the contrary, Telefónica, aside from its agreement to participate in Unisource (25 percent) in order to offer global network services, a key piece of its strategy of participation in the structuring of the Pan European market, has made cellular mobile (60 percent of Telefónica Romania) and radiopaging (15 percent of Contactel-Portugal) investments.

At the time of privatization, the operators in developing countries usually face significant unsatisfied demand and provide low quality service. Those factors, no doubt, condition the time horizon for expected recovery of investment, pushing it out to the long term. As for Telefónica, despite this element, which is a relevant factor in the final decision of whether or not to commit to a foreign investment project, the company is convinced that the historic opportunity to enter these growing markets probably will not come around a second time. This perspective is confirmed clearly, from looking at the operating results achieved in recent years by the Group's enterprises. For instance, in the 1990-1994 period, the operating companies in which Telefónica Internacional participates have, jointly made investments in telephone plant of over $5 billion, and in coming years they hope to double that figure.

This investment effort, obviously, has translated into a significant growth of the respective networks as well as in degree of digitalization, thereby complying with the promises about attending to demand and improving quality that were made to the different Latin American communities in which Telefónica offers service. Among the operating results, the installation jointly by the Telefónica Internacional Group of more than three million lines since acquisition of ownership, stands out. That achievement has required a 51 percent increase in installed plant. In addition, the Group has completed a major modernization by removing over 600,000 analog lines. In fact, the great extension of telephone service, with important improvements in ratios of penetration in all types of services (basic, cellular, data, etc.), was the common thread noted in all the countries in which Telefónica has taken a position, expecting a future of sustained growth.

Those results have been well received by the stock markets, as measured by the substantial price appreciation of the stocks of those companies in the Group that are quoted on an exchange, such as CTC and Telefónica de Argentina. This positive stock market performance creates notable hidden values for Telefónica. The investments have risen 230 percent on average over the cost of acquisition, while the annual average internal rate of return on the portfolio has exceeded 50 percent.

Consortia and Alliances: the Perspective of Telefónica

One of the essential elements of Telefónica's strategic approach to international expansion is the active role given in each project to local as well as strategic partners. That role depends on the complementarities that they contribute, in each case, to facilitate and improve the management of the investment.

The opening sections of this paper have explained the advantages inherent in the collaboration of third parties, independent of their shareholder position, how they help deal with the difficulties that arise in every investment project, in particular if made abroad, and how they compensate for the internal weaknesses of the strategic partner who leads the effort or takes the initiative in the project. The difficulties and weaknesses come in many shapes and forms: a limited capacity to finance, an inability to provide the human resources needed to accomplish the investment independently, technological inadequacy, or lack of knowledge of the socio-economic and political scene. These failings could create barriers to an entry into the market in a manner that would achieve adequate penetration, and set up barriers to a reasonable adaptation and integration of the personnel that must move to other countries. Thus, the formation of consortia to arrange and manage direct investments in the telecommunications sector has constituted a fundamental tool which Telefónica, and many other international operators, have utilized, continually, in order to gain access to new markets and to share all sorts of risks (political, economic, and legal).

Within the consortium, it is important to distinguish the participation of the local partners from the other strategic partners (operators in the case of the telecommunications sector). Partners have different motivations and interests in the project. As can be appreciated from Figures 16 and 17, Telefónica, in almost every instance, in its international investments, counts on the participation of local partners. Generally, those are well-known business groups in the country. On many occasions, they have construction or banking as a core business activity.

The reason should be obvious why a construction company has an interest in the telecommunications sector. For one, it is becoming more common to see construction firms engaging in highly diversified activities, so that they may offset, as much as possible, the typical cyclical fluctuations inherent in the construction business. In addition, the telecommunications sector, which requires for its development major investments in infrastructure, represents, for construction companies, a business opportunity, especially in the area of investment in external plant.

For the strategic partner, this profile of the local partner can be highly beneficial. From the local partner, the strategic partner gains a good understanding of the local business scene, and benefits, too, from the experience this type of firm has in

TELEFÓNICA INTERNACIONAL: SHAREHOLDINGS & MAIN PARTNERS

COMPANY	BUSINESS	OWNERSHIP	CONTROL	OTHER STRATEGIC PARTNERS	MAIN LOCAL PARTNERS	CORE BUSINESS OF LOCAL PARTNERS
CTC	Telecommunications	43,6%	Yes	None	Chilean Pension Funds (14,9%)	Equity & Fixed Income Investments
TASA	Telecommunications	22,0%	Yes	None	Citicorp (16,7%) Banco Rio (9,6%) Techint (5%)	Banking Banking Construction
CANTV	Telecommunications	6,4%	No	GTE (20,4%) AT&T (4,8%)	Electricidad de Caracas (6,4%) Republic of Venezuela (49%)	Electricity
CPT + ENTEL PERÚ	Telecommunications	31,5%	Yes	None	Banco Wiese (1,75% Grafña y Montero (1,75%)	Banking Construction
TLD-PUERTO RICO	Long Distance	79%	Yes	None	Puerto Rico Telephone Authority	-
TELEFÓNICA ROMANIA	Cellular Service	60%	Yes	Radiocomunicatii (20%) Rom Telecom (20%)	Radiocomunicatii (20%) Rom Telecom (20%)	Telecommunications Telecommunications
CONTACTEL	Paging	15%	No	CPRM Marconi (51%)	Promindustria (15%) Banco Português de Investimento (9%)	Banking Banking
COCELCO	Cellular Service	31%	No	CTC Celular (95)	Grupo Sarmiento (50,1%) Grupo Ardila Lülle (9,9%)	Banking Beverages
PUBLIGUÍAS	Yellow Pages	51%	Yes	Publicar (19,6%)	Lord Cochrane (20,4%)	Printing
SINTELAR	External Plant	25%	No	Sintel (50%)	-	-

FIGURE 16

OTHER SIGNIFICANT TELECOM INVESTMENTS IN LATINOAMERICA WITHOUT PRESENCE OF TELEFONICA INTERNACIONAL

COUNTRY	COMPANY	BUSINESS	STRATEGIC PARTNERS	LOCAL PARTNERS	CORE BUSINESS OF LOCAL PARTNER
ARGENTINA	Telecom Argentina Movicom Compañía de Teléfonos del Interior	Telecommunications Cellular Service Cellular Service	France Telecom (19,5%) STET (19,5%) BellSouth (30%) Motorola (n.a.) GTE (23%) AT&T (10%)	Pérez Companc (15%) JP Morgan (6%) BGH Grupo Macri Diario Clarín (22%) Benito Roggio (20%)	Maritime transportation Banking Banking Construction Media Construction
MÉJICO	TELMEX IUSACELL	Telecommunications Cellular Service	Southwestern Bell (10%) France Telecom (5%) Bell Atlantic (40%)	Grupo Carso (6%) Grupo Peralta (60%)	Industrial holding Industrial holding
COLOMBIA	CELUMOVIL	Cellular Service	AT&T & McCaw (12,5%)	Grupo Santo Domingo (62%)	Industrial holding
VENEZUELA	TELCEL	Cellular Service	BellSouth (44%)	Grupo Cisneros (32%)	Industrial holding

FIGURE 17

373

the management of human resources—a vital element in improving the communications between employees and top management, with the objective of turning the employees into participants in the newly defined strategy. For local partners whose core business is in the financial arena, their interest lies in obtaining business derived from the need of private telecommunications companies to externally finance their investment plans, which are usually large, thanks to the backward state of infrastructure that normally exists under the circumstances.

The strategic partner may have to work in a country with recent experience of hyper inflation, where the interest rate and exchange risks are high, the accounting systems are complex and peculiar, and the changes in taxation, exchange control, and regulation of foreign investment are frequent. If so, it would be extremely advantageous to have the participation of and even the sharing of responsibilities with (at least initially) a local partner that has not only experience in this sort of circumstance but also the human resources prepared to resolve these sorts of difficulties.

In every case, in spite of the existence of cultural, linguistic and other affinities with the country in which the investment originates, it will always be advantageous to count on the collaboration of a local partner, not only to allow a rapid entry into the market, but also for understanding of the local political and business picture. Frequently, moreover, the local partner selected, through its own businesses, offers stable channels of distribution, institutional relations, and a wide list of clients, both commercial and high income residential, whose sharing with the consortium is vitally important for the rapid development of the network and achievement of a large scale commercialization of different services. For all those reasons, the selection of the right local partner is very important. Even though, to the local community and to the authorities, the strategic partner is responsible for management, the complementarities that the local partners bring to the picture play a significant role in the success of the investment project, always to the mutual benefit of the partners.

In the configuration of the consortium, more than one strategic partner might participate, as has been the case of several consortia formed to effect a privatization (Telecom Argentina with the participation of STET and France Telecom, or Telmex with the presence of Southwestern Bell and France Telecom). The objectives of strategic partners in collaboration are different than those of local partners. In this sense, Telefónica's approach, no doubt, is similar to that of other operators. Basically, it centers on the sharing of complementary abilities in technology, management and development of infrastructure, know-how in commercialization and introduction of services, and contribution of qualified human resources.

Of course, depending on the breadth of the project, the participation of each partner may or may not be similar in the form in which shared risk, the classic objective of this type of operation, is assumed in different manners by each participant. Nevertheless, recent experience in the processes of privatization demonstrates the great complexity implied in project management shared by more than one foreign operator, each of which has a distinct business culture, not to mention divergent long term interests. Collaboration with local partners, on the other hand, produces fewer conflicts, perhaps because of the lower strategic content of the arrangement.

The consortium, is put together in the context of development of a project of local character. Should the selection of the other strategic partner be guided solely by criteria of diversification of economic risks and acquisition of sufficient financial capacity to respond to a privatization which offers handsome possibilities of profit? On the contrary, we should make a rigorous analysis to determine which partner is ideal for each project, orienting the selection toward the search for operating synergies. From Telefónica's point of view, that analysis, though directed at configuring a consortium to develop a concrete investment, should take on the perspective of formation of alliances with a more global approach, whether in lines of business or in presence in different geographic areas. In other words, in spite of the fact that the reason for taking action, at any given moment, is a local project, the approach to selection ought to be global, in order to obtain, from the potential strategic partners, synergies of greater scope than those achieved from the pure investment in a particular operator, or in a specified market. These synergies should involve a greater integration of activities, sharing of markets and interchange of experience.

The international position that Telefónica now has, especially in Latin America, confers upon it a privileged position in terms of being able to analyze the possibility of establishing strategic alliances. The business opportunities that Telefónica, as well as the right strategic partner, can take advantage of in an increasingly global sector, are varied. Among the outstanding synergies and opportunities are the following:

- To complement Telefónica's investments with those in other markets in the region (such as Mexico, Brazil, Colombia, etc.).

- To carry a greater volume of international traffic, above all transit traffic, and to facilitate faster interconnection of networks between the companies participating in the alliance. The integration and coordination of this business makes it possible for the component firms of the alliance and its participating companies to maintain a unified position when negotiating correspondent agreements with third parties.

- Optimization of cellular networks, improving interconnection, increasing the mobility of clients by means of roaming accords, and facilitating one contract for service in a large geographic area (one stop shopping).

- Making use of experience in different services of a more advanced character such as PCS, virtual private networks, mobile data transmission services, outsourcing, calling cards, etc.

- Joint design and introduction of infrastructures and services at a regional level.

- Joint exploitation of future multimedia businesses, taking advantage of different internal technological developments and those derived, from the point of view of producing content for delivery, from being positioned in markets with a common language.

- Geographic mobility of human resources, not only to implant techniques of management and services already tried elsewhere, but also to jointly commit to new investment projects.

- Establishment, within the framework of the alliance, of a strategy of a common business culture.

- Putting in place common information and management systems in order to homogenize the processes, and to create technological platforms.

- To increase negotiating leverage against vendors, for the coordination of supplies, which, eventually, should permit an optimization of processes, such as the management of inventories.

In sum, opportunities to strengthen competitive position are important, and they are achieved through synergies that translate into greater profits and cost savings that would be difficult to realize under independent management. Those are the principal accomplishments that, not only Telefónica but also the balance of the important international operators, are achieving currently from establishing alliances or cooperative agreements.

As for the future, the map of telecommunications is still in a first draft. For one thing, the geographic diversification of some international operators, just as their presence in different lines of business, appears to indicate that it is difficult for two companies to totally complement each other so that both companies emerge simultaneously strengthened by their alliance. The need to establish strategic agreements with different partners for different lines of business and different geographic areas seems unavoidable, at least in the next few years, in order to place the firm in the best position to participate in the configuration of the telecommunications sector over the intermediate term. This is a sector that, in the opinion of some experts, will be dominated by a few megaoperators coexisting with an aggregation of regional or local operators that will have a greater or lesser degree of dependency on the megaoperators. Right now, the future composition of these megaoperators is difficult to predict, but it seems evident that they will not be constituted solely by the traditional telecommunications operators, but will include enterprises with interests in different businesses, such as multimedia services, cellular telephony, information processing, and the communications media.

Despite all discussion of the advantage of alliances, haste in signing an accord with an inadequate partner, aside from carrying with it the costs inherent in making the transaction, can generate a high opportunity cost. That follows from having underestimated other potential candidates who, as a result of this lapse of judgment, will reach accords with other operators, thus leaving the first operator out of the picture altogether, or at least in a weaker bargaining position when it comes to future negotiations.

In this race to make alliances, the picture that develops could look like that of the first important telecommunications privatizations, in that those who first position themselves or reach agreements will have the best chance for survival and growth.

Chapter 29

Thoughts of an Ex-PTT Minister

Barton Dominus

"What a waste of time," thinks the former Minister of Posts, Telegraph and Telephone (PTT). "I have to listen and smile and nod, while this bunch of academics tells me about Strategic Alliances and the Telecommunications Revolution. I've brought my country and my family through the Real Revolution, and more, and these academics are going to tell me about alliances." He nods politely and smiles as the First speaker, the University President, continues his invocation to the Muses of Communications and Alliances, to favor and foster the new and more peaceful world order.

The former Minister is a man faithful to his country, his party, and his family. He had been Deputy Director, then Director, and finally Minister of PTT for nearly a decade. Now, he no longer dreams of being Prime Minister himself or of running any of the really important Ministries, say Internal Affairs or National Defense. His best hope is for a judgeship or appointment to one of the permanent international councils.

The Second speaker, an Eminent Guru on privatization and consultant to several newly-democratic governments, with ties to academia (several books, etc.), looks trim, lean, urbane, and with a healthy tan. "Retirement couldn't be that bad," the Minister thinks. "Write a book, serve on some Boards, consult, spend more time with my grandchildren..." he smiles.

The Eminent Guru, he recalls, is given to quick solutions, feeling that change is best done suddenly—despite subsequent discomfort. "This builds national character and unity," the Guru says. Of course his Eminence doesn't have to suffer these discomforts himself. Many of his (former) clients have, however.

Some, such as the Newly Democratic State, the former Minister's nearby neighboring country, take a perverse pleasure in things being more discomforting than perhaps is necessary. The former Minister listens intently to the Eminent Guru's litany: "Join the Telecommunications Revolution. Don't Let Your Country Fall Behind in the Infobahn Race."

"Like the rallies I remember attending in my youth," the Minister thinks. He briefly pictures an army of consultants, looking like Junior Eminent Gurus, in serried ranks, their MBAs rolled up into megaphones, shouting, "Cut rates! Upgrade technology! Open markets! The Age of Telecommunications is Nigh!"

"Maybe," thinks the former Minister, "maybe not. After four years of my Ministry, the five billion I bring into the Treasury every year pays for our entire Coast Guard and National Police.

"Right now, my former Ministry provides twenty-five thousand skilled, stable jobs to loyal citizens and their families, and in turn, those citizens provide jobs for another seventy-five thousand families. The multiplier effect. (I know some economics, too, damn hotshots.) One hundred thousand families, loyal families, depended on me. Open our country to foreign competition, cut our rates, and how many of these loyal citizens will end up on the streets or in the opposition—and their relatives and friends as well?

"Invite competition to cut rates? No!" thinks the former Minister angrily. "MCI or AT&T or Sprint or British Telecom, they're all too hungry. Too much invested for the amount of business. Too much capacity for the amount of traffic on their networks. Too inexpensive to put cable in along previously-used rights-of-way. Too easy to have extra bandwidth available. As fast as they put in fiber-optic cable, the capacity of already-installed base increases. Additional traffic is pure profit, so they're willing to buy it with low rates.

"Supply creates its own demand—Quesnay?" he wonders, searching his memory of his student days. "We'll see if the Frenchman was right.

"Those lunatic Americans have unleashed insane competition in their own country and on the world. Now they want the rest of us to do the same. Imagine, three long distance carriers in the States. Each with its own network and cables. How inefficient. And the local carriers want to get into the same damn businesses.

"We can't deal with just one carrier in the states: MCI or AT&T or Sprint. No, we have to do business with all three. We don't choose who handles our calls there. It's assigned by lot according to how much traffic each has generated with us. Now the British have followed the Yanks. These Anglos always seem to end up doing the same thing—the curse of their common language.

"Inviting them to compete here, with us, is like inviting the sharks to dinner. They'll end up with the whole meal, including the plate and the cook. Fortunately, national telecommunication markets are closed to foreigners until 1998. After that, there's the 'Japanese Solution' to stop them," he almost says out loud.

"The Japanese Solution: delay. Delay at each and every step in the interconnection process. Delay access, connection, installation, switching. The Japanese Solution: To use permit requirements, zoning laws, environmental studies, labor, whatever, to slow down the inevitable pace of deregulation, competition, lower revenues, and loss of control.

"Eventually, we'll have to give in and open up our markets, like we had to with Salt and Tobacco. By then it will be someone else's problem.

"I have a lot of support on this. My fellow Ministers are my natural allies and have been so (more or less) for a century and a half. A Strategic Alliance? Of Course! We all want to modernize and we all want to keep destructive competition under control. Our Ministries have done so in the past, successfully, and we will continue to do so in the future. In the meantime, I'll keep doing what I am doing. What's worked before seems to be working now," reflects the former Minister of PTT, his anger vented.

Speaker Two is succeeded by speaker Three, the Nobel Prize winning Director of the prestigious industrial research and development lab. Words like Superhighway, Internet, University of the Future, and Tele-Education float back and forth through the air, kept in constant motion by the speaker's obvious enthusiasm and commitment to his belief.

But the former Minister sees through this Internet Gibberish. "Bah. Professors trading papers, students trading manifestos, and teenage boys trading dirty pictures. Who pays for it? We do. The state does by subsidizing the universities' use of the internet. God help me if I endorse these new technological marvels here and try to bring them into every home. The priests/rabbis/mullahs would have my manhood."

The Fourth speaker, an expert representing a cable consortium, began her talk on The Electronic Highway. Her words, "Superhighway...changes everything," echo in the former Minister's ears yet one more time.

"It certainly does change everything," he thinks. "And not always for the better. Look at the French and their minitel system. How much has it cost? Billions. What do people use it for? To look up phone numbers: men wanting women and women wanting men. One of the most popular 'services' of the French system.

"These cable companies won't go after the local traffic at first. Too little revenue and too expensive to service. No. They're starting with video on demand to take business away from video rental stores," he muses.

"You can't trust the cable companies. Too close to the entertainment business. They're always falling into bed with lots of other partners and then falling out again. Unfaithful lovers. Better to keep them tightly reined in," thinks the former Minister.

The Fifth speaker, the former Minister is glad to see, is his old friend, the Director General of Telefabrikan SA. The former Minister's country has been a customer of Telefabrikan since its first switchboard in the capital in 1887. Thirty-five percent of his engineers had worked with Telefabrikan engineers and fifty percent of his senior technicians had been Telefabrikan trained. A mix of American and Swedish hardware filled out this country's infrastructure.

The former Minister is familiar with their history together. He knows that during the "troubles" of 1905-1907, Telefabrikan SA had extended his country badly needed credit and equipment. Also during the late embargo, Telefabrikan SA had made sure that untraceable replacements were obtainable to his government.

For fifteen percent of Telefabrikan's new Long Line, Switch and Cellular production capabilities, his country is the exclusive licensee from Telefabrikan for their sales, distribution, etc. rights in his country's former overseas colonies. His country was the first to set up a Cellular Network using Telefabrikan's new Cellular switches (run by his brother-in-law).

Telefabrikan has had three large manufacturing facilities in the former Minister's country since 1921 and is building a fourth in his home province. They are training Ministry engineers and technicians on this next generation of switches, repeaters, etc. It is always a good deal for both of them. "Ah! Another Strategic Alliance," smiles the former Minister, as his friend describes the pan-continent development consortium of which his country is (also) a member.

Telefabrikan had another business venture with his Ministry, a joint venture to upgrade the telecommunications system in the capital city and its surrounding area. The capital was fortunate to have been laid out in the 1880s with a grid pattern, major boulevards, and easily accessible rights of way. This was true of the countryside surrounding the capital also. Its railroad and canal lines had for generations served to make connecting the country easier. The network of roadbeds and canals extended east into what is currently the nearby Newly Democratic Country's westernmost province.

Formerly, it had been his country's easternmost province. Lost in the Peace of 1908, "the Easterners" were linguistically, religiously, and ethnically much closer to his people than to the mass of citizens of the Newly Democratic Country. He had blood relatives among them, who, even now, were being persecuted and discriminated against, occasionally even murdered.

As part of his country's "open door" policy, they had offered to interconnect all of the Eastern province with modern equipment through his capital's new fiber optic hub. This way his country could control communications in the Eastern province and help preserve the culture and historic ties. Who knew how long this wave of peace would last, and when, once more, the Eastern province would become one with the homeland. The naive do-gooders who made up the government of the Newly Democratic State might be inclined to say yes.

The former Minister of the PTT knew, above all, the importance of absolutely secure information channels. He would accept joint ventures as long as he and his ministry retained ultimate control. He remembers hearing about how British control of the cables in W.W.I. and American control of the airwaves during W.W.II. gave each of those countries control over what information could be sent and received by his countrymen.

"Even the Americans don't let outsiders own more than twenty percent of any communications company," he thinks. "Why should we be generous?"

His country had eighteen other population and business centers with outmoded equipment. The business communities were complaining. So were his colleagues in other Ministries, who couldn't keep in touch with their people or send faxes, much less hook up into networks. There were over a dozen companies besides Telefabrikan seeking joint ventures to upgrade his country's technology base, if he'd simply share the revenues with them.

The hungriest were the former Regional Bell Operating Companies (RBOCs), the Baby Bells. Their shareholders and management knew that their local monopolies would be over when, soon, both long distance carriers, and cable companies, began offering local access.

Shareholders, Management, and Employees sought to be seen advocating, embracing, and proclaiming their companies' new competitive attitudes before their current monopolies disappeared. With a typically American "can-do" attitude, management's mission became "Leadership," and the company's goal, "Customer First." Employees were "Empowered" to somehow advance the "Cultural Revolution."

One indicator used by shareholders of the RBOC's presumed business prowess was its overseas aggressiveness. The RBOC's senior managers needed to show deals. The result: loyal employees came to the former Minister's country hungry for business. Their agreements were long, complex, and detailed, of the sort to give delight to the legalist's heart, and befitting that (one-time) most regulated of industries.

"'As for revenues and losses from these overseas adventures...well, perhaps the projections were a bit optimistic. They would pay out eventually...might need additional capital...several times...management wants it...Strategic Alliance, Important country...hero at my company, with my family...' might well think a newly-inspired, former, what did my aide call them? Bellhead," muses the former Minister.

"That, and the fact that they were throwing off a lot of cash from their current monopolies, led to the RBOCs negotiating poorly, overpaying, and over committing. Good," thought the former Minister. "Now we'll get them involved in our infrastructure development."

As expected, the Sixth speaker is the dynamic Head of Overseas Investments of the Baby Bell. "We are all looking for deals ranging from infrastructure development to turnkey operations. Privatize. Let us invest and we'll show you," he promises, "technology, skills, training, everything you want." The Head previously had been an investment banker and then senior staff at a major consultancy.

The former Minister thinks, "We'll get them to put up the money while we supply the labor, at union scale, of course. They'll put in the money, our loyal union labor will do the work, and my friend the Director General will supply the materials. Then, in three or four years, when the sharks are competing in the Baby Bell's home markets, its surplus cash flow has ceased, revenues from their venture here have not materialized, and they are required to invest more to complete the job, then, we will buy them out very cheap. Far better than nationalization...Strategic Alliances."

The former Minister smiles and thinks, "If God did not wish them shorn, why did he make them sheep.

"As for the old equipment that the Baby Bell replaces, the cross-bar stuff can be used in the countryside. It's old, but it still works. We have plenty of technicians who know how to maintain it and peasant boys they can teach. My government will call it an example of Technological Transfer. The newer, electronic equipment we can re-sell or use at our telephone subsidiaries in Former Colonies Overseas."

By reason of historical relations, his country had a major stake in the telecommunications enterprises of a number of Former Colonies Overseas. Many of their engineers, administrators, and technicians were trained by his countrymen. His country had supplied technology and financing to them for decades, and sanctuary to their politicians for centuries.

"Ten years ago," he thinks, "they were ten years behind us, five years ago, five years behind us. Now they are only a year or two behind. Our roots go deep. Almost every family in each of the Former Colonies Overseas has some of their wealth invested in our subsidiaries...just for insurance. Our future and theirs have been linked for three hundred years. More Strategic Alliances.

"It's true that we don't own the cables, we lease them from two American carriers (always two, never one), but it's not as secure as our own cable would be. We can always have our own cable put in, but even that can be cut. We keep the Americans out of our business in the Former Colonies Overseas by continuing to lease their undersea cables, but not inviting them in to do more. When they get in, they'll go after my big money first, my international business market, undercutting prices and giving away bandwidth and services to the big companies. By giving them a long-term agreement for cable services, I keep them out of the Former Colonies Overseas. These, too, are Strategic Alliances.

"I'm no longer Minister of Posts, Telegraph and Telephone," he reflects, "now I'm Minister of Communications." The Party Leaders and the Prime Minister himself have rewarded him. As Minister of Communications, his portfolio now includes Radio, Cable, Wireless, and even Satellite—all communications except those of Internal Affairs and National Defense. His new Ministry is also a member of the government's Executive Council (along with National Defense and Internal Affairs and a few others). The new Minister of Communications appreciates the confidence of his colleagues in the Executive Council, feeling that by this expression they are adding strength to the country.

The new Minister has a vision that he is only now able to explore. That is for his country to own a satellite, in geosynchronous orbit above his homeland. In this way, communications in his country and to the rest of the world could never be shut off by any third party. The Minister feels that such a project would prove of interest to his counterparts at Internal Affairs and National Defense.

"An alliance with them should prove possible...A Strategic Alliance, of course. The Prime Minister will like that. He likes signs of cooperation among his Ministers," he thinks, as he pictures himself standing at the Prime Minister's right during next year's Patriot's Day Parade. The new Minister, himself the Final speaker, stands:

> Fellow delegates, I am delighted to reaffirm my country's commitment to advancing the telecommunications revolution and to the development of the international telecommunications highway.

My country, as you know, has a dozen strategic alliances in place, and seeks more to cement relationships between countries and among people. We've demonstrated our commitment with real projects, real partners, and real investors.

My recent appointment as Minister of Communications affirms my country's clear direction, and its belief in the similarities and convergence of all communications channels, including cable, which will now get more attention and encouragement.

The Minister of Communications sits down and thinks, "This job was a lot easier for my predecessor ten years ago. We had a system that worked very well, then. If you had the money you could get the phone—if you were patient, or were willing to arrange for a few favors. And if not—that's what the mails were for. It was better for the poor to write letters, anyway. It taught them literacy."

Chapter 30

Conclusion

Leonard S. Hyman

Privatization has its odd aspects. Private investors, after all, founded many of the world's great utilities. Governments took over the utilities when the private managements ceased to manage well, ran out of money to fund expansion, milked the companies rather than provided good service, or came to represent exploitation (especially foreign exploitation) in the eyes of the public. Now, governments want to dispose of state-owned utilities because those firms provide poor service, lack money to expand, put the needs of entrenched bureaucracies ahead of the public interest, and represent sources of badly needed cash if sold. The new, private owners, though, sometimes smug in their superiority and ignorant of history, could, conceivably, trigger a new wave of nationalizations in the future, if they lose their dynamism over time, as do so many successful firms, and end up providing as mediocre as service as their predecessors. Except, this time around, many of the local governments have gotten smarter. Local governments have introduced competition into the public utility sector to reduce the potential for exploitation, to spur on the companies to greater efficiencies, to keep the utility managements on their toes, to assure that consumers as well as investors reap the benefits of privatization.

Odd, too, are the supposedly compelling reasons for privatization. Governments are just as capable as shareholders of finding excellent managers, providing them with incentives, and authorizing them to run the company in the right way. If lack of profitability renders the company incapable of raising capital for expansion, the government, as owner of the company, surely can raise prices as easily as the government, as regulator, can allow the privatized firm to raise prices. Somehow, though, the government does not take action when it can. The real problem, which cannot be solved through better management or rational pricing, rather, may be that an expanding utility consumes cash and may do so for decades. By privatizing the utility, by selling it, the government converts that utility holding into an immediate source of cash, which can be deployed into areas of social need that the private sector will not serve.

Turning a local governmental agency—often poorly run—into a private company is a difficult task, requiring tough management decisions, a change in corporate culture, and dealing with outside investors, and adjustment to regulation. The new owners need to not only learn the local markets but also to make the commercial alliances required in an ever more global business environment.

Some privatizations are high risk operations, although one would never know it from the comments made by investors in them. Somehow, investors believe that having some international agency involved reduces the risk, because no rational government would tangle with an international agency. Proper hedging, too, reduces currency risk, but hedging has costs. The right local partner removes political risk, yet the right partner in the eyes of the present regime might be the wrong partner in the eyes of the next government. In reality, the key to success is whether the consumer has the money to buy the utility's output, which, in turn, depends on the state of the national economy. You cannot squeeze water from a stone. When the Mexican economic miracle ended with a crash, people worried about maintaining the public credit, about political unrest, about the stability of the banking system, about unemployment and illegal immigration, not about how much money investors in private enterprise lost. In some privatization auctions, the eager winners will end up the losers, their money down the drain, victimized by poor economic conditions, or unreasonable regulation, or changes in the rules.

Yet, privatization is a powerful catalyst. Changing ownership changes policies, and changes expectations. Privatizations have produced more efficient organizations more capable of meeting the demands of customers, introduced millions of people to share ownership, introduced new managerial skills to local industry, and connected local markets to world markets. Privatizations have provided governments with cash to meet pressing social needs.

Privatization, in the end, may not prove the panacea for all the ills of the public utility sector, but with so much need for infrastructure investment, privatization may prove the only practical way to raise the money.

APPENDICES

Appendix A

Worldwide Statistics

Compiled by Robert Hyman

Table A-1. Electricity Consumption

	Total Electricity Consumption (not as Primary Energy) TWh		Growth Rates for Electricity Consumption % per annum	Electricity Consumption per Capita MWh per Capita		Growth Rates for Electricity Consumption per Capita % per annum
	1990	**2020**	**1990-2020**	**1990**	**2020**	**1990-2020**
North America	3,475.5	4,650	1.0	12.60	14.20	0.4
Latin America	598.1	2,350	4.7	1.34	3.27	3.0
Western Europe	2,468.4	3,900	1.5	5.44	7.97	1.3
Central and Eastern Europe	362.0	600	1.7	3.61	5.35	1.3
CIS	1,718.4	2,400	1.1	5.95	7.03	0.6
Middle East and North Africa	311.4	1,350	5.0	1.15	2.47	2.6
Sub-Saharan Africa	224.6	700	3.9	0.45	0.58	0.9
Pacific	1,407.0	3,050	2.6	2.52	3.93	1.5
Centrally Planned Asia	699.0	2,650	4.5	0.56	1.61	3.6
South Asia	343.3	1,350	4.7	0.30	0.70	2.9
World	11,607.7	23,000	2.3	2.19	2.84	0.9

Source:
World Energy Council, Energy For Tomorrow's World, *1993.*

Table A-2. Worldwide Generating Capacity and Production in 1990

Region	Capacity		Production			Capacity by Energy Source		
	Total (Million kw)	Per Capita (watts)	Total (Billion kwh)	Per Capita (kwh)	Per kw of capacity (kwh)	Thermal (%)	Nuclear (%)	Hydro and Other (%)
Africa	72.7	116	315.1	503	4334	72.0	1.3	26.7
USA and Canada	879.5	3181	3512.8	12705	3994	68.6	13.8	17.6
Latin America and Caribbean	163.7	368	608.0	1368	4448	42.5	0.0	55.5
Asia	572.9	185	2572.2	829	4490	70.7	8.0	21.3
Europe and USSR	1011.4	1280	4535.9	5739	4485	60.2	16.4	23.4
Oceania	45.8	1711	189.6	7094	4140	72.1	0.0	27.9
World	2746.1	521	11733.9	2227	4273	64.5	12.3	23.2

Sources:
United Nations, 1990 Energy Statistics Yearbook
World Bank, World Population Projections, *1992–1993 edition.*

Table A-3. Electricity by Country (1990)

Country	Per Capita		Generating Capacity By Energy Source			
	GDP ($)	Elec Prod'n (kwh)	Total (Thou. of MW)	Thermal (%)	Nuclear (%)	Hydro etc (%)
Bangladesh	190	76	2.5	90.9	0.0	9.1
Nigeria	230	103	4.0	53.0	0.0	47.0
Kenya	380	126	0.7	24.9	0.0	75.1
Indonesia	490	248	11.5	82.8	0.0	17.2
Egypt	700	760	11.7	76.6	0.0	23.4
Panama	1980	1200	1.0	44.5	0.0	55.5
Chile	2130	1395	4.1	43.9	0.0	56.1
Brazil	2540	1478	52.9	12.6	1.2	86.2
S. Africa	2600	4580	25.9	94.0	3.7	2.3
Mexico	2680	1422	29.3	68.5	2.3	29.2
Romania	3000	2772	22.9	75.6	0.0	24.4
Turkey	3100	1026	16.3	58.4	0.0	41.6
Portugal	5580	2755	7.4	54.4	0.0	45.6
Spain	11100	3866	43.3	46.8	16.1	37.1
UK	15000	5558	73.1	78.7	15.5	5.8
France	15500	7434	103.4	21.9	53.9	24.2
Australia	18200	9047	36.8	79.6	0.0	20.4
Switzerland	18700	8320	16.3	6.1	18.1	75.8
Canada	19500	18166	104.1	30.0	13.0	57.0
USA	22100	12125	775.4	73.8	14.0	12.2
Japan	23700	6940	194.8	64.2	16.2	19.6

Sources:
United Nations, 1990 Energy Statistics Yearbook
World Bank, World Population Projections, *1992-1993 edition*
1993 World Almanac

Table A-4. Worldwide Production of Electricity 1970-1990

Region	(Billions of kwh and %) Production			Annual Rate of Growth	
	1970	1980	1990	1970–1980	1980–1990
Africa	87.4	188.2	315.1	8.0%	5.3%
North America	1898.0	2839.9	3698.5	4.1	2.7
South America	107.6	268.2	422.3	8.0	4.6
Asia	612.2	1339.5	2572.2	8.1	6.7
Europe	1407.4	2175.1	2809.9	4.4	2.6
Oceania	69.9	122.6	189.6	5.8	4.5
USSR	740.9	1292.1	1726.0	5.7	2.9
World	4923.4	8225.8	11733.9	5.3	3.6

Sources:
United Nations, 1990 Energy Statistics Yearbook
United Nations, Statistical Yearbook *(various dates)*

Table A-5. World Natural Gas Consumption, 1970–1990 (Terajoules)

Region	1970	1980	Annual percent change, 1970–1980	1990	Annual percent change, 1980–1990
Former USSR	5,945,000	13,710,000	8.7%	26,623,000	5.6%
North America	24,863,000 (e)	23,258,000	-0.5%	23,064,000	-0.1%
OECD Europe	2,634,000	7,566,000	11.1%	10,592,000	3.4%
Asia/Pacific	509,000 (e)	2,483,000	17.2%	6,046,000	9.3%
Middle East	640,000 (e)	1,425,000	8.3%	3,886,000	10.6%
Latin America	987,000 (e)	2,215,000	8.4%	3,404,000	4.4%
Non-OECD Europe	1,478,000 (e)	2,803,000	6.6%	3,047,000	0.8%
Africa	101,000 (e)	732,000	21.9%	1,453,000	7.1%
World	39,275,000 (e)	54,206,000	3.3%	78,076,000	3.7%

Note: (e) Estimate.
Sources:
Organization for Economic Co-Operation and Development/International Energy Agency,
   Oil and Gas Information: 1989–1991, *1992.*
Organization of Petroleum Exporting Countries, "Opec Natural Gas Exports: Past, Present, and Future",
   Opec Review: An Energy and Development Forum, *Spring 1992.*
British Petroleum, BP Statistical Review of World Energy, *June 1987.*

Table A-6. Supply and Consumption of Natural Gas for Selected Countries, 1990 (Terajoules, unless otherwise stated)

Country	GDP per capita (U.S. $)	Gas usage per capita (Megajoules)	Gas production per capita (Megajoules)	Gas usage % of total energy needs	Sectors using natural gas (%)					
					Industry	Residential	Commerce and public	Electric generation	Energy sector	Other
Netherlands	14,600	95,891	170,020	45.4	28.2	25.3	—	5.0	3.3	38.2
Canada	19,500	91,216	150,529	30.1	36.1	20.5	15.0	3.3	24.1	1.1
USA	22,091	74,096	70,175	25.1	34.9	23.2	13.9	14.9	10.1	3.0
New Zealand	12,200	52,986	52,986	36.2	29.2	2.2	3.1	30.8	1.4	33.3
UK	15,000	38,060	33,166	26.0	25.9	49.0	5.8	1.9	6.4	11.0
Italy	14,600	27,038	10,386	24.9	37.5	39.7	—	20.5	0.7	1.6
Ireland	9,690	24,812	26,349	22.7	42.8	6.3	4.6	44.8	—	1.6
France	15,500	23,859	2,080	20.2	45.4	26.4	24.4	1.6	0.5	1.8
Norway	17,400	23,549	266,550	11.5	—	—	—	—	100.0	—
Japan	23,736	16,243	655	13.4	2.8	—	—	72.3	0.7	24.3
Spain	11,100	5,661	1,288	7.6	75.3	7.8	3.3	5.4	0.7	7.5
Turkey	3,100	2,141	127	6.3	23.5	1.4	—	74.5	0.6	0.0

Sources:
Organization for Economic Co-operation and Development/International Energy Agency,
  Oil and Gas Information: 1989-1991, 1992.
United Nations, 1990 Energy Statistical Yearbook, 1992.
World Bank, World Population Projections: 1992-93 Edition.
1993 World Almanac

Table A-7. Natural Gas Usage

	Natural Gas Consumption Mtoe		Growth Rate of Natural Gas Consumption % per annum	Per Capita Natural Gas Consumption toe		Growth Rate of Per Capita Natural Gas Consumption % per annum
	1990	2020	1990–2020	1990	2020	1990–2020
North America	497	601	0.6	1.80	1.84	0.1
Latin America	80	296	4.5	0.18	0.41	2.8
Western Europe	254	354	1.1	0.56	0.72	0.8
Central and Eastern Europe	64	105	1.7	0.64	0.94	1.3
CIS	569	744	0.9	1.97	2.16	0.3
Middle East and North Africa	117	412	4.3	0.43	0.76	1.9
Sub-Saharan Africa	4	29	6.8	0.01	0.02	2.3
Pacific	94	216	2.8	0.17	0.28	1.7
Centrally Planned Asia	14	126	7.6	0.01	0.08	7.2
South Asia	25	94	4.5	0.02	0.05	3.1
World	1,718	2,977	1.9	0.32	0.37	0.5

Note: toe = tonnes oil equivalent
Source:
World Energy Council, Energy for Tomorrow's World, 1993.

Table A-8. Worldwide Main Telephone Lines

Region	Total Main Lines		Average annual growth (%)	Main lines per 100 inhabitants	
	1981	1991	1981–1991	1981	1991
Africa	4,137,000	9,616,000	8.8	0.8 (e)	1.5
Asia	63,792,000 (e)	117,515,000	6.3 (e)	2.3 (e)	3.8
Europe	135,543,000 (e)	222,896,000	5.1 (e)	20.8 (e)	28.4
USA and Canada	118,124,000	155,473,000	2.8	45.8 (e)	55.6
Oceania	6,648,000	10,032,000	4.2	27.5 (e)	37.3
Latin America and Caribbean	16,253,000	30,452,000	6.5	4.1 (e)	6.8
World	344,918,000	545,984,000	4.7	7.7 (e)	10.3

Sources:
Siemens, International Telephone Statistics, *various editions.*
(e) Estimated.

Table A-9. Telephones by Country (1990)

Country	GDP per Capita ($)	Main Lines			Cellular Mobile Subscribers (Thousands)	Calls per Main Line	Residential	
		Per 100 Inhabitants	Total (Thousands)	Connected to Electronic Switching Systems (%)			Main Lines per 100 House-holds	% of Main Lines
Rwanda	220	0.1	10.4	–	–	1987	0.2	38.9
Gambia	230	1.1	9.8	96.4	–	–	7.6	63.7
Uganda	290	0.1	28.3	55.8	–	5865	0.4	37.7
China	370	0.5	6850.3	–	18.3	280	0.5	22.3
Papua NewGuinea	730	0.8	30.0	–	–	9825	0.8	16.7
Peru	900	2.6	575.2	–	8.5	3357	9.1	71.9
Thailand	1450	2.4	1356.5	65.0	66.3	–	7.5	65.0
Costa Rica	1810	10.2	307.9	21.8	–	4598	32.0	66.7
Chile	2130	6.2	811.8	21.8	18.5	2047	22.8	73.1
Iran	2490	4.3	2426.8	11.3	–	–	11.3	54.2
South Africa	2600	9.6	3212.4	44.9	7.0	–	49.2	69.1
Mexico	2680	6.5	5189.8	28.4	60.0	1305	22.7	70.9
Uruguay	2970	13.4	415.4	55.1	–	–	35.2	77.1
Turkey	3100	12.1	6893.3	63.5	31.8	–	42.3	67.9
Hungary	3270	8.3	869.9	5.5	2.6	1523	18.5	81.0
Portugal	5580	11.7	1158.0	33.4	6.6	–	28.2	76.7
Greece	7650	38.5	3948.7	–	8.7	2397	83.3	69.3
Spain	11100	33.2	12914.0	28.3	54.7	–	78.5	71.7
Singapore	12700	46.8	1267.3	81.4	51.0	3671	112.0	55.2
Netherlands	14600	46.7	7019.0	–	79.0	1093	86.5	76.0
Switzerland	18700	58.0	3942.7	54.3	125.0	914	–	-
Canada	19500	56.9	15295.8	–	583.0	–	112.9	71.0
USA	22100	52.1	130424.3	95.6	5300.0	3595	95.4	68.3
Japan	23700	44.2	54480.0	–	867.0	1333	88.5	67.9

Sources:
AT&T, The World's Telephones, *1993*
International Telecommunications Union, Yearbook of Common Carrier Telecommunication Statistics: 1981–1990
1993 World Almanac
Siemens, International Telecom Statistics, *various dates*

Table A-10. European Water and Sewerage Statistics (1989 data)

	GDP per Capita ($US)	Water			Sewerage			
		Total population served by a piped public water supply (%)	Urban population served by a piped water supply (%)	Rural population served by a piped water supply (%)	Urban population served by a sewerage network (%)	Urban population lacking adequate disposal means (%)	Nation Rural population served by a sewerage network (%)	Rural population lacking adequate disposal means (%)
Turkey	1,394	69.0	72.8	66.0	69.0	0.0	20.0	10.0
Poland	1,926	79.9	93.1	55.8	79.0	0.0	6.2	0.0
Czechoslovakia	2,588	77.1*	89.0*	76.0*	75.0	0.0	45.0	0.0
Portugal	4,325	58.0	97.0	50.0	83.0	0.0	9.0	0.0
Ireland	9,721	90.6	98.7	80.5	99.4	0.0	23.2	0.0
Israel	10,297	99.9	100.0	98.0	90.0	0.0	60.0	0.0
UK	14,914	99.0	99.5	91.5**	99.0	0.0	90.0	0.0
France	17,008	98.0	100.0	95.0	100.0	0.0	63.0	0.0
West Germany	18,981	97.8	100.0	97.0**	97.0	0.0	93.7	0.0
Sweden	22,524	86.0	100.0	75.0	100.0	0.0	18.0	0.0

All tables of water statistics in this file and all other files on the disk were compiled by Robert Hyman.
*Data may be unreliable
** Public supply system only

Sources:
World Health Organization, Water and Sanitation Services in Europe
United Nations, Statistical Handbook 1992

Table A-11. Effects of improved water and sanitation on sickness (data compiled 1990)

Disease	Millions of people affected by illness	Median reduction attributable to improvement (%)
Diarrhea	900 (cases per year)	22
Roundworm	900	28
Guinea worm	4	76
Schistosomiasis	200	73

Table A-12. Effects of water supply and sanitation improvements on morbidity from diarrhea (data compiled 1985)

Type of improvement	Median reduction in morbidity (%)
Quality of water	16
Availability of water	25
Quality and availability of water	37
Disposal of excreta	22

Table A-13. Availability of water by region

Region	Annual internal renewable water resources per capita (cubic meters)	Percentage of population living in countries with scarce annual per capita resources (less than 2000 cubic meters)
Middle East and North Africa	1,000	71
South Asia	4,200	0
Other Europe	4,600	21
East Asia and the Pacific	5,300	6
Sub-Saharan Africa	7,100	24
Eastern Europe and former USSR	11,400	22
Canada and the United States	19,400	0
Latin America and the Caribbean	23,900	4
World	7,700	12

Table A-14. Water availability

Country group	Per capita annual internal renewable water resources, 1990 (cubic meters)	Per capita annual water withdawal, year of data (cubic meters)	Sectoral withdrawal as a share of total water resources (%)		
			Agriculture	Domestic	Industry
Low income	4,649	498	91	4	5
Middle income	12,597	532	69	13	18
High income	10,528	1,217	39	14	47
World	7,744	676	69	9	22

Source (Tables A-11, A-12, A-13, and A-14): World Bank, World Development Report, *1992*

Table A-15. Water supply and sanitation coverage by region, 1980–1990, and coverage for 2000 at current rates of progress (Population in millions)

Region/sector	1980			1990			2000		
	% coverage	Number served	Number unserved	% coverage	Number served	Number unserved	% coverage	Number served	Number unserved
Africa									
Urban water	83	99.41	20.36	87	176.21	26.33	76	253.01	79.48
Rural water	33	109.83	223.00	42	172.05	237.59	47	234.27	262.32
Urban sanitation	65	77.85	41.92	79	160.01	42.53	73	242.17	90.32
Rural sanitation	18	59.91	272.92	26	106.51	303.13	31	153.11	343.48
Latin America and the Caribbean									
Urban water	82	194.11	42.61	87	281.95	42.13	89	369.79	47.00
Rural water	47	58.71	66.20	62	76.80	47.07	77	94.89	27.95
Urban sanitation	78	184.61	52.08	79	256.02	68.06	79	327.40	89.39
Rural sanitation	22	27.48	97.43	37	45.83	78.04	52	64.18	58.66
Asia and the Pacific									
Urban water	73	401.09	148.35	77	586.11	175.07	71	771.71	314.43
Rural water	28	510.52	1,312.78	67	1,406.60	692.80	99	2,302.68	10.11
Urban sanitation	65	357.14	192.30	65	494.77	266.41	58	632.40	453.16
Rural sanitation	42	765.79	1,057.51	54	1,133.68	965.72	65	1,501.57	819.22
Western Asia									
Urban water	95	26.16	1.38	100	44.25	0.17	100	67.26	0.00
Rural water	51	11.19	10.76	56	14.34	11.26	57	17.48	13.18
Urban sanitation	79	21.76	5.78	100	44.42	0.00	100	67.26	0.00
Rural sanitation	34	7.46	14.49	34	8.70	16.90	32	9.94	20.72
Global totals									
Urban water	77	720.77	212.70	82	1,088.52	243.70	77	1,456.27	445.83
Rural water	30	690.25	1,612.74	63	1,669.79	988.72	89	2,649.33	321.55
Urban sanitation	69	641.39	292.08	72	955.22	377.00	67	1,269.05	633.05
Rural sanitation	37	860.64	1,442.35	49	1,294.72	1,363.79	58	1,728.80	1,242.88

Source:
United Nations, Achievements of the International Drinking Water Supply and Sanitation Decade 1980–1990, 1990

Table A-16. Percentage increase in the number of people served and unserved by water supply 1980–2000

Region/sector	1980–1990		1990–2000 (projected)	
	Increases in number served (%)	Increases in number unserved (%)	Increases in number served (%)	Increases in number unserved (%)
Africa				
Urban water	77	29	44	203
Rural water	57	7	36	10
Urban sanitation	106	2	51	112
Rural sanitation	78	11	44	13
Latin America and the Caribbean				
Urban water	45	-1	31	12
Rural water	31	-29	24	-41
Urban sanitation	39	31	28	31
Rural sanitation	67	-20	40	-25
Asia and the Pacific				
Urban water	46	18	32	80
Rural water	175	-47	64	-99
Urban sanitation	39	39	28	70
Rural sanitation	48	-9	32	-15
Western Asia				
Urban water	69	-88	52	-100
Rural water	28	5	22	17
Urban sanitation	104	-100	51	0
Rural sanitation	17	17	14	23
Global totals				
Urban water	51	15	34	83
Rural water	142	-39	59	-67
Urban sanitation	49	29	33	68
Rural sanitation	51	-6	34	-9

Source:
United Nations, Achievements of the International Drinking
Water Supply and Sanitation Decade, 1980–1990, *1990*

Table A-17. Water Requirements for Selected Industries in the World
(Water requirements for unit of product produced)
(data post 1960)

Industry, product and country	Unit of product (ton, except as specified)	Water required per unit (liters)
Canned Food		
Tomatoes, whole, Cyprus		2,000
Peas, Cyprus		10,000
Carrots, Cyprus		16,000
Grapes, Cyprus		30,000
Average for fruits, vegetables and juices, United States		24,000
Meat packing, United States	ton of prepared meat	23,000
Meat preserving, Israel	ton of prepared meat	10,000
Canned fish, Canada		58,000
Chickens, United States	per bird	25
Turkeys, United States	per bird	75
Sugar, France	ton of sugar beets	10,900
Sugar, Great Britain	ton of sugar beets	14,900
Sugar, Israel	ton of sugar beets	1,800
Sugar, United States	ton of sugar beets	6,000
Beer, France		14,500
Newsprint, Canada		165,000 to 200,000
Ammonia (naptha, reforming), Japan		255,000
Caustic soda (Solvay process), United States		60,500
Caustic soda (Dual process), Federal Republic of Germany		160,000
Polyethylene, Federal Republic of Germany		231,000
Sulphuric acid, Federal Republic of Germany		83,500
Dyeing textiles, France		180,000
Iron and steel products		
Martin process (open hearth), France		15,000
Thomas process (Bessemer converter), France		10,000
Rolling and drawing mills, United States	14,700	
Blast furnace smelting, United States		103,000
Automobiles, United States	vehicle	38,000
Electric power (conventional thermal), United States	kilowatt-hour	200
Laundry, Cyprus	ton of washed goods	45,000

Source: United Nations, Guidelines for the Preparation of National
Master Water Plans, *1989*

Appendix B

Selected Privatizations

Compiled by Leonard S. Hyman

Since 1980, various nations have sold off close to $100 billion of utility assets to private investors. Many countries have auctioned off the rights to participate in utility industries opened up for the first time to competition or to private participation. In addition, countries have permitted new investment groups to provide services, often choosing the investment group through competitive bidding or negotiation. Each of those procedures constitutes privatization, in one way or another. A list of every one of those efforts would be either endless or incomplete. The compilation of significant privatizations that follows is incomplete, in the sense that it concentrates on sale of existing government utilities, rather than on the granting of new licenses to provide additional services. A number of government utilities were sold over a multi-year period. The listing shown is in the first year of sale of government owned shares to a private entity. In some instances, where the government controlled utility already had private shareholders, the privatization date shown is that of an offering of part of the government's shares to the public, the sale of control shares to investors, or of a sale of new shares to the public. A number of countries have sold some stock to the public but retained voting control. Is that a true privatization? Probably not, unless the utility is run and regulated as if it were a private entity, or unless the government intends to sell the rest of its shares in the near future.

Table B-1. Utility Privatizations by Year, Country and Percentage of Stock Sold

Year and Country	Telecom	Electric	Gas	Water
1980 Chile		Two small distribution utilities		
1981 United Kingdom	Cable & Wireless-first tranche of sales that eliminate government position by 1985			
1982 Chile		Chilmetro-9%, Chilquinta-10%, contributions reimbursable in stock, through 1985		
1984 United Kingdom	British Telecom-50%, balance sold by 1993			
1986 Chile		Chilgener-35% (100% by 1988) Chilmetro-63% nongovernment (100% by 1987) Chilquinta-63% nongovernment (100% by 1987)		
United Kingdom			British Gas- 100% sold	
1987 Canada	Teleglobe- 100% to Memotec (renamed Teleglobe)			

Table B-1. Utility Privatizations by Year, Country and Percentage of Stock Sold

Year and Country	Telecom	Electric	Gas	Water
1987 *(continued)*				
Chile		Endesa-20% (100% by 1989)		
Japan	Nippon Tel & Tel-12 %, subsequent offerings made, but government retains control			
Spain	Telefónica-small offering to establish New York market, government retains control			
1988				
Austria		VKW-100% Verbund-49%		
Canada	Terra Nova Tel-100% to Newfoundland Tel		BC Gas-100% to Inland Gas	
	Northwest Tel-100% to BCE			
Chile	Cía. Teléfonos de Chile- 32% to Bond Corp, subsequent sales and change of control to Telefónica			
Jamaica	Telecom of Jamaica-13% to public, subsequent sales through 1991 to Cable & Wireless			

Table B-1. Utility Privatizations by Year, Country and Percentage of Stock Sold

Year and Country	Telecom	Electric	Gas	Water
1988 *(continued)*				
Spain		Endesa-first offering more subsequently, government retains control		
1989				
Austria		EVN-25%, more subsequently		
Chile	Entel-private sale of 30% to Telefónica and Santander	Pehuenche-private sale to Endesa		
Korea		Korea Electric Power-21% sold		
United Kingdom				Water industry of England and Wales-100%
1990				
Argentina	Entel divided into two, 60% control sold to Telefónica and Stet privately, subsequent public offerings made			
Canada	Telus (Alberta Government Telephones)-60%, more later			
Germany		W. German utilities begin purchase of E. German utility properties	E. German Verbundnetz Gas- to Ruhrgas group	

Table B-1. Utility Privatizations by Year, Country and Percentage of Stock Sold

Year and Country	Telecom	Electric	Gas	Water
1990 *(continued)*				
Israel	Bezek- 6%, more later but government retains control			
Malaysia	Telekom Malaysia-22%			
Mexico	Teléfonos de Mexico- voting control of 20.4% to Grupo Carso/ Southwestern Bell/France Telecom, balance sold later			
New Zealand	Telecom of New Zealand- sold to Bell Atlantic/ Ameritech, with later public offering			
United Kingdom		Regional electric companies of England and Wales- 100%		
1991				
Philippines		Manila Electric		
United Kingdom		National Power- 60% (balance in 1995)		
		PowerGen- 60% (balance in 1995)		
		Scottish Power- 100% Scottish Hydro- 100%		
Venezuela	CATV-40% to GTE group			

Table B-1. Utility Privatizations by Year, Country and Percentage of Stock Sold

Year and Country	Telecom	Electric	Gas	Water
1992				
Argentina		Edesur-51%		OSN-30 year water concession to Lyonnaise des Eaux
		Edenor-51%		
		Individual power stations sold		
			Transportadora del Sur-70%	
			Trans. del Norte-70%	
			MetroGas-70%	
			Other gas utilities-70%	
Australia	Aussat- to to Optus (BellSouth/ Cable & Wireless group)			
Canada	Telesat- 53% to telcos	Nova Scotia Power-100%		
Malaysia		Tenaga Nasional- 23%		
Puerto Rico	Tel. Larga Distancia- 80% to Telefónica			
United Kingdom		N. Ireland Electricity- private sale of some assets		
1993				
Argentina		Transener-65%		
Canada			Alberta Energy- 36% government stake	

Table B-1. Utility Privatizations by Year, Country and Percentage of Stock Sold

Year and Country	Telecom	Electric	Gas	Water
1993 *(continued)*				
Hungary	Matav-30% to Deutsche Telekom/ Ameritech			
Korea	Korea Telecom-10%, more later			
Mexico				Mexico City privatizes management of water system
Singapore	Singapore Telecom-11%			
Turkey		Kepez Elektrik-11%		
		Cukurova Elektrik-25%		
United Kingdom		Northern Ireland Electricity-100%		
1994				
Australia		Gladstone Power Station-to Comalco/ Northern States Power		
Brazil		Cía. Energetica de Sao Paulo (CESP)-nonvoting preferred		
China		Huaneng Power Intl- 25%		
		Shandung Huaneng Power Development		
Cuba	Emtel Cuba-49% to Grupo Domos (Mexico)			
Denmark	Teledanmark-48%			

Table B-1. Utility Privatizations by Year, Country and Percentage of Stock Sold

Year and Country	Telecom	Electric	Gas	Water
1994 *(continued)*				
Germany		Complete privatization of E. German utilities, control sold to W. German utilities, with some ownership by PowerGen/ Northern States Power Bayernwerk-control to Viag		
Indonesia	Indosat-25%			
Latvia	Lattelkom-49% to Cable & Wireless group			
Netherlands	Koninklijke PTT Nederland (KPN)-30%			
Pakistan		Hub River project-National Power (UK)/ Xenel(Saudi Arabia group leads private financing of new project, some shares in public sale		
Peru	Entel and Cía. Peruana de Teléfonos-35% government stakes to Telefónica group			
Thailand		Electric Generating Co.- 50%		

Sources
Privatization Yearbook *(various years)*, Financial Times, *prospectuses, brokerage reports, and other references.*

Appendix C

Market Performance of Privatized Firms as of Selected Dates

Leonard S. Hyman

By and large, the shares of privatized utility companies have performed well, often better than the market by a substantial margin. How well they did depended on how poorly the government judged the value of its assets, whether the government really intended to obtain the highest value possible in the sale or had other motives, and what management accomplished after the privatization. Over time, though, market performance of the existing companies' shares should converge to the average, as competitive forces or firmer regulation erodes some of those unusually high profits earned by privatized monopolists. Furthermore, over time, the governments seem to get a better handle on how to price the shares, making spectacular share price performance less likely in the future.

The following tables show percentage price increases of U.K. utilities since privatization compared to that of the London stock market, and the compound annual price gains (in dollars) since privatization for selected telecommunications stocks compared to price gains in the same periods for the New York market averages. With the exception of Nippon Tel and Tel, every utility or utility group significantly outperformed the market averages.

Table C-1. The Profitability of U.K. Privatizations as of June 10, 1993

Company	Industry	Year of Privatization	% Increase in Share Price Since Privatization Date for	
			Privatized Company	Stock Market*
British Telecom	Telecom	1984	216	142
British Gas	Gas utility	1986	116	77
BAA	Airports	1987	202	23
North West Water	Water utility	1989	85	22
Thames Water	Water utility	1989	93	22
National Power	Electric generation	1991	105	16
PowerGen	Electric generation	1991	115	16
Scottish Power	Electric utility	1991	32	13
Scottish Hydro	Electric utility	1991	43	13

* *Market measured by the FTSE 100 index.*
Source: Financial Times.

Table C-2. Profitability of U.K. Privatizations as of Dec. 22, 1994

Company or Sector	Year of Privatization	Price Performance % Relative to Market* Since Date of Privatization
British Telecom	1984	110
British Gas	1986	120
Water Sector	1989	135
Electricity Sector	1990	170

* *Stock market as measured by the FT-A All Shares Index.*
Source: Financial Times.

Table C-3. Profitability of Telecommunications Privatization Offerings Measured in Dollar Terms as of Sept. 1, 1994

| Company | Country | Offering Date | Compound Annual % Increase in Dollar Price since Date of Privatization for | |
			Privatized Company	New York Shares*
DDT	Japan	9/93	183.3	2.6
Cía. Teléfonos de Chile	Chile	7/90	53.6	6.8
Telefónica de Argentina	Argentina	12/91	49.4	8.2
Telekom Malaysia	Malaysia	9/90	46.7	9.4
Telecom New Zealand	New Zealand	7/91	28.9	5.5
Teléfonos de México	Mexico	5/91	28.6	4.3
Telecom Argentina	Argentina	2/92	23.5	14.8
Cable & Wireless	United Kingdom	11/81	21.9	11.0
STET	Italy	7/91	18.8	7.2
British Telecom	United Kingdom	12/84	15.3	11.3
Telefónica de España	Spain	6/87	9.9	7.0
Nippon Tel & Tel	Japan	2/87	2.6	7.6

* *Stock market measured by S&P 500 index.*
  Source: Infrastructure Finance, Financial Times, *S&P.*

Appendix D

Selected Bibliography on Privatization

Andrew S. Hyman

Clarke, Thomas and Christos Pitelis, editors, *The Political Economy of Privatization*, New York: Routledge, 1993.

Discusses the political and organizational issues related to privatization around the world.

Ernst and Young, *Privatization: Investing in State-Owned Enterprises Around the World*, New York: John Wiley & Sons, Inc., 1994.

Outlines financial opportunities in the privatization market. Contains glossary and annotated bibliography.

Gayle, Dennis J. and Jonathan N. Goodrich, editors, *Privatization and Deregulation in Global Perspective*, New York: Quorum Books, 1990.

Analyzes examples of privatization around the world. Extensive bibliography.

Gómez-Ibáñez, José and John R. Meyer, *Going Private: The International Experience with Transport Privatization*, Washington, D.C.: The Brookings Institution, 1993.

Covers urban transit, highways, rail and air transport. Balanced coverage with discussion of benefits *and* potential problems.

Gormley, William T. Jr., editor, *Privatization and Its Alternatives*, Madison, Wisconsin: The University of Wisconsin Press, 1990.

Discusses the role privatization has played and can play in education, housing, and law enforcement.

Henney, Alex, *Privatise Power: Restructuring the Electricity Supply Industry*, Policy Study No. 83, London: Centre for Policy Studies, May 1987.

Outlines how to set up a competitive, private, electric utility industry in Britain. Contains bibliography and glossary.

Henney, Alex, *A Study of the Privatisation of the Electricity Supply Industry in England and Wales*, London: EEE Limited, 1994.

Detailed analysis of the privatization with extensive coverage of the problems encountered. Extensive discussion of the financing of the privatization, and possibilities for the future.

Lord, Rodney, editor, *Privatisation Yearbook 1994*, London: Privatisation International, 1994.

Discusses and analyzes annual privatizations on a country-by-country basis.

MacAvoy, Paul W., W.T. Stanbury, George Yarrow, and Richard Zeckhauser, editors, *Privatization and State-Owned Enterprises: Lessons from the United States, Great Britain and Canada*, Boston: Kluwer Academic Publishers, 1989.

Analyzes the performance record of state-owned corporations. Analyzes privatization experiences and respective political/organizational aspects. Bibliography.

Neuberger, Julia, editor, *Privatisation: Fair Shares For All or Selling the Family Silver*, London: Papermac, 1987.

Authors from the left, right, and center discuss the economic and social implications of privatization in the United Kingdom.

Organisation for Economic Co-operation and Development, *Regulatory Reform, Privatisation and Competition Policy*, Paris: Organization for Economic Cooperation and Development, 1992.

Discusses the state of policies to promote economic competition and reduce the government's economic role in OECD countries.

Pirie, Madsen, *Privatization*, Aldershot, England: Wildwood House, 1988.

Briefly discusses the reasons for privatization. Deals extensively with various ways to privatize industries and opportunities for privatization, with an emphasis on Britain.

Robinson, Colin and Allen Sykes, *Privatise Coal: Achieving International Competitiveness*, Policy Study No. 85, London: Centre for Policy Studies, July 1987.

Discusses the need for privatization of the British coal industry and the potential benefits. Glossary.

Savas, Emanuel S., *Privatization: The Key to Better Government*, Chatham, New Jersey: Chatham House Publishers, Inc., 1987.

Discusses the need for privatization and how it has and can be implemented in various cases.

Suleiman, Ezra N. and John Waterbury, editors, *The Political Economy of Public Sector Reform and Privatization*, Boulder, Colorado: Westview Press, 1990.

Studies political impact of privatization in many nations. Extensive coverage of privatization in the developing world.

World Energy Council, *Energy for Tomorrow's World: The Realities, the Real Options and the Agenda for Achievement*, New York: St. Martin's Press Inc., 1993.

Projects how the energy industry will look in the future. Discusses economic and environmental concerns around the world. Bibliography and statistical appendices.

Appendix E

Accounting and Financial Analysis

Leonard S. Hyman

Accounting and financial analysis procedures vary from country to country, but international investors like to set the accounts into a standard format, and companies that list their shares on a stock exchange in the United States must produce a summary set of accounts using United States Generally Accepted Accounting Principles (USGAAP). Good accounting procedures, too, are a necessity in operating a modern corporation, and many utilities under government ownership lacked a rigorous accounting system. No privatized utility can run successfully without a carefully devised accounting system. No privatized utility can successfully raise capital in world markets without an easily understood system of accounts that can be utilized to value the securities of the firm.

SECTION ONE: SOME BASICS
Before plunging into analysis of what standard accounts require and what investors want, it would be worthwhile to consider some basic concepts.

Regulation
A utility, in the old sense, is supposed to be a *natural monopoly*, meaning that one producer can serve customers more efficiently than can many competing producers. In addition to avoiding the obvious inconvenience of having five or six utility companies dig up the streets, the natural monopoly provides *economies of scale*—that is, one large utility can produce and sell its product more cheaply than could a number of small producers. Because a utility has a monopoly, a *regulatory agency* assures that the utilities do not take advantage of their customers. The agencies set service standards and prices. The price (rate) is set to permit the utility to collect enough money to cover all operating expenses, including taxes, and to have enough *operating income* left to provide a fair *rate of return* on the money invested in the business. Investors supply the money used to build the plant and to buy the equipment that serves the customers (the *rate base*). The rate of return is determined from the utility's *cost of capital*. For example, suppose that a utility has invested $1,000 in facilities to serve its customers. The company borrowed $500 on which it is paying 10 percent interest ($50 a year). Holders of the utility's common stock furnished another $500. The regulators note that the loan costs 10 percent. After a lengthy hearing, the regulators

decide that common stockholders are entitled to a return of 15 percent on their investment ($75 a year). Thus, the cost of capital, as calculated below, is 12.5 percent, the rate of return that the utility is allowed to earn.

Type of Capital	Amount of Capital	Cost of Capital	Dollar Return	
Debt	$ 500 x	10% =	$ 50	
Stock	500 x	15% =	75	
Total	$ 1,000		$ 125	and: $\dfrac{\$125}{\$1,000} = 12.5\%$

Regulatory agencies rarely set rates more often than annually. Certain major expenses, however, can move up or down rapidly in the course of a year. A utility might earn too little when these expenses rise, or too much when they fall. To avoid having frequent rate hearings to adjust price for these sudden shifts in expenses, most agencies allow the use of *automatic adjustment clauses* which pass on to customers changes in certain expenses.

The standard regulatory framework is changing. Technological developments have encouraged competition which requires a new look at pricing the product. In addition, regulators are seeking alternative methods of regulation that will give utilities the incentive to run more efficiently, and help customers use electricity better. The old style rate of return regulation is giving way to alternatives.

Finances

Utility facilities are enormously expensive to build. Rarely can utility companies set aside from the year's income enough money to pay for constructing a new plant. To pay for the plants, the companies often have to borrow money and to sell new shares of stock to outsiders (*external financing*). Thus, the profits from new business that is served by the new plant have to be shared by an increased number of holders of the company's bonds and stock. If too many new securities are sold and if business does not grow as expected, the share of profits left for the holders of old securities might actually be less than before the expansion. *Dilution* takes place when so many new shares have to be sold to pay for expansion that earnings per share of stock are less than they would have been had no expansion and financing taken place. Dilution usually occurs when the *market value* of the stock (the price at which it sells) is less than the *book value* (the amount of money per share that common stockholders have already invested in the business plus any earnings that have been retained or saved by the company). As a result, investors and management carefully watch the ratio of *market* value to *book* value—the market price of the stock stated as a percentage of its book value. Other things being equal, a utility is better off if it can finance as much of its expansion as possible from internal sources when interest costs are high and stock prices are low.

Ratio Analysis

The financial reports of a corporation have three key parts. The *income statement* shows revenues and expenses for the year, and the net income, which is what is left over after expenses are paid. The *balance sheet* provides a statement of assets (what is owned), money owed, and money put in by shareholders. The *statement of cash flows* tells how the company raises and disposes of cash in a particular accounting period.

The balance sheet shows the sources of all money used to build the company since it was formed (the *capital*) and the percentage of capital that was borrowed and the percentage that came from shareholders (the *capitalization ratio*). If a large percentage of funds came from borrowing, the company is said to be *leveraged*. If something goes wrong, the shareholders will not be paid dividends or get back their investments until creditors (those who have lent money to the company) have been repaid. Bondholders judge the quality of their securities by whether shareholders have invested a sufficient cushion of money for bondholders to fall back on if something goes wrong and by the *pretax interest coverage ratio* ("coverage"), which measures how much income is available to pay interest charges. If $100 of income is earned and interest charges are $20, then the coverage ratio is five-to-one (5x). Financial organizations rate investment quality of bonds. Many investors are not allowed to own bonds rated below certain levels because they are not considered to be prudent investments.

Some companies use conservative accounting procedures that tend to show the maximum expenses that can be written off in a period, and do not count income until the money is in the till. The reported income is then likely to be below that of a comparable company using liberal accounting procedures. Regulatory agencies establish accounting procedures for utilities. Some agencies are more cautious than others. Several items make a big difference in determining how solid are earnings. *Quality of reported earnings* is the term that describes the overall conservatism of an income statement.

Finally, to determine how profitably stockholders' money is being used, we must find out how much income is earned on every dollar invested, or the *return on equity*. If a company earns $150 for stockholders who have invested $1,000, the return on equity is 15 percent.

Capital Markets

Most of the money supplied to a utility from outside sources is in the form of borrowings or of equity capital (money invested by stockholders who own the business). Borrowings usually come from banks or from investors who buy commercial paper (*short term debt*), or in the form of bonds or debentures (*long term debt*). In the case of long term debt, the creditor lends money for a long period (perhaps 20 years) and receives a bond that will *mature* (be paid off) on a specified date. When owners of bonds need cash before the maturity date, they sell the bonds in the marketplace. Bondholders have no assurance that the market price will equal the price paid when the bond was issued or will equal the value of the bond at maturity (*face* or *par value*). Meanwhile, the bondholder receives a fixed interest payment (often call the *coupon*) each year. The return that the bondholder earns is called *yield*. The simplest yield is the *current yield*, the coupon as a return on the market price of the bond. If a bond sells for $100 and has a coupon of 12 percent ($12), the current yield is also 12 percent. If the same bond with the 12 percent coupon ($12 in interest) sells at $80, the current yield is 15 percent. When the bond is selling below par, $80 in this example, the investor will not only receive $12 a year in interest, but will also receive $20 more when the bond is finally redeemed (at $100 par) at maturity. In that case, the correct yield to use is the *yield to maturity*, a calculation of return that takes into account both the current return and the increase in price as the bond approaches the maturity date. In general, yield to maturity is lower for high rated (high quality) bonds. That is, when risk is lower, return is lower.

Preferred and *preference* stocks also pay fixed dividends. Many preferred and preference stocks remain outstanding for the life of the corporation, i.e., they have no fixed date for repayment of investment to their owners. The shareowners must sell the shares in the market when they need to raise cash. The return is measured by the *dividend yield*, which is the annual dividend divided by price.

The *common stockholders* are the owners of the business. The stockholders' investment in it is called *equity*. In order of priority, interest is paid first, then preferred and preference dividends, then dividends on common stock, if anything is left. The same order applies if the company goes out of business. First, all debts are paid in full. Then preferred and preference shareholders get their investments back. Finally, if any funds remain, the common stockholders take what is left. When something goes wrong, common stockholders' money is used to pay the holders of bonds and preferred stock. When business is good, the common stockholders collect the profits. If a company earns $1 million and has one million shares of common stock, it has *earnings per share* of $1. The company will keep some of the profits for the business (*retained earnings*) and pay the balance as *dividends*. The *payout ratio* is the dividend as a percentage of earnings. The price of a common stock is usually valued at a *multiple* of earnings, also called the price-earnings (P/E) ratio. For instance, if the stock of a company earning $1 a share sells at $7, its P/E ratio is seven-to-one, or seven times earnings (7x). Investors often pay a higher P/E for the stocks of companies whose earnings are expected to rise rapidly. The second common measure of value is the dividend yield—the dividend return on the price of the stock. The stock selling for $7 and paying a dividend of 63¢ a share annually yields 9%. Shares of companies that are expected to raise their dividends rapidly often sell at lower dividend yields. A company with a high payout ratio may not be able to raise its dividend for lack of earnings from which to pay the additional dividend. As a result, shares of that company may sell at a high dividend yield. In other words, investors will pay a higher P/E ratio and settle for a lower current dividend yield if they expect substantial improvement in the future. Investors also consider the risk level of the stock and will pay a higher P/E and accept a lower dividend yield from the investment with the lower risk.

Movements in interest rates affect bond and stock prices. When investors can earn a high return on money in the bank, for instance, they will not buy a stock or bond until its price has declined to a point at which the dividend yield or the yield to maturity is high enough to compete with returns offered elsewhere. On the other hand, when interest rates decline, investors bid up the prices of stocks and bonds until returns on them drop to levels that are close to interest rates. The market is a two-way street.

SECTION TWO: DIFFERENCES IN ACCOUNTING SYSTEMS

Differences In Accounting Systems

Accounting formats differ from country to country, but many of the variations involve how the items are arranged, rather than differences in principles. Real differences involve accounting concepts rather than location of items on the page.

Anyone well versed in accounting can figure out standard sets of accounts from various countries, as long as the underlying principles are similar—sometimes they are not. The reader needs to know the basis for the accounting system, and the purpose of the system. Here are key questions that must be answered:

Are the accounts for tax or for corporate reporting purposes?

In some countries, including the United States, the accounts shown to the income tax authorities may differ from the accounts given to the owners of the business. On the tax accounts, the business takes advantage of all the rules that allow it to show higher expenses and to defer the reporting of income in order to reduce reported income and thereby reduce taxes paid. Those procedures used to reduce taxes may not reflect what is really happening at the business, and the firm's accountants will not certify them for use by investors.

Are the accounts on a cash or on an accrual basis?

Most corporations try to match up revenues and the expenses attributable to those revenues (*accrual accounting*). Cash accounting only shows transactions that produce cash inflows or outflows in the accounting period. For instance, the corporation, this year, sells products, pays the employees and suppliers who helped to produce the product this year, but collects payment from the buyers next year. In cash accounting, the corporation would report all the expenses this year, because it paid cash to employees and suppliers, but it would not report any revenue and therefore would incur a loss. Next year, the corporation would report the revenue from the sale of the products, but would show no expenses, because it paid all the expenses last year. The corporation would show a big profit, because it has a lot of revenue and no expenses. That procedure would paint a misleading picture, though, because the revenues and expenses are part of the same transaction. In accrual accounting, the corporation would show all the revenues from the sale, even if it collects the money in the next accounting period, and all the expenses involved in that sale, even if the corporation were to pay some of the bills in another accounting period. Most large corporations throughout the world use accrual accounting.

What items does the corporation capitalize?

Some expenditures are to make purchases that will last many years (machinery, for instance) while other expenditures are directly connected to what is produced in the year. Items that last a long time are capitalized, that is, put on the books as assets and written off gradually over many years as they are used up. That seems simple. If a corporation builds a new plant that will last for decades, the corporation does not claim that the entire cost of the plant is an expense allocable against the year's production. It capitalizes the plant, and allocates part of the cost to each year's costs until the plant has worn out. Some expenditures, however, might be considered for a capital asset in one country, and considered an expense in another. Those items could be large, and their treatment needs to be understood when examining financial statements.

Are the accounts consolidated?

Often large corporations own or control other corporations. In the United States and Canada, the parent corporation shows its accounts to include the results of the subsidiaries and affiliates, thus giving shareholders a complete view of the operations. That procedure is called consolidation. In numerous other countries, the parent reports its own results, but omits information about its subsidiaries or affiliates. That omission often gives the shareholders and creditors a misleading view of the corporation.

Have the accounts been adjusted for inflation?

Inflation changes the value of assets over time, reduces the value of debt, and allows businesses to make profits just because the price of the product goes up after it is produced. In most industrialized countries, in which inflation has been a minor annoyance, corporations do not adjust their accounts to reflect the impact of inflation. In countries in which high rates of inflation prevail, accountants adjust the financial statements to reflect the impact of inflation. The adjustments vary from country to country, change whenever the accountants come up with a better way, and generally, confuse and confound those not used to such procedures. Adjustments usually center on the value of assets, the correct depreciation expense for such assets, benefits that accrue to shareholders by borrowing money, and losses of value to the business caused by keeping cash on hand. Some accounting rules force the company to restate last year's reported results for the value of money in the current year. Often, the difference between the results shown using inflation-adjustment accounting and that which would be shown if the company used U.S. or European procedures is enormous.

SECTION THREE: THE STATEMENT OF INCOME AND RETAINED EARNINGS

The income statement covers a specific period, and shows the amount of money that customers paid for services within that period (revenues) and the costs that were incurred by the firm to provide those services (expenses). The difference between revenue and expense is the profit or net income that is left for the owners of the business. Some of the income is paid to owners in the form of dividends. The rest is kept by the firm for use in the business (retained earnings). In addition to annual statements, most companies provide income statements on a quarterly basis.

Simplified Statements

The following is an example of a standard income statement for an industrial concern:

Sales (revenues)	$1,000
Cost of sales (expenses directly associated with production of product)	500
Depreciation (wear and tear on machinery)	100
Interest (on borrowed money)	100
Total Expenses	700
Pretax income	300
Income taxes	100
Net income (profit)	$ 200

Income statements for utilities are often recast for regulatory purposes as follows:

Revenues	$1,000
Operating Expenses: Production, maintenance, etc.	500
Depreciation	100
Income taxes	100
Total operating expenses	700
Operating Income	300
Interest expense	100
Net Income (profit)	$ 200

The difference exists because the utility regulator may be concerned with the return on capital—the interest paid to creditors of the firm and the profits available for stockholders. In our simplified statement, operating income, which is after deduction of taxes but before interest expense, represents the income available to pay the owners of the capital that has been invested in the business.

A number of utilities own non-utility subsidiaries. The accountants insist that the income statement add together the utility and non-utility businesses. The statement of income that includes all operations is "consolidated," and might be presented in one of several formats. If we take the two statements shown above, we could add them together in several ways, including:

Standard Format		Utility Format	
Utility revenues	$1,000	Utility revenues	$1,000
Industrial sales	1,000	Industrial sales	1,000
Total revenues	2,000	Total revenues	2,000
Expenses: Cost of sales	500	Expenses: Cost of sales	500
Production, maintenance, etc.	500	Production, maintenance, etc.	500
Depreciation	200	Depreciation	200
Operating expenses	1,200	Operating expenses	1,200
Income before interest and taxes	800	Pretax operating income	800
Interest expense	300	Income taxes	200
Pretax income	500	Operating income	600
Income taxes	200	Interest expense	300
Net income	300	Net income	300

Although the utility accounting format makes sense for regulatory purposes, most utility-type companies outside the United States have adopted the standard industrial format for accounting purposes. Each country, and each industry will produce a variation on the standard format. The example that follows is for an electric utility, but the same procedures apply to water, natural gas and telecommunications corporations.

Utility Income Statement

The actual income statement is complicated, as can be seen in the following example:

Statement of Income
($ Thousands)

	Year Ended December 31,	
	1994	**1995**
Operating Revenue	$500,000	$550,000
Operating Expenses		
Fuel	200,000	245,000
Purchased & Interchanged Power	40,000	10,000
Other	50,000	60,000
Maintenance	40,000	50,000
Depreciation and Amortization	35,000	40,000
General Taxes	30,000	31,000
Total Operating Expenses	395,000	436,000
Operating Income	105,000	114,000
Other Income	4,000	5,000
Pretax Income before Interest Charges	109,000	119,000
Interest Expense		
Interest on Long-Term Debt	23,000	28,000
Other Interest	4,000	4,000
Capitalized interest	(5,000)	(6,000)
Total Interest Expense	22,000	26,000
Pretax Income	87,000	93,000
Income Taxes	27,000	29,000
Net Income	60,000	64,000
Preferred Dividend	8,000	8,000
Balance Available for Common Stock	52,000	56,000
Average Shares Outstanding During Year	9,000	10,000
Earnings Per		
Average Common Shares Outstanding	$5.78	$5.60
Statement of Retained Earnings		
Balance, Beginning of Year	138,000	158,000
Add:		
Net Income After Dividends on Preferred Stock	52,000	56,000
Deduct:		
Cash Dividends on Common Stock	32,000	34,000
Balance, End of Year	$158,000	$180,000

The utility sells a certain amount of electricity in the year at particular prices. Receipts from customers produce *Operating Revenue*. The costs of paying employees, suppliers, and taxes—expenses involved in producing the electricity—are called *Operating Expenses*. The major item is almost always Fuel that is burned in the boiler to generate the electricity. Sometimes a utility buys power from other utilities because it does not have a generator in operation or because the power produced by the other utility is cheaper. That power is *Purchased and Interchanged Power*. The utility may sell power to other electric companies. Such interchange power receipts are shown as part of revenues. *Other* expenses associated with operations includes salaries and miscellaneous items.

Maintenance Expenses are small repairs and regular overhauls of equipment. Plant and equipment wears out over time or becomes obsolete and eventually must be replaced by more modern and efficient equipment. The company estimates how long the equipment is expected to last and spreads the cost of the purchase over the productive life of the asset. For example, if a machine costs $100,000 and will last for 20 years, the company will show an expense of $5,000 (one-twentieth of the purchase price) each year. That expense is called *Depreciation*. *Amortization* is the spreading over time of the cost of some other expenditure or loss that already took place. For instance, if a storm did enormous damage, the regulator might tell the utility to set up a storm damage account, and then amortize the expense over five years, that is, only show one fifth of the expense in each year. Unlike other expenses, depreciation and amortization does not entail paying out money when the expense is shown on the income statement.

General Taxes includes taxes on real estate and on the company's revenues, and are often levied by state and local governments.

Total Operating Expenses is subtracted from *Operating Revenue* to produce *Operating Income*.

Other Income includes the income from various affiliated companies, interest earned on investments, and a variety of other items.

Pretax Income before Interest Charges is the sum of *Operating* and *Other Income*. This is an important figure for creditors, because it shows how much income is available to pay interest charges.

Interest Expense is divided into Interest on *Long-Term Debt* and *Other Interest*. The latter is usually interest on bank loans and on commercial paper. Some companies subtracted out interest earned on investments to produce a *Net Interest*. Many utilities deduct from the current year's interest charges an amount equal to interest expenses on debt incurred to raise funds for plant that is under construction, variously titled, but called *Capitalized Interest* in this statement. (In the United States, the terms used have included *Interest During Construction* and *Allowance for Funds Used During Construction*. In the United States, the amount is clearly shown in the statements. That is not the case elsewhere.)

A utility may have a substantial amount of money tied up for years in a facility under construction. That money had to be raised by means of borrowing or by sale of stock. The utility pays interest on borrowed money, and stockholders also expect a return on their investment even though the plant is not yet operating. How can the utility recover those costs involved in raising money to build the power plant? The answer, in many cases, is to add the cost of the money to the cost of the power plant. Once the plant is completed, the utility earns a return on the money used to pay suppliers of machinery, bricks, and construction services, plus a return on the money paid to the suppliers of capital. Furthermore, the utility will recover, by means of depreciation, all the costs of the plant, including the cost of capital.

Interest Capitalized is a mechanism whereby the cost of money is added to the plant account on the balance sheet. The cost of money raised to build the power plant (AFUDC) is added to company income and thus increases the stockholders' equity shown on the right side of the balance sheet. Because the balance sheet must balance, under the double entry system, a similar sum is added to the plant account on the assets side of the balance sheet. Money is raised either from stockholders or from creditors (lenders). Accordingly, *Interest Capitalized* serves two purposes. One purpose is to allow the utility to recover costs of plant (by means of depreciation) and earn a return on capital costs incurred while a facility is under construction. A second purpose is to remove from the income statement the effects of expenses that have nothing to do with operations for the current year.

When *Total Interest Expense* is subtracted from *Pretax Income Before Interest Charges*, then *Pretax Income* remains. Once *Income Taxes* are paid, *Net Income* is left. This is the money left for the owners of the business. All owners, however, are not equal. The owners of preferred stock must be paid fixed *Preferred Dividends* before the common stockholders are paid.

The *Balance Available for Common Stock* is a residual. To calculate the income available per share of common stock, we must know how many shares are outstanding. The number of shares outstanding changes during the year as shares are repurchased or new shares are issued. Standard practice is to use *Average Shares Outstanding During the Year* to calculate per share data.

When income available for all common stock is divided by the average number of shares of common outstanding during the year, *Earnings Per Average Common Share Outstanding* results.

What happens to the income left after common stockholders have been paid? That is shown in the *Statement of Retained Earnings*. The *Net Income After Dividends on Preferred Stock* is added to the *Balance of Retained Earnings at the Beginning of the Year*. From the *Total, Cash Dividends on Common Stock* must be subtracted, leaving the *Balance at the End of the Year*.

Consolidation

Electric utilities might own subsidiaries that furnish services to the electric utility. Sometimes a holding company owns the electric utility and an affiliated firm that sells services or products to the electric utility. How does the group of corporations present its accounts? The group does not add up the revenues and expenses of the component companies because that would constitute double counting. One does not make money selling to oneself. The answer is to consolidate the results. For instance, the holding company owns a utility that buys its coal from a mine owned by the holding company. The holding company has to issue its accounts and could add up the result as follows:

	Coal Mine	Electric Company	Total
Revenues	$100	$1,000	$1,100
Expenses	50	600	650
Fuel Costs	—	100	100
Total Expenses	50	700	750
Profit	50	300	350

The fact of the matter is that the group only collected $1,000 in revenue, from the customers of the electric company. That is all the money that came in the door. As for expenses, the total company may show $750 including fuel, but we know that only half the cost of the coal represents expense, and the rest is profit. One has to remove the effect of selling from one affiliate to another. The means to do so is by consolidating, rather than adding:

	Coal Mine	Electric Company	Eliminate Intra-Company Transactions	Consolidated Results
Revenues	$100	$1,000	($100)	$1,000
Total Exp.	50	700	(50)	650
Profit	50	300	—	350

To put it simply, if the utility had owned the coal mine, there would have been no pretense that a sale had been made, and we could have ended up in the same place as the consolidated results without the complications.

SECTION FOUR: THE BALANCE SHEET

The balance sheet shows the property and cash owned by a firm and the amounts owed to it (assets). The money that a firm owes and the source of the money used to purchase those assets (liabilities and capital) are also shown. Data are given as of the end of business on a stated day—usually the end of the year or the end of an accounting period.

The Utility Balance Sheet

The balance sheet of a utility is similar to that of an industrial company except that industrial companies generally put current assets and liabilities at the top of the balance sheet. Assets owned by the utility are shown on the left side (or top half) of the balance sheet.

Balance Sheet Assets
($ Thousands)

	December 31,	
	1994	**1995**
Utility Plant and Equipment		
In Service	$1,000,000	$1,160,000
Less Depreciation	250,000	290,000
Net Plant in Service	750,000	870,000
Construction Work in Progress	100,000	120,000
Net Utility Plant and Equipment	850,000	990,000
Other Property and Investments	10,000	10,000
Current Assets		
Cash and Temporary Investments	5,000	6,000
Accounts Receivable	25,000	28,000
Materials and Supplies	50,000	55,000
Total Current Assets	80,000	89,000
Deferred charges and Miscellaneous Assets	20,000	20,000
Total Assets	$ 960,000	$1,109,000

Liabilities and Capital

	December 31,	
	1994	**1995**
Capitalization		
Common Stock	$115,000	$ 171,000
Retained Earnings	158,000	180,000
Preferred Stock	90,000	90,000
Long Term Debt	400,000	480,000
Total Capitalization	763,000	921,000
Current Liabilities		
Accounts Payable	17,000	14,000
Accrued Expenses	10,000	4,000
Bank Loans and Commercial Paper	40,000	20,000
Long Term Debt Payable in One Year	30,000	30,000
Total Current Liabilities	97,000	68,000
Deferred Credits and		
Miscellaneous Liabilities	100,000	120,000
Total Liabilities and Capitalization	$960,000	$1,109,000

The asset side of the balance sheet shows the cost of what the company owns plus what is owed to it by others plus the value of some money that the company has already paid for future expenses.

The major items on a utility's balance sheet usually represent physical plant (machinery, buildings, and land) that is being or will be used to serve the customer. *Utility Plant and Equipment* is divided into several categories. The first is the cost of plant that has been completed and is *In Service*. That cost includes not only the money paid to the manufacturers of building products and machinery and to construction workers but also the return that was paid to those who supplied the money.

Physical plant wears out over time or machinery may lose value because it is obsolete. Every year the firm reduces the value of a piece of machinery to reflect the aging process by adding to a reserve for *Depreciation*. *Net Plant in Service* represents the original cost of the plant less the depreciation reserve.

Most utility companies have plant under construction to meet the growing demands of their customers. Machinery, buildings, and equipment that are part of an incomplete project are called *Construction Work in Progress*. The sum of all the money invested in plant, less depreciation, is *Net Utility Plant and Equipment*.

Many utilities have invested in other businesses. Those investments are shown under *Other Property and Investments*.

The company's plant account often is called fixed assets because the property cannot be easily moved and cannot be converted quickly into cash. *Current Assets*, on the other hand, includes cash, items that can be quickly converted into cash, and accounts that will be paid to the company within 12 months.

The utility maintains *Cash and Temporary Investments* to pay expenses. Customers are charged for services used and, until the bills have been paid, the money owed to the company represents *Accounts Receivable*. The utility keeps an inventory of spare parts, office supplies, emergency materials, and a supply of fuel for its power plants, all of which are included in *Materials and Supplies*. The total of those items makes up *Total Current Assets*.

Deferred Charges and Miscellaneous Assets represent money that has already been paid for something that applies, at least in part, to some future period. For example, the utility paid an underwriter (investment banker) to market some bonds. The money received from the sale of the bonds will be used by the utility for a 20-year period. The expense should, therefore, be spread over the 20 years. Accordingly, the total underwriting expense becomes a deferred charge. Each year, one twentieth of the total is shown as an expense while the deferred expense item on the balance sheet is reduced by an equal amount. In another example, the company incurs some major expense because of a storm or because of the scrapping of some big project. The regulators might want that expense to be spread over several years so that consumers do not have to pay sharply higher rates in a single year to offset the total charge. The regulator tells the utility to defer the charge and to write it off (that is, to reduce the total by a specific amount) over several years. The amount of the writeoff becomes part of each year's expenses. Other miscellaneous assets also appear at the bottom of the balance sheet, some of them extremely large.

The *Total Assets* are the sum of the preceding items.

The *Liabilities and Capital* side of the balance sheet shows the amounts that owners invested in the business and the amounts the business owes to its creditors. The utility accounts usually begin with a statement of *Capitalization*, which shows the amount that has been invested in the business for the long term. Money that cannot be taken out of the business before an appointed time (usually more than one year from the date of the balance sheet) is included in this section.

Common Stock is the value assigned to the shares. Some common stock has a nominal or par value ($1 a share, for example), which is a holdover from the early days of corporate organization. When such shares are sold to the public, the price paid is usually well over par value. The difference between par value and the price for the stock is called paid-in surplus. For example, if stockholders purchasing 1,000 shares had invested $6,000 for a stock with a $1 a share par value, the common stock account would look like this:

Common Stock ($1 par value, 1,000 shares outstanding)	$1,000
Paid-in surplus	5,000

Usually, part of the year's income is paid to stockholders as dividends and part is retained for future use. The portion not distributed is *Retained Earnings*. Numerous variations exist on the components of the funds provided by common shareholders including reserve accounts that are not common in the industrialized world. Those reserves plus the sum of retained earnings, paid-in capital, and par value, or the sum of common stock and retained earnings, is common stockholders' equity. In other words, the money that common stockholders have invested in the business plus the income that could have been paid to common shareholders but was retained instead is their contribution to the capital of the enterprise.

Purchasers of *Preferred Stock* receive a fixed dividend that must be paid before common stockholders can receive a dividend. If the company goes out of business, preferred stockholders must be paid in full before holders of the common stock are paid. In those ways, preferred stock is similar to debt. But the rights of preferred shareholders are junior to those of debt holders, and in that way, preferred stock is similar to common stock.

Long Term Debt is money borrowed for more than one year (sometimes 10 to 30 years).

The sum of common equity, preferred stock, and long term debt is the permanent capital or *Total Capitalization* of the utility.

The company has obligations that must be paid within 12 months of the date of the balance sheet. Those obligations are *Current Liabilities*.

Accounts Payable consist of bills that the company must pay within the year (usually sooner). Such bills could be for supplies and other services. *Accrued Expenses* are known expenses that the company must pay in the near term, although bills have not yet been received. For example, a utility may show money owed to employees for work already performed as an accrued expense before the paychecks are actually written. Taxes may also be treated in that way. Utilities generally raise money by selling long term securities. The utility often borrows from banks or sells short term commercial paper until it becomes convenient to repay those loans by selling long term securities. *Bank Loans and Commercial Paper* can vary greatly from period to period, depending on when long term offerings are planned. *Long Term Debt Payable in One Year* represents a bond issue that will be due for payment within 12 months of the date of the balance sheet.

The total of the items in *Total Current Liabilities* should be compared with total current assets to determine whether current liabilities are covered by current assets. The difference between current assets and current liabilities is called working capital.

Deferred Credits which could be deferred income, are similar to the deferred charges on the assets side of the balance sheet. For example, customers may pay for something in advance. The company collects the cash from the customers, but does not show the income from the transaction until the service is performed. In addition of course, the company may lump together many miscellaneous liabilities in this item.

Total Liabilities and Capitalization must, of course, equal total assets.

Consolidation

Often, the corporation owns other corporations. In financial parlance, the parent company owns subsidiaries. The subsidiaries have assets and liabilities, and may even have their own debt outstanding. As an example, the parent company raises $1,000 by selling stock to investors, another $1,000 by selling bonds to investors and invests $1,000 in the common stock of two subsidiaries. Each of the subsidiaries then sells $1,000 worth of bonds to investors in order to raise more capital, and then invests $2,000 in plant and equipment.

Working out the asset side of the balance sheet, each of the subsidiaries has $2,000 of plant and equipment for a total of $4,000. The parent company has $2,000 of assets, consisting of stock in the subsidiaries. On the liabilities side, each subsidiary has $1,000 of debt and $1,000 of equity (a total of $2,000 debt and $2,000 equity) and the parent has $1,000 of debt and $1,000 of equity. Should we add up the figure for the subsidiaries and the parent to get a total? The answer is no. We sense that doing so would be wrong by looking at the assets. The combined group really has $4,000 worth of plant and equipment and nothing else. On the liability side, three corporate utilities have borrowed $3,000 in total but they have only raised $1,000 from shareholders, when the parent company sold stock. The accounts have to be consolidated, not added:

	Subsidiary One	Subsidiary Two	Parent	Consolidating Adjustment	Consolidated
Assets:					
Plant and Equipment	$2,000	$2,000	0		$4,000
Common Stock Investments	0	0	$2,000	($2,000)	0
Total	$2,000	$2,000	$2,000	($2,000)	$4,000
Liabilities:					
Debt	1,000	1,000	1,000	0	$3,000
Common equity	1,000	1,000	1,000	($2,000)	1,000
Total	2,000	2,000	2,000	($2,000)	$4,000

Regulators and creditors of the subsidiaries will look at the balance sheet of the subsidiaries, but common stockholders of the parent will be concerned with the consolidated statement.

SECTION FIVE: THE STATEMENT OF CASH FLOWS

The balance sheet tells what the company owns and owes at the end of a given day. The income statement helps to determine how profitable the operations of the firm were for a given period. The statement of cash flows analyzes the cash received and disbursed in a given period. There are several kinds of cash statements: the statement of change in financial position, the statement of source of funds used for construction, and the statement of cash flows.

Variations On A Theme

Let us start with simplified examples. The company collects $1,000 in cash profits from its business operations during the year, and pays a $500 dividend to stockholders. Cash in the bank at the beginning of the year is $3,000. Stock worth $3,000 is sold to raise money. The company buys a new machine costing $6,000. No money is owed on a current basis at the beginning of the period. (Current assets consisted of $3,000 cash in the bank. There are no current liabilities. Working capital is $3,000 at the beginning of the year.) Here is how the statements should appear.

Statement of Changes in Financial Position

Sources of Funds	
Profit	$1,000
Sale of stock	3,000
Total Sources of Funds	$4,000
Uses of Funds	
Purchase of machine	$6,000
Dividend	500
Total	6,500
Increase (decrease) in working capital	(2,500)
Total Uses of Funds	$4,000

To examine how the company got the money it needed for construction (or buying the machine), we could recast the statement as follows:

Statement of Sources of Funds Used for Construction

Sources of Funds	
Profits	$1,000
less Dividends	500
Earnings retained in the business	500
Sale of stock	3,000
Decrease in working capital	2,500
Funds Used For Construction	$6,000

Nowadays, however, firms prefer to focus on the movement of cash, not one particular use of the cash. Thus, firms prepare a statement of cash flows. Remember that a number in parentheses indicates a reduction of the corporation's cash. Cash equivalents are items that can be turned into cash immediately at no real cost (usually liquid investments such as government short term debt).

Statement of Cash Flows	
Cash flows from operating activities	
Profits	$1,000
Change in current assets and current liabilities	
(Working capital)	0
Net cash provided by operations	1,000
Cash flow from investing activities	
Purchase of machinery	(6,000)
Cash flow from financing activities	
Sale of stock	3,000
Dividends	(500)
Net cash from financing activities	2,500
Net change in cash and cash equivalents	(2,500)
Cash and cash equivalents at beginning of year	3,000
Cash and cash equivalents at end of year	500

Variations are possible, too, so the above statements should be viewed as skeletal examples. The *Statement of Changes* in *Financial Position* and the *Statement of Sources of Funds for Construction* have the advantage of simplicity in concept and terminology. Unfortunately, many accounts have opted for the third method, the *Statement of Cash Flows* which mixes cash flows from operations with changes in working capital, calls spending on machinery a negative cash flow, and puts dividends and stock sales into one category.

The Statement Of Cash Flows

We now look at the statement of a normal utility. Keep in mind that terminology and minor items will differ from company to company.

Statements of Cash Flows (for the Year 1995)
($ Thousands)

Cash flows from operating activities	
Net income	$64,000
Items not requiring (providing) cash	
Depreciation	40,000
Deferred credits	20,000
Interest capitalized	(10,000)
Changes in current assets and liabilities	
Accounts receivable	(3,000)
Materials and supplies	(5,000)
Accounts payable	(3,000)
Accrued expenses	(6,000)
Net cash provided by operating activities	97,000
Cash flows from investing activities	
Construction expenditures	(180,000)
Allowance for funds used during construction	10,000
Other investments	0
Net cash used in investing activities	(170,000)
Cash flows from financing activities	
Dividends on preferred and common stock	(42,000)
Redemptions	
Bank loans and commercial paper	(20,000)
Long term debt	(30,000)
Issuances	
Long term debt	110,000
Common stock	56,000
Net cash provided by financing activities	74,000
Net change in cash and equivalents	1,000
Cash and equivalents at beginning of year	5,000
Cash and equivalents at end of year	6,000

The statement begins with a grouping entitled *Cash Flows from Operating Activities*, which is basically what is left over from the year's revenues after the expenses that require cash outlay (such as interest on debt, payments for fuel, or salaries) are paid. The first item is the *Net Income* which is reported before adjusting for any items that do not result in cash. To that we must add expenses that do not require cash outlays, or subtract reported income that does not bring in any cash. *Items Not Requiring (Providing) Cash* follow. Usually the largest such item is *Depreciation*. Any Number of other expense categories could follow, but the bulk of them involve *Deferred Credits* which usually consists of deferred taxes, that is, taxes that are shown as expenses in the income statement but which will not be paid until some time in the future. For most utilities, the biggest addition to income that involves no current cash inflow is the *Interest Capitalized*. Note that this is the first line in parenthesis, meaning that it has to be subtracted from the cash inflows shown above it.

The accounting format just marches on, but we need to stop here for a minute. The items through line 6, the cash flows from operating activities, add up to $114 million. The income statement for 1995, reported $550 million of revenue. Out of those receipts, after paying expenses, the utility has generated $114 million to buy new equipment, pay debts, or declare dividends. Some of the cash produced has to be used to prepare the business for the future, or to pay off obligations incurred in the past. The utility might have to pay some suppliers that it kept waiting last year, or buy extra coal ahead of time because it looks as if there might be a coal strike next year. That cash is not free for any use.

Change in Current Assets and Liabilities is the next grouping. An increase in *Accounts Receivable* means that the customers owe more to the utility (which presumably has to take cash out of its own bank account to pay suppliers until it gets paid by the customers). In this case, accounts receivable have increased. Utilities have to keep a large stockpile of fuel and parts to ensure continuous operation. *Materials and Supplies* have risen, requiring cash to pay for them. Suppliers have to be paid, and when *Accounts Payable* are brought down, that too requires cash as in this example. (Of course, if the utility lets the accounts payable run up, then it would be reducing cash outflow, at least until the company had to pay its bills.) Finally come *Accrued Expenses* which, are expenses that the utility has not gotten around to paying. When accrued expenses increase, the utility has saved cash, at least until time of payment. In our example, the utility is reducing the account, paying the expenses.

The total of changes in assets and liabilities is ($17 million), that is, the total reduces cash by $17 million. Adding up the cash flows from operating activities and from changes in assets and liabilities, we come to *Net Cash Provided by Operating Activities*, a total of $97 million.

Companies do more than work with what they have on hand or what comes from the year's operations. They make investments to enlarge their productive capability, as an example, or sell off properties when they decide to get out of a business. *Cash Flows from Investing Activities* includes such purchases and sales. For most utilities, *Construction Expenditures* is a large figure, given the need to expand facilities to meet the demand of new customers. The construction figure, though, includes the capitalized interest, which does not represent an outflow of cash. Therefore, *Interest Capitalized* must be removed from the total construction figure, and the net outflow of cash for construction (not shown in the statement) really is $170 million. If the company has made *Other Investments*, that would show as an outflow of cash, and if it had sold investments, doing so would have added to cash. Altogether, that adds up to *Net Cash Used in Investing Activities*, at total of $170 million.

So far, the utility has laid out $73 million more than it has taken in. Where does the money come from?

Cash Flows from Financing Activities accounts for how the utility raises much of its cash needs. As a start, though, the utility has shareholders that expect *Dividends on Preferred and Common Stock*, which are paid out during the year and represent a drain on cash. Some of the utility's debt has to be repaid, and *Redemptions* require cash. The utility might pay down *Bank Loans and Commercial Paper* or *Long Term Debt*, or redeem preferred stock or even buy back shares of common stock. On the other hand, *Issuances* of securities bring in cash. This utility sold *Long Term Debt* and *Common Stock* in order to raise funds. The utility could have sold a new issue of preferred stock, or taken out a bank loan, too. The *Net Cash Provided by Financing Activities* adds up to $74 million, which is $1 million more than the shortfall we calculated previously. In other words, the financings raised more than what was spent, and the extra $1 million is the year's *Net Change in Cash and Equivalents*. If that sum is added to the *Cash and Equivalents at Beginning of Year*, we end up with *Cash and Equivalents at End of Year*.

SECTION SIX: RATIO ANALYSIS
The balance sheet, income statement and funds statement provide the raw material needed to analyze the finances of the corporation.

The Balance Sheet
The plant account is the most important section on the asset side of the balance sheet and should be examined to determine how much plant is actually in service and how much is under construction. In some jurisdictions, the regulator will not allow the company to earn a return on plant that has not been put into service, that is, a return on construction work in progress (CWIP). If a large part of the utility's assets are under construction, and the construction program is behind schedule, the utility might be put under financial pressure while trying to finance the project.

For that matter, if the CWIP is not included in the rate base (i.e., is not earning a return), the utility might need a large price increase—possibly too large for the regulators to grant all at once—upon completion of the plant. Also, we want to compare the proposed spending program with the plant already in place. A huge spending program in relation to present facilities means that the rate base will grow rapidly, probably faster than operating income will grow unaided by rate relief. That means that rate of return on rate base will drop unless the utility gets a substantial amount of rate relief, which is difficult to obtain all at once. For a quick analysis, compare the capital spending program on utility plant with the gross plant of the utility (the sum of plant in service and construction work in progress before depreciation and amortization) at the beginning of the period.

That ratio, then, should be compared with those for other utilities. The higher the ratio of spending to plant, the more likely it is that the utility will require substantial amounts of outside financing to complete the capital expenditure effort and large rate hikes to offset the costs of the new capital. A high ratio, in short, could indicate future financial strains and regulatory problems. Here is an example:

1. Utility plant at original cost (gross plant in service)	$1,000
2. Less depreciation	200
3. Net utility plant in service	800
4. Construction work in progress	300
5. Net utility plant	1,100
Gross plant = line 1 + line 4 =	$1,300

$$\text{CWIP as \% of net plant} = \frac{\text{line 4}}{\text{line 8}} = \frac{\$300}{\$1,300} = 23\%$$

Construction program for next three years:

6. Capital expenditures	400
7. Interest capitalized	100
8. Total	$ 500

Construction program as % of beginning of period gross plant =

$$\frac{\text{Line 8}}{\text{Line 1 + line 4}} = \frac{\$500}{\$1,300} = 38\%$$

The capitalization also deserves attention, for both financial and regulatory reasons. When a large proportion of the capital is provided by debt, the company is said to be leveraged. The covenants or indentures that govern the company's borrowing put limits on how much debt can be sold. Many companies borrow large amounts of short term debt. Some have a permanent layer of short term debt and thus always owe money to banks or to other short term lenders. Short term debt has a different call on assets (if something goes wrong) than does long term debt, but the obligation to pay is still there.

Some companies exclude short term debt from their calculations of capitalization ratios. Doing so can be misleading. Here is an example of how inclusion or exclusion of a large amount of short term debt affects capitalization ratios.

	Amount	Capitalization Ratio or % of Total
With short term debt		
Common equity	$ 500	41.7%
Preferred stock	100	8.3
Long Term debt	400	33.3
Short term debt	200	16.7
Total	$1,200	100.0%
Without short term debt		
Common equity	$ 500	50.0%
Preferred Stock	100	10.0
Long term debt	400	40.0
Total	$1,000	100.0%

Are current assets sufficient to pay current liabilities? In an emergency, selling properties could take a long time, but current liabilities would still have to be paid when due. Current assets include cash or items that can be converted quickly into cash. Therefore, the greater the ratio of current assets to current liabilities, the easier it would be for the utility to meet its obligations.

The ratio of current assets to current liabilities is called the current ratio. The difference between current assets and current liabilities is working capital.

Current assets $5,000
Current liabilities   2,000

Current ratio $= \dfrac{\$5,000}{\$2,000} = 2.5$, or 2.5 to 1

Working capital = $5,000 − $2,000 = $3,000

A large amount of short term debt may create additional risk for the utility. Because short term interest rates are unstable, the company's income could be affected by the rise and fall of interest costs. A large amount of short term debt also creates financing inflexibility. To pay its debts, the utility might be forced to offer long term securities at an unfavorable time, and might not even be able to raise sufficient funds.

Capitalization plays a role in regulation. Regulators want the utility to raise money in the least expensive fashion to keep down the rates charged to customers. Regulators believe that debt financing is cheaper than equity financing, because creditors have a protected position and therefore settle for lower profits than stockholders, who take the risks. Interest charges, moreover, reduce income taxes, so part of the cost of debt can be offset through lower taxes. Here are costs of capital for two capitalizations:

	Amount		% Cost		After Tax Return Calculated by Regulators	Pretax Return (35% Tax Rate) Paid by Consumers
Debt	$ 300	x	10%	=	$ 30.00	$ 30.00
Equity	700	x	15%	=	105.00	161.55
Total	$1,000				$135.00	$191.55
Example B: High Leverage						
Debt	$ 700	x	10%	=	$ 70.00	$ 70.00
Equity	300	x	15%	=	45.00	69.23
Total	$1,000				$115.00	$139.23
Ratio of A to B					117%	138%

The problem with this type of calculation is that regulators rarely consider the price of added risk to shareholders that comes from high leverage. Nor do regulators consider Modigliani and Miller's admonition that the pretax cost of capital for a corporation does not change with the corporation's capitalization.

The preceding examples reveal a conflict of interest. The regulator wants the utility to finance by means of debt to keep down the cost of capital. On the other hand, the utility may want to keep down the use of debt because too much debt increases the risk and may increase interest costs enough to offset savings derived from the lower equity ratio. For example, assume that two utilities have $1,000 of capitalization, one borrowed $300 and the other $700, and a storm wipes out $200 of each company's assets causing the companies to go out of business. Before stockholders receive anything, owners of debt must be paid in full. What would be left for stockholders?

	Low Leverage	High Leverage
Original assets	$1,000	$1,000
less: Storm damage	200	200
Assets available for distribution	800	800
less: Payment of debt	300	700
Assets available for distribution to stockholders	500	100
Original stockholder investment	$700	$300
Loss of investment	200	200
Loss as % of investment	29%	67%

The Income Statement

Balance sheets change slowly, but income statements change rapidly. Those changes can tell a great deal about the utility and the direction in which it is going. Investors, though, should be cautious about applying many standard analyses of operations to utilities, because location of operation, type of fuel, and whether the utility is vertically integrated will affect the results of the analyses. Thus, our analysis focuses on financial matters.

Because of the capital intensive nature of the utility business, depreciation is a major item on both the income and the cash flow statements. The composite book depreciation rate is the rate of depreciation of plant in service as shown on the books of the corporation. The book depreciation rate is a straight line rate for most utility companies. Furthermore—and this is a key point—the rate of depreciation usually must be approved by the regulatory agency that has jurisdiction over the company. Depreciation is a cost of doing business that must be offset by revenues. The higher the depreciation rate, the more the customer must pay in current utility bills. At the same time, a higher depreciation rate increases cash flow, thereby allowing the utility to finance internally more of its expansion and to have less dependence on the capital markets.

Different kinds of utility plants require different depreciation rates. A telephone company might use 7 percent, an electric or gas company 3 percent or 4 percent, and a water company an even lower rate. Even within an industry, the appropriate rate will vary. A hydroelectric company depreciates a dam more slowly than another company depreciates a coal burning plant. Similar utilities, however, may have different book depreciation rates. A higher rate is favorable for investors, because it creates a greater cash flow.

Owners of debt and preferred stock examine the income statement to determine the safety of their investments. *Pretax interest coverage* how much money is available from earnings to pay interest charges—is one of the standards used to determine the strength of a debt security. Although many persons think of a corporation's assets as protection for debtholders, what would the assets be worth if they could not generate income? Pretax income is used for the analysis because interest charges must be met before any income taxes can be paid.

There are numerous ways of calculating interest coverage, some of which are prescribed by government agencies. There are two easy ways to do so. The first is to examine how many times interest expenses are covered by the operations of the utility. The second is to consider how many times interest expenses are coveraged by the entire reported income of the corporation. The former ratio is a more conservative one, because total pretax income from all sources is more likely to contain temporary income, and income from accounting procedures rather than from sale of a product of services. In other words, it is less likely to be real income. As an example, the income statement shows:

Revenues	$1,000
Operating Expenses	700
Operating Income	300
Other Income	50
Pretax Income Before Interest Charges	350
Interest Charges	100
Pretax Income	$ 250
Income Taxes	100
Net Income	$ 150

Using the formula for interest coverage from operating income, we get:

$$\frac{\text{Operating income}}{\text{Interest charges}} = \frac{\$300}{\$100} = 3.0\text{x}$$

Using the formula for interest coverage from pretax income before interest charges, we find:

$$\frac{\text{Pretax Income Before Interest Charges}}{\text{Interest charges}} = \frac{\$350}{\$100} = 3,5\text{x}$$

Analysts must be careful when using those formulas or comparing ratios from company to company, or even from year to year for the same company. Analysts must know whether capitalized interest has been subtracted from the interest expenses. The formula needs to use the interest actually being paid out, and that is before subtracting capitalized interest.

Common stockholders require a different set of analyses. *Earnings per share* (EPS) analysis is based on the average number of shares outstanding during the year. Because utility companies often sell common stock, using year-end shares could be misleading. For example, only a portion of the money received from the sale of shares may have been put to work to produce income during the entire year.

That point is illustrated in the following example, which shows two identical companies, each of which started the year with 800 shares outstanding and ended the year with 1,000 shares. Company A sold new stock at the beginning of the year and had 1,000 shares outstanding for almost the entire period and, therefore, had use of the money from the new shares for almost the full year. Company B sold new shares at the end of the year and had use of the funds for just a few days.

	Company A	Company B
Net income for year	$1,000	$1,000
Year-end shares outstanding	1,000	1,000
EPS based on year-end shares outstanding	$ 1.00	$ 1.00
Average shares outstanding	999	801
EPS based on average shares outstanding	$ 1.00	$ 1.25

If EPS is calculated on the basis of shares outstanding at the end of the year the investor could conclude incorrectly that the shares of both companies have equal earning power. In all likelihood, Company B, once it puts into use the cash derived from the sale of stock near the end of the year, will show greatly improved earnings per share in the following year?

What happens to earnings? A portion of earnings is retained and the rest is distributed as dividends to stockholders. The dividend payout ratio is the standard measure of how much of the earnings available to common stockholders is paid out in the form of dividends.

Reported EPS	2.00
Dividends	1.20
Payout ratio (Div.)/(EPS)	60%

$$\text{Dividend payout ratio} = \frac{\text{Common stock dividends}}{\text{Earnings available to common stock}}$$

The payout ratio is one indication of how well the dividend is covered by earnings. Unfortunately, the tendency exists to look at the ratio for a single year and to forget that utility earnings have become less stable in recent years because of the timing of rate relief and the sensitivity of earnings to weather conditions. Investors in utilities expect stable or growing dividends. Companies do not raise or lower dividends to maintain a stable payout ratio. A company maintains a stable dividend and lets the payout ratio fluctuate. Most companies have a target payout ratio, which represents an average goal. Moreover, the higher the payout ratio, the less able the company will be to raise the dividend, and the smaller the funds the company will retain to finance future growth.

The Cash Flows Statement

In a period of high cost money, the need to borrow money or to sell stock at inconvenient times in the market cycle could have a serious effect on profitability. On the other hand, if a business can generate cash from operations, that money could be invested in profitable ways. Even in the best of times, utilities may require new cash because operations for the year do not generate sufficient funds to finance the purchase of expensive equipment that can serve customers for 30 years. Customers cannot be expected to pay so much for services in a single year that the utility can meet its needs for the next three decades.

The cash flows can be analyzed conveniently by rearranging them into a simplified format:

Uses Of Funds

Capital expenditures (after subtracting interest capitalized	$1,000
Interest capitalized	200
Total expenditures for plant account	$1,200
Refunding	50
Working capital and misc.	50
Total uses of funds	$1,300

Sources Of Funds

Retained earnings*	$ 100
Income deferrals	(5)
Depreciation and amortization	205
Deferred expenses	150
Total internal sources of funds	450
Debt 400	
Common stock	300
Preferred stock	150
Total sources of funds	$1,300

$150 net income for common stock minus $50 dividend.

Internal sources of funds as a percentage of expenditures for plant account =

$$\frac{\$450}{\$1,200} = 37.5\%$$

Internal sources of funds (less interest capitalized) as a percentage of expenditures for plant account (less interest capitalized) =

$$\frac{\$450 - \$200}{\$1,200 - \$200} = \frac{\$250}{\$1,000} = 25.0\%$$

The next step is to calculate how much of the money spent for construction came from internal sources. In the above example, the answer seems to be 37.5 percent. Part of the earnings, however, came from a non-cash source, interest capitalized. Again, part of the expenditures for plant may not represent cash outlay, but are for interest capitalized. Therefore, a second ratio can exclude interest capitalized and show that 25.0 percent of cash expenditures for construction (i.e., what was actually paid to the suppliers and builders) came from internal sources.

Sometimes, it is helpful to look at the cash flow from operations before it is dispersed. A strong cash flow is a valuable asset to any business if properly deployed. To do so, add up:

Net income for common stock	$150
Depreciation and amortization	205
Income deferrals	(5)
Deferred expenses	150
Cash flow from operations	$500

This number tells how much cash comes in from the day to day business of the company. The number excludes non-recurring items, such as profit on sale of property, or writedowns of asset value that involve no cash loss at time of the writedown. One can even calculate cash flow per average share outstanding in the same way as net income per share is calculated. Earnings per share can be compared to cash flow per share, and one might prefer to invest in the company that has more cash flow behind each dollar of earnings per share, or behind every dollar of dividends paid.

That brings up the question of how money should be raised. If an industrial firm builds a factory that will last for 10 years, the company might borrow money from the construction and pay the loan over a 10 year period. Because the firm is unlikely to build a plant each year, the loan will probably be paid from the proceeds of the operation. The loan, in short, will be self-liquidating. Utilities, on the other hand, may borrow annually, plow all cash back into plant, and raise funds to repay the loan from sale of additional securities.

Inflation adds to the problem. A utility's cash flow from internal sources is derived from a return on and depreciation of the original cost of assets, (unless the local government allows inflation adjustments for regulatory purposes). Original cost is not adjusted for increases in price levels. Accordingly, the utility can only recover by means of depreciation the actual cost of the asset, not the cost of replacement at current price levels. The utility has to sell additional securities to raise cash with which to replace the asset. (A number of countries have refused to adjust utility assets or earnings for inflation, in the past, with disastrous consequences.)

How is that problem different from that of other businesses? Most other businesses do not have so much of their money invested in long-lived fixed assets. Other businesses can raise prices on inventory so that the firms can replace the inventory with a like quantity of more expensive goods. Businesses can also raise prices, if the competition allows, to make sure that they have enough cash to replace fixed assets that now cost more. The utility, of course, cannot raise prices at will. So long as regulation and depreciation are based on original cost of property, the utility has a hard time meeting its needs from internal sources in an inflationary economy.

Other Ratios

In our previous examples, we have examined ratios derived entirely from a single financial statement. Yet, several key ratios use items from several financial statements.

Investors and regulators want to know rates of return—how much profit is made for every dollar invested. When creditors lend the business $100 in return for $10 a year of interest plus repayment of the $100 principal at the end of a given period, they accept a 10 percent return ($10 a year for every $100 borrowed). When a stockholder puts money into a new business expecting the business to earn $20 for each $100 invested by stockholders, the investor expects a 20 percent return ($20 a year for every $100 invested). Shareholders also expect to sell their shares for at least $100, so that the $20 a year does not have to be offset against a capital loss. If the business is set up with $100 from creditors, who expect a return of $10 a year, and with $100 from stockholders, who expect a return of $20 a year, the return on the total investment of $200 is:

Debt	$100	x	10%	=	$10
Equity	100	x	20%	=	20
	$200				$30

and:

$$\frac{\$30}{\$200} = 15\%$$

Determining the profitability of the utility in the same manner as the regulators make the calculation is a useful exercise. Unfortunately, procedures vary from country to country. Usually, regulators look at return on capital invested in the business, or return on equity. To approximate those calculations, consider a utility that has the following income statement and balance sheet:

Income Statement

Revenues	$1,000
Operating Expenses	700
Operating income	300
Other income	50
Pretax income before interest charges	350
Interest charges	100
Pretax income	250
Income Taxes	100
Net income	150
Preferred dividends	50
Net income for common stockholders	100

Balance Sheet

Assets		Liabilities and Capital	
Net utility plant	$2,500	Common stockholders equity	$ 700
Other assets	100	Preferred stock	600
Total assets	$2,600	Debt	1,200
		Total capital	2,500
		Other liabilities	100
		Total liabilities	$2,600

The *return on capital* consists of the earnings made on capital (net income for common stockholders plus dividends on preferred stock plus interest on debt) as a percentage of total capital, or:

$$\frac{\$100 + \$50 + \$100}{\$2,500} = \frac{\$250}{\$2,500} = 10.0\%$$

The *return on common equity* consists of the profit earned by common shareholders as a percentage of common stockholders equity or:

$$\frac{\$100}{\$700} = 14.3\%$$

SECTION SEVEN: MARKET AND PER SHARE RATIOS AND RATINGS

The financial statements tell us how much the company earns, where the money comes from and where it goes, and how much has been invested in the business. Statements do not tell us the present worth of nor do they indicate how much investors are willing to pay for the flow of cash coming to them from the business. Statements cannot tell us what the company would have to pay for additional funds, nor do they show the amount that could be realized from sale of the business. Managements need that information to make investment decisions, and regulators need the information to determine the utility's cost of capital.

Common Stock

The common stockholder is concerned with stock price, dividend, earnings per share and book value per share.

Price of stock in market	$32.00
Earnings per share (EPS)	4.00
Dividends per share	2.40
Book value per share	30.00

The *price/earnings ratio*, P/E, or multiple for the stock is the price divided by earnings per share. In the above case:

$$\frac{\text{Price}}{\text{Earnings per share}} = \frac{\$32}{\$4} = 8x$$

Generally speaking, the market is willing to pay a higher multiple for each dollar of earnings when the company is extremely solid (risk is lower) or when earnings are growing rapidly. In the case of a rapid-growth company, investors may be willing to pay 16 times earnings on the theory that earnings are increasing so fast that by next year earnings will have doubled. Accordingly, the multiple is actually just eight times earnings for next year. In some instances the investor will pay a higher multiple because net for the current year is unduly depressed and will spring back quickly. Conversely, the investor may pay a low multiple if this year's earnings are unduly high and are expected to fall.

Because many utility stocks are purchased for current income, the *Dividend Yield* is an important element in the investment decision. Although the price-earnings ratio is meaningful, there can be temporary distortions in earnings per share (caused by weather, delays in rate relief, plant breakdowns, etc.). Investors could view the dividend as an indication of normalized earning power. If so, then it might be better to examine the dividend yield in relation to that of other stocks. The dividend yield is:

$$\frac{\text{Dividends per share}}{\text{Price}} = \frac{\$2.40}{\$32.00} = 0.075 = 7.5\%$$

Other things being equal, the investor will accept a lower current dividend yield from an investment in a strong company with good prospects of growth than from an investment in a weaker company with poorer prospects. A lower risk produces a lower return. The prospect of more income in the future will induce investors to accept less income in the present.

The *Total Return* for a stock is the current dividend yield plus growth in value of the shares. Thus, assuming that earnings, dividends and stock price move together over time, a stock with a 7.5 percent dividend yield and a 5 percent anticipated growth rate would have an expected total return of 12.5 percent per year.

Investors often look at the *Book Value* of a stock. (Book value is the total amount of stockholders' equity, as shown on the books of the corporation, divided by the number of outstanding shares of common stock.) In many businesses, book value is only of academic interest, because changes in the value and earning power of assets make it likely that a purchaser of the corporation would pay far more or far less than book value for outstanding shares. In the utility business, rates of return often are allowed on book value, and, therefore, book value is a key to the potential earning power of the company. The market/book ratio is:

$$\frac{\text{Price of stock}}{\text{Book value of stock}} = \frac{\$32}{\$30} = 1.067 = 106.7\%$$

The *Market/Book Ratio* indicates to existing shareholders whether new common stock financing will increase or will dilute book value and earning power of their shares. The ratio also indicates to regulators whether return being earned is satisfactory (i.e., high enough to bring the stock at least to book value). In the following example, new stock offerings are made at 50 percent, 100 percent, and 150 percent of book value. The regulator allows the company to earn a 15 percent return on equity.

	Before Stock Offering	Situation After $1,000 Is Raised by Sale of Stock at		
		50% of Book Value	100% of Book Value	150% of Book Value
Common equity	$1,000	$2,000	$2,000	$2,000
Number of shares	100	300	200	166.7
Book value per share	$10.00	$ 6.67	$10.00	$12.00
Net income	$ 150	$ 300	$ 300	$ 300
Earnings per share	$ 1.50	$ 1.00	$ 1.50	$ 1.80

A low market price/book value ratio means that new financing will be dilutionary. On the other hand, if the ratio is low, the company probably is underearning and potential for improvement exists. The investor must judge whether financing plans will lead to considerable dilution and whether potential for improvement can be realized within a reasonable time.

Sometimes it is easier to calculate ratios from information per share than to go to the statements of the company. The *Return on Book Value* is roughly equivalent to return on equity:

$$\frac{\text{Earnings per share}}{\text{Book value per share}} = \frac{\$4}{\$32} = 0.133 = 13.3\%$$

The Return on Book Value is not necessarily identical to return on equity, because the numerator is based on average shares outstanding and the denominator on year end shares, but it is close enough for most purposes.

The *Dividend Payout Ratio* approximates the percentage of earnings available to common stock that is paid out in dividends:

$$\frac{\text{Dividends per share}}{\text{Earnings per share}} = \frac{\$2.40}{\$4.00} = 0.60 = 60\%$$

Again, the calculation may not produce exactly the same results as using the total dividends paid as a percentage of reported net income, but it is good enough to use.

The various market ratios are affected by the prospects of individual companies and by alternative investments that are available. A change in prospects for a company or for an entire industry will cause investors to pay higher or lower P/E ratios or to accept lower or higher dividend yields. A change in the returns offered by alternative investments would have the same effect.

The following table illustrates the effect on stock price and ratios of a shift in bond yields from 10 percent to 13 percent to 8 percent, in cases where the alternative is to invest in bonds and investors demand a dividend yield on stocks one percentage point below the interest rate on bonds.

	10% bond yield	13% bond yield	8% bond yield
Dividend per share	$2.40	2.40	$2.40
Earnings per share	4.00	4.00	4.00
Book value	30.00	30.00	30.00
Stock price	26.67	20.00	34.29
Dividend Yield	9.00%	12.00%	7.00%
P/E ratio	6.67x	5.00x	8.57x
Market/book ratio	88.90%	66.70%	114.30%

Fixed Income

Bonds provide a fixed return (interest) if held to maturity. The *Coupon Yield* is based on the face value of the bond. For example, the 12 percent series first mortgage bond, due January 1, 2000, pays 12 percent a year on every $100 of face value. On January 1, 2000, the investor will get back $100 for every $100 face value of bonds issued. Some investors do not choose to hold the bond to maturity and, therefore, sell at whatever market price is offered. The price offered rises and falls with interest rates. Suppose the market for a bond is as follows:

Years to maturity   = 20
Coupon   = 12%
Price of bond per $100 of face value   = 90%

If the payment of a bond at maturity is ignored, the Current Interest Yield is calculated as:

$$\frac{\text{Coupon rate}}{\text{Price of bond}} = \frac{12}{90} = 0.133 = 13.3\%$$

If the acceptable interest rate on the above quality of bond rises to 15%, the price for the bond would have to decline to $80 to give new investors a 15% return.

$$\frac{\text{Coupon}}{\text{Price}} = \frac{12}{80} = 0.15 = 15\%$$

The current yield, however, does not really indicate the total return picture. If investors hold the bond to maturity, they receive not only the coupon every year, but also an extra $10 (in the first case) or $20 (in the second) because they paid less than $100 for the bond. That capital gain is really part of the return expected by investors. The return that includes both coupon and capital gain (or loss) is *Yield to Maturity*. Tables provide accurate yields to maturity. The investor, however, can calculate an approximate yield to maturity.

Where:
   $100 = Face value of bond
     C = Coupon rate (for each $100 of face value)
     P = Price of bond
     Y = Years to maturity

The approximate yield to maturity (A) equals

$$\frac{C + \left(\frac{100 - P}{Y}\right)}{\left(\frac{100 + P}{2}\right)}$$

In the above example where P = 80:

$$A = \frac{12 + \left(\frac{100 - 80}{20}\right)}{\left(\frac{100 + 80}{2}\right)} = \frac{13}{90} = 0.144 = 14.4\%$$

and in the example where P = 90:

$$A = \frac{12 + \left(\frac{100 - 90}{20}\right)}{\left(\frac{100 + 90}{2}\right)} = \frac{12.5}{95} = 0.132 = 13.2\%$$

Yields calculated by the above formula should be regarded as approximations, and used only when bond tables are not available.

Bonds have quality *Ratings* determined by rating agencies. In the United States, the largest agencies—Moody's and Standard & Poor's—use letter guides, in declining order of quality:

Moody's	S&P	Comment
Aaa	AAA	Best quality, extremely strong
Aa	AA	High quality, very strong ability to pay.
A	A	Upper medium grade, strong capacity to pay.
Baa	BBB	Medium grade, adequate strength.
Ba	BB	Speculative, future not assured.
B	B	Speculative, undesirable as an investment

A plus or minus or a number (the lower the better) after the letter rating is often added to indicate further gradations in quality. Ratings below Baa and BBB are not considered to be of investment quality. Bonds with ratings that begin with the letter C (not shown here) are of companies in or near bankruptcy or are extremely speculative in nature. Many investors are prohibited by law from buying bonds with ratings below certain limits. The ratings for particular issues may differ from rating agency to rating agency. As a rule, ratings do not differ sharply, but it is not unusual for a bond to be rated Aa by one agency and A by another. That is called a split rating.

The market demands a higher yield from riskier bonds. Therefore, bonds with lower ratings generally provide higher yields to maturity than bonds with higher ratings. A drop in rating (the ratings are re-examined and revised periodically) can lead to a drop in bond price (to produce the higher interest rate). Accordingly, investors watch the trend in financial ratios for the companies in which they invest.

Utilities also seek to keep financial ratios at levels that will retain or improve ratings. A lower bond rating might make the bond difficult to sell to certain investors and might force those investors to sell the bonds if the rating fell below desired levels. When investors expect a bond rating to change, they adjust the price that they will pay for the bond (thus requiring a different yield). Accordingly, some bonds provide yields that seem out of line with their present ratings.

Preferred stocks are like bonds in that they pay fixed dividends, but most preferred stocks have no set life. A preferred stock may remain outstanding for the life of the corporation, or it may have some sort of redemption feature that calls for the redemption of the stocks by a certain year. For the standard, non-redeemable preferred stock, investors simply calculate a dividend yield:

$$\frac{\text{Dividend}}{\text{Market Price}}$$

When the preferred has redemption features, investors will have to make calculations similar to those for bonds. Preferred stocks have ratings, too, and investors will want to compare ratings and yields, to make sure that they are getting a higher yield if they are buying a lower quality preferred.

As a final point, the difference in yield between rating groups varies over time. When the market is worried about the state of the economy and the ability of weaker companies to weather the storm, a greater yield differential often exists between low and high quality fixed income securities. At such a time, investors see greater risk in low quality securities and demand to be compensated accordingly.

Appendix F

Regional Map

North America

Latin America and the Caribbean

Western Europe

Central and Eastern Europe

Commonwealth of Independent States

Middle East and North Africa

Sub-Saharan Africa

Centrally Planned Asia

South Asia

Pacific Countries

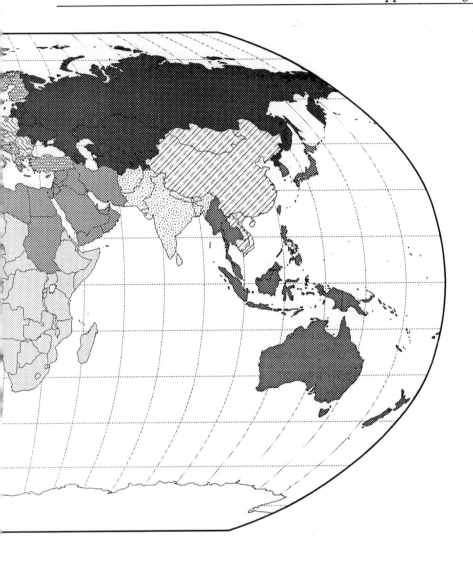

Appendix G

Author Biographical Information

Rosemary Avellis Abrams is a Senior Analyst in the Defined Asset Funds Research Department of the Private Client Group at Merrill Lynch in Princeton, N.J. Prior to joining Merrill Lynch, Abrams was an Associate Director at Standard & Poor's Corporation responsible for assigning ratings on debt and preferred securities by Bell Regionals, independent telephone companies and cellular telephone companies. She spent 11 years as a common equity analyst at Merrill Lynch, responsible for coverage of the telecommunications and electric utility industries, and six years at a regional brokerage firm covering electric and telephone regulatory issues. Abrams is a member of the New York Society of Security Analysts (NYSSA) and the Association for Investment Management and Research (AIMR). She is the co-author of the book *The New Telecommunications Industry: Evolution and Organization*, published by Public Utilities Reports, Inc.

Gerald R. Alderson is President and Chief Executive Officer of KENETECH and most of its wholly owned subsidiaries, including KENETECH Windpower. He has a broad business background both in entrepreneurial enterprises and in established companies. Alderson is a founder of US Windpower, Inc. (subsequently KENETECH Corporation), The First Enterprise Bank, Civic Bank of Commerce, Energy Finance Corporation, RMR Corporation, TXL Corporation and Genstar Container Corporation (now a subsidiary of General Electric Credit Corporation). He is currently chairman of The Business Council for a Sustainable Energy Future. Alderson's educational background includes a BA in economics, cum laude, from Occidental College and an MBA, with high distinction, from the Harvard University Graduate School of Business.

John Baker has had a career in both the public and private sector. An Arts graduate from Oxford University, he spent ten years each dealing with transport policy and finance and then went on to urban regeneration and social housing. He moved into the energy sector in 1979 as Company Secretary to the Central Electricity Generating Board. Appointed to that Board in 1980, he became Corporate Managing Director, responsible for commercial matters and then on to management of the privatization program. Most recently, he served as Chief Executive of National Power, from its beginning in 1990, until March of 1995. He is also a Non-Executive Director of Royal Insurance and a Member of the European Advisory Council of Air Products, Inc. and the Bankers Trust.

Francisco Blanco, since joining Telefónica Internacional as Deputy Director of Investments, has participated in the privatization process of Telefónica de Argentina, Compañia Anonima de Telefonus de Venezuela , ENTEL-Peru, Compañia de Telefonus del Peru. Blanco is a founding member of the Spanish Association for Investor Relations and served as Vice Chairman on behalf of Telefónica de España. He has been a professor of Economics at the Universidad Autónoma de Madrid since 1989. Blanco is the author of several studies and articles about mergers and acquisitions, valuation of companies, privatization and investor relations.

José Luis Martín de Bustamante, until his retirement in 1993, was the Chairman and Chief Executive Officer of Telefónica de Argentina. A native of Spain, he began his career as a planning engineer for Telefónica de España in 1954. While associated with Telefónica de España, he held the positions of Director of the North Region, General Inspector, Deputy General Manager and head of several central departments. During his service with the company, he was particularly involved in the automation of telephone services and installation of the first coaxial cables. Bustamante was named Engineer of the Year in 1993 and is the recipient of the Gran Placa del Mérito de Telecommunicación and of Engineering as well as a degree in telephone traffic engineering and another in theology.

Barton Dominus has specialized in marketing and information technology management for more than 30 years. He currently serves as a consultant to clients that include MCI, AT&T, US West and APA, developing marketing strategies and plans, initiating product development and market research programs, and developing databases. Prior to this, he served as President of B&D Marketing. Dominus received his BA in economics from Bard College in 1964, studied econometrics at New York University in 1969 and received his MBA in information and communications systems from Fordham University in 1991.

James T. Doudiet is President of J.T. Doudiet Associates, Inc., a firm specializing in analyzing financial, strategic and regulatory issues in the electric utility industry. Prior to forming the firm, he spent 26 years as a financial executive in the industry and as an investment banker serving the industry. Doudiet has held the Chief Financial Officer position with Northern States Power Company and Northern Indiana Public Service Company. He has also served as Treasurer and Financial Vice President for Pacific Gas and Electric Company and as a Managing Director in investment banking with Dean Witter. As a utility executive, he was responsible for the full range of financial functions including strategic planning, regulatory affairs, investor relations, financing and administration. In the investment banking industry, he worked on financing, mergers and acquisitions and structuring unregulated power projects. He graduated from the University of California at Berkeley with a BA in mechanical engineering and an MBA in finance.

Sylviane Farnoux-Toporkoff, Ph.D. is a Professor of Economics at the University of Paris (Institute of European Studies) and serves as a special consultant to the European Commission in Brussels. She is the author of several books, including *Telecommunications in Transition; Cooperation and Competition in the Field of Telecommunications;* and *Promotional Sales.* Farnoux-Toporkoff has served as director of more than 20 research projects concerning deregulation, telecommunications and trade for the EC Commission DG XIII and was a principal organizer of a series of international meetings of industry and government leaders. In 1986, she received her Ph.D. in economics at the Paris I Pantheon Sorbonne.

Roger D. Feldman is a partner and head of the Project Finance Group of McDermott, Will & Emery's Washington, D.C. office. He practices in the area of finance and regulation of electric power and other energy sources. Prior to this, he served as Deputy Administrator for Finance and Environment of the Federal Energy Administration and currently serves on the Environmental Protection Agency's Financial Advisory Board. He has chaired American Bar Association Committees on Energy Law, Alternate Energy Sources, and Energy Finance. He serves on the Boards of the National Independent Energy Producers, the Competitive Power Policy Forum, and the Cogeneration Institute. In 1990 he was named Cogeneration Professional of the Year by the Association of Energy Engineers. Feldman received his BA from Brown University in 1962, his LL.B. from Yale Law School in 1965 and his MBA from Harvard Business School in 1967.

Angel García-Cordero is the founder and head of ANTA Financial Advising, a Spanish registered assets management group which specializes in trading and management of financial derivatives. He has extensive experience in telecommunications, regulation, privatization and finance through his work with Telefónica de España, and as a licensed broker, president and founder of the Investor Relations Association of Spain. Prior to founding ANTA, García-Cordero also served as director of a Telefónica subsidiary in the US, and was manager of Investor Relations at Banesto. He holds a degree in business administration as well as accounting and auditing from Madrid's Complutense University.

David L. Haug is Executive Vice President, Strategic Development and Acquisitions, for Enron Power Corporation and Managing Director of Enron Power's development group. Haug specializes in structuring project financings and acquisitions and plays a leading role in the development, contracts and financing of Enron Power's projects worldwide. He was instrumental in structuring and negotiating Enron Power's 1,725-megawatt Teesside, England project. Prior to joining Enron Power, Haug was a lawyer in the Houston and London offices of Vinson & Elkins, specializing in project finance, mergers and acquisitions, venture capital, and later a business and finance consultant to power and biotechnology development companies. He has a BBA (Finance), a BA and law degrees from the University of Texas.

Alex Henney studied engineering at the Universities of Bristol in England and Virginia in the US, as well as business administration at the London School of Economics. Following a varied career in industry, McKinsey & Company and the government, he was appointed as the consumer director on the London Electricity Board in 1981. He was invited to be chairman of the Electricity Supply Working Group of the Center for Policy Studies and in 1987 published *Privatize Power*. Henney has been an advisor to electric companies, independent power producers, large customers and government agencies on various aspects of competitive power markets.

Andrew S. Hyman is a graduate student at the University of Illinois, where he is presently studying the economics of inland water transportation. He received a MPP degree from Vanderbilt University and a BS from Tufts University. He has contributed statistical work to *America's Electric Utilities: Past, Present and Future*, and wrote a report about mobile air pollution sources for the Israel Union for Environmental Defense.

Robert C. Hyman is a student at Harvard University, majoring in earth and planetary sciences. He previously compiled the Chronology for the fifth edition of *America's Electric Utilities: Past, Present and Future*, and helped to develop a computerized inventory of water pollution sources for Westchester County, New York.

Don D. Jordan, since being elected in 1977, has held the title of Chairman and Chief Executive Officer of Houston Industries, Inc. He also serves as Chairman and CEO of three HII subsidiaries: Houston Lighting & Power, KBLCOM Inc., and Houston Industries Energy. He has also served as past chairman of the Edison Electric Institute, past chairman of the Electric Power Research Institute and has served as Vice Chairman of the National Electric Reliability Council. Jordan received a BBA in Industrial Management in 1954 from the University of Texas and his JD in 1969 from the South Texas College of Law.

Viswanath Khaitan joined Scudder, Stevens & Clark in 1987 as an analyst responsible for the utility and transportation industry sectors. He is a managing director of the firm. Prior to joining Scudder, Khaitan was associated with First Chicago Investment Advisors responsible for securities analysis of the utility industry. He has also worked as a management consultant to the utility industry. Khaitan holds an MBA from Northwestern University, an MS from the Illinois Institute of Technology and an undergraduate degree from Jadavpur University in Calcutta, India. He has a CFA and is a member of the Association for Investment Management and Research.